D1488569

This book examines the intellectual confrontation between priest and Free-thinker from 1660 to 1730, and the origins of the early phase of the Enlightenment in England.

Through an analysis of the practice of historical writing in the period, Dr Champion argues that historical argument was a central component for displaying defences of true religion. Taking religion – and specifically defences of the Church of England after 1660 – as central to the politics of the period, the first two chapters of the book explore the varieties of clericalist histories, arguing that there were rival emphases upon *regnum* or *sacerdos* as the font of true religion. The remainder of the book examines how radical Freethinkers like John Toland or the third Earl of Shaftesbury set about attacking the corrupt priestcraft of established religion. Arguing against the secular interpretation of Freethinkers, the later chapters examine how the radicals developed a theory of religion that not only condemned corrupt Christianity, but also importantly promoted a reforming civil theology. Using an analysis of 'other' religions the Freethinkers insisted, following James Harrington's thought, that all societies needed a form of public religion.

Cambridge Studies in Early Modern British History

THE PILLARS OF
PRIESTCRAFT SHAKEN

Cambridge Studies in Early Modern British History

Series editors

ANTHONY FLETCHER
Professor of Modern History, University of Durham

JOHN GUY
Professor of Modern History, University of St Andrews

and JOHN MORRILL
Lecturer in History, University of Cambridge, and
Fellow and Tutor of Selwyn College

This is a series of monographs and studies covering many aspects of the history of the British Isles between the late fifteenth century and the early eighteenth century. It includes the work of established scholars and pioneering work by a new generation of scholars. It includes both reviews and revisions of major topics and books which open up new historical terrain or which reveal startling new perspectives on familiar subjects. All the volumes set detailed research into broader perspectives and the books are intended for the use of students as well as of their teachers.

For a list of titles in the series, see end of book.

THE PILLARS OF PRIESTCRAFT SHAKEN

The Church of England and
its Enemies, 1660–1730

J. A. I. CHAMPION

*Lecturer in History, Royal Holloway and Bedford
New College, University of London*

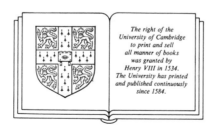

The right of the
University of Cambridge
to print and sell
all manner of books
was granted by
Henry VIII in 1534.
The University has printed
and published continuously
since 1584.

CAMBRIDGE UNIVERSITY PRESS

Cambridge
New York   Port Chester
Melbourne   Sydney

Published by the Press Syndicate of the University of Cambridge
The Pitt Building, Trumpington Street, Cambridge CB2 1RP
40 West 20th Street, New York, NY 10011–4211, USA
10 Stamford Road, Oakleigh, Victoria 3166, Australia

First published 1992

Printed in Great Britain at the University Press, Cambridge

A catalogue record for this book is available from the British Library

Library of Congress cataloguing in publication data
Champion. J. A. I.
The pillars of priestcraft shaken: The Church of England and its
enemies, 1660–1730/J. A. I. Champion.
p.   cm. – (Cambridge Studies in early modern British history)
Includes bibliographical references and index.
ISBN 0 521 40536 X (hardback)
1. Church of England – Apologetic works – History. 2. Anglican
Communion – Apologetic works – History. 3. Dissenters, Religious –
England – History. 4. Free thought – England – History. 5. Church of
England – Controversial literature – History. 6. Anglican Communion –
Controversial literature – History. 7. Enlightenment – England.
8. England – Intellectual life – 17th century. 9. England –
Intellectual life – 18th century. I. Title. II. Series.
BX5092.C42   1992
283′.42′09032 – dc20   91–18221   CIP

ISBN 0 521 40536 X hardback

CE

For Sylvia

CONTENTS

ACKNOWLEDGEMENTS

In writing this book I have incurred many debts and made many friends. My main thanks and appreciation must go to Mark Goldie, who has directed my studies in one form and another for most of the 1980s while I was both an undergraduate and research student at Churchill College, Cambridge: he has managed to combine enthusiasm with inspiration, and the necessary scholarly chiding with charm. Thanks, too, must be gratefully extended to John Marshall and Robert Iliffe, for the frequent and valuable conversations or 'cabals' we have had. Perspectives, objectives and intentions have not always been harmonious but, for me at least, the outcome has always been fruitful. In undertaking research, friends are as important as colleagues. Getting away from, as well as being immersed in, work is essential: so thanks to those who have at different times put up with my obsessions, irritability, untidiness and depressions – in particular, Matthew Arcus, Bernard Attard, Michael Berlin, George Conyne, Heather Creaton, Stewart Eames, Andrew Hanham, Shelagh Johnson, Derek Keene, Tamas Liptak, Jon Luke, Olwen Myhill, Tony Trowles, Tim Underhill, and Mary Wilmer.

In general my work could not have been so efficient and effective without the co-operation and dedication of the staff of all the libraries I have used: but special thanks are due to the people of the Rare Books Rooms in the University Library, Cambridge. Throughout my research they have been consistently friendly, informative, tolerant and helpful: in the last few months of my original research I must have tried their patience to the limit. In the process of converting my work from thesis to book I have had the advice and help of many people who gave up their time to read and criticize. In particular, Silvia Berti and Michael Hunter gave accurate and stimulating comments. Participants of the various seminars at the Institute of Historical Reseach and the Institute of Romance Studies in London, and of others in Oxford and Leiden, where some of the ideas in this book were tested, should also be acknowledged. A special mention should be made for all those who attended the Foundation for Intellectual History Seminar in the Summer of 1990 in Leiden: a more splendid and fertile environment I have not encountered. Conversations and correspondence with Professor Richard Popkin have proved invaluable in developing new approaches to early modern unbelief. For allowing me to test my ideas on them, many thanks must also be extended to all the students I have taught in Cambridge and London. While acknowledging all those who have read, criticized, applauded and condemned my work, I accept the end result replete with its quirks, grumblings and idiosyncrasies as entirely my own responsibility. Many thanks also to the Isobel Thornley Bequest Fund, who gave a generous grant in aid of publication.

A final acknowledgement must go to those who have had to put up with me at closest quarters: my partner Sylvia Carter, who has suffered the burdens of living with someone obsessed at times with the past rather than the present, with a stern, patient, and loving good humour. Also to my family who have always been there when I needed them.

ABBREVIATIONS

All references are to the editions I have used, and they are not necessarily the first editions. Unless otherwise stated, both primary and secondary material was published in London. All citations remain orthographically and grammatically as they were in the originals.

CNM	J. Toland, *Christianity Not Mysterious* (1696)
DNB	*Dictionary of National Biography*
HJ/CHJ	*(Cambridge) Historical Journal*
HPT	*History of Political Thought*
HT	*History and Theory*
JEH	*Journal of Ecclesiastical History*
JHI	*Journal of the History of Ideas*
JHP	*Journal of the History of Philosophy*
JWCI	*Journal of the Warburg and Courtauld Institute*
OED	*Oxford English Dictionary*
PP	*Past and Present*
SVEC	*Studies in Voltaire and the Eighteenth Century*
TAPS	*Transactions of the American Philosophical Society*
TRHS	*Transactions of the Royal Historical Society*

------------------- ≪ 1 ≫ -------------------

Introduction

RELIGION AND HISTORY FROM RESTORATION TO ENLIGHTENMENT

When Hilkiah the high priest found the original complete book of the Mosaick Law, he was not reprimanded and discouraged from producing it but had it carried immediately by Shaphan the scribe to good King Josiah, and found presently a reformation according to it undertaken by him.[1]

Religion is the pillar on which the great fabric of the microcosm standeth. All humane societies, and civil associations, are without Religion, but ropes of sand, and stones without mortar, or ships without pitch.[2]

That religion doth now consist, not so much in obeying the dictates of the Holy Spirit, as in defending Men's own fantastical opinions; Charity is now no part of religion, but discord and implacable hatred pass under the masque of Godly zeal.[3]

Writing in the late 1670s to the libertine Rochester, Charles Blount (1654–93), early deist and Freethinker, commented upon Averro's idea that the whole world was deceived by religion, 'for supposing that there were but three laws, viz. that of Moses, that of Christ, and that of Mahomet: either all are false, and so the whole world is deceived; or only two of them, and so the greater part is deceived'.[4] This idea of religion as the politic device of the three great impostors is most commonly attributed to the radical French treatise *Le Traité des trois imposteurs* published in 1719. The French text is considered by scholars of eighteenth-century ideas to be one of the primary documents of Enlightenment Freethought; or as the introduction to the treatise succinctly commented, 'a complete system of

[1] W. Whiston, *Primitive Christianity reviv'd* (5 volumes, 1711–12), I: Appendix: An Account of the Convocations Proceedings with Relation to Mr Whiston', 3.
[2] A. Ross, *Pansebeia: Or a view of all Religions in the World* (6th edition, 1696), 'Dedication to the Worshipful Robert Abdy'.
[3] B. Spinoza, *A Treatise Partly Theological and Partly Political* (1689), 156.
[4] C. Blount, *The Oracles of Reason* (1693), 123–4, and following.

1

atheism'.[5] As the title of the work suggests, the author (or authors) of the work indicted all organized religion (Judaism, Islam and Christianity being merely the main examples) as fictional imposture. All religion is the combination of human ignorance, historical circumstance and priestly corruption. Priests and monarchs have (and by implication always will have) created false revelations to gain political obedience from an ignorant and fearful laity. Prejudice, passion and fear were the components of popular belief: theology was human contrivance. As one historian has commented, the *Traité* was a digest of all the most radical irreligious arguments of the period.[6] In both the published and clandestine work, the sacred histories of Moses, Christ and Mohammed are given a Machiavellian turn.[7] The theologies of the Judaeo-Christian orthodoxy were exposed as corrupt opinion rather than transcendent divine truth: the orthodox idea of the soul, of heaven and hell, and the very conception of a divinity, were products of the 'absurd imagination'. The 'empire of fable' described the nature of all organized religion rather than the empire of truth.[8] In France this work was perennially popular throughout the eighteenth century and has perhaps become identified as the epitome of the Voltairean assault upon the Church of the *ancien régime*. In English historiography the work is virtually unknown.[9]

[5] In the manuscript collection of the British Library there is an early eighteenth-century text titled 'The Famous Book De tribus Impostoribus', an edition 'faithfully Englished – with a preface, annotations and additions'. See BL Stowe 47. There is also a late eighteenth-century French manuscript and a Latin version 'De Tribus Impostoribus', dated 1709. See BL Sloane 2039 and Add. 12064. The only other known English manuscript is in the Bamberger Collection at the Hebrew Union College, Cincinnati: it is a variant of the Stowe item in a different hand.

[6] See I. O. Wade, *The Clandestine Organisation and Diffusion of Philosophic Ideas in France from 1700 to 1750* (Princeton, 1938), chapter 5. Importantly on the authorship of the *Traité* see S. Berti, 'The first edition of the *Traité des trois imposteurs*, and its debt to Spinoza's *Ethics*', in M. Hunter and D. Wootton (eds.) *Atheism from the Reformation to the Enlightenment* (Oxford, forthcoming). For a thorough examination of the *Traité*, see S. Berti, *Trattato dei Tre Impostori. (La Vita e lo Spirito di Spinoza)* (Turin, in press). Many thanks to the author for allowing me to see a copy of this text which will be translated into English and published by Van Gorcum, Assen.

[7] See N. Machiavelli, *The Discourses* (Harmondsworth, 1978), and *The Prince* for a political account of Moses and the Italian Church: for the English background, see F. Raab, *The English Face of Machiavelli* (1964).

[8] Stowe 47, folios 27v, 30r.

[9] This is even more intriguing than it might at first appear: importantly, as Popkin and others have shown, there was an orthodox worry about the existence of such a work in the 1650s and 1660s. Indeed, Richard Smith's 'Observations on the Report of a Blasphemous Treatise by some affirmed to have been of late years published in print of Three Grand Impostors', written and circulated prior to 1671, bears some striking resemblances to the introductory dissertation that traditionally accompanied the French treatise. See R. H. Popkin, 'Spinoza and the Conversion of the Jews', in C. de Deugd (ed.), *Spinoza's Political and Theological Thought* (Amsterdam, 1984); J. A. I. Champion, 'Legislators, Impostors and the Politic Origins of Religion', in S. Berti, F. Charles-Daubert and R. H. Popkin (eds.), *Contexts of*

Why then, given that the concern of this book is to examine the confrontation between priest and Freethinker in England between 1660 and 1730, have I started with a brief account of a French work published in 1719? My point is historiographical. Analyses of the *Traité des trois imposteurs* are almost exclusively Francocentric if not Francophone. Although the most recent scholarship has indicated that the composition of the treatise is a bricolage of classical, Renaissance and materialist sources (ranging in time and place from the Roman Cicero, the Italian Vanini, to the English Hobbes), discussions of the intellectual context which generated the work describe it as uniquely Continental. The only discussion of the treatise with reference to England is to be found in the speculations of M. C. Jacob concerning the involvement of the radical Republican writer John Toland (1670–1722) with the Franco-Dutch coterie that was involved, if not in the composition, then certainly in the circulation of the *Traité*.[10] The lack of emphasis upon the English connection is puzzling; and not just for chauvinistic reasons. The conundrum has, I believe, two elements. First, this lack of emphasis is a reflection of the paucity of sources: as noted above, there are only two surviving English translations of the *Traité*, compared with a massive distribution in France.[11] Given the profound irreligion of the text, it seems odd that so few copies exist in England, but even more curious that there is little or no reference to the existence of such a radical work, even by hostile orthodox contemporaries. While it is perhaps valid to argue that the *Traité* was not a specific source that radicals in England had access to, or even that Churchmen needed to rebut, it is certainly not acceptable to argue that the central ideas of the work were elusive in England. The second element in the conundrum is that the main components of the *Traité* were manifest in England prior to the publication of the French work in 1719. The radical and public discourse against 'priestcraft' conducted by Republicans like Toland against the Church of England between 1680 and 1720 pre-empted the *Traité* in developing ideas of organized religion as imposture, and the political accounts of Judaism, Christianity and Islam. It will be the ambition of this book to argue that if there was a discourse directed against the English clergy by a body of radical Republican theorists that publicly pre-empted the clandestine literature of French atheism, then it is perhaps time to re-examine the commonplace characterization of the nature of what has been succinctly identified as the 'crisis' of the European mind and the 'origins' of the Enlightenment as a Continental rather than English moment.

The period from the Restoration to the early years of the Hanoverian

Imposture (Leiden, 1991). Professor Popkin and I intend to publish the Smith Mss. (BL Sloane 388, and Sloane 1024) in the near future.
[10] See M. C. Jacob, *The Radical Enlightenment* (1981), passim, but see in particular 216–20.
[11] See Wade, *Clandestine Organisation*, 124–41; the research of S. Berti and F. Charles-Daubert will bring the location of manuscripts in Europe up to date.

monarchy has been commonly termed an age of transition, from the prerogatives of faith to the claims of reason.[12] According to this interpretation the shackles of established religion were unlocked, banishing the dark shadows of superstition and Christian mystery. Recent work has tended, at least in dealing with the political and institutional conflicts of the period, to reject this proleptic and whiggish vision by reaffirming the centrality of religious controversy.[13] While there has been much scholarly endeavour in delineating the evolutions, contortions and contradictions of civil political ideas during the period, there has been only a frugal examination of the arguments and languages of religious thought.[14]

Contemporary intellectual history of the seventeenth and eighteenth centuries is preoccupied with the history of liberty, and with issues of political sovereignty and obligation. One result of this pattern in the history of political thought has been the concentration upon the great texts of the period. For example, Thomas Hobbes' *Leviathan* (1651) has been treated almost exclusively as a founding text of modern political philosophy: this interpretative enterprise has been possible because only Books I and II (the

---

12 See G. R. Cragg, *The Church and the Age of Reason* (1965); this commonplace is also the premise of much work undertaken upon studies in the origins of the Enlightenment, such as P. Gay's magisterial but flawed *The Enlightenment An Interpretation*, (2 volumes, 1967-), see especially vol. I: *The Rise of Modern Paganism* 149, 313, 319–28, 338–9, 343. E.g. 'In Great Britain the Anglican Church had been deprived of most of its power after the Restoration, even over its own affairs'; see also R. Zaller, 'The Continuity of British Radicalism in the Seventeenth and Eighteenth Centuries', *Eighteenth-Century Life* 6 (1980–1); J. H. Pruett, *The Parish Clergy under the Later Stuarts* (Illinois, 1978), 2. For a more sensitive study see R. Porter and M. Teich (eds.), *The Enlightenment in National Context* (Cambridge, 1981).

13 See, for example, G. A. Holmes, *British Politics in the Age of Queen Anne* (1967); J. Miller, *Popery and Politics 1660–1688*, (Cambridge, 1973); W. Speck, *Tory and Whig: The Struggle in the Constituencies 1701–1715* (1978); G. V. Bennett, *The Tory Crisis in Church and State. The Career of Francis Atterbury* (Oxford, 1975). The most recent contribution to a re-emphasis upon the importance of religious affairs is J. C. D. Clark's *English Society 1688–1832* (Cambridge, 1985), which, although laudable in its willingness to take religious polemic seriously, has certain dubious methodological pronouncements which mar the value of the work.

14 It would entail a footnote of epic proportions to document the bibliographical state of scholarship on the political thought of the period: a selection of the notable works includes J. G. A. Pocock's *The Ancient Constitution and the Feudal Law* (Cambridge, 1957); Pocock, *The Machiavellian Moment* (Princeton, 1975); Pocock, *The Political Works of James Harrington* (Cambridge, 1977); J. Dunn, *The Political Thought of John Locke* (Cambridge, 1968); J. P. Kenyon, *Revolution Principles: The Politics of Party 1689–1720* (Cambridge, 1977); R. Tuck, *Natural Rights Theories* (Cambridge, 1979); of the few recent works that have dealt with the religious complexion of ideological debate, the most notable are M. C. Jacob, *The Newtonians and the English Revolution 1689–1720* (Harvester, 1976), and *The Radical Enlightenment* (1981); J. R. Jacob, *Henry Stubbe, Radical Protestantism and the Early Enlightenment* (Cambridge, 1983); M. A. Goldie, 'John Locke and Anglican Royalism', *Political Studies* 31 (1983). For a more general discussion see J. Obelkevich, L. Roper, R. Samuel (eds.), *Disciplines of Faith: Studies in Religion, Politics and Patriarchy* (History Workshop: 1987).

political parts) of *Leviathan* have been the subject of investigation at the expense of the second half of the work which deals with (in modern terms) the marginal issues of theology and is thus considered theoretically redundant for the concerns of modern secular society.[15] Modern history of political thought (even given Pocock's, Dunn's and Skinner's injunctions on the necessity of a rigorous contextualism) studies politics in a modern sense: theology, religion and the Church are excluded from this secular idiom.[16]

Between 1660 and 1730 the Church of England retained its social power. The Restoration in 1660 was heralded by a reassertion of the political role of the Church. Francis Atterbury, in sermonizing upon the blessed memory of the martyred Charles I, gave an apt description of Anglican perceptions of the Restoration. He wrote, 'At last the storm ceased, the clouds dispersed, and the sun shone out again in his strength; the Royal family returned, and with it our old constitution in Church and state.'[17] The Clarendon Code enshrined the principles of Anglicanism with severity. The cause of monarchy and Church were firmly riveted together against all challenges.[18] The Church reacted sternly against any attempt to loosen its monopoly of clerical authority. The dynamic between the claims of a liberty for religious

---

[15] Please note, throughout this book I use the C. B. Macpherson (Penguin) edition of *Leviathan*.
[16] For example, H. J. Laski, *Political Thought in England from Locke to Bentham* (1920) and C. B. Macpherson, *The Political Theory of Possessive Individualism: Hobbes to Locke* (Oxford, 1962). See also H. T. Dickinson, *Liberty and Property* (1977). For a general assault upon this position see M. P. Thompson, 'The reception of Locke's *Two Treatises of Government* 1690–1705', *Political Studies* 24 (1976) and Clark, *English Society 1688–1832*, 42–64. See also J. Dunn, 'The Politics of Locke in England and America in the Eighteenth Century' in J. W. Yolton (ed.), *John Locke: Problems and Perspectives* (Cambridge, 1969), plus the anticlerical dimensions discussed in R. A. Ashcraft and M. M. Goldsmith, 'Locke, Revolution Principles, and the Formation of Whig ideology', *HJ* 26 (1983).
[17] F. Atterbury, 'On the Martyrdom of King Charles' in *Sermons and Discourses on Several Subjects and Occasions* (9th edition, 1774), IV, 15. For a general contemporary account, see G. Burnet, *History of My Own Times* (1724), I, 91–218; there is some debate over the theological tenor of the Church's restoration. R. S. Bosher, *The Making of the Restoration Settlement* (1951) argues in favour of Laudian victory, while I. M. Green, *The Re-Establishment of the Church of England* (Oxford, 1978) suggests a more moderate settlement. See also R. A. Beddard 'The Restoration Church' in J. R. Jones (ed.), *The Restored Monarchy* (1979), 155–76. The most recent account is J. Spurr, *The Restoration Church of England 1646–1689* (Yale, forthcoming) that argues for the robustness and continuity of Anglicanism. Spurr's emphasis is upon the survival of sacerdotal conceptions over the commonly accepted latitudinarian moralism. Many thanks to Dr Spurr for allowing me to read his typescript. See also J. Spurr, 'Latitudinarianism and the Restoration Church' *HJ* 31 (1988), Spurr '"Rational Religion" in Restoration England', *JHI* 49 (1988); and Spurr, 'The Church of England, Comprehension and the Toleration Act of 1689', *English Historical Review* 104 (1989) and 'Schism and the Restoration Church', *JEH* 41 (1990).
[18] See D. Witcombe, *Charles II and the Cavalier House of Commons* (Manchester, 1966) and D. Lacey, *Dissent and Parliamentary Politics in England 1661–1689* (New Jersey, 1969). See G. Burnet, *History of My Own Times*, I, 93, where Burnet reported Charles II's opinion that 'he thought government was a much safer and easier thing where authority was believed infallible, and the faith and submission of the people was implicite'.

toleration, the idea of comprehension within a broad Church settlement, and arguments for the necessary exclusivity of the Anglican Church, provided the axis for both religious and political disputes during the period.[19] With the accession of William and Mary the close identification between Church and state became blurred: after the failure of Lord Nottingham's comprehension scheme, the 1689 Toleration Act established some measure of religious liberty. Many churchmen lamented the decline of their monopoly of theological and moral discipline, but the Church of England still remained a potent if threatened force in society. This book is concerned with the intellectual confrontation between those who defended, and those who attacked, the position the Church held in society. It is the intention of this work to focus in detail upon the religious nexus of debate identified in the clash between Freethinker and priest over the nature of true religion. The relationship between Church and state, and the very definition of these institutions, was a catalyst of political change. Debates about the nature of monarchical sovereignty necessarily intersected with discussions about the competence and independence of the Church. Conformity to the Church settlement was analogous to political obedience, while theological innovation was often considered a form of secular sedition. To define the sacerdotal competence of the priest in a certain manner held implications for conceptions of civil authority. To argue for one form of Church government was to negate the legitimacy of a related form of civil administration. There was no conceptual separation between issues of Church and state, religion and politics.

Issues of theological belief and religious duty permeated almost every facet of seventeenth- and eighteenth-century life. The child was ushered into the world with the incantations of religious ceremony. The pace of life, be it rural or urban, was set by theological co-ordinates. Catechisms, prayers, festivals and Holy Communion marked the passage of the religious year.[20] The focal

---

[19] On the exclusion crisis see J. R. Jones, *The First Whigs: The Politics of the Exclusion Crisis 1678–83* (Durham, 1961); J. P. Kenyon, *The Popish Plot* (1972); F. S. Reynolds, *The Attempted Whig Revolution 1678–81* (Illinois Studies 21, 1937); O. W. Furley, 'The Whig Exclusionists: Pamphlet Literature in the Exclusion Campaign 1679–81', *CHJ* 13 (1957); B. Behrens, 'The Whig Theory of the Constitution in the Reign of Charles II', *CHJ* 8 (1941); see in particular Henry Care's *The Weekly Pacquet of Advice, Or the History of Popery* (1678–83).

[20] For a useful introductory survey, see B. Reay, 'Popular Religion' in B. Reay (ed.), *Popular Culture in Seventeenth-Century England* (1985). For a late manifestation of popular religious enthusiasm, see the case of the French Prophets. Thomas Emes was led by spiritual fervour to proclaim his own resurrection just before his death on 22 December 1707. Emes' prophecy of his regeneration on 25 May 1708 convinced Sir Richard Bulkeley along with many thousands of others. On the expected date over 20,000 people assembled at Bunhill Fields: the government was so intimidated that troops were sent to quell the threat of insurrection. See H. Schwartz, *The French Prophets* (1980), especially 79–124; R. Porter, 'The Rage of Party: A Glorious Revolution in English Psychiatry?' *Medical History* 27

point of this society was the Church and the parson. The sermon confirmed both the injunctions of Christ and the political order in the minds of the congregation. The distribution of the Eucharist was symbolic of the moral, social and political status of the individuals in a community.[21] The Church was teacher (the pulpit was the most effective means of communication with the populace), landowner and judge.[22] As Richard Steele wrote in 1713 on the extent of clerical authority: 'You have almost irresistible power over your congregations for circumstances of education and fortune place the minds of the people, from age to age, under your direction.'[23]

The hegemony of the Church and churchmen (of whatever theological complexion) did not go unchallenged. While there were furious debates within Anglican circles between High Church and Erastian versions of Church government, there were also assaults upon the idea of a Christian confessional state from without. This book intends to examine how radicals like Henry Stubbe, Charles Blount and John Toland set about undermining the clerical edifice, and to explore the historical polemics they mustered in their assault on Christianity. These men congregated in the coffee-houses, the republics of Freethought, rather than before the priestly pulpit, to discuss subversive manuscripts such as Stubbe's account of the history of Mahomet, or the clandestine *Spaccio della bestia trionphante* written by Bruno and circulated by Toland.[24] John Toland (1670–1722) is one of the most

(1983). For a general discussion of religious belief see M. Eliade, *The Sacred and the Profane: The Nature of Religion* (1959).
21 See P. Laslett, *The World We Have Lost* (1979), especially chapter 3: 'The Village Community', 55–84, 184–6.
22 For a general discussion, see K. V. Thomas, *Religion and the Decline of Magic* (1978), especially 179–182; on the extent of the Church's moral supervision of its parishioners, see K. Wrightson and D. Levine, *Poverty and Piety in an English Village: Terling 1525–1700* (New York, 1979) and K. Wrightson, *English Society 1580–1680* (1982), especially chapter 7: 'Learning and Godliness', 183–222.
23 J. H. Pruett, *The Parish Clergy*, 155; see also the Republican Thomas Gordon's recognition of the useful propagandist role of the clergy; he wrote: 'It is my opinion, that a parochial clergy are of infinite use, where they take pains by their example and instructions to mend the hearts of the people, where they teach them to love God, and their neighbour, and virtue, and their country, and to hate no man' (*The Works of Tacitus*, III, 221). For a contrary appraisal, see James Hamilton to John Locke on 8 February 1694 in *The Correspondence of John Locke*, ed. E. de Beer, volume V, 11. He wrote: 'But thoe I am my self of the Church of England, I am loathe to have my Children tutor'd by any of the Clergy, for most of them, have still a hankering after *jure divino* and passive obedience principles, and are over tenacious as to indifferent ceremonys, and very fond of the nicetyes in religion, which are matters I would have none of my Children trouble theyr heads about.'
24 The history of these coffee-house meetings and clubs is obscure and little studied: much of the subversive reputation may be due to the paranoia of the clergy rather than evidence of a solid nature. The most serious discussions can be found in the works of both M. C. Jacob and J. R. Jacob. For an account of an early Whig club, see the Green Ribbon Club, Pepys' Library, Magdalene College, Cambridge, Ms. Misc. 7 f. 484 and J. R. Jones 'The Green Ribbon Club' in *Durham University Journal* (1956); of the 'College', see Jacob, *The Radical Enlightenment* (1981), 117–18, and S. Daniel, *John Toland* (McGill, 1984), 147, 213. See also M. A.

important figures of this tradition. He travelled widely throughout Britain and abroad. His foreign visits took him to The Hague, Rotterdam and Hanover. The list of his patrons, colleagues and associates is a pantheon of radicalism including, for example, Spencer Compton, later the Speaker of the House of Commons, the Republican Rector William Stephens, Anthony Collins, Matthew Tindal, the 'atheistical' Lord Macclesfield, John Methuen, the Duke of Newcastle, the printer John Darby, the City of London Alderman, Sir Robert Clayton, and most importantly, the third Earl of Shaftesbury, Anthony Ashley Cooper. As will be illustrated below, Toland's contribution to the anticlerical attack took a variety of forms. He collaborated with other writers, for example with John Trenchard and Walter Moyle in the standing army debate, and with Shaftesbury in tracts of the late 1690s. He was a central figure in the circulation and translation of subversive manuscripts.

As a biographer and editor of works, Toland is an interesting and important figure. In particular his editions of Milton, Ludlow, Sidney and Harrington between 1697 and 1700 point to the political traditions he applauded. As well as contributing to the Standing Army debates, the issue of occasional conformity, the Hanoverian succession, and the Sacheverell affair, Toland complemented these political works with his own original researches, writing extended dissertations upon theology, natural philosophy, druidical religion and the metaphysics of antiquity. These works were both published and secretly disseminated.[25] Like the earlier Freethinker, Charles Blount (d. 1693), Toland combined the talents of the plagiarist with originality of purpose. Toland's relationship with such men as the Earl of Shaftesbury and the commonwealthsman Robert Molesworth is testimony both to his political commitments and his undervalued importance in the political and religious controversies of the period.[26]

The task of this book will be, then, to explore this 'age of transition' not in the sense of discussing the 'birth of modernity', but examining how the

Goldie, 'The Roots of True Whiggism 1688–1694', HPT 1 (1980). See, on the provincial influence of the Calveshead Club, T. Hearne, Remarks and Collections I, 179–80 and II, 90; E. T. Thompson (ed.), Letters of Humphrey Prideaux to John Ellis 1674–1722 (Camden Society, 1875), 162. Hearne (Remarks, II, 90) also makes reference to the existence of two anticlerical London clubs, 'The Blasphemy Club and the Devil's Lighthouse', which were founded with the purpose 'to run down all religion and carry on all manner of debauchery'.

[25] For a general account of Toland's life and contacts, R. Sullivan, John Toland and the Deist Controversy (Harvard, 1982) and Jacob, Radical are the most comprehensive. See Wade, Clandestine Organisation, 15, 80, 37, 237–8, for the distribution in France of some of Toland's works such as Nazarenus (1718), Pantheisticon (1720) and The Primitive Constitution of the Christian Church (1726).

[26] For evidence of the close intellectual relationship between Molesworth and Toland, see the latter's copy of M. Martin's A Description of the Western Islands of Scotland (1716) BL C.45.c.1, which contains marginal notes and commentaries by both men, for example 78, 83, 239.

Freethinkers set out to challenge the sanctity of the Church. That is to explore what literary or intellectual means the radicals employed to attempt to render the clerical vision moribund.[27] Implicit in this investigation will be the insistence that the Christianity or Anglican identity of the period was not simply entertained as a collection of propositional beliefs. Religious belief was a complex fabric of doctrine, devotion and institution. It was not enough to subscribe to the Thirty-nine Articles, worship by the Book of Common Prayer or believe in the Trinity. Christian belief also included and absorbed ideas about the legitimacy of government by bishops, the sanctity of Churches, and the truth and authority of the Scriptures. There was, as Greenleaf has commented in another context, a 'hinterland of beliefs'. For the radical Freethinker, however, the whole panoply of corrupt religion (be it Jewish, Christian or Muslim) was reduced to the issue of the authority of the priest and the clergy: the very notion of *sacerdos*. Their objection was practical rather than philosophical. As Thomas Pope Blount wrote 'these Spiritual Machiavellians' corrupted civil society: 'their chief business is to give a helping hand towards making Princes Arbitrary'.[28] All the radical objections against Christianity came to a head in their hostility to the role of the Church in politics. For example, in this light, we might read Hobbes' *Leviathan* (1651) as an indictment, not of disobedient subjects, but of disobedient priests who challenged their ghostly authority against the civil sovereign. Priesthood, not divine ontology, was the rub. Rather than deny God, as this book will show, the radicals were concerned to debunk the false authority of the Church. In examining the discontinuity between the age of faith and the age of reason, the investigation at least for the English context will not address how the voice of reason constructed philosophical and propositional arguments against the existence of God, but how a group of like-minded Republicans compiled a coherent strategy for arraigning the 'political' power of the Church of England.[29]

Commencing with a disenchantment with the authority of the priest, the radical polemic against priestcraft tended to redefine traditional conceptions of the exclusive 'truth' of Christian belief. This development provided the foundation for what would later become known as an anthropology of religion or the modern idea of *Religionswissenschaft*.[30] This study will then eschew the traditional epistemological investigation of the radical assault

---

[27] See J. Miel, 'Ideas or Epistemes: Hazard versus Foucault' in *Yale French Studies* 49 (1973), 236–8.

[28] T. P. Blount, *Essays on Several Subjects* (1691), 12, 52.

[29] The premise that Freethought or Enlightenment rested upon a rational conception of God (or the non-existence of God) is central to the recent arguments of Kors and Wootton. See note 40 below.

[30] See P. Harrison, *'Religion' and the Religions in the English Enlightenment* (Cambridge, 1990), passim.

upon the Church in favour of (in a very loose sense) a sociological examination of the conflict. Thus, the intention is not to assess the veridical nature of either radical or clerical statements about God, Scripture or organized religion, but to examine the confrontation in terms of competing human claims to the authoritative interpretation in these issues. The clash between Freethinker and cleric ultimately concerned who gave the more credit-worthy account of the truth – rather than the truth itself. Let me clarify the point. Many recent studies have insisted that the achievement of late seventeenth-century English thought was the epistemological separation of reason and revelation. As Emerson has written, English deism belongs 'to a European debate about knowledge more than to an English debate about social and political order ... the deistic controversy was about the shape, size, and character of the intellectual world and about how one was to know it'.[31] In this reading of the crisis the achievement of deism was to absolve and correct the epistemic sin of the age of faith. Elevating the claims of reason and logic, the writings of Locke (the *Essay Concerning Human Understanding*) and Toland (*Christianity Not Mysterious*) simply showed contemporaries that theological mystery was wrong. This pointed out the Church capitulated to the logic of reason. In contradiction to this view, it will be the argument of this book that this interpretation is in some sense a misreading of the 'political' context of post-Reformation debates about knowledge. The conflict was not just about the competing epistemological hierarchy of revelation and reason but about who or what institution held the authoritative interpretation of truth. Charles Blount, paraphrasing Hobbes' thought, pointed to the general issue when he commented:

When we believe another man's Revelation, not from the reason of the thing reveal'd but from the Authority and good opinion of him to whom it was so revealed, then is the speaker or enthusiast the only object of our Faith, and the honour done in believing, is done to him only, and not to him that revealed it: so on the contrary, if Livy says the Gods once made a Cow speak, and we believe it not; herein we distrust not God, but Livy.[32]

The issue was, as Blount commented, about 'the Authority and good opinion' of the speaker, rather than 'the reason of the thing reveal'd'. The question that the radicals posed was not 'what is the truth' but rather 'how have the priesthood gained a monopoly over what is considered and accepted as the truth'. This was not a purely epistemic debate but attempted to address

---

[31] R. L. Emerson, 'Latitudinarianism and the English Deists' in J. A. Leo Lemay (ed.), *Deism, Masonry, and the Enlightenment. Essays honoring Alfred Owen Aldridge* (Newark, 1987), 28, 31.
[32] C. Blount, *The Last Saying and Dying Legacy of Mr Thomas Hobbs of Malmesbury* (1680).

the social 'power' that lay behind the priestly claim to be sole interpreters of true knowledge.[33]

This book will, then, treat the deist controversy not just as an argument in favour of the competence of human reason, but as an attack upon the perceived injustice of the distribution of authority in society. Since the 'power' of the Church and priest was entrenched in the whole conception of a Christian identity it was not enough to claim the 'truth' of reason as a simple proposition to topple their authority. The radical attack developed a broader historical perspective. Insisting that contemporary Christianity was corrupt, they turned to the past to exemplify how this corruption had been historically generated. This intellectual confrontation between priest and radical will be examined by considering its impact on the historiography of the period. Both the clergy and their radical assailants shared a common need to be seen to be defending a true and objective set of beliefs about religion. The simple claim to be good, religious and true was not enough: the ability to present a cogent and credible version of the past could shore up such a claim. Churchmen and Freethinkers wished to secure moral convictions in their audiences: one acceptable and even commonplace method of doing so was by writing historical defences of their positions. Because the controversialists of the period considered it necessary to supplement pure theological or philosophical argument with historical perspectives, this work sets out to explore precisely how churchmen and radicals engaged each other in their rival interpretations of the past. Such an enquiry follows the precedent set by J. G. A. Pocock's *The Ancient Constitution and the Feudal Law* (1957) and focuses upon the historiographical traditions of the period as a juncture where historical and political theology met. While Pocock's programme undertook to examine the civil and legal idioms of historiography, my concern is to explore religious histories, initially the histories of episcopacy, of the early Church of England, and of the Reformation, but most pertinently the Freethinking counter-histories of priestcraft, classical theology and superstition. As Pocock has shown, historical traditions and the idea of institutional continuity were (and are) an essential feature of all societies: the idea of the past and the establishment of lineage with this past was elemental in a Christian society. Christianity has a specific temporal teleology ranging from the institutions of Christ to the Last Judgement. The true Christian society has to define itself within terms of this history. The legacy of Christ as an historical (as well as spiritual) event could only be reconstructed by historical investigation. The Christian past was a necessary determinant (for

---

[33] For an interesting discussion of the idea of social power see M. Braddick, 'State Formation and Social Change in Early Modern England: A Problem Stated and Approaches Suggested', *Social History* (1991).

the Christian) of the morality or truth of the present. For the seventeenth-century Christian an essential part of religious experience was the continual re-evaluation of the present in terms of the past. As history was used by churchmen to authorize the present, so was it employed by the Freethinkers as a tool of criticism.[34] In order to see how men like Blount, Toland and Trenchard rewrote the past, it will be necessary to give some sense of the Christian interpretation by first examining a selection of the clerical histories of the period.

While the past held a natural authority, the reconstruction of this past into historical writing was governed by rules inscribed in humanist tradition. In discussing the necessary combination of factual and evaluative statements in the histories of the period, some attempt will be made to re-examine the Whiggish story of the rise and origins of modern historical scholarship which is still commonly thought to have started in the early modern period.[35] In contradiction to this, I wish to argue that the developments in the writing of history were perceived as a means to securing a credible defence of ideological opinions rather than forging more modern ways of writing history. As each disputant attempted to render their prospect of the past authoritative, the need to define credible, true and good history became more pronounced. The apparatus of scholarship (testimony, documents and evidence) became entangled in the business of controversy. Thus, in addition to the contribution of J. G. A. Pocock, D. C. Douglas' *English Scholars 1660–1730* (1951) has provided an historiographical framework for this work. While Douglas has dealt admirably with the scholarly achievements of the historians of the period, this book intends to place these achievements in the context of religious debate.

One of the most elegant and thought-provoking accounts of the disconti-nuity in European culture and society between 1680 and 1730 was the study written by Paul Hazard in 1935, *La Crise de conscience européenne.*[36] In this examination Hazard argued for a shift in the way Europeans constructed their worldviews, exemplified most succinctly in his assertion that one day Europe thought like Bossuet, defender of the Church and indicter of heresy and schism, and the next day like the shibboleth of Enlightenment thought Voltaire.[37] Unashamedly idealist as his account was, Hazard portrays the achievement of the period as the progress and unshackling of reason in

---

[34] See J. G. A. Pocock, 'Time, Institutions, and Action: An Essay on Traditions and Their Understanding' in *Politics, Language, and Time* (1972), and 'English Historical Thought in the Age of Harrington and Locke', *Topoi* 2 (1983); A. Richardson, *History Sacred and Profane* (1964); for an excellent treatment of later historiography based on Pocockean premises, see J. Burrow, *A Liberal Descent* (Cambridge, 1983).

[35] See most recently P. Avis, *Foundations of Modern Historical Thought from Machiavelli to Vico* (1986), Introduction, 1–29.

[36] Hazard's work was translated into English in 1953: there have been numerous editions since.

[37] Hazard, *The European Mind*, Preface, i.

history. The clerical world was unpicked by a collection of great minds. Although primarily Continental, Englishmen like Newton, Locke and even the minor luminary Toland, acted as tributaries to the common stream of rationality. Natural philosophy, travel literature and history lit the beacons of reason that illuminated the shadows of ignorance. Reason replaced revelation.[38]

That there was a transition or crisis in European thought and society is now unchallengeable. The nature of this transition and how to interpret it is less certain. In general the period has been considered as a 'moment' at the origins of modernity: either as the birth of a fledgling reason, or as the emergence and triumph of a hidden atheism.[39] As asserted by my opening paragraphs a recurrent theme of these writings is the concern to emphasize the centrality of the French context. Indeed eighteenth-century intellectual studies have been dominated by the need to understand the French Enlightenment, and in particular the relationship between this culture and the coming of the French Revolution of 1789.[40] There have, however, been some notable attempts to examine or address the idea of an English Enlightenment, although in the memorable phrase of one of the more thoughtful assessments, when doing so an ox sits upon one's tongue.[41] This literature has one broad common theme: that is, if one is to write of an

---

[38] Hazard, *The European Mind*, 46–7, 85, 145–6, 159, 498–9.

[39] The first case is presented most cogently by Gay, *The Enlightenment*; the second perhaps by D. Berman, *A History of Atheism* (1988). Both strands of interpretation share a common Whiggism redolent of the late Victorian secularist writings of Robertson or Bury. See, for example, J. M. Robertson, *A History of Freethought. Ancient and Modern to the Period of the French Revolution*, 2 volumes (1936). For an account of nineteenth-century Freethought, see E. Royle, *Radicals, Secularists and Republicans. Popular Freethought in Britain 1866–1915* (Manchester, 1980). The most recent consideration will be *Atheism from the Reformation to the Enlightenment*, eds. M. Hunter, and D. Wootton (Oxford, forthcoming). Many thanks to Michael Hunter for allowing me to read typescripts of the contents.

[40] See M. Buckley, *At the Origins of Modern Atheism* (New Haven, 1987); and A. Kors, *A History of French Atheism* in 2 volumes, vol. I (Yale, 1989) and 'The Preamble of Atheism in Early-Modern France' in A. C. Kors and P. J. Korshin (eds.), *Anticipations of the Enlightenment in England, France, and Germany* (Philadelphia, 1987). For some eminently sensible comments upon the historiography of this problem, see S. Gilley, 'Christianity and the Enlightenment', *History of European Ideas* (1981). See also J. E. Force, 'The Origins of Modern Atheism', *JHI* 50 (1989).

[41] The first suggestive remarks upon the English Enlightenment were made by F. Venturi in his essay, 'The European Enlightenment' in *Italy and the Enlightenment* (1972), see 5–9. This essay was originally published in Italian in 1960. Venturi's researches were followed up in his *Utopia and Reform in the Enlightenment* (Cambridge, 1971). The first extended piece on the idea of an English Enlightenment was J. G. A. Pocock, 'Post-Puritan England and the Problem of the Enlightenment' in P. Zagorin (ed.), *Culture and Politics* (California, 1980). More recently see R. Porter and M. Teich (eds.), *The Enlightenment in National Context* (Cambridge, 1981), article by Porter; J. A. Gascoigne, *Cambridge and the Age of the Enlightenment* (Cambridge, 1989), esp. 1–21; J. G. A. Pocock, 'Clergy and Commerce: The Conservative Enlightenment in England' in *Età dei Lumi. Studia Storici sul settecento Europeo in onore di Franco Venturi* (Naples, 1985).

Enlightenment in England then it should be delimited by the words 'conservative', 'polite' or 'sociable'. As Pocock would have it: the English
Enlightenment was inscribed from within the prophetic.[42] In England,
according to this interpretation, the *Aufklärung* was generated from within,
and broadly assimilated by a civic Protestantism.[43] Unlike France where the
priest held intellectual power and political authority, in England it was the
cleric who drafted the first essays in reason: in doing so religion rather than
being crushed was made 'reasonable'.[44] In England, then, deist and Christian
worked hand in glove.[45] There has, however, been a revision of this notion of
the 'conservative' Enlightenment. M. C. Jacob argues for a duality between
a conservative (or Newtonian) and a radical (pantheistic) Enlightenment.[46]
Jacob's argument rests upon her conception of the triumph of 'liberal
Christianity' after the Glorious Revolution of 1689. Parliamentary sovereignty, Newtonian science, and a latitudinarian conception of the Church of
England dominated the early eighteenth century. Ranged against this 'liberal
Christianity', for Jacob, was a radical, clandestine, and shadowy coterie of
materialists. This radical Enlightenment 'tended inevitably in a socially
levelling direction because it undermined the theoretical foundations for
established Churches and their priestly caste'. It was this English attack
directed against the 'new order' of a rational Christianity that laid the
foundations for the 'High Enlightenment' of 'the great salons of Paris and
that is best represented in the writings of Baron d'Holbach and his atheistic

42 See Pocock, 'Post-Puritan England', 91; see also R. Porter, 'The Enlightenment in England',
    6: 'The simple fact is that Enlightenment goals – like criticism, sensibility, or the faith in
    progress – throve in England *within* piety. There was no need to overthrow religion itself
    because there was no Pope, no Inquisition, no Jesuits, no monopolistic priesthood with a
    stranglehold on children through education and on families through confession.'
43 See Gascoigne, *Cambridge and the Age of the Enlightenment*, 21; for this author it was left to
    the Cambridge clergy in particular to 'absorb the Enlightenment into the stream of English life
    rather than leave it to become a potentially subversive and even revolutionary movement'.
44 See, for example, the remarks of N. Hampson,, 'The Enlightenment in France' in Porter and
    Teich, (eds.), *The Enlightenment*, 47; 'The religious thought of the Enlightenment in France
    was ... influenced, if not conditioned, by the practicalities of power ... [So] the deism of the
    philosophes took on an anticlerical, and in some cases an anti-christian edge that was
    unnecessary in England or the Netherlands and unpolitic elsewhere.' To me it seems rather
    contradictory to argue (1) that in France the clergy were so strong they had to be the focus of
    attack, and then (2) that the clergy in England were so weak that they dictated and absorbed
    the Enlightenment.
45 It is interesting to speculate upon the issue of deist versus churchman after the 1720s,
    particularly in view of J. C. D. Clark's insistence that the Church of England remained a
    vigorous and undiluted confession (that is resolutely sacerdotal rather than latitudinarian)
    until the 1800s. Perhaps the question should not be whether the radicals were assimilated in
    this period but whether they were defeated.
46 See M. C. Jacob, *The Radical Enlightenment* (1981); also restated in 'Hazard Revisited' in
    M. C. Jacob and P. Mack (eds.), *Politics and Culture in Early Modern Europe* (Cambridge,
    1987). It is interesting to note, however, that Pocock (the originator of the clerical
    Enlightenment) is keen to explore the investigations of Jacob's work: she is constantly cited
    with approval in his main discussions of the issue.

friends'.[47] In Jacob's assessment it is clear that there is a profound gap between the desires of the English radicals and those of even the rational churchmen: here infidel confronted priest. Although it seems clear that Jacob's speculations about the shadowy links between English Freethought, Continental Freemasonry and the French salons of the 1770s are dubious, and that she has understated the persistence of High Church sacerdotal Anglicanism, her implicit suggestion that there is some historical connection between English Republicanism and Enlightenment Freethought is valuable. The precise nature of this connection remains in Jacob asserted rather than explored since it is her intention to explore the 'origins' of the 'high Enlightenment' rather than the contextual intentions of English radicals between 1680 and 1730. This suggested link (both historical and conceptual) between the Republicanism of the 1650s and the 1700s is thought-provoking, although I will argue below that Jacob's levelling conception of Republicanism has forced her into characterizing the radical Enlightenment as a democratic and liberal phenomenon against the grain of the sources.

Underpinning the central notion of a conservative or clerical Enlighten-ment is the suggestion that Christianity and the power or authority of the priest was on the wane in England by 1700, unlike the French experience.[48] In understating the central role (and power) of the Church, this interpreta-tion correspondingly makes an under-assessment of the radical agenda of the Freethinkers between 1680 and 1730. To put it succinctly: if there was no religion, then anti-religious opinions had no significance. The issue of the persistence of religion is, then, a central theme of this book.[49] In stressing the

---

[47] Jacob, *Radical Enlightenment* 22, 25, 72–3, 83, 84, 142–5; and *Newtonians* 51–2, 74, 141, 143–4. Jacob's account of the latitudinarian triumph of 1689 is highly contentious: the scholarship of G. V. Bennett, G. Holmes, M. A. Goldie, and most recently J. Spurr, clearly argues against such a clear-cut victory.

[48] The most recent assertion of the decline of religion is C. J. Sommerville, 'The Destruction of Religious Culture in Pre-industrial England', *Journal of Religious History* (1988). Arguing for both an institutional and individual secularization, Sommerville insists (at 77) that religion was divorced 'from all areas of social and cultural life', and that Englishmen had 'abandon[ed] the security of ecclesiastical establishment in favour of an appeal to popular opinion'. Sommerville's general point about the change from a broad religious culture to one where religious belief was considered as private belief is an interesting one: whether this transition can be identified in the early eighteenth century is another matter.

[49] Clark, *English Society* has most recently proposed the dominance of what he terms the 'confessional state' throughout the eighteenth century. His emphasis upon the importance of the religious context is in general terms commendable: his reading of the radical attack upon the role of the priest is misconceived. See below, 18–20. It is significant that the rebuttals of Clark's arguments have avoided engaging in any profound sense with his religious her-meneutic. See, for example, J. Innes, 'Jonathan Clark, Social History and England's Ancien Regime', *PP* 115 (1987). Clark's reply, 'On Hitting the Buffers: The Historiography of England's Ancien Regime. A response', *PP* 117 (1987), again re-asserts the persistence of the confessional state, and clarifies (at 205) his treatment of radicalism in commenting: 'We are not measuring a correlation between "heterodoxy" and "political radicalism"; we are exploring the ramifications of the first when not conceptualized by the second.'

religious context, the intention is to place the study of the radical assault upon the 'halo of sanctity' within the broad historiographical rethinking that has been undertaken within the last few years. This reorientation looks backward to the seventeenth century, as well as forward to the eighteenth. Traditionally the seventeenth century has been considered as the theatre for constitutional and political innovation: the era of revolutions and social change. In many respects, as one recent historian has phrased it, the seventeenth century is fractured, 'broken in the middle', by the great upheaval of the 1640s. Restoration England heralded the age of party and political stability. The confrontation of sovereignty between king and Parliament was resolved finally in 1689: politics achieved autonomy from religious reference.[50] The scholarly reinterpretations of the pre-revolutionary period now tend towards emphasizing the religious context of the conflict. Interregnum accounts deal centrally with religious themes. It is even now possible to write a 'politics of religion' in the post-Restoration period.[51]

The most revisionist suggestion of recent years has been that in treating the seventeenth century as an 'essential unity' the emphasis must be laid upon the continuity of crises that was the English experience in the period. Scott identifies three 'crises of popery and arbitrary government of 1637–42, 1678–83, and 1687–9, [that] were fundamentally about religion'.[52] This series of crises of popery can be legitimately extended from 1689 to the 1720s if we widen the ambit of 'popery' to encompass the central idea of the sacerdotal authority of the Church of England. This wider reading of popery, particularly for the post-1689 period, suggests that what was at issue in the three crises as reread by Scott was not just the link between a corrupt theology and arbitrary civil authority drawn from the Continental model of Catholic absolutism but the central relationship of Church and state. The conflict was not between monarch and Parliament but between *sacerdos* and

[50] See M. G. Finlayson, *Historians, Puritanism, and the English Revolution: The Religious Factor in English Politics before and after the Interregnum* (Toronto, 1983).

[51] On the religious dimensions of the 1640s see J. S. Morrill, 'The Religious Context of the English Civil War', *TRHS* (1984) and 'The attack on the Church of England in the Long Parliament' in D. Beales and G. Best (eds.), *History, Society and the Churches* (Cambridge, 1985); works on the religious experiences of the Interregnum are legion – the best place to start is C. Hill, *The World Turned Upside Down* (1975), and B. Reay and J. F. L. McGregor (eds.), *Radical Religion in the English Revolution* (Oxford, 1984). On the Restoration, see T. Harris, P. Seaward and M. A. Goldie (eds.), *The Politics of Religion in Restoration England* (Blackwell, 1990).

[52] See J. Scott, 'England's Troubles: Exhuming the Popish Plot' in Harris, Seaward and Goldie (eds.), *Politics of Religion* at 110, and 'Radicalism and Restoration: The Shape of the Stuart Experience', *HJ* 31 (1988) at 458–60. The case for a thriving and coherent Church of England has been put most elegantly and convincingly by J. Spurr: apart from his series of articles, see *The Restoration Church of England 1646–1689* (Yale, forthcoming). Many thanks to the author for allowing me to read his typescript prior to publication.

regnum. Clearly Scott's emphasis upon the real danger of the French or Spanish example of popish tyranny intermeshed with this English debate which lay ambiguous since the days of the Reformation. In this reading the period post-1689 saw the battle moving in even more closely upon the very nature of *sacerdos*. The anti-popish criticism of the theology and discipline of the Laudian Church evolved into a fully blown anticlericalism by the 1700s. So the hostility of the late sixteenth century of, for example, the Marprelate tracts which, while indicting episcopacy, still upheld *sacerdos* in the Church, became the Erastian radicalism of Blount or Toland which denied the very notion of *sacerdos*.

The attack of the Freethinkers, of the deists, or of the radical Republicans, should then be appreciated as part of the continuing problem of the relations between priest and civil society that periodically convulsed England in the seventeenth century. Interestingly, although the majority of historical studies have avoided such a suggestion, it was an argument put forward by at least one contemporary. William Stephens, the radical Whig cleric, in his *An Account of the Growth of Deism in England* (1696) gave precisely this analysis of the irreligion of the 1690s. The premise of his argument is couched in the language of popery which was defined not in specific Roman Catholic terms but as a 'device of the Priesthood, to carry on a particular interest of their own'. Popery was a phenomenon not just of the Italian Church but also the 'Protestant High-Priests'. In anecdotal form Stephens narrated how an individual might come to deism. It was a tradition for young gentlemen to travel abroad as a device to appreciate the corruption of the Roman Catholic Church and priesthood. Such a young gentleman travelling in the days of Charles I would return to England and

with those very eyes which he had so lately cleared up in Italy and France, he could not forbear to see that both these Protestant Parties [the Laudian and the Presbyterian], under the pretence of religion, were only grasping at power, and that the controversy at bottom, was not who's Religion was best, but only what sect of clergy should make the best market of the meer lay-men.[53]

This perception set the individual on to a 'further step towards Deism'. The last step of the Freethinking path was to consider that if modern priests behaved in such a manner it was probable that the 'antient clergy' were of a similar inclination. Thus the Scriptures might be forged to uphold the interest of the priest rather than religion. This led Stephens to the remarkable statement, 'and if Jesus Christ their patron, laid the foundation of those powers, which both Popish and Protestant Clergy claim to themselves from

---

[53] W. Stephens, *An Account of the Growth of Deism in England* (1696), 6. Another text that insisted upon the continuity of the High Church policies of the 1630s and 1680s was William Denton's *Some Remarks Recommended unto Ecclesiasticks* (1690). See below, chapter 3, 95–6.

under him, I think the Old Romans did him right in punishing him with the death of a slave'.[54] Stephens completed this analysis by suggesting that such sharp invective 'against the Clergy' made him 'almost a Christian: for he who loveth the institution of Christ, but cannot respect those who are the ministers thereof'.[55] This anecdotal account of the passage from believer to Freethinker by Stephens neatly illustrates the domestication of popery in the course of the seventeenth century. It also suggests that the most significant element in the Freethinking attack was its anticlericalism rather than irreligion.

The most recent contradiction of the commonplace historiographical neglect of religious belief and Church politics is J. C. D. Clark's *English Society 1688–1832* (1985). Writing against both the Whiggish and *marxisant* histories of secularization Clark has forcefully and convincingly reaffirmed the centrality of the Church. The broad argument of his book is important to historians of politics and political thought: the illustration of the persistence of the confessional state until Catholic emancipation in 1828; the rejection of the historiographical fiction of a Lockean consensus in eighteenth-century political ideology, the consequent emphasis upon the vigorous tradition of *de jure divino* Filmerism in grand political thought, and the resilience of equivalent ideas in popular culture, are all crucial scholarly arguments. The most important (and certainly most applaudable) thesis of *English Society 1688–1832* is for the theological tenor of all political, social, and cultural structures during the period. George Lawson's dictum, 'that politics, both civil and ecclesiastical, belong unto theology, and are but a branch of the same' fully displays Clark's position.[56] Since religion was so

---

[54] Stephens, *An Account*, 7.   [55] Stephens, *An Account*, 25.

[56] Clark, *English Society*, 136–7, and passim. Clark, however, is mistaken to attack the *marxizant* historians for failing to examine religion and theology seriously: the work of Hill is evidence enough of a devout interest in religious matters. See also E. P. Thompson (another favourite target of Clark's venom), 'The Peculiarities of the English' in *Poverty of Theory* (1978) at 80, which pre-empts many of Clark's strictures against economic reductionism: 'The religious conflicts of the English Revolution were not "economic aspirations" diluted with illusions but conflicts about Church authority and doctrine.' The issue of the interpretation of religion is an enormous problem. For a general discussion of the method adopted in this book see R. A. Nisbet, *The Sociological Tradition* (1967), 221–3; J. Thrower, *Marxist-Leninist 'Scientific Atheism' and the Study of Religion and Atheism in the USSR* (Berlin, 1983), xvii–xviii, passim; and *The Alternative Tradition: Religion and the Rejection of Religion in the Ancient World* (The Hague, 1980), 7–10, 15–35; Q. Hoare and G. Nowell (eds.), *Selections from the Prison Notebooks of Antonio Gramsci* (1971), 326–43; J. V. Fermia, *Gramsci's Political Thought* (Oxford, 1981); G. A. Williams, 'The Concept of "egemonia" in the Thought of Antonio Gramsci', *JHI* 21 (1960); J. Larrain, *The Concept of Ideology* (1979); P. Berger, *The Social Reality of Religion* (1968); K. Nielsen, *An Introduction to the Philosophy of Religion* (1982). The most recent discussion with particular relevance to seventeenth- and eighteenth-century thought is J. S. Preus, *Explaining Religion: Criticism and Theory from Bodin to Freud* (Yale, 1987), which identifies the naturalistic, rather than reductionist, explanation of religion. Contrary to Clark's position in *English Society* (see below) Preus argues (at page xix) that 'religion and the study of religion enjoy no

central to seventeenth-century political culture we need to take its significance as a starting-point from which to examine and locate the precise critical attentions of the radicals who attempted to destroy clerical power. Given that this book intends to counter the traditional secular account of the Freethinking challenge to the Church, the problem of how to evaluate religious belief becomes even more acute. In emphasizing the persistence of theology Clark has gone some way towards revising the commonplace view of the men of reason establishing an easy ascendency over a waning religious order by insisting that early modern political radicalism originated in theological heterodoxy. However, the general tenor of his work (in chapter 5, 'The Ideological Origins of English Radicalism') is to marginalize the religious thought of men like James Harrington, John Toland and the Third Earl of Shaftesbury. Although Clark notes the logical connection between Republicanism and anticlericalism in the need of the radicals to argue against the prevalent *de jure divino* claims of the status quo, in defining Republicanism as religious heresy he has to some extent given himself grounds to ignore it since he claims the dominance of Christianity.[57]

Since the central polemic of Clark's work is against the prevailing materialist assumptions of modern historians and the resultant secular idiom in which historiography had placed the radicalism of the period, he objects to the commonplace analysis of religion as the ideological expression of a rising bourgeoisie or the legitimation of capitalist property relations. In his view historians have concentrated upon elements of the radical polemic which could be identified as modern (the rights of revolution, parliamentary reform, or the rise of liberalism) which has led to a neglect of religion, or to the other sin of interpreting religion in terms of economic structure and political change. Clark's own strictures insist upon the centrality of the theological component of commonwealth ideology. He shows clearly the general radical uninterest in issues of parliamentary reform and government structure. In place of the Whiggish interpretation Clark proposes an understanding of radicalism that directed its strength in undermining the role of the Church of England in society. Broadly characterized, the Republican programme as presented by Clark is crudely Erastian: a negative movement

privileged status. Despite the claim that religion is sui generis (whatever meaning one attaches to that notion), it seems self-serving rather than rationally persuasive to argue that religion can therefore be understood only from within a religious perspective'.

[57] Clark, *English Society*, 277–348; for a discussion of the relationship between politics and religion for an earlier period, see J. F. McGregor and B. Reay (eds.), *Radical Religion in the English Revolution* (Oxford, 1984). For valuable general discussions see M. Godelier, *Perspectives in Marxist Anthropology* (Cambridge, 1977), 'Fetishism, Religion, and Marx's General Theories concerning Ideology', 169–86; K. Marx and F. Engels, *On Religion* (Moscow, 1976), in particular Engels' essays on 'Bruno Bauer and Early Christianity' and on the origins of Christianity. Note also E. P. Thompson, 'The Peculiarities of the English' in *The Poverty of Theory* (1978).

concerned more with destroying the past than providing the conditions for the future. Since the traditional order survived intact and solid, until the 1830s, radicalism was necessarily (in Clark's view) a failure. For Clark, one need spend no historical acuity on failure. While sensibly deconstructing the commonplace assumption that anticlericalism implies secularism, Clark seems blind to the premise of his own work that religion implies Anglicanism.[58]

This book is concerned with the historical dimensions of the disputes between priest and deist, how these disputes were presented as impartial history, and the development of Freethinking ideas of religion. The starting-point for the study is a discussion of received ideas of the practice of history in the Restoration period placed firmly in the context of religious and intellectual debate. Historiography in the period was caught between the pure rhetorical model of the humanist notion of *res gestae*, and the modern idea of history as an autonomous mode of empirical discourse or *disciplina*. The argument is premised on the humanist insistence that 'history is or should be the best philosophy, or ethics in perfection', that apologists in the period accepted implicitly the Renaissance aspiration to use history as an instrument of moral and civic persuasion, but grafted on to this an empirical idea of probable and certain evidence.[59] If the historiography of the period does begin to adopt a more empirical and autonomous stance this was, as I

[58] In devaluing Republican theology as unimportant heterodoxy, Clark has fallen into the same snare he so capably identified in others: radical religious belief remains unexplored. Admittedly, Clark would insist that the opinions of infidels like Toland and Blount should not be called religious, but it is the claim of this book that such expressions were religious, not in the sense of appealing to a Christian God, but to a more universal and naturalistic transcendent principle. Both the reductionist interpretative strategies and Clark's revisionism are incapable of comprehending the spiritual dimension of Republicanism, which, I argue, can be ultimately identified in the espousal of civil religion in the thought of such central characters as Harrington, Toland and Moyle. Clark insists that 'the historian is under no obligation to explain religion in terms of something else'. The interpretation of religion, despite this methodological naïveté, is a difficult problem. We are forced (by the claims of religion itself) either to accept religion in its own terms as true, or (if we cannot accept the truth of this or that religion) then in terms of something else. Clark is unashamedly committed to the first strategy: for him all other paths smack of reductionist materialism. But if we are to take religion seriously we must approach all religion with similar gravity and be committed to a position of severe relativism (which Clark evidently is not), or else fall into the circular argument of insisting that one religion is right because all others are wrong.

[59] As one recent commentator has written: 'If the early modern period is to be seen as harbouring the beginnings of modern historiography, the explanation lies not in early modern historiographers trying to write like nineteenth- and twentieth-century ones but in their failure to sustain the convention of received modes of historical argumentation.' C. Cordren, 'From Premise to Conclusion: Some Comments on Professional History and the Incubus of Rhetorical Historiography', *Parergon: Bulletin of the Australian and New Zealand Association for Medieval and Renaissance Studies. Festschrift for Professor Sir Geoffrey Elton* 6 (1988), 10–11. See P. Millard (ed.) *Roger North: The General Preface and Life of Dr John North* (University of Toronto, 1984), 76.

argue, an attempt by its practitioners to gain the moral high ground for their particular principles: a fact that opponents were swift to point out.

As history was an essential means for making moral defences of ideological positions, so religious histories assumed a high profile. A secure and authoritative history of the Church had been an ambition of Anglican apologists since the days of the Reformation. Because the overarching purpose of this book is to explore the radical Republican and Freethinking attacks on the Church of England, chapter 3 sets out to give a necessarily selective but illustrative account of the rival type of clerical histories written in the Restoration. This chapter does not claim to present a systematic and comprehensive account of Church apologetics, but to give some sense of the ideological dimensions of commonplace ecclesiological argument. Accepting that much clerical dissension revolved around the axis of Reformation theorizing about the relative hierarchies of *regnum* and *sacerdos* the intention has been to illustrate the wide spectrum of different and opposing interpretations. Peter Heylyn has been chosen as a representative of the High Church defence of an independent clerical authority *in extremis*. Without wishing to make precise historical claims for Heylyn's vision of the Church as an accurate representation of the nature of Restoration ecclesiastical politics, ideologically Heylyn was taken by men of unimpeachable radicalism like Locke and Sidney to be typical of the High Church position.[60] To balance this clericalist defence of the independence of priest and Church from civil sovereignty the persistent importance of the Reformation and its associated ecclesiologies is illustrated by a detailed examination of the two major scholarly histories: Edward Stillingfleet's *Origines Britannicae* (1685) and Gilbert Burnet's *History of the Reformation* (1679–1714). These two works, both accepted in England and on the Continent as works of profound scholarship, are taken as epitomes of the early modern fusion of history as a rhetorical and empirical science. Although presented as impartial matter of fact, the works were identified by contemporaries as controversial. In particular, the disputes displayed in the historical treatment of the English Reformation and Archbishop Cranmer indicate the growing conflict between the latitudinarian defence of the royal supremacy and the High Church objections to the Erastian implications of this scheme.

While chapter 3 involves a selective rather than all-encompassing account of the complex history of Restoration apologetics, the intention is to describe the general shape of ecclesiological argument which radicals like Toland, Tindal and Gordon reacted against. Certainly the ecclesiological ideas proposed by theologians like Heylyn and Burnet were not innovative but firmly rooted in themes defined in the English Reformation. Reformation ecclesiologies had concentrated upon jurisdictional issues: questions of the

60 See M. A. Goldie, 'John Locke and Anglican Royalism', *Political Studies* 31 (1983), passim.

relative hierarchies of the Church or state. In order to sanctify the English Reformation, early Anglican apologists such as Jewel had defended the Church of England as a theological renovation of the Primitive Church, conducted under the aegis of the jurisdictional *dominium* of the imperial royal supremacy. Implicit in this ideological defence was the insistence that although the Church abdicated a false popish *jurisdictio* it necessarily retained its spiritual *auctoritas*. Anglican apologists from Jewel to Burnet were careful to point out that the civil sovereign could claim no spiritual competence: while the clergy could not challenge monarchical jurisdiction, *regnum* certainly did not imply *potestas ordinis*.[61] Within the logical terms of this defence, with its different components (broadly the royal supremacy and the idea of a clerical *sacerdos*), there were various ways Anglicanism could be presented, as the painstaking ecclesiological manœuvres of the sixteenth and seventeenth century illustrate.

The rest of the work is devoted to the various assaults upon the Church and its clericalist histories. In chapter 4 the focus is upon the Trinitarian disputes of the 1690s. I show how the Unitarian polemicists displayed a history of monotheistic Islam to indict the deviations of orthodox Anglicanism. From a consideration of the Unitarian use of the pattern of Islam the chapter continues to explore the radical usage found in Henry Stubbe's manuscript account of Mahomet and John Toland's *Nazarenus* (1718). These men extended Unitarian reformism to an open assault upon Christianity in the development of an idea of civil theology. The following chapter is concerned to document the varieties of histories the Freethinkers and Republicans constructed to indict the corruptions of a religion founded upon the principle of priestcraft. Using a much ignored text, Edward Herbert's comparative study of heathen theologies, *The Antient Religion of the Gentiles* (Latin version published at Amsterdam 1663, and an English translation at London 1705), the chapter illustrates how the Restoration Freethinkers adopted the history of paganism. I show how Charles Blount's historical polemic in such works as *Great is Diana of the Ephesians* (1680) and *Anima Mundi* (1679), drew upon and radicalized Herbert's more eirenic arguments. This involves a revaluation of the general intellectual relationship between Herbert and Blount and also the suggestion that the *Dialogue between a Tutor and a Pupil* (1768) traditionally attributed to Herbert was in fact the product of Blount's pen. Following from this analysis the chapter continues to deal with the radical statements of John Toland's *Letters to Serena* (1704) – which combined (amongst other sources) both Herbert's researches and Blount's adaptation – and John Trenchard's *A Natural*

---

61 The literature on the history of religious thought from the Reformation to the eighteenth century is manifold; the best survey is W. Cargill Thompson, 'The Two Regiments', (unpublished PhD, Cambridge, 1960).

History of Superstition (1709). In narrating the heathen origins of natural worship and the historical decline of this unsacerdotal religion the radicals attacked Christianity.

In chapter 6 the Republican applause for the ancient model of civil religion is discussed along with their prescriptions for the replacement of Anglicanism by a national Church devoted to the pursuit of virtue rather than mystery. The focus is upon the transmission of the historical model of the politic legislator in the classical writings of men like Cicero, Plutarch, and Dionysus of Halicarnassus, and Renaissance works like Machiavelli's *Discourses*, to such Republican texts as James Harrington's *Oceana* (1656, but importantly in John Toland's 1700 edition) and most importantly Walter Moyle's *Essay on Roman Government* (written mid-1690s, published 1726). In arguing this point my suggestion is that Republicanism in the period (J. G. A. Pocock's Neo-Harringtonians, C. Robbins' commonwealthsmen, Z. Fink's classical Republicans, and M. A. Goldie's true Whigs) should be given a broader definition, and one that envelops the religious dimension to their thought. The final chapter investigates the relationship between Republicanism and deism, arguing, contrary to modern secularistic interpretation, that the civil theologies promoted by such men as Harrington, Toland and Shaftesbury were profoundly religious enterprises. In particular, the chapter will focus upon an important but under-studied work, Shaftesbury's *An Inquiry Concerning Virtue* (1699), which is of especial interest because of John Toland's involvement in its unauthorized publication and its centrality to the tradition of civil theology.

The polemical thrust of the second half of this work is to revise the commonplace historiographical description of the radical tradition as a secularistic and modern project. In both the Marxist and Whiggish visions the radicals evangelized the process of secularization: divinity and transcendent principle were banished from social, political, and economic life. It would be more fruitful to consider the ecclesiological ideas of the radical tradition than to confront their supposedly modern political theory. While the rise of deism and the origin of the Enlightenment has been characterized as a 'trial of God', a more informative description would be as a 'trial of the priests'. Recently historiography has been concerned to consider the continuity (or lack of it) of the radical theorizing of the English Revolution with the radicalism of the Restoration and after. In terms of the grand themes of political theory (the right of revolution, the extent of suffrage and franchise, and political obligation) the Good Old Cause appears to have withered with the return of the Stuart monarchy. It has been a mistake of current historiography to search for some pre-type of modern rights theories (at least within Republican environs). In eschewing Lockean individualism, theorists like Harrington, Toland and Shaftesbury promoted more holistic conceptions of the relationship between individual and community. This conflation of ethics and politics can be most readily identified if we take seriously the radicals' religious opinions. The radical anticlericalism of the 1690s is also an easy route to establish continuities with the revolutionary traditions of the 1640s and 1650s. The radical programme was not to destroy religion, but to deprive the corrupt Christian priesthood of all independent political power. The traditional interpretative fault has been to mistake the deconsecration of Anglicanism for a desecration of all religion, and therefore by necessity a secularistic movement. For the Republican, the Anglican priest was an instrument of both irreligion and social tyranny. To overthrow priestcraft was to purify both religion and society.[62]

---

[62] The lineage with the radical traditions of both the Levellers and Winstanley are evident, particularly in the shared themes of the divinity of 'reason' and the socially corrosive role of the priesthood: see J. C. Davis, 'The Levellers and Christianity' in B. Manning (ed.), *Politics, Religion, and the English Civil War* (1973); B. Manning, 'The Levellers and Religion' in J. F. McGregor, B. Reay (eds.), *Radical Religion in the English Revolution* (Oxford, 1984); the seminal discussion of continuities is C. Hill, 'From Lollards to Levellers' in M. Cornforth (ed.), *Rebels and their Causes* (1978). See also C. Robbins, *The Eighteenth Century Commonwealthsmen* (Cambridge, Mass., 1959); C. Hill, *Some Intellectual Consequences of the English Revolution* (1980), 8–9, 27, 44, 87; M. C. Jacob, *Radical Enlightenment* 65–86, 201–2, 262; M. C. Jacob and J. R. Jacob (eds.), *The Origins of Anglo-American Radicalism*, (1984); J. G. A. Pocock (ed.), *Three British Revolutions: 1641, 1688, 1776* (Princeton, 1981); R. Zaller, 'The Continuity of British Radicalism in the Seventeenth and Eighteenth Centuries', *Eighteenth Century Life* 6 (1981); J. F. Maclear, 'Popular Anticlericalism in the Puritan Revolution', *JHI* 17 (1956).

Ars historica

RHETORIC, CREDIT AND HISTORICAL SCHOLARSHIP, 1660–1730

Viscount Bolingbroke insisted in his *Letter ... Concerning the True Use and Advantages of the Study of History* (1735) that the love of history was inseparable from human nature. He wrote:

The child hearkens with delight to the tales of his nurse: he learns to read, and he devours with eagerness fabulous legends and novels: in riper years he applies himself to history, or to that which he takes for history, to authorised romance: and even in age, the desire of knowing what happened to other men, yields to the desire alone of relating what has happened to ourselves. Thus history, true or false, speaks to our passions always.

Bolingbroke complained that history was often read as idle diversion, merely to increase learning: he explained, 'we effect the slender merit of becoming great scholars at the expense of groping all our lives in the dark mazes of antiquity'. The true purpose to the study of history was not pedantic scholarship but, 'a constant improvement in private and public virtue'.[1] During the Augustan era the value of history as a form of instructive knowledge was repeatedly affirmed. Historical writing was considered as a particularly competent means to display precepts of prudence and morality. Charles Leslie, eminent non-juror, insisted in his *Dissertation upon Ecclesiastical History* (1704), that while a 'picture allures more than description; and matters of fact beyond many arguments: discourse tells us of things, but history shews them to us'.[2] This view contradicts that of many modern historians who have suggested that the seventeenth century saw the eclipse of exemplary uses of history, and the move towards a modern idea of historical objectivity. Modern historians have been led astray by a conflation of the meanings of 'truth' and 'objectivity'. The period saw the practice of history expanding from the purveyance of moral injunctions, to legitimating social

---

[1] I. Kramnick (ed.), *Lord Bolingbroke. Historical Writings* (Chicago, 1972), 7–8.
[2] C. Leslie, *Theological Works*, 7 volumes (Oxford, 1882), I, 411.

practices and institutions such as the Church of England. As historical writing became more entrenched in these ideological conflicts it developed a more complex and sophisticated set of rules to secure the position of history as a medium for the dissemination of ethical precepts. The religious past was particularly important: as Charles Leslie wrote, 'of all history, the ecclesiastical is the most beneficial, as much more as the concern of the Church are beyond that of the state, our souls above that of our bodies, and our eternal state more than the moment we have to stay in this world. Secular history may make us statesmen and politicians; but the ecclesiastical will make us wise unto salvation'.[3] Historians and churchmen argued that scholarly research could resolve disputes about the true model of Church government and discipline. William Lloyd, Bishop of St Asaph, and close associate of the latitudinarian divine Edward Stillingfleet, composed his *Historical Account of Church Government* (1684) with the aim of refuting hostile anti-episcopalian visions of the history of the Church of England. Sir Roger Twysden, in defending the legality of the Anglican Reformation against papist charges of schism, explicitly denied he was dealing with dogmatical complexities, asserting that the controversy could be resolved through historical enquiry. He wrote: 'I began to cast with myself how I could historically make good that I had thus asserted, which in general I held most true, yet had not at hand punctually every circumstance, law, and history that did conduce unto it; in reading therefore I began to note apart what might serve for proof any way concerning it.'[4] The picture of Sir Roger Twysden or William Prynne, a more extreme case, ravenously poring over a pile of musty old tomes, gleaning them for relevant examples to validate their beliefs, is an accurate description of the practice of history in the period.

RELIGION, HISTORY AND TRUTH: THE PURSUIT OF IMPARTIALITY

The ecclesiastical histories of the period contained the ubiquitous assertion that authors wrote impartially. This claim interlocked with the contrary insistence that opponents' works were fictional. On the one hand the 'impartial' historian suggested that his work was 'true' because it was real, it was simply a direct representation of what actually happened. On the other hand the opponent was caricatured as constructing an historical past; such history was the fabrication of an interested imagination. By implication men

---

[3] *Ibid.*, 411–12. See also Richard Baxter: 'He that is but furnished with the historical knowledge of past matters of fact and then impartially readeth over the book itselfe, will have cause to thank God that he hath a clearer expository light than most expositors give him and that he hath escaped their obscuring self devised expositions', cited in W. M. Lamont, *Richard Baxter and the Millennium* (1979), 67.

[4] R. Twysden, *An Historical Vindication of the Church of England* (1675), III, 195–8.

should only be convinced by the truth; conversely to be duped by fictitious material was to endanger one's salvation. It was strategically imperative that a writer present his work as a 'fair and impartial history'.[5]

Characters as theologically opposed as Peter Heylyn and Thomas Fuller both claimed to be serving truth with impartiality. Thomas Fuller wrote of his own work, 'my Church history was so far from prostituting herself to mercenary embraces, she did not at all espouse any particular interest, but kept herself a virgin'.[6] Peter Heylyn in a vituperative attack on Fuller's work proclaimed that 'truth is the mistresse which I serve'; he decried Fuller's history as subversive of both Church and state.[7] The injunction to conduct a sincere search after the truth was ingrained in histories of the period. The claim to impartiality was linked to the moralistic intention of the history: a work was considered impartial, or true, only if it had a congruency with the ethical or theological framework of truth. Implicit within this assumption was that false precepts could only be maintained historically upon forged or fictitious evidence. Edward Stillingfleet's motivation was to rescue the history of the Church, 'from those fabulous antiquities which had so much debased the value and eclipsed the glory of it'.[8]

One of the most important pieces of historical scholarship was Gilbert Burnet's three-volume *History of the Reformation* (1679–1714) which was written with didactic intentions: such was its efficacy that it received institutional applause from both Houses of Parliament in 1680. Burnet, insistent that his work had instructive purposes, published an abridgement in 1682. Although the reduced work could not engender the same extent of authority as the complete work, it was still an efficient means of conveying true knowledge in a palatable form to the populace. Burnet's work was not to be considered,

> only as a tale of what was transacted in former times ... It becomes most profitable, when the series and reasons of affairs, and secret counsels and ends, together with the true characters of eminent men, are rightly presented to us, and so upon the light which is given to us of past times, we may form prudent judgements of the present time, and probable conjectures of what is to come; and may both enlighten our understandings more by giving us a freer prospect of humane affairs, and may better direct us in our conduct.[9]

Burnet's work 'took quiet possession of the belief of the nation at home, and of a great part of Europe abroad, being translated into four languages'.[10] The work had been composed as a warning to the nation against the

5 J. Inett, *Origines Anglicanae*, 2 volumes (Oxford, 1704, 1710), II, ii, xxiv.
6 T. Fuller, *The Appeal of Injured Innocence* (1659), Dedication: 'To the Right Hon. George Berkeley'.
7 P. Heylyn, *Examen Historicum* (1659), Sig. A4.
8 E. Stillingfleet, *Origines Britannicae* (1685), i.
9 G. Burnet, *The Abridgement of the History of the Reformation*, Sig. A3v.
10 G. Burnet, *The History of the Reformation*, III, Introduction, iii.

encroaching dangers of popery, during the attempted exclusion of James, the Catholic Duke of York, from the British throne. While the *History of the Reformation* inspired great public praise, it also attracted many attacks intended to undermine its prescriptions. Burnet, later Bishop of Salisbury, in his response to these attacks, made it a common theme to present an image of scholarly moderation. While willing to have his mistakes corrected where uncovered, he reserved hostility for the petty cavils of theological opponents whose only purpose was to devalue his authority and integrity. Burnet was adamant that his work contained no deliberate, nor important distortions. The analogy between the value of true history and good money was drawn; he wrote:

History is a sort of trade in which false coyn and false weights are more criminal than in other matters; because the errors may go further and run longer; tho' these authors colour their copper too slightly to make it keep its credit long. If men think there are degrees of lying, then certainly these that are the most loudly told, that wound the deepest, that are told with the best grace, and that are transmitted to posterity under the deceitful colours of truth, have the blackest guilt.[11]

The appendix to the second volume of the history contained lists of such corrections sent to Burnet by Thomas Baker, member of the High Church and later non-juror. It was part of Burnet's strategy for objectivity that his desire for public and detailed correction was loudly proclaimed. In this way he implored impartial critics to render his work even more authoritative. This strategy did not pass unhindered.[12]

One of the most damaging assaults on Burnet's historical fidelity was Anthony Harmer's *A Specimen of Some Errors* (1693). 'Anthony Harmer' was a pseudonym for Henry Wharton (1664–95), chaplain to the High Church Archbishop William Sancroft. Wharton was an extremely productive historian, his great scholarly contribution being the two folio volumes of medieval Church and monastic history *Anglia Sacra* (1691). This work lauded the history of the spirituality of the medieval Church, directly contrary to the commonplace post-Reformation denunciation of the era as heralding the rise of superstition, and the ascendancy of popery.[13] Wharton insisted it was his right to examine the claims Burnet had made for the impartiality of the *History of the Reformation*.[14] He wrote:

This examination will be so much the more necessary and serviceable, by how much the history hath obtained the greater reputation in the world: since where any history

11 G. Burnet, *Reflections on Mr Varillas' History of the Revolution* (1689), 9–10.
12 Note that the Cambridge University Library's first edition of Burnet's *History of the Reformation* belonged to the High Church man Thomas Baker. There are many marginal corrections and additions in his hand.
13 For an account of Wharton, see G. D. D'Oyly, *The Life of William Sancroft*, 2 volumes (1821), passim. Also D. C. Douglas, *English Scholars 1660–1730* (1951), 139–55, on *Anglia Sacra* at 144–52.
14 Wharton, *A Specimen*, iv.

acquireth (as this has most deservedly) such as universal reception; as to be read, and esteemed by all at home, to be translated into other languages abroad, to be accounted the most perfect in its kind; that the universal reputation will the more effectually contribute to the propagation of the errors contained in it.

Wharton quantified Burnet's inconsistencies and manipulations, concentrating in particular upon his manuscript sources. Burnet had included large appendices of unpublished records supplementing his historical veracity. Wharton insisted, on the contrary, that the collections were worthless because there 'appears just reason to suspect the care and fidelity of the transcriber'.[15] Wharton informed the reader 'that of those which I have examined, I found near as many to be false as true'. Wharton examined Burnet's work page by page, line by line, and word by word. In referring throughout the examination to 'the Historian', as he catalogued the misdemeanours of the *History of the Reformation*, Wharton implied that Burnet did not merit the privileges the title of historian endowed. Wharton identified and displayed eighty-nine faults in Burnet's evidence: a damning blow to one who proclaimed the purity and truth of his scholarship so loudly.

Wharton exclaimed that his cause was that of historical fidelity, and his intention to undermine Burnet's 'credit'. He wrote:

Now to mistake and report falsely the dates of publick instruments is not a matter of light moment. For these will necessarily betray both writers and readers into infinite other mistakes, while they endeavour to adapt things and the circumstances of them to the supposed, but mistaken time of other actions. Besides all this diminished the credit of any history, so that in all other matters the reader cannot safely rely upon it, when he knows the negligence of the Historian in any part of it.[16]

Burnet swiftly identified Wharton's intention. In a letter to William Lloyd, the Bishop of Lichfield and Coventry, Burnet commented, 'as to the charge of falsehood that comes over so often, that it is plain by his frequent repeating it, that he intended it should stick'.[17] Burnet, anxious to rebuff Wharton's threat to his credit, produced written testimony from a Mr Angus, his transcriber, to the effect that he was willing to swear on oath that his copies of the manuscripts had been correct. Burnet supplemented this with a statement that he had double-checked all his references 'so that I may sincerely say that I writ that work with the same fidelity that I should have given evidence upon oath in a Court of Judicature'. Burnet rather paradoxically interpreted Wharton's work as testimony to the value of his own work. The mistakes identified in the *Specimen* were of such a minor status that they indicated that everything essential to Burnet's argument was sound.[18] In the retrospective third volume of his history (1714), Burnet identified Wharton as the author of *A Specimen*, suggesting that the attack had been inspired by

15 *Ibid.*, 26.   16 *Ibid.*, 26.   17 G. Burnet, *Letter to the Bishop of Coventry* (1693) 7.
18 *Ibid.*, 8, 13–14.

personal malice. Wharton had approached Burnet after 1689 in the hope that the bishop might be able to procure him clerical advancement. Burnet was unresponsive to these requests: Wharton's criticisms were devalued because constructed for personal revenge.

A common characteristic of historical works of the period, as the case of Burnet and Wharton indicates, was the fashion for extensive line-by-line analysis of opponents' works. In the early Restoration, the rival visions of Peter Heylyn and the Presbyterian Henry Hickman resulted in each man publishing extremely detailed dissections of opponent texts. Francis Atterbury and William Wake took it in turns to publish histories, and then comb the replies, sentence by sentence, to expose inconsistency and contradiction. Many works were simply long lists of mistakes, prefaced by the authorial injunction that the reader in face of the evidence should ignore the prescriptions of the work under examination. Burnet was a typical exponent of the practice. His *History of the Reformation* had been originally published in refutation of the French republication of an earlier Jesuit work written by Nicholas Saunders, which treated the English Reformation as heretical schism. Included at the rear of Burnet's first two volumes were detailed analyses of the mistakes in Saunders' work.[19] Another historian, the Frenchman Varillas, had his work subjected to a similarly anatomical investigation by Burnet's pen. Instead of eulogizing the actions of the Reformation, Varillas contradicted Burnet in his history of Protestant heresies, *Histoire des revolutions arrivée l'Europe en matière de religion* (1686–8, 6 volumes). Between 1687 and 1689 Burnet published three long volumes against Varillas's work.[20] Each of these works set out to destroy Varillas's 'credit', and discover him as a 'false coyner', a man who issued 'romantick impostures'.[21]

One of Burnet's most common charges, against such men as Varillas and Heylyn, was that they gave no voucher for their statements.[22] The development of citations, footnotes, and appendices crammed full of musty manuscripts has been heralded as the birth of modern objective scholarship. What I would argue is that the practice originated in the attempt to accredit a particular text with authority: the reference to hard empirical documents created an image of transparent truth. Jean Leclerc in his *Parrhasiania* (1700) noted that 'tis a common question, whether those who write ancient history, or at least a history of which there are no living witnesses, ought to cite the authors, whom they made use of, in every page or in every article'.[23]

Leclerc discussed the variant ideas presented on the issue; some thought

---

[19] Burnet, *History of the Reformation*, I, 272–304; II, 383–416.
[20] See G. Burnet, *Reflections on Mr Varillas* (1689), *A Continuation of the Reflections* (1687), *A Defence of the Reflections* (1687).
[21] *Ibid.*, 32–3.   [22] *Ibid.*, 30; *History of the Reformation*, I, Introduction, Sig. bv.
[23] J. Leclerc, *Parrhasiania* (1700), 107.

the reader ought to rely simply on the honesty of the writer, or that a list of source material ought to be placed at the end of the text. Leclerc was insistent that reference had to be continually made throughout an historical work. He explained, 'for the republic of letters is at last become a country of reason and light, and not of authority and implicit faith as it has been too long'. With a description of the material used the reader could check the veracity of the relation. The contrary reasoning was that, if an historian omitted reference to primary manuscripts and vouchers then either he had something to hide or was writing fiction. Leclerc continued, 'we therefore maintain, that if a man avoids to quote his vouchers, the reason of it is, because he would not have anyone to examine the history, as he relates it, by comparing the narration with that of other historians who writ before him'. Without footnotes it was too easy for the devious historian to foist a fraud upon the helpless reader. Leclerc complained, ''tis easy for a man to sham a romance upon the world without fear of discovery, and to give his history, whatever turn he pleases, the suspicious reader does not know where to take his word, and immediately throws aside a book upon which he cannot safely depend'.[24]

While Burnet appreciated that the demand for his *History* meant an abridgement was necessary, he was unhappy that the 'great collection' of records included in the original 'for my justification' had to be abandoned: everything written in the *Abridgement* (1682) had to be taken upon trust.[25] In the introduction to the first volume of his *History* Burnet had castigated Peter Heylyn, for 'he never vouched any authority'.[26] It was this type of assault that Burnet intended to avoid by self-consciously parading a large manuscript collection at the end of his work. He wrote:

I know it is needless to make great protestations of my sincerity in this work. These are of course, and are little considered, but I shall take a more effectual way to be believed, for I shall vouch my warrants for what I say, and tell where they are to be

---

[24] *Ibid.*, 108–10. If we simply look at the function of citations as persuasive mechanisms we can understand the preoccupation authors had with referring the reader to the original sources. Consider a seventeenth-century reader examining a work upon a contentious theme, for example the historical narration of the rights of the monarchy over the Church. We encounter a description of events that suggests the king's authority is supreme over all other powers both civil and spiritual, and that the Church is simply an appendage of the civil state. This is a view we have always been taught is incorrect. We examine the text: the author has written a 'true' account, following documents and contemporary descriptions to which he has given us directions. We may not be convinced by reasonable argument, but someone declaring 'look this is how it was done, here are the manuscripts to prove it' is less easily dismissed. In this way the reader was led to depend upon the expertise of the historian.

[25] Burnet, *Abridgement of the History* (1682), Sig. A4r–v.

[26] Burnet, *History of the Reformation*, I, Sig. bv. Henry Hickman, Heylyn's redoubtable Presbyterian opponent, had similarly taunted the High Church man with the same charge. Hickman wrote about one of Heylyn's unhelpful references: 'Who these are I know not, nor have any direction to find them out, but a blind one in the margin, v.Synod.Rem. which I am not scholar enough to make use of, if the Synodolia Remonstentium be intended, why is not the page in which those words occur quoted? Can the historian imagine his readers do so

found. And having copied out of Records and Mss. many papers of great importance, I shall not only insert the substance of them in the following work, but at the end of it shall give a collection of them at their full length, and in the language they were originally written: from which the reader will receive full evidence of the truth of this history.[27]

Burnet intended to convince the reader of the 'truth' of his position: this conviction was to be achieved through displaying empirical evidence which was a 'more effectual way to be believed'.

In the first volume of the History, Burnet noted that his research had the full support of such eminent divines as Stillingfleet, Lloyd and Tenison. These men, who would hold some of the highest clerical offices in the country, accrued authority to his work. Burnet omitted to point out that even with this backing he had been banned from one manuscript collection. Renowned throughout Europe the Cottonian library contained Saxon works, Hebrew texts, Greek originals, plus primary authorities for every period of English History. Burnet desired to use this collection, but Sir John Cotton (1621–1701) was reluctant to allow him access. Although Sir John was a scholar, a man who encouraged learning, and who made arrangements just prior to his death to open the library to the public, he objected to Burnet, conceiving Burnet as 'being no friend to the prerogative of the Crown, nor the constitution of the Church'.[28] Burnet could bring no argument to sway Cotton. He was thus forced to enter the library illegally, under the cover of night, aided by Cotton's unfaithful nephew Sir John Marsham. This vision of a reputable cleric stealing into the library after the witching hour to transcribe manuscripts faithfully, in order to warn the nation against the impending threat of popery, is a delightfully apt one to characterize the practice of Augustan history.

HISTORICAL REVOLUTION: RHETORIC, PERSUASION AND PROBABILITY

In order to comprehend the persuasive and didactic purpose of historical writing we need to explore seventeenth-century ideals of historiography, bearing in mind Bolingbroke's dictum that the correct purpose of historical research was not meticulous erudition, but prudential instruction. This distinction is one which modern historians of history have failed to grasp. There are many works commenting on early modern historiography, all committed to narrating the growth of the 'modern discipline'. The most

abound in leisure, as to read over a Book of so great a bulk, as the Synodolia to find out one phrase?' Hickman, *Historia Quinqu-Articularis* (1659), 15.
[27] Burnet, *History of the Reformation*, I, Sig. cr.
[28] Burnet, *History of the Reformation*, III, Introduction, i, ii.

recent work, B. Shapiro's *Probability and Certainty* (1983), suggests the seventeenth century saw the practice of history joining hands with that of the scientist in following the ideal of dispassionate investigation. For both disciplines the method lauded was that of ' impartial accuracy', 'accurate reporting' and the 'requirements of scholarship'.[29] J. Preston has commendably set out to examine the problem of 'bias' in Restoration ecclesiastical historians. However, he represents the works of the period as attempting to grapple with the 'complexity and difficulty of the problem of objectivity', constructing 'new expedients' to ward off bias. Preston epitomizes the proleptic notions of modern historiography.[30]

The case for the origins of modern historical method arising in the early modern period has been forcefully argued by F. Smith Fussner in *The Historical Revolution* (1962). Again the scientific ideal is lauded. His subjects are berated for not consciously articulating their historical methodology. Fussner's work heralds the advent of the use of primary material, the 'awareness of process', and the inevitable secularization of belief. 'Science, not religion, was the new and revolutionary force in human society.' A more recent work, A. B. Ferguson's *Clio Unbound* (1974), is a more sensitive attempt than that of Fussner; it is still constrained by the implicit need to document the progress and origins of the 'modern sense of history'. The work condemns the early modern historian for entertaining incomplete notions of causality, for being innocent of methodological theory, for irritating 'modern tastes' with an 'indigestible lump of ecclesiastical apologetics' and, finally, for not studying social and cultural issues.[31]

[29] See B. Shapiro, *Probability and Certainty in Seventeenth-Cemtury England* (Princeton, 1983), especially chapter 5 'Historical Method', 119–63, i.e. 117–20, 126, 139–40, 147; on the connection between humanism and the rise of modern science, see B. Shapiro and F. R. Frank, *English Virtuosi in the Sixteenth and Seventeenth centuries* (Los Angeles, 1972); also G. Wylie Sypher, 'Similarities between the scientific and historical revolutions at the end of the Renaissance', *JHI* 26 (1965); see A. Richardson, *History Sacred and Profane* (1964), 41, commenting on the Restoration period as 'a kind of twilight period, an age of half seeing, between the fading brilliance of the medieval world system and the dawn of our modern historically minded age'.

[30] See his concluding remarks: 'It is the contention of this writer that some English Church historians of the later seventeenth century showed increasing awareness of the difficulty of the problem of bias and adjusted their methodology in an attempt to solve or at least reduce the problem. In doing so they disclosed attitudes towards historiography that foreshadowed some nineteenth-century developments, and in stressing the importance of sources, they anticipated contemporary practices in historical writing'. J. H. Preston, 'The Problem of Bias in Ecclesiastical History' in *JHI* 32 (1971), 204, 208, 217.

[31] F. Smith Fussner, *The Historical Revolution* (1962), 27, 32–37, 60–91, 92–113, 274; A. B. Ferguson, *Clio Unbound* (North Carolina, 1974), xv, 2, 83. Note G. R. Elton's hostility to the latter work which he castigates for its 'astonishingly anachronistic air. In fact the twentieth century keeps sticking its superfluous nose into the discourse', *HT* 20 (1981) 94. For other works that rest upon proleptic premises, see D. R. Kelley, *The Foundations of Modern Historical Scholarship* (New York, 1970), J. H. Preston, 'Was There an Historical Revolution?', *JHI* 38 (1977); J. Levine, 'Ancients, Moderns and History: The Continuity of

All the above works appear to be the result of a Rankean or positivistic belief in the inevitable progress of knowledge. The mythology of prolepsis is evident. The evaluation of past historical work is conducted in terms of the current status of historical method. Modern history is practised in terms of pseudo-scientific objectivity; its social function is confined in general, to academic circles. The early modern mind perceived 'history' as a means of access to religious and moral rectitude: because of this, historical method and writings, like Burnet's *History of the Reformation*, became entrenched in the ideological conflicts of the period.[32] It will be central to my argument that methodological apparatus, both implicitly accepted, and explicitly forged, was linked to the ideological function of historical discourse. The intellectual disunity of the period meant that participants had to search for some form of authoritative leverage in polemical debate, for a form of knowledge that could be deployed and maintained with a status of certainty and objective truth. History was a means of creating assurance in an audience. Thus, in an age of religious disunity, the past, and the presentation of the past, became a displaced crucible for ideological dispute. The internecine struggle between different interests in turn led to redefinitions, and increasing sophistication, in the techniques created for cementing the mandatory value of historical discourse.[33]

Historical Writing' in P. J. Korshin (ed.), *Studies in Change and Revolution* (Menston, 1972); J. H. Franklin, *Jean Bodin and the Sixteenth-Century Revolution in the Methodology of Law and History* (New York, 1963); F. J. Levy, *Tudor Historical Thought* (California, 1967); Levi Fox (ed.), *English Historical Scholarship in the Sixteenth and Seventeenth Centuries* (Oxford, 1956). The most recent example is P. Avis, *Foundations of Modern Historical Thought from Machiavelli to Vico* (1986).

One of the more sensitive studies, A. M. Momigliano, 'Ancient History and the Antiquarian' in *Studies in Historiography* (1969), 1–40, promotes a more sophisticated argument. Momigliano suggests that during the seventeenth century the distinction between historian and antiquarian, or between collecting facts and interpreting these facts, became more pronounced. Following this development he argued that, threatened by the accusations of historical Pyrrhonism in the German universities, historiography evolved from the Renaissance rhetorical tradition of *ars historica*, to a more empirical notion of *ars critica* or textual criticism. While accepting Momigliano's thesis for the general shape of Continental historiography, I would dispute its aptness in the English context. My case is that there were crucial rhetorical elements within the development of a critical discipline in historical writing, that is in Momigliano's terms *ars historica* and *ars critica* became entangled, rather than separated. The dynamics of English historiography developed within a context of polemical dispute, rather than the purely academic or intellectual threat of scepticism.

32 See K. V. Thomas, *The Perception of the Past in Early Modern England* (The Creighton Trust Lecture, 1982); H. White, *Tropics of Discourse. Essays in Cultural Criticism* (Baltimore, 1978), especially chapter 5, 'Fictions of Factual Representation'; L. Jardine, *Francis Bacon and the Art of Discourse* (Cambridge, 1974). E. Said, *Orientalism* (1978), 9–10, is useful on the distinction between pure and political knowledge: 'The determining impingement on most knowledge produced in the contemporary West ... is that it be non-political, that is scholarly, academic, impartial, above partisan, or small minded doctrinal belief.' Said attacks the liberal consensus that true knowledge is fundamentally non-political. J. G. A. Pocock, *The Ancient Constitution and the Feudal Law* (Cambridge, 1987), has recently pointed out the inherent Whiggish dangers of a history of historiography.

33 For general accounts of the epistemological crisis of the seventeenth-century mind see:

The early modern idea of the methods and value of historical writing was entrenched in the canons of literate society. A brief examination of curricula and the prescriptions of educationalists reveal the determining influence of the thought, principles, and texts of classical antiquity. The *trivium* at Cambridge University focused upon learning the techniques of grammar, rhetoric and dialectic – traditions which were a legacy of the humanist preoccupation with pagan learning. Rhetoric and oratory, that is, the correct use of words, were a central feature of university education in the period.[34] Rhetoric involved not only methods of communication, but also those of persuasion. Early modern ideas of history were part of this tradition. The works commonly employed to teach the principles of the *ars dicendi* were classical texts like Cicero, Quintilian and Aristotle. The principles of classical rhetoric were also disseminated to the seventeenth century in a form directly linked to historical methods in the works of ancient historians such as Polybius, Sallust, Thucydides, Dionysus of Halicarnassus and Lucian. The works of these authors were the common stock of the libraries of literate individuals. In order to understand seventeenth-century attitudes to history these works and their relationship with the ingrained ideas of the function of rhetoric must be defined.[35]

The premises of rhetoric were based on the relationship between the expert, or the authority, and the uninitiated audience. The intention of the *rhetor* was to persuade the audience that the thesis proposed was a 'true' one. The process was one of cultivating a conviction in the minds of the listeners or readers that the speaker was communicating a valid and correct proposition. In this relationship the *rhetor* has to establish authority in two forms. The creation of conviction in the speaker's personal authority was a condition of persuading the audience of the authoritative value of the thesis proposed. The rhetorical relationship is intent, in tandem, at establishing both the 'credit' of the opinion and the utterer. If we examine one of the most influential classical texts, Aristotle's *Rhetoric*, this will become evident. In 1651 Thomas Hobbes anonymously published a translation and abridgement of Aristotle's *Rhetoric*. The latter was republished, with the

H. Van Leeuwen, *The Pursuit of Certainty in English Thought 1630–1690* (The Hague, 1963); R. Popkin, *The History of Scepticism from Erasmus to Spinoza* (1979); R. S. Carroll, *The Commonsense Philosophy of Bishop Edward Stillingfleet* (The Hague, 1975); H. Baker, *The Wars of Truth* (Massachusetts, 1969).

34 W. T. Costello, *The Scholastic Curriculum at Early Seventeenth Century Cambridge* (Cambridge, 1958), at 39–51; Jardine, *Francis Bacon and the Art of Discourse*, passim. On linguistic theory, see M. Cohen, *Sensible Words* (Baltimore, 1977).

35 See P. Burke, 'A Survey of the Popularity of Ancient Historians 1450–1700', *HT* 5 (1966) and 'Tacitism' in T. A. Dory (ed.), *Tacitus* (1969); J. W. Johnson, 'The Classics and John Bull 1660–1714' in H. T. Swedenborg (ed.), *England in the Restoration* (California, 1972); R. S. Ogilvie, *Latin and Greek. A History of the Influence of the Classics on English Life from 1600–1918* (1967); J. Johnson, *The Formation of English Neo-Classical Thought* (Princeton, 1967). G. Kennedy, *Classical Rhetoric and its Christian and Secular Tradition from Ancient to Modern Times* (North Carolina, 1980).

authorship acknowledged, in 1681. Hobbes conceived the work as supplementary to his *Leviathan* (1651); in the latter work he had demonstrated 'in the state of nature, the primitive art of fighting to be the only medium whereby men procur'd their ends'. In the *Art of Rhetoric* he intended to show 'what power in societies has succeeded to reign in its stead. I mean the art of speaking, which by the use of the commonplaces of probability, and knowledge in the manners and passions of mankind, through the working of belief is able to bring about whatsoever interest'.[36] Hobbes complimented the ancients for their perspicacity in insisting that the rhetorical art was necessary to politics. Hobbes followed Aristotle in defining rhetoric as 'that faculty, by which we understand what will serve our turn, concerning any subject to win belief in the hearer. Of those things that beget belief; some require not the help of art; as witnesses, evidences, and the like, which we invent not, but make use of; and some require art and are invented by us.' For Aristotle the techniques of persuasion were a form of demonstration, 'for we chiefly believe a thing when we suppose it to be demonstrated'. The central rhetorical principle was for the speaker to present 'what is like to truth. For men are sufficiently inclin'd to truth. Wherefore he who attains easily to probability by conjecture, takes the same course to find out the truth.' Intrinsic to this action was that the oration 'is so pronounced that the orator may be thought a person worthy to be credited. For we believe the vertuous more easily and sooner, and barely in all things; but absolutely in these things where there is not that certainty, but a suspense of judgements, and a difficulty of determination, in regard to the various opinions of men.'[37]

Classical historical writing was founded on these rhetorical principles.[38]

---

36 T. Hobbes, *Art of Rhetoric* (1681), Sig. A3v. See W. J. Ong, 'Hobbes and Talon's Ramist Rhetoric in English', *Transactions of the Cambridge Bibliographical Society* 1 (1951) esp. 261–2. The idea of manipulative rhetoric, or the creation of false ideologies, is a central, if understudied, theme of Books III-IV of *Leviathan*. This is a polemic that links Hobbes firmly with the later writings of Toland, in particular his *Christianity Not Mysterious*: see below.

37 Hobbes, *Art of Rhetoric*, iii; Aristotle, *Rhetoric: Or the True Grounds and Principles of Oratory* (1681), 4, 5, 8. See Bacon: 'For as knowledges have hitherto been delivered, there is a kind of contract of error between the deliverer and the receiver; for he who delivers knowledge desires to deliver it in such a form as may be best believed, and not as may be most conveniently examined; and he who receives knowledge requires present satisfaction', cited in Jardine, *Bacon*, 174. See also Toland: 'Humane authority is also call'd *Moral Certitude*; when I believe an intelligible relation made by my friend, because I have no reason to suspect his veracity, nor he any interest to deceive me', *Christianity Not Mysterious*, 15.

38 T. P. Wiseman, *Clio's Cosmetics* (Leicester, 1979), 1–8. For general discussions of the rhetorical heritage of antiquity and its relationship with historical method see: N. Struever, *The Language of History in the Renaissance* (Princeton, 1970), 5–40; P. Burke, *The Renaissance Sense of the Past* (New York, 1966); L. B. Campbell, *Tudor Conceptions of History and Tragedy in a Mirror for Magistrates* (Berkeley, 1936); M. Gilmore, *Humanists and Jurists* (Harvard, 1963); B. R. Reynolds, 'Latin Historiography: 1400–1600', *Studies in the Renaissance* 2 (1955): L. Janik, 'Lorenzo Valla: The Primacy of Rhetoric and the Demoralisation of History', *HT* 12 (1973); B. Reynolds, 'Shifting Currents in Historical Criticism', *JHI* 13 (1953); G. H. Nadel, 'The Philosophy of History before Historicism', *HT*

The contribution of the oratorical traditions to the practice of history in the ancient world was the use of rhetorical finesse to render persuasion more effective, by creating a narration that 'sounded' like the truth. The role of the historian in classical antiquity mirrored that of the orator in providing incentive for virtue. If the ancient historian was committed to the role of presenting paradigms of morality as a didactic function, then the author, by default, had to employ the persuasive tools of rhetoric.[39]

These classical ideas carried much weight during the Augustan era. There was an extensive interest in, and publication of, the histories of antiquity during this period. The works of Sallust, Tacitus and Plutarch retained a perennial attraction for the *literati* of Europe. Works were published in both Latin and vernacular editions. These works shared the common premise that history was an instructive discourse. Thomas Hobbes translated the *Eight Books of the Peloponnesian Warre ... Written by Thucydides* in 1634. He willingly recommended Thucydides' books, 'as having in them profitable instruction for noblemen, and such as may come to have the managing of great and weighty actions ... For in history, actions of honour and dishonour doe appear plainly and distinctly, which are which; but in the present age they are so disguised, that few there be, and those very carefull, that be not grossely mistaken in them.' Hobbes was to insist that Thucydides' work was superior even to that of Polybius. Thucydides managed to combine both truth and eloquence in his writings, a beneficial mixture, 'for in truth consisteth the soule, and in eloquution the body of the history. The latter without the former, is but a picture of history; and the former without the latter, unapt to instruct.'[40] According to Hobbes, Thucydides had avoided instructive digression which was the role of the philosopher, instead by means of 'cohærent, perspicuous, and perswasive' narration he had conveyed his precepts to the reader. This was executed so skilfully that 'the narration itself doth secretly instruct the reader, and more effectually then possibly can be done by precept'.[41] Hobbes applauded Thucydides for being able to convey moral statements to men without them mobilizing opposition to such instruction.[42] It was Hobbes' contention in *Leviathan* (1651) that

3 (1963–4); G. Gentile, 'Eighteenth-Century Historical Methodology: De Sovia's *Institutions*', HT 4 (1964–5); G. H. Nadel, 'History as Psychology in Francis Bacon's theory of history', HT 5 (1966).
39 Kennedy, *Classical Rhetoric*, 38–9.
40 T. Hobbes, *Eight Books of the Peloponnesian Warre ... Written by Thucydides* (1634), Epistle Dedicatory, Sig. A2r, 'Of the Life and History of Thucydides' Sig. br. a2v.
41 *Ibid.*, 'Of the Life and History of Thucydides', Sig. a3r.
42 Thucydides' history was a replacement for experience; the reader was placed in the position of spectator. Hobbes declared: 'For he setteth his Reader in the assemblies of the people, and in the senates, at their debating; in the streets, at their seditions; and in the field, at their battels. So that looke how much a man of understanding, might have added to his experience, if he had then lived, a beholder of their proceedings, and familiar with the men, and the

one of the causes of sedition in the 1640s was that the men of action had been educated in rebellious principles through reading malevolent ancient history.[43]

History as a substitute for experience was the central motif of Polybius' method; history was to perform therapy on the ills of the body politic.[44] A competent English version of Polybius was executed by Sir Henry Sheeres in three volumes in 1693–8, with an introductory preface by John Dryden. According to the latter, Polybius was the 'clearest and most instructive of all historians'. So much so that even as a young boy Dryden had been able to extract counsels of prudence from the histories.[45] Dryden continued in rapture: 'Tis wonderful to consider, with how much care and application he instructs, counsels, warns, admonishes and advises, whensoever he can find it a fit occasion: he performs all these ... in the nature of a common parent of mankind.' Polybius was ever diligent in drawing the truth up from the bottom of the deepest well, commending the study of history with the love of virtue.[46] The value of truth in history in the Polybian scheme was to fulfil the utilitarian function of disseminating moral patterns to the reader. This model of historical enquiry had been commended by such disparate figures as Jean Bodin, William Camden, John Milton and Thomas Hobbes.[47]

This relationship between the role of the historian as reflector of truth, and the reader as receiving the lessons of this truth, was the essence of early modern history. These ideas are embodied in the work of Degory Wheare (1573–1647), first Camden Prælector of History at Oxford 1625–47. In 1634 Wheare published at Oxford his *Reflectiones Hyemales De Ratione et Methodi Legendi: Utrasques Historias Civile et Ecclesiasticus*. The work was popular. It was translated in 1684 by Nicholas Horseman; a further edition was enlarged and expanded by Edmund Bohun in 1694. The latter work was prefaced with an instructive discourse by Wheare's successor Henry Dodwell (1641–1711). That this work was published in 1634, and still merited two

business of the time, so much almost may be profit now, by attentive reading of the same here written', Hobbes, *Eight Books ... by Thucydides*, 'To the Readers', ii.

[43] Hobbes, *Leviathan*, 369–70.

[44] Isaac Casaubon had written an expert and scholarly Latin edition of Polybius' histories in 1609, complete with an eulogy of the historian's skills. In 1634 Edward Grimston had attempted an English translation, with rather inadequate results.

[45] Sheeres, *Histories of Polybius*, I, 'The Character of Polybius and his writings', Sig. A2v, B1v–B2r.

[46] *Ibid.*, Sig. B2r, B7v, B8r.

[47] See J. Bodin, *Method for the Easy Comprehension of History*, ed. B. Reynolds (New York, 1945); L. F. Dean, 'Bodin's *Methodus* in England before 1625', *Studies in Philology* 38 (1943); J. A. Bryant, 'Milton and the Art of History', *Philological Quarterly* 24 (1950); E. M. Tillyard, *Milton's Private Correspondence* (Cambridge, 1932). For an interesting contemporary work, see T. Heywood, *The Two ... Histories both Written by C. C. Sallust* (1608), in particular the prefatory 'Of the Choise of History, by way of Preface, dedicated to the courteous reader' which translated portions of Bodin's work.

further editions in the 1680s and 1690s would imply both the continuity of attitudes to historical method, and that Wheare's work is a convenient epitome of these attitudes.[48] Wheare deployed the Ciceronian maxim 'that history is the register and explication of particular affairs, undertaken to the end that the memory of them may be preserved, and so to universals may be the more evidently confirmed by which we may be instructed how to live well and happily'. History was the mistress of life, a fruitful granary of didactic examples, and prudence. While moral philosophy aided men to the improvement of civil society by the use of precept, history achieved the same purpose by the instrument of example. He wrote: 'For the principle end of history is practice, and not knowledge or contemplation. And therefore we must learn, not only that we may know, but that we may live well and honestly.' Wheare insisted that readers should glean the pages they read in search of true moral insight; these examples ought to be placed in commonplace books for ready instruction.[49] Particularly commended was the study of ecclesiastical history; it was the readers' 'most indispensible duty to turn over the ecclesiastical history night and day'. Wheare insisted that individuals had a duty to acquire 'civil knowledge'; and although political experience was necessary and indispensable to this search, history was an important supplement. Henry Dodwell, in his prefatory 'Invitation to Gentlemen to Aquaint themselves with Antient History', seconded Wheare's notion that the application of history was 'more fitted for the use of an active than a studious life'.[50] Dodwell's work was an exhortation to the youth of the 1690s to leave the study and become, like the Pythagoreans, 'useful citizens'. Dodwell conceived of a Platonic unity between contemplation and practice, which could be achieved through the correct direction and application of historical reading.[51]

The postulate of the impartial, independent and veracious historian was central to the ideological function of the early modern historian. The claim to be unmasking, reflecting, and transmitting the truth, free from partial interests, was an ideological disclaimer. Under the guise of impartiality the historian was free to institute his own 'colour' of truth as objective. The assertion was that the historian could transcend his cultural and political identity in the name of universal truth. Such a claim to have direct access, via

---

48 On Wheare, see C. Hill, *Intellectual Origins of the English Revolution* (Oxford, 1965), 54, 72, 176–77, 211, 310. See H. Prideaux, 5 January 1679, commending Wheare's work, *Letters of Humphrey Prideaux*, 63–4; and John Locke, 'Some Thoughts concerning the Reading and Study for a Gentleman' in P. Desmaizeux (ed.), *A Collection of Several Pieces of Mr John Locke* (1720), 239, where he strongly recommends Wheare's work.
49 Wheare, *Reflections*, 15, 20, 299, 304, 324, 341, 362.
50 *Ibid.*, 'Mr Dodwell's Invitation', Sig. A4r.
51 *Ibid.*, Sig. A5v, A3r–v, A7r.

historical investigation, to the 'truth' (to knowledge about the correct model of morality) in the context of seventeenth-century polemics was a persuasive strategy. The claim to be an 'historian' was to manufacture integrity and moral authority: the practice of history became entangled in the tendrils of ideology.

Historians of the period were aware that the claim to be writing true history was not enough assurance, in itself, that a text was veracious. To create a standard of rectitude they constructed a system for distinguishing between valid and corrupt works. This method of legitimating historical texts was not only for the practising historian, but more importantly for the direction of the reader to 'true' principles. Since the premise of history was that the reader ought to be persuaded by prescriptive texts, many of the works discussed the standards to be employed by the reader in judging the quality of the history. The historian had to keep a balance between his presentation of the facts and his use of rhetorical techniques: a balance between the process of licit and illegitimate insinuation. Edmund Bolton, author of *Hypercriteria* (1622), noted that 'the judgements of interested authors are commonly not judgements so much as prejudices ... iniquities practis'd in this point are not more ordinary than odious, and are some times laid on so impudently thick, that with less than half an eye the paintings are discernible'.[52] The aim of 'candid and sincere' history was not to impose on the reader. The Huguenot refugee René Rapin-Thoyras commented in his *Modest Critick* (1691) that good history 'ought to leave my heart free, to judge the better of what it tells me. Eloquence, which by its character, is an art that imposes, may steel upon my liberty, by striving to persuade me beyond my will.'[53] The limits of legitimate discourse between the necessities of a persuasive medium, and the burgeoning dangers of misuse of these skills were firmly inscribed in the methodological texts of the time. Ultimately it was the duty of the reader to 'judge' whether the work was competent. The judicial activity of the reader was the result of the balance between belief in the credit of the history and a wariness against being imposed upon by fictional testimony.[54]

[52] E. Bolton, *Hypercritica: or a Rule of Judgement* (Oxford, 1622), 233, in J. Haslewood (ed.), *Ancient Critical Essays* 2 (1815).

[53] R. Rapin-Thoyras, *The Modest Critick: or Remarks on the Most Eminent Historians* (1691), 71–2 translated by J. Davies of Kidwelly from French. Note that the work was originally translated in 1680 under the title of *Instructions for History*. The work is an abridgement of both classical (Lucian and Dionysus of Halicarnassus) and 'Spanish and Italian modern' (Francis Patrizi, Agostino Muscardi, Paolo Beni and Lewis Cabrera) historical methods. On Rapin-Thoyras, see R. Gwynn, *Huguenot Heritage* (1986).

[54] See, for example, Languet de Fresnoy, *A New Method For Studying History* (2 volumes, 1730), I, 259, who insisted that the best method for the reader to follow was that of Aristotle and take the middle road. He wrote: 'We must not be too credulous on the one side, nor on the other hand too much affect a pyrrhonism, that is doubting of everything. In truth, if on the one side too great a credulity causes us to slip into errors, and makes us take up for true,

Contrary to the claims of historians, Francis Osborne, in his popular work *Advice to a Son* (1658), insisted upon the 'great uncertainty in history'; such relations were constructed more for the interest of particular men, that that of the truth.[55] Osborne advised his son not to follow the injunctions of history 'beyond the pillars of possibility'; in this manner Osborne offered his son what might be called a constructive scepticism in historical method.[56] Although the medium of historical writing was implicitly susceptible to the distortions of prejudice, there was a type of knowledge that could be accepted if submitted to the realm of 'likelihood'. This point is crucial to an understanding of early modern attitudes to the function of history. This concept is alien to modern minds, constrained by 'scientific' claims to 'objectivity': the assertions of positivism can gain no interpretative access to the form of knowledge suggested by the historical method of the Augustan era. The idea of the 'pillars of possibility' is the central motif. Precepts and narrations were constructed from probability, credit and proof: this edifice was of a similar proportion to the structure of classical rhetoric.

Bolton lamented that many 'have let their credit split in pieces' in defence of false notions of liberty, prerogative and faith. The antidote to this position was to rely upon a concatenation of witnesses, testimony and 'natural' narrative, which would combine to create a work with valid 'probability'. Part of the reader's duty was to assess the credit of the author he was examining. Du Fresnoy wrote, 'before we read therefore an Historian we should be acquainted with him, and nothing can better tend to our giving a true judgement of the facts he relates than to know his character, his interests, his passions, the circumstances of his life, and the conjectures in which we find him'.[57] Writers who upheld 'uncertain probabilities' and 'tinsel arguments' were ridiculed by Jean Leclerc. The historian ought to use no other than solid reasonings; if these were not extant then he should operate within the realm of probability. In this manner the writer was to create a foun-

things the most dubious and false; on the other hand, an incredulity which we may entertain in the study of history, shall hinder us from reaping any benefit.'
55 F. Osborne, *Advice to a Son* (Oxford, 1658), 73, 74. See also the hostile injunctions of C. Agrippa, *The Vanity of Arts and Sciences* (1684), 2, 8, 27, against the insidious dangers of false history which was worse than the 'mad dreams of poets'.
56 Osborne, *Advice to a Son*, 79; on the term 'constructive scepticism', see R. Popkin, *The History of Scepticism* (1979).
57 Bolton, *Hypercritica*, 245; du Fresnoy, *A New Method For Studying History*, I, 275. See also J. Locke, *An Essay Concerning Understanding* (1690), IV, chapter 15.4, discussing the grounds for probability: 'First, the conformity of anything with our own knowledge, observation, and experience. In the testimony of others, is to be considered: (1) the number, (2) the integrity, (3) the skill of the witnesses, (4) the design of the author, where it is a testimony out of a book cited, (5) the consistency of the parts and circumstances of the relation, (6) contrary testimonies.'

dation for his narrative out of 'certain incontestable matters of fact in which all the world are agreed'.[58]

The insistence upon the 'likelyhood' of an historical narrative was a reaction against the poetic tradition of discourse, which suggested that precepts could be transmitted in parable or fable. It was one of the stock dismissals of incorrect histories to term them 'romances' or fictions, rather than histories. Richard Braithwaite noted that poetical histories themselves operated within a structure of probability. Hesiod's accounts of Hercules and Cerberus were set down with 'probable coherence, that if the matter itself did not imply an impossibility, one would certainly be induced to beleeve so concordant a history'.[59] Narrative had to conform to the constraints of consistency and reality. Braithwaite applauded the historian who 'can joyne profit with a modest delight together in one body or frame of one united discourse, grounding his story upon an essential truth' as the most valid model; the next type of true model was the man who could 'proportion' his text 'to a likeness of truth'. The dylogistic model was the historian who observed 'neither mean nor measure, but gorge their own insatiable appetites with full messes of untruths (without probability)'.[60]

The structure of witnesses and testimony joined together to create a creditable and probable narrative which would convince the reader of the authority of history. The idea of 'probability' is crucial to this persuasive scheme. The modern perception of the word is linked with the idea of statistical regularity, and the notion of a form of mathematical demonstration. The Augustan use of the word implies a type of moral commitment to the statement uttered. To say that something was 'probable' implied both approval of its intent, and that the action was broadly conformable to the realities of the world.[61] Probability could be created by the credit of the

---

[58] Leclerc, *Parrhasiania*, 58–61.

[59] Braithwaite, *A Survey*, 123. For a general discussion see L. J. Davis, 'A Social History of Fact and Fiction: Authorial Disavowal in the Early English Novel' in E. Said (ed.), *Literature and Society* (1980); M. E. Novak, *Realism, Myth, and History in Defoe's Fiction* (Nebraska, 1983). A useful epitome of the tensions between factual and fictional discourse is Daniel Defoe's *The Life and Strange Surprising Adventures of Robinson Crusoe* (1719), which Defoe presented as a 'just history of fact, neither is there any appearance of fiction in it'. Defoe was attacked by the converted deist Charles Gildon in *The Life and Strange Adventures of Mr D ... de F ...* (1719) which condemned Defoe's manipulative and false history. Defoe was to defend his 'emblematic history' in *The Serious Reflections ... of Robinson Crusoe* (1720). For Defoe historical writing was a valid mode of literary discourse, useful for conveying moral or religious principle to the reader.

[60] Braithwaite, *A Survey*, 239.

[61] Aristotle wrote: 'That being probable that for the most part and most usually happens to be; not simply, as some would have it to be; but as being that, which in those things that may be otherwise has the same relation to probable, as universal to particular.' Hobbes, *Art of Rhetoric*, 13. See also John Locke's notions on probability and witnesses in the *Essay Concerning Human Understanding* (1690), IV, chapters 15 and 16, at IV, 16.xi defending history: 'I would not be thought here to lessen the credit and use of history: it is all the light

historian, by the type of language used, from the issues presented, 'additional proofs' of probity could be effected by witnesses, oaths and testimonies. The intention was to imprint the issue discussed in the minds of the audience; as Aristotle explained:

That which we call a probable proposition, is that which when we have declared to the hearers, they retain the examples of the thing spoken in their minds ... and therefore we are to observe this diligently always in our orations, whether we have left the auditors conscious of the thing of which we discours'd to 'em. For it is most likely that they give greatest credit to those things.[62]

The deployment of 'testimony' was essential to the procedure of inducing conviction in the audience. It was this that was crucial to the *a priori* of historical method. The definition posited by Aristotle was: 'Testimony is a voluntary concession of a known thing. Now of necessity it must be either probable or improbable or doubtful to be believed, and in a like manner the witness must be either credible, or not to be believed or of doubtful credit.'[63] Testimony was adduced to support a case by creating the semblance of truth: in the practice of historical writing the statements of witnesses performed the role of anchoring the text in probable reality, giving it relevance to the universal issues of morality. The claim to be deploying valid witnesses was a rhetorical one, and so the character and motivations of the testimony had to be rendered free from the taint of interest in order to become persuasive. On the contrary, those who wished to undermine a case could do so effectively by contradicting the credit of the witnesses.[64]

As I have already shown, ideas of rhetorical persuasion were a commonplace in the mentality of the seventeenth century. The structure of an historical text was orientated to develop a conviction in the reader, which

we have in many cases, and we receive from it a great part of the useful truths we have, with a convincing evidence.'

[62] Aristotle, *Rhetoric*, 236–7.   [63] *Ibid.*, 248–9.

[64] The ability to confer credit on a thesis was given further treatment in Aristotle's *Rhetoric* IV, chapter 23, 'Of Confirmation'. Here 'just and profitable proofs' drawn from examples, common opinions, and recapitulations were to be deployed, see Aristotle, *Rhetoric*, 271–3. For a further discussion of the idea of 'probability', see I. Hacking, *The Emergence of Probability* (Cambridge, 1984), especially 11–39. Note also the case of the Newtonian and friend of Gilbert Burnet, John Craig, and his *Theologia Christiane Principia Mathematica* (1699), edited by G. Nadel in *History and Theory*, supplement 4 (The Hague, 1964). This work attacked monkish histories, and created a mathematical method for calculating the probability of historical data. He argued that 'after 3150 years from the birth of Christ the probability of his written history will vanish'. It was thus likely that Christ would return to earth before this date. Note F. Atterbury, *The Epistolary Correspondence*, (4 volumes, 1789), I, 86–7: Atterbury to Trelawny, 11 March 1701, reporting the indictment of Craig's work alongside that of Toland's *Christianity Not Mysterious* (1696) in the Lower Convocation Committee for inspecting books. He wrote: 'I bring in tomorrow a book of one Craig, a Scotch-man, chaplain to the Bishop of Sarum, to prove, by mathematical calculation, that, according to the pretension of the probability of historical evidence, in such a space of time (which he mentions) the Christian religion will not be credible. It is dedicated to the Bishop.'

would act as an incentive to some form of prudence or virtue.[65] This image of the reader in judicial guise, vacillating between one opinion and another, according to the nature of probable 'instances' encountered, is an informative one for the practice of Augustan historical discourse.

CREDIT AND 'MATTER OF FACT': THE CONVOCATION CRISIS

The major objective of the historian was to establish the competence of his own credit, while undermining his opponent's integrity. For example, Francis Atterbury in his *Rights, Powers, and Priviledges of an English Convocation* (1700) set out to diminish the authority of 'those designing writers who ... raise to themselves a character of impartiality, of a singular integrity, and courage. Their own virtues also shine to advantage ... and withal they imitate ... how fit they are to be advanced to a post, wherein they may correct such enormities.'[66] Atterbury defended the independent rights of the clergy from the Erastian claims of such men as William Wake and Gilbert Burnet, whose historical researches tended to suggest that ultimately the Church was reliant upon secular authority. Atterbury, with typical astuteness, pointed out that the claim to impartiality was a very effective means of imposing upon the reader. He wrote that it was important to ask of Burnet,

if the main facts he professes to relate, and the colours he gives to those facts are right; if there be no premeditated omissions, or disguises of material truths; no designed compliance with popular mistakes and prejudices; if that air of impartiality which at first sight seems to run through the relation, be undissembled, and not only a more artificial way of conveying false principles and characters into the mind of the reader.'[67]

The process of exposing historians' manipulations had the double benefit both of undermining their visions of the past, and of also accruing more credit to the historian who effected the critique.

The claims to truth and probability were essential to conveying a political or theological precept in historical form. In order for the message to be

[65] Hobbes was to describe this process of conviction commenting on Aristotle's *Rhetoric*; he wrote: 'That the judge, while he hears the facts proved probable, conceives it as true. For the understanding has no object but truth. And therefore by and by, when he hear an instance to the contrary; and thereby find that he had no necessity to think it true, presently changes his opinion, and thinks it false, and consequently not so much as probable. For he cannot at one time think the same thing both probable and false: and he that says a thing is probable, the meaning is he thinks it true, but finds not arguments enough to prove it' (*Art of Rhetoric*, 97–8).

[66] F. Atterbury, *Rights, Powers, and Privileges of an English Convocation* (1700), Sig. A8v. For an account of the importance of 'matter of fact' in the polemics of dispute in issues of natural philosophy, see S. Shapin, 'Pump and Circumstance: Robert Boyle's Literary Technology', in *Social Studies of Science* (1984), and S. Shapin and S. Schaffer, *Leviathan and the Air Pump* (Princeton, 1985), passim.

[67] Atterbury, *Rights of Convocation*, 243–4.

accepted by a reader as truthful, the language of credit had to be employed. There was an implicit link between the stated value of 'evidence' and its ability to persuade the reader: evidence was the route to proof of a particular case. Francis Atterbury's dispute with Wake's assertion that the clerical convocation was an appendage of the civil state, was couched in the terms of proof, demonstration, and probability. Atterbury suggested that Wake's opinions were innovatory and contained little 'truth or probability'. Atterbury intended to throw light upon these false claims. The metaphor of displaying an issue in full light is central to the idea of transparent and veracious history. Atterbury deployed his own 'evidence' to justify his opinion of the rights of the convocation. Wake's 'cloud of witnesses' did not enlighten Atterbury, they only served 'to darken and confound the point we are in pursuit of, not at all to clear it'.[68] Edward Stillingfleet was convinced that the bond between testimony and probability was sufficient to establish a morally certain form of knowledge; 'sufficient probation' could only be established on the solid ground of consistent 'evident demonstration'.[69] For Stillingfleet mere probability was not to qualify as true testimony. The points of antiquity were not to be decided, 'in the field, nor at the bar, nor by a majority of voices, but depend upon the comparing of ancient histories, the credibility of testimonies, and a sagacity in searching, and skill in judging concerning them'.[70]

Empirical evidence or 'matter of fact' was conceived as a sure method of resolving issues in contention. Charles Leslie insisted that serious breaches in both doctrine and discipline could be best healed by appeal to the arbitration of empirical research. He declared that the answer lay in 'matter of fact ... for plain matter of fact will not bend, or suffer us to dodge and fence with it, as we may do for ever about poor criticism of words, and speculations of our own inventing'.[71] Burnet held a similar attitude, he commented: 'The truth is, reason is a tame thing which bends easily to a man of wit and fancy; but facts are sullen things, they are what they are.'[72] While Kennett in his work against Francis Atterbury, *Ecclesiastical Synods* (1701), premised his arguments on these very grounds; he wrote, 'matters of notion and bare speculative points, are liable to alternate disputes for ever: but matters of fact and express authorities, are evidence of proof and demonstration'. Kennett suggested that there were only two methods which could undermine the

---

[68] *Ibid.*, 73, 132.   [69] E. Stillingfleet, *Origines Britannicae* (1685), 262.   [70] *Ibid.*, iii.
[71] Leslie, *Theological Works*, I, 412–14. W. H. Greenleaf, *Order, Empiricism, and Politics: Two Traditions of Political Thought 1500–1700* (Oxford, 1964), 173, writes on the historiography of the late Restoration: 'The result was a more extensive and reliable mass of historical data as an empirical basis for discussion and as a force of authoritative examples and precedents.' Although Greenleaf is correct to stress the empirical element, he fails to set this within a context of authority and credit.
[72] Burnet, *Letter to Thévenot*, 20–1.

empirical case, 'one to prove a falsehood in the citations, and a wrong term in the application of them; another to represent it as a moot case, and to produce as much evidence on this side, as had been given on that'. Atterbury, according to Kennett, had not attempted to justify his case in abstract terms about the nature of the Church as a society of Christians, but had built his defence upon, 'statutes ... Records ... rolls and registers'.[73] His argument was to 'stand or fall upon the truth and application of these authorities': it was to this enterprise that Kennett devoted his work. Historical enquiry was an arena where there was the possibility of a final resolution, but also of certain refutation. Kennett commented on Atterbury's presentation of evidence,

> I must needs own, those authorities are so confidently cited, affirmed, and repeated; that I took them long upon content, and believed them very genuine, and fairly thought I could suspect nothing, but the mighty assurance of the voucher; and even that upon first thought inclin'd me to suppose, he was most certainly in the right and might be depended on. Till at length, inclination to be a little curious, and good tolerable opportunities to be well informed, have put me upon searching his margins and references, and upon collecting his multitude of collections with books and papers, from which they were, or ought to have been taken.[74]

Once again the picture is of an individual being confronted with a mass of marginal references and footnotes, attempting to form his opinions in relation to their content. The superficial attraction of Atterbury's case was, according to Kennett, a carefully fabricated illusion. He criticized Atterbury's scholarly integrity: 'Upon view I am now entirely satisfied, that no one writer ever managed an historical argument with more slightness and superficial touch; or indeed with more falsehood and deceit.'[75]

The value of historical discourse to Kennett was that it was a superior method of communication since it was firmly rooted in empirical fact, accessible to everyone. He wrote, 'falsehoods in philosophy and speculative points, may have imposed upon successive ages; but a forged history never stood the test of any one generation: people may for a while read, and take for granted; but when they come to examine and compare, they despise the story, and suspect the teller of it'.[76] Kennett intimated that Atterbury's manipulation of historical writing was symptomatic of the complexion of his devotion, 'for another Church of traditions and legendary Tales; than for our Church, that can be supported by nothing but sincerity and truth'.[77]

---

73 W. Kennett, *Ecclesiastical Synods* (1701), 29, 108.
74 *Ibid.*, 108. For a modern example of this metahistorical rhetoric, see J. C. Rule, 'Bibliography of Works in the Philosophy of History 1945–1957', *HT* supplement 1 (1961), Index, s.v. 'fact, historical ...' (see also: 'objectivity', 'reality', 'science,' 'truth'), and 'verification (justification, evidence) of historical statements and theories ...' (see also: 'fact', 'logic', 'probability', 'science').
75 *Ibid.*, 108–109.   76 *Ibid.*, 175.   77 *Ibid.*, 153.

Atterbury in turn suggested that Kennett was too reliant upon 'fact' to support his case: he had constructed a factual account to fit with his conceptions of just Church government. He complained that facts were produced 'purely to establish rights on them; and having laid down his historical grounds therefore does, in every instance, proceed to draw his conclusions from them'.[78]

The dispute over the value and persuasive authority of 'matter of fact' became integrated with the Convocation controversy. The polemical issue was concerned with whether the Convocation, and ultimately the clerical order, had authority and power independent of the civil administration. Traditional scholarship has suggested that the crisis was inspired by the publication of Francis Atterbury's *Letter to a Convocation Man* (1696). Recent research has relocated the origins of the debate in the earlier 1690s. The crucial publication was Humphrey Hody's *The Unreasonableness of Separation* (1691). Hody, a Fellow of Wadham College, Oxford had published a medieval manuscript referred to as the 'Baroccian Ms', as an attempt to defend the deprivation of those bishops who had refused the Oath of Allegiance to the monarchy after the Glorious Revolution of 1689. The ancient manuscript supposedly gave precedents for such practice from the early Church. The deployment of the manuscript engendered immediate and outraged replies from such men as the High Church Thomas Browne, Nathaniel Bisbie, Simon Lowth and, most expertly, from Henry Dodwell. Goldie has examined the debate thoroughly, illuminating both the chronology of publications, and the intricacies of argument and counter-argument. Hody's publication was inspired by the need for a 'scholarly defence of the deprivations'. In the course of the exchange this language of scholarship became inextricably linked with the language of polemics.[79]

Hody insisted that the evidence of the 'Baroccian Ms' ought to have been persuasive to those men who considered the practice of antiquity a valid model. Hody directed this accusation in particular at Henry Dodwell, 'who before was so full of his history and examples, begins now not to esteem them ... He is now for rules, not examples: and he has good reason for it for rules he makes of his own, but examples he cannot'.[80] We have already encountered Henry Dodwell declaring his appreciation of the didactic uses of history. Dodwell was a scholar, appointed Camden Professor of History at

---

[78] Atterbury, *Rights*, 154. See also I. Basire, *The Ancient Liberty of the Britannick Church* (1661), 22; T. Jones, *Of The Heart* (1678), 45, 52.

[79] M. A. Goldie, 'The Nonjurors, Episcopacy and the Origins of the Convocation Controversy' in E. Cruickshanks (ed.), *Ideology and Conspiracy: Aspects of Jacobitism 1689–1759* (Edinburgh, 1982), 21. See also G. V. Bennett, *The Tory Crisis in Church and State*, chapter 3; N. Sykes, *From Sheldon to Secker* (Cambridge, 1959), chapter 2; Douglas, *English Scholars*, chapter 10; G. Every, *The High Church Party*, chapters 5, 8.

[80] H. Hody, *Reflections on a Pamphlet Entitled Remarks on the Occasional Paper Numb. VII* (1698), 18.

Oxford in 1688. The deposition of the Catholic James II saw Dodwell refuse the Oath of Allegiance. After he was deprived of his Professorship at Oxford in 1691, he turned his scholarship towards a defence of those clergy who had suffered similarly deprivation.[81]

In his *A Vindication of the Deprived Bishops* (1692) Dodwell objected to Hody's profligate use of 'instances'. Hody's work had simply been a list of all precedents that favoured his case. Dodwell's complaint was that Hody had assumed a *de facto* rectitude to anything that had happened, simply because it had happened. He wrote:

> Whether they did well or not in it, is not here so much as attempted to be proved; only as it is presumed to be well done, barely because it was done in so many instances, and no publick opposition made against it. But if matters of fact so nakedly mentioned must be urged for precedents, it will be impossible to make any thing of this way of arguing from history. What history is there, that in a succession of nine hundred years, does not afford examples against examples? And how can it be understood which are rather to be followed as examples, if no more be considered concerning them but barely this, that they were examples? How easy were it for the historian, by this way of reasoning, to justify, as our Brethren do, the wickedest things that can be.[82]

Dodwell suggested that the truth of historical example came not from the *de facto* quality of the action, but through conformity with an external standard of rectitude. Dodwell dismissed the value of the 'naked matter of fact' and instead sought prescriptive value in the connections between principle and actions. Valuable historical example was derived from the history of men of 'true' principles. Dodwell rejected Hody's examples as malicious, because they enshrined incorrect theological principles.

The imperative was to find 'matters of fact' which embodied true opinion which could thus become persuasive. Simon Lowth, another non-juror, in his *Historical Collections Concerning Church Affairs* (1696) and *Ekalogai: or Excerpts from the Ecclesiastical History* (1704), set out to provide a detailed collection of counter examples to Hody's scheme. He wrote that his 'method' was to relate 'naked history' and 'bare matter of fact'.[83] In the earlier work Lowth had accepted Hody's criticism that the issue should be conducted in terms of 'instances'; he qualified this with Dodwell's point that the 'instance' employed should be moral.[84] The value of historical example had reached such an authority that Hody issued a challenge, in his *Case of Sees Vacant* (1693), to his non-juring opponents to produce 'one single instance' in favour of their case.[85] The challenge was repeated in his later work *Reflections on a Pamphlet* (1698) where he reiterated the 'argumentativeness

---

[81] For an account of Dodwell see *DNB*.
[82] H. Dodwell, *Vindication of the Deprived Bishops* (1692), 11.
[83] S. Lowth, *Ekalogai* (1704), xxvi.   [84] S. Lowth, *Historical Collections* (1696), Sig. A2v.
[85] H. Hody, *Case of Sees Vacant* (1693), 'To the Reader', ii–iv.

of such facts'; he restated the challenge thus, 'the Dr. challenges Mr Dodwell and his whole party (... and desire they take notice of it) to produce him any one single instance from the time of Aaron, the first high Priest of the Jews, or a Bishop disown'd by the generality of the Catholick Church, for this reason, because put into the place of another deposed by civil authority'. If they could do so Hody declared that he would 'own myself obliged for the instruction'.[86]

Hody had reviled Simon Lowth's work: he was a 'foul mouthed collector' whose work was a 'long wild rage of impertinences'. According to Hody, Lowth had attempted to impose upon readers with 'tricks and shuffles'. Hody advised the reader to examine his work side by side with the execrable Lowth's: it would be apparent to the impartial man that Hody's work contained the 'phænomena of history'. This notion of the 'phænomena' of history indicates the appeal to the idea of empirical resolution of ideological disputes. Gilbert Burnet insisted that Hody's scholarship had provided this factual resolution to the debate, he commented on Hody's *Case of Vacant Sees*, 'Dr Hody has fully ended the argument that he had begun, from the practice of the Church; and that in so convincing a manner, the matter of fact seemed not capable of a clearer proof ... We know the reason why it is not answered is, because it cannot be answered. Men may wrangle on eternally in points of speculation; but matters of fact are severe things, and do not admit of all that sophistry.'[87]

Dodwell (and the non-juror scholars in general) was insistent that Hody's 'sacred instances' were nothing of the sort. Dodwell's attack was to undermine Hody's credit, by suggesting that he had manipulated his evidence. Hody rested the authority of his case on the relevance and antiquity of the 'Baroccian Ms'. Dodwell, Thomas Browne and Nathaniel Bisbie questioned both of these assertions. Dodwell argued that the manuscript was too inconsequential to be classified as 'evidence'. He doubted the integrity and competence of it as testimony. The issues presented in the ancient manuscript extended no further than the Greek Church of the fourth century. Dodwell insisted that the text could therefore have no application to the model of the ancient Catholic Church. Dodwell suggested an alternative: the correct model and precedent ought to be derived from the actions of St Cyprian, 'not only because they are the ancientest, indeed the first we know of ... but because we have withal in him the most distinct account of the sense of the Church in his age of such facts, and of the principles on which they proceeded.'[88]

In his *An Answer to a Treatise* (1691) Nathaniel Bisbie thrust an even

---

[86] Hody, *Reflections* (1698), 17 and *Case of Sees*, 'To the Reader', iii–iv.
[87] Hody, *Reflections* 20, 27–8, 15.
[88] Dodwell, *Vindication of the Deprived Bishops*, 4–6, 16, 22.

more damning counter argument against Hody's use of the manuscript in suggesting that Hody had deliberately suppressed an appendix to the original work, which directly contradicted the principles he wished to draw from the account. Hody claimed that the manuscript presented evidence for obligation to a bishop who had replaced another (unjustly deprived by either ecclesiastical or secular authority). Bisbie showed that the probable author of the 'Baroccian Ms' was Nicephorus Callistus 'the worst greek author extant, 'till Mr Hody is pleased to publish some other'. Even if this research was not enough to neutralize the value of the text for Hody's case, Bisbie published a set of canons which were formerly appended to the manuscript. With this addition the manuscript became relevant only to the legality of obligation in the case of synodial deprivation. It had been Hody's intention to defend obligation in actions of civil deprivation. Bisbie sarcastically complimented Hody's prudent concealment of the canons, since they in themselves were a 'sufficient answer' to his claims.[89] Dodwell in the second part of his *Vindication* had also identified this deliberate suppression of evidence. Dodwell proved that the manuscript had been written in the context of the schism originating in the deprivation of Michael Palælogus by Patriarch Arsenius employing synodical methods. The precedent of the work could have no application to the disputes of the 1690s which were about the validity of lay deprivation.[90] The non-jurors attempted to assimilate the authority of the manuscript to their case. The suppressed canons appended to the 'Baroccian Ms' became 'approved facts' which contradicted Hody's arguments. The value of Hody's scholarship was repeatedly undermined by the non-jurors' persistent republication of the canons.

Humphrey Hody, with his impartiality under public threat, replied to these charges, not in terms of the legality of his case, but with arguments defending his scholarship. In the *Letter from Humphrey Hody to a friend* (1692), Hody declared

> when I transcribed our treatise out of the Baroccian Ms. I did it as an historian, or a philologer, or whatsoever else you will call it not imagining then, I should ever send it abroad upon such an occasion; if therefore the aforesaid Canons do truly belong to the treatise, it is to be imputed to an error and mistake of my judgement, and not to an ill design, that they are omitted.

Hody was still insistent that the canons were no part of the original text: the two different parts were written in distinct hands. The canons were not relevant to the main issue since they only dealt with the regulation of private conventicles, rather than deprivations.[91]

---

[89] N. Bisbie, *An Answer to a Treatise* (1691), 22, 29–30. The canons are at 31–2. See also N. Bisbie, *Unity of Priesthood Necessary to the Unity of Communion in a Church* (1692).
[90] Dodwell, *Vindication*, 2nd part, 33–106.
[91] H. Hody, *A Letter from Mr Humphrey Hody to a Friend* (Oxford, 1692), 4–6, 8–9.

Hody was well aware that the authority of the manuscript was central to the legitimacy of his defence of the deprivations of the 1690s. He reversed the charge of manipulation against his opponents, commenting acidly: 'Five hundred to one, but a month or six weeks hence we may have a report spread abroad, that advice has been sent from Paris, that the aforesaid canons are found in the Ms. there in the self same manner as at Oxford. A spurious letter, as from some considerable man, the librarian himself, or some other, will do very well for the purpose.' Hody stalwartly insisted that even if this did happen it was still not persuasive evidence, because both works could have been copied from a single defective source. Hody attempted to deflect assaults upon his credit, while still upholding the value and relevance of the manuscript to the debate. The non-jurors' objections, as far as Hody was concerned, were a result of their stubborn spirit of contrariety. As he lamented, 'it is not your carrying a light that will make a man follow you; not the shewing him the road, that will make him go right, unless he has a will to be directed'.[92]

The controversy of the early 1690s over the status of non-juring Churchmen, was framed in terms of historical evidence. Rational theological debate was supplemented by the display of manifold empirical histories. The authenticity of manuscripts, the identification of handwriting, schemes of evidence and testimony were central to the mechanics of polemical discourse. Hody's challenge to the non-jurors to produce one 'instance' in their favour was readily accepted by such men as Atterbury, Lowth and Jeremy Collier. The early eighteenth century saw the hierarchy of the Church of England filled by clerics of Gilbert Burnet's complexion: historical defences of the Anglican establishment flooded the printing presses. The works of White Kennett, William Wake and Edward Gibson were to provide erudite, complete and interminably lengthy justifications of their model of Church government.

This chapter has focused upon the metahistorical principles of the early modern period. Placing the developments in theories of both reading and writing history within the context of religious polemic and apologetic, the intention is to challenge the received Whiggish idea of an historical revolution. From the variety of sources (from Braithwaite's handbook for the gentry, to Leclerc's eighteenth-century orations on history) I have suggested that the changes, and *perhaps sophistications*, in historical writing were not progression towards the modern idea of history as an autonomous mode of discourse, but evolutions of an acknowledged humanist tradition adapted to the controversial needs of the age. From one viewpoint, the modern could argue that a revolution had occurred (new methods of philology, manuscript discoveries, and citations, were apparent). Douglas and Momigliano have

[92] *Ibid.*, 15–16, 18.

discussed the scholarly and antiquarian developments of the discourse. However, even honorary moderns, like Locke and Toland, were committed to history as an instrument of humanist edification. The significance of the epistemological status of historical method should be assessed not in terms of its contribution to 'progress', but placed firmly in the context of religious debate.[93]

93 As already noted above, Locke, particularly in the *Essay*, recommended the didactic value of history. John Toland is perhaps an even more persuasive case. S. Daniel, *John Toland: His Methods, Manners, and Mind* (McGill, 1984) gives the most detailed discussion of this facet of Toland's polemic, although Daniel's notion of Toland as an 'historian-exegete' lacks an explicatory humanist framework, (see 28, 56–8). Toland's promotion of history as a weapon against priestcraft (i.e. as a hypothetical rather than categorical activity) was central to his polemic. In *Christianity Not Mysterious* Toland's epistemological category 'Evidence', was not mere philosophical investigation, but practical advice on how to attain just moral precepts; see *CNM*, 14, 16–19, 21–2. It seems likely that Toland was following Hobbes (compare *Leviathan*, 410 with *CNM*, 14–16) rather than Locke. I do not intend to trace the penetration of historical ideas down into the realms of the popular press since the research of B. Capp and M. Spufford have admirably illustrated this dissemination. B. Capp, *Astrology and the Popular Press: English Almanacs 1500–1800* (Cambridge, 1981), M. Spufford, *Small Books and Pleasant Histories* (1981). For literacy and popular readership, see D. Cressy, *Literacy and the Social Order* (Cambridge, 1980), and C. J. Sommerville, *Popular Religion in Restoration England* (Gainsville, 1977).

3

Arimathea to Cranmer

The disputes and wranglings of informed historical opinion during the period were manifold. Saxonist confronted Saxonist, the pedant of monasticism vied with the antiquarian of diocesan rights. One convenient means of access to the disputes of the period can be found in William Nicolson's *English Historical Library* (1696–9), in essence little more than a partisan bibliography of the current refinements in historical learning. Nicolson's work, in effect and design, was a handbook of the fruits of true research, and by implication of the correct interpretation of the past. Edward Gibson writing to Thomas Tanner in May 1696 commented upon Nicolson's draft,

that part which I have seen is drawn up gentleman-like (as you know he does everything) but contains little in substance, but what you and I know already. 'Tis a book very likely to take, and will be a good manual to inform the generality of mankind what has been done in our English affairs, whether topographical or historical.[1]

Although Nicolson's work was little more than a reference work (without any great academic insights), it enabled the uninitiated laity to come to a 'true' perception of the past.

The work consisted of three parts: Book I dealt with topographical and geographical matters, Book II with ecclesiastical history, and the third with a description of the contents and locations of public records. The second book identified the important polemical foci of scholarly debate. The general premise of the *English Historical Library* had been the search for true, impartial and disinterested history.[2] Nicolson insisted on the need for a 'general Examen, a sort of an Universal Index Expurgatorius, that points at the mistakes and errors of every page of our several historians'. The intention

---

[1] F. G. James, *North Country Bishop: A Biography of William Nicolson* (Yale, 1956), 86, citing Tanner Ms. 24. folio 120.
[2] See Nicolson's citation of Lucian's model of the unbiased historian: *English Historical Library* (3 volumes, 1696–9), I, Preface, Sig. Ar–v.

of the work was to winnow the 'good sterling History' from the chaff of 'romance or Buffoonry'.[3] Thus addressing the 'England Protestant Reader' he presented his catalogue of worthy ecclesiastical historians.[4] The bare bones of English Church history were displayed and a canon of good histories provided to fill this form with persuasive description. The origins of the English Church were examined in the form of a bibliographical commentary upon the traditions of Joseph of Arimathea and King Lucius, and the usurping attempts of Augustine. Edward Stillingfleet's *Origines Britannicae* (1685) was unequivocally recommended as the best scholarly work which 'perfected all the collections of former writers on that subject'.[5] History from Augustine to the Reformation was described briefly, but dismissed as a tale of papal dominance, Catholic accretions and popish superstition. The greatest eulogies were reserved for the account of the English Reformation. The primary text was John Foxe's *Acts and Monuments* (1570).[6] Although Foxe's work was the seminal text in its narration of Protestant suffering and the triumph of the true religion, the demands of faith and the requirements of scholarship were in conflict. There were some few errors in Foxe's account.[7] The true monument both to erudition, truth and faith was Bishop Burnet's *History of the Reformation* (first 2 volumes, 1679–80) which was recommended in unreserved terms, while other histories like Peter Heylyn's were rejected for their partiality.[8] Nicolson staunchly defended Burnet's work from all malicious assaults upon his integrity and learning.[9]

The Protestant canon created by Nicolson in his bibliography was convicted by the High Church man Francis Atterbury, in his *Rights of Convocation* (1700), of dangerous latitudinarian principles. Nicolson's impartiality was impugned. As a young scholar Nicolson had certainly entertained no latitudinarian inclinations; Thomas Hearne suggested that he was a youth of devout High Church beliefs. By the 1690s Nicolson was in correspondence with men of a Whiggish tenor like Edward Gibson, White Kennett and William Wake. The publication of the *English Historical Library* and Atterbury's hostility towards it pushed Nicolson further into latitudinarian circles. After his consecration as Bishop of Carlisle both his London and provincial diaries are testimony to his frequent contact with men of the highest eminence, such as William Lloyd, Bishop of Worcester,

---

[3] *Ibid.*, I, Preface, Sig. A5r.   [4] *Ibid.*, II, 88.   [5] *Ibid.*, II, 18–20.

[6] Nicolson noted on the 1684 edition of Foxe that 'the publishers had well nigh prevail'd with King Charles the Second to revive Queen Elizabeth's order and A. B. Parker's canon, for having a set of these volumes in the common halls of every Archbishop, Bishop, Dean, Archdeacon, etc.' (*ibid.*, II, 81–2).

[7] *Ibid.*, II, 82.

[8] *Ibid.*, II, 94–7. Nicolson argued that this partiality was displayed in the fact that Heylyn had employed only Laudian transcripts made from the Cottonian Library.

[9] *Ibid.*, II, 100, 102, 103.

Gilbert Burnet, Bishop of Salisbury, and Archbishop Tenison.[10] On 29 January 1702 Bishop Lloyd presented Nicolson with Kennet's recently published Whiggish Church history of Convocation; the following day Kennet himself sent Nicolson another copy. In February 1702 Nicolson proudly distributed copies of his own *Scottish Historical Library* to Tenison, Burnet and Lloyd. In June of the same year Nicolson recorded in his diary that the dinner conversation at Lambeth Palace with Tyrrell, Burnet and Evelyn had been much concerned with the 'Atterburians'. By mid-1704 Nicolson was in open conflict with Atterbury and his faction, in particular over his appointment as Dean of Carlisle. In his diary Nicolson noted and denied the accusation that his hostility towards Atterbury had been inspired by 'measures from Lambeth'.[11] Although it would be foolish to press the point too far, it is clear that Nicolson's bibliographical exercise launched him into the heart of the ecclesiological wranglings of the period. In intention a follower of historical veracity, in his creation of a Protestant canon he had become identified with the Whig-latitudinarian cause. The contents of this historical canon display the contributions of scholarship to ecclesiastical ferment.

The position of the Church of England was ambivalent; it had at the same time, to uphold its authority as a valid institution, while distancing itself from the heritage of Roman Catholicism. While historical continuity with the early Church argued against the charge of innovation, this connection with the past had to be divorced from Catholic tradition. The issue was further complicated by Roman polemicists who were insistent on displaying the Catholic lineages of the Anglican Church. Men such as Baronius and Cardinal Bellarmine had supplemented their arguments against the reformation of theology and Scripture with historical example. Such works as Nicholas Saunder's *De Origine et Progressu Schismatia Anglicanae* (1585) and Thomas Stapleton's translation of Bede's *Ecclesiastical History* (1565) with an appendix that suggested the Augustinian plantation of the faith of Rome in England was the first reception of Christianity, necessarily provoked some 'historical' response from the apologists of Anglicanism.

PETER, PAUL OR JOSEPH: THE GENESIS OF THE CHURCH

One of the most frequently discussed histories was the account of the regal supremacy of King Lucius, and the tradition that the British nation was converted to Christianity by Joseph of Arimathea. The historical narration of

---

[10] See G. Holmes and C. Jones (eds.), *The London Diaries of William Nicolson 1702–1728* (Oxford, 1985), 216, 225; 'Bishop Nicolson's Diaries' by the Bishop of Barrow-in-Furness, *Transactions of the Westmorland and Cumberland Archaeological and Antiquarian Society* (1901), 38, 39, 40, 42 and (1902), 113.

[11] G. Holmes and C. Jones, (eds.), *The London Diaries* 12 November 1704, 225.

the early conversion of the British Isles was an important ideological tool against papal pretensions. Belief in the traditions of Joseph of Arimathea and King Lucius penetrated deep into the historical mentality of the period. The Anglican vision of the origins of the Church of England was constructed in opposition to powerful Catholic interpretations like Robert Parsons' *A Treatise of Three Conversions* (1603). Parsons' work argued that the English Church was subject to Rome because she owed the institution of her faith to St Peter. This foundation was later reinforced by Pope Eleutherius and St Augustine. The Anglican apologists swiftly replied to this work with counter-assertion, Matthew Sutcliffe in his *Subversion of Robert Parsons* (1606) insisted that Parsons' claims were 'dreams and fancies', that his 'proofes stand upon conjectures'. The arguments and testimonies for St Peter being in England were weak and frivolous.[12] Francis Goodwin, Bishop of Hereford, in an appendix to his *Catalogue of the Bishops of England* (1615) entitled 'A Discourse concerning the First Conversion of this Island of Britain into the Christian religion', further denigrated Parsons' assertions. He argued that the testimony for the Petrine conversion rested upon the bare report of Simon Metaphrastes, who was a 'notable lyer ... of notorious untruthes'.[13]

Goodwin was persuaded by the evidence that St Peter had never visited British shores: the proofs were more 'pregnant' for St Paul's visitation. The first conversion was made by Joseph of Arimathea. He wrote 'for Joseph of Arimathea, the testimonies of his coming here, and his actions here, they are so many, so cleere and pregnant, as an indifferent man cannot but discerne, that there is somewhat in it, our conversioner mentioneth them so faintly.'[14] Goodwin brought forth 'evidence' that would advance the 'credit' of the history: the charters giving twelve hides of land to the monastery Joseph founded at Glastonbury were particularly convincing. He produced even more tangible evidence in the form of an 'ancient inscription engraved in brasse, heretofore fixed upon a pillar of St Joseph's Chapell'. The inscription was transcribed for the benefit of the reader.

Joseph of Arimathea's conversion of England has many variants. The most common was that Joseph had been a disciple of the apostle Philip who had sent him in AD 63 to convert Britain, shortly after the death of Christ. A further tale was that Joseph had been imprisoned after the crucifixion of Christ, but had managed to retain a chalice of Christ's blood which he had transported to Britain where he founded a monastery at Avalon with the permission of King Aviragus. This tradition was to blend and blur with the Arthurian myth of the Holy Grail.[15] The main source for the tradition was

---

12 M. Sutcliffe, *The Subversion of Robert Parsons* (1606), Epistle Dedicatory, Sig. A2r–A3v, 4.
13 F. Goodwin, *A Catalogue of the Bishops of England* (1615), 3.   14 *Ibid.*, 6, 8.
15 J. A. Robinson, *The Glastonbury Legends* (Cambridge, 1922), 28–50.

William of Malmesbury's *De Antiquitate* written in the mid-thirteenth century. This work in itself was a blend of earlier traditions; in the seventh century Isidore of Seville had referred to the idea of St Philip preaching to the Gauls. A similar reference had been made by Freaugulfus, Bishop of Lisieux, in the ninth century. William of Malmesbury was to conflate all these earlier stories with the history of the monastery at Glastonbury and the tradition of the Charter of St Patrick.[16] The tradition of Joseph of Arimathea was deployed by Goodwin as central to his notion of the continuity of the Anglican Church. This continuity was further reinforced by the example of King Lucius and British independence at the time of Augustine.

Parsons had insisted that Pope Eleutherius converted the British king to Catholicism, and that therefore the British Church owed allegiance to the papacy. Goodwin replied by illustrating the continuity of Christian belief between the time of Joseph and Lucius, and that the latter had been converted by an indigenous Christianity. If there had been any correspondence between Lucius and the papacy it was a relationship of brotherhood rather than subjection. Goodwin produced a letter from the Pope to King Lucius in which the former referred to the latter as a 'vicar and lieutenant immediate of God, subject to none other but God himself'. Lucius was the first model of the Godly Prince. According to Goodwin's narration Lucius was to renounce his crown and become the apostle of German Christianity.[17] Goodwin dealt with Parsons' claims for the Augustinian conversion in a similarly hostile manner. Augustine was treated as a model of the pomp and pride of the modern papacy. The British clergy were portrayed as bravely denouncing the attempts of the interloper. In Augustine the reader could find 'a true picture of a proud priestly spirit full fraught with malice and revenge (as is always ye case) when they have power to exercise it, under ye disguise of piety and religion: or (when is ye best pretence of all) ye interest of ye Church, by which is meant only themselves, and ye bigoted tools of their own mischief'.[18] Goodwin intended to convince the reader that the 'historical' claims of the Catholic Church to authority over the Church of England were false.

This earlier three fold tradition of Joseph, Lucius and Augustine was altered by the close focus of historical scholarship. The two greatest works of original research were Henry Spelman's *Concilia* (1639) and James Ussher's *Britannicarum Ecclesiarum Antiquitates* originally published in the same year, but also importantly republished in 1687.[19] Spelman's work was a comprehensive collection of statutes, letters and unpublished manuscripts concerning the history of the British Church, focusing in particular upon

---

[16] *Ibid.*, 34–7.   [17] Goodwin, *A Catalogue*, 34, 35.   [18] *Ibid.*, 44.
[19] A second volume of Spelman's work was posthumously published in the early years of the Restoration under the guidance of the High Church scholar William Dugdale; see *DNB*.

evidence for an early institution. In the introductory *Apparatus* Spelman discussed the available evidence for the Arimathean conversion of England. One of his findings was that the brass plate upon which Goodwin had laid so much importance was in fact a medieval production. James Ussher took up the same theme in his work. He carefully examined the genesis and variant mutations of the Arimathean tradition, the extent of Lucius' conversion to Christianity, and Augustine's invasion of the British Church. These works were perennially popular. Rather than examine them in detail I wish to show how they were used by later polemicists.[20]

An example of the polemical usage of this earlier scholarship is Thomas Jones' *Of The Heart and its Right Sovereign* (1678). Jones was rector of Oswestry, and Chaplain to the Duke of York, although he was vocally anti-Catholic. Jones presented the 'true' origins of Christianity in England, arguing that the faith was received in Britain before St Peter's visit to Rome. In the same thrust he suggested that St Augustine's actions were a direct invasion of British liberty. Following the erudite antiquarian research of Archbishop Ussher, Jones recounted how the faith had been brought to British shores by Joseph of Arimathea. Although he rejected the many fabulous accounts of miracles, revelations and visions that accompanied Joseph's foundation of the monastery at Glastonbury, the evidence of extant manuscripts and charters indicated the truth of the history.[21] Further credit was brought to the tradition because it had been brought to 'publicke test and examination in several general synods of Europe'. The 'renowned Ussher', citing the impartial testimonies of the Councils of Pisa and Constance, of Gildas and the Early Fathers, Theodoret and Nicephorus, insisted that the Arimathean tradition was 'far out of doubt and question'.[22]

Jones argued for an indigenous Christianity in Britain, to counter the Catholic precedent of the relationship between Pope Eleutherius and the British monarch King Lucius. The papists had claimed that Eleutherius had converted Lucius to Christianity, and that therefore the British Church was subject to Rome. Jones argued that there had long been a Christian tradition in Britain, and that the case of Lucius provided a parochial equivalent of the Constantinian model. The evidence, as Jones argued following Ussher, clearly indicated that the Pope had referred to Lucius as the 'vicar' of his kingdom. Jones continued to anatomize the invasions of popery into British liberty; in particular the attempt by Augustine in the early seventh century.

---

20 See H. Spelman, *Concilia* (1639), 'Apparatus de exordia christianae religionis in Britannis'; the brass plate and criticism are at 7–10; J. Ussher, *Britannicarum Ecclesiarum Antiquitates* (1687), 1–31. On Ussher, see also R. Buick Knox, *James Ussher Archbishop of Armagh* (Cardiff, 1967), 98–113; and Ussher's *A Discourse of the Religion Anciently Professed by the British and the Irish* (1687).

21 T. Jones, *Of the Heart and Its Right Sovereign* (1678), 124–6, and passim.

22 *Ibid.*, 128–9, 131.

The intruder had allied with pagans and the pride of the Saxon kings in an attempt to eradicate the 'true' religion.[23] The polemical point of Jones' presentation of the early history of the British Church was to legitimate the Reformation in terms of a reclamation of 'primitive liberty'. This renovation was effected by the authority of the Christian magistrate. Jones was careful to elevate the right of the secular authority over that of the Church; it was only the anti-Christian Church which attempted to dominate the civil power. As he wrote, 'the Christian Mitre attends the Crown'.[24]

Edward Stillingfleet's *Origines Britannicae, or the Antiquities of the British Church* (1685) subjected Ussher's work to important revisions. The design of this work was 'to give as clear and distinct a view of the state and condition of the British Churches, from their first plantation to the conversion of the Saxons'.[25] Stillingfleet had three intentions: '1. To examine the tradition, concerning Joseph of Arimathea, and his brethren coming hither to plant Christianity. 2. To shew that there was a Christian Church planted here, in the apostles times, and within that compass that Gildas speaks of. 3. To prove the great probability, that St Paul first founded a Church here.'[26] Stillingfleet's argument was that although orthodox opinion was misguided in the precise nature of early British Christianity, they were right in asserting that there had been an early conversion. This was to be proved with the mechanism of historical probability.

Stillingfleet epitomized the researches of Spelman and Ussher in arguing that the myth of Joseph of Arimathea was the product of monkish fable.[27] The probable origin of the tradition was due to the actions of the Saxon Christians, who under the threat of persecution had fled to inaccessible areas of the country such as the Isle of Avalon. These men had been elevated into legends by interested monks who had intended to protect privileges they had usurped from the local laity. Stillingfleet cited Spelman's opinion that the brass plate at Glastonbury was no more than 300 years old.[28] Stillingfleet deployed all the fabulous variants of the story embodied in the tales of the Holy Grail found in Capgrave's *Vita Josephi*, or the evidence of the Charter of St Patrick. The latter manuscript had been used by the Catholic historians, the Jesuit Matthew Alford (1587–1652) and the Benedictine Serenus Cressy (1605–74), to suggest that Joseph, inspired by the Archangel Gabriel, had

---

23 *Ibid.*, 143–7, 216, 220. The myth of the continuity of the British Church was fostered by Jones who compared the suffering of the English Church to the persecutions of the early Church, see 236, 238, 295–300, 301, 306–14.
24 *Ibid.*, 365, 413–14, 416.
25 Stillingfleet, *Origines Britannicae*, i.
26 *Ibid.*, 6.
27 *Ibid.*, 9.
28 *Ibid.*, 11–12.

founded a church at Glastonbury for the worship of the Virgin Mary.[29] Stillingfleet noted that the charter was dated AD 425, which pre-empted the system of dating, which as Mabillon had shown, was a later practice. Internal evidence also suggested the document was untrustworthy. The Charter of King Ina which declared that the church was dedicated to the Virgin was shown to be a forgery. Selden's research, into seals and document composition, indicated that the charters were products of the twelfth century. Stillingfleet commented, 'I do not question that King Ina did found a monastery there, where there had been an ancient Church in the British times. But I see no ground to believe, that either Joseph of Arimathea, or St Patrick, or St David had ever been there.'[30]

Stillingfleet insisted that the legend of Arimathea had been constructed by the monks of Glastonbury to elevate the importance of their establishment during the time of Henry II. The latter had confirmed the monks' claims, 'and from thence grew to be the common opinion of the nation, and was pleaded for the honour of it in the councils of Pisa, Constance, Siena, and Basil'. There was not only insufficient evidence in the testimonies, but also 'improbable circumstances' in the story. Having deconstructed the Arimathean myth, Stillingfleet set out to construct a more 'probable' replacement, 'built on the testimony of Ancient and credible writers, and [which] hath a concurrent probability of circumstances'.[31]

The primary evidence for Stillingfleet's vision of early Christianity in England was taken from the venerated authority of Eusebius. The latter 'affirms it with so much assurance', that some of the Apostles preached the Gospel in the British Islands. Theodoret's testimony indicated that St Paul had travelled around Europe; Stillingfleet insisted that 'there cannot appear any improbability that he should come into Britain, and establish a Christian Church here'.[32] The evidence presented by Stillingfleet for Paul's conversion seems unconvincing today: however, to Stillingfleet and his contemporaries it seemed more 'probable' and secure than the tales of Joseph. One of the premises of this probability was that there had to be a pre-papal source for British Christianity. A recent commentator has insisted that Stillingfleet had employed a 'better informed and more critical scholarship' than former

---

[29] S. Cressy, The Church History of Brittanny [sic] (1668), II, chapter 8. This work was borrowed largely from Alford's Annales Ecclesiae Britannicae in manuscript. Note also that there was a 'Second Part of the Church History of Brittany' in manuscript deposited at the Bendictine Monastery at Douai; see DNB.

[30] Stillingfleet, Origines Britannicae, 15–17, 18–23, 26. See on Stillingfleet's epistemological theory R. S. Carroll, The Commonsense Philosophy of Bishop Edward Stillingfleet (The Hague, 1975). It should be noted that this work does not deal with the status of historical knowledge, or the persuasive role of 'probability'.

[31] Stillingfleet, Origines Britannicae, 28, 35.   [32] Ibid., 37, 41.

men.[33] Although Stillingfleet certainly spent more time and thought on his work than others, he did not advance a purely scholarly opinion but employed sophisticated polemical technique to legitimate the Anglican settlement. In a similar manner Stillingfleet de-Catholicized the tradition of Lucius. Stillingfleet argued that Lucius' conversion was not necessary for the triumph of Christianity in England because the authority and competence of the Church was already established through the apostolic succession. Stillingfleet was insistent that neither 'our religion, nor our government need such fictions to support them'. He discounted Geoffrey of Monmouth's account of Lucius' transformation of the pagan religion into a Christianized form. He was against such a narration because it implied that there was 'no Church here before'. Stillingfleet was certain that there was pre-Lucian Christianity. He suggested that there was a place for training godly men at the University of Cambridge: these men had been responsible for Lucius' conversion.[34] More importantly, Stillingfleet maintained that there was an unbroken succession of British bishops during this period. He made a close identification between the origin of Christianity and the government of the Church by bishops. The next issue Stillingfleet confronted was the nature of episcopal government. Were the bishops created by sacerdotal ordination, or by the consent of the civil order? The evidence indicated that the people did have some part in the creation and election of bishops, but that this was only a power of 'nomination' while the real right of episcopal election lay within the episcopal body. Stillingfleet thus argued that the legitimacy of the British Church lay upon the legality of a fully competent episcopacy. Just as other provinces held self-determination, so the British Church had independent authority. He wrote: 'British Churches had as great privileges and as just rights ... as the African Churches.'[35] The 'Cyprian Privilege' was once again deployed against a papal assertion of jurisdiction of the Church of England.[36]

The final evidence of British independence was from the narrative of Augustine's attempted usurpation of the Church of England. He wrote, 'it remains only that we consider the liberty, or independency of the British Churches; of which we have no greater proof than from the carriage of the British Bishops, towards Augustine the monk when he came in full power from the Pope to require subjection from them'. Stillingfleet readily countered the papist claims of Alford and Cressy by displaying the evidence

[33] G. Williams, 'Some Protestant Views of Early British Church History', *History* 37 (1953). Williams argues that Stillingfleet's Pauline thesis was accepted by scholars until the middle of the nineteenth century.
[34] Stillingfleet, *Origines Britannicae*, 58, 65, 67, 69. [35] *Ibid.*, 77, 96–7, 101.
[36] For an earlier use see the works of Archbishop Laud. Note also that Heylyn referred to the latter as 'Cyprianus Anglicanus'.

of the 'Dinoth Ms'. This was a contemporary seventh-century document that had been first deployed by Spelman in his *Concilia*. The manuscript clearly indicated that the British bishops resolutely rejected Augustine's attempt to establish 'subjection' to the papal see under the 'cloak of ecclesiastical unity'. The Catholic historians Alford and Cressy had both suggested that the work was a forgery, specifically created to deny papal claims. Stillingfleet argued for the authenticity of the work, especially when it was supplemented by Bede's declaration that the British clergy would not own Augustine as their archbishop. Thus, although Stillingfleet had earlier argued in *Irenicum* (1661) that episcopacy was not the *esse* of a legitimate Church, his history argued that in the specific case of England, episcopacy was the traditional (and therefore legal) mode of ecclesiastical government.[37] It appears that by the time Stillingfleet composed *Origines Britannicae* he had altered his opinion as stated in *Irenicum*. In the latter work Stillingfleet had argued the cause of 'moderation' against the rival claims of Presbyterians and Episcopalians. The central argument of *Irenicum* was that there was no universally binding *de jure divino* model of Church government: the apostolic age left no evidence of such a prescriptive model, neither did Scripture. This was an epistemological statement: there simply was not enough 'evidence' to reconstruct the true pattern of Church government. The 'testimony of Antiquity' was defective, ambiguous, partial and contradictory; he wrote: 'Now all those uncertain and fabulous narrations as to persons then, arising from want of sufficient records made at those times, make it more evident how incompetent a judge antiquity it is as to the certainty of things done in

---

[37] *Ibid.*, 356, 358, 360–4. I have argued that Stillingfleet's defence of British independency rested upon his idea of the competence of episcopacy to legislate and create a Church. There were further attacks upon this position not merely from Catholics, but lack of space debars me from exploring these histories. The Presbyterian interest argued against the validity of episcopal government by deploying the historical example of the early Scottish Church. Their point was that originally Christianity in Scotland had been founded upon a system of independent Churches known as Culdees. They argued that popish episcopacy had been imposed upon the Scots by the advent of the Catholic Palladius. This case was argued in a number of works such as D. Blondel's *Apologia* (Amsterdam, 1646), John Selden in a preface to R. Twysden's *Historia Anglicanae Scriptore Decem* (1650), and R. Baxter's *Treatise of Episcopacy* (1681). The seminal defence of Anglican episcopacy was written by William Lloyd, Bishop of St Asaph, in his *An Historical Account of Church Government* (1684). Lloyd was a colleague of Stillingfleet, to whom (along with Henry Dodwell) the work was dedicated. Lloyd argued that the Presbyterian case was premised upon false and fictional history (A3r–v, A5v–A8v). In chapter 7 he focused upon the notion of Church government by 'Culdees' (133ff.) His argument was that the term Culdee, or Keldee, had reference to monks rather than the clergy. He showed that the usage of the word was not common until the sixteenth century. The original inspiration for the idea of Church government by Culdess was the self-interest of the monk John of Fordon, who had fabricated such an illustrious past to elevate the prestige of his own order. It is important to note that the idea of Culdees was further deployed against the Church of England for different intents by John Toland in his *Nazarenus* (1718). See W. Reeves, *The Culdees of the British Isles* (Dublin, 1864).

Apostolical times'. Stillingfleet's insistence was that in the face of this historical uncertainty the idea of a transcendent true model of Church government should be shelved: instead, the legitimate form of ecclesiological settlement was to be defined quite properly by the authority of civil sovereignty. Church government was inherently mutable. Having disposed of the issue of *de jure divino* government by apostolic prescription, towards the end of *Irenicum* Stillingfleet focused in detail on the nature of Church government in England. His intention (backed by the impartial opinions of learned divines and scholars like Cranmer, Whitgift and Hooker) was to justify episcopal government not *de jure divino* but as a 'very lawful and useful constitution'.[38] By the time he wrote *Origines Britannicae* it is apparent that Stillingfleet now believed that there was enough 'probable evidence' to make a certain case for episcopacy as the original form of Church government, legally constituted in England. Stillingfleet's statements in the later work are powerful evidence of the persuasive role history could play in forming individual beliefs. It also seems clear the *Origines Britannicae* is not necessarily at odds with the argument of *Irenicum*. In the latter work Stillingfleet set about addressing a specific question about the obligation of the individual to the legally established Church settlement. Given the epistemological relativism of men's opinions ('for as long as mens faces differ, their judgements will') and Stillingfleet's concomitant scepticism about the possibility of 'an universal harmony in the intellectual world', coupled with his doubts about the quality of evidence for a *de jure divino* model for Church government, he chose to answer the question 'what is the legitimate model?' not in terms of a prescriptive historical dissertation but by an analysis of the logics of authority and sovereignty within the idea of political and religious societies. If history could not persuade, then reason must. By the time Stillingfleet composed *Origines Britannicae*, having endured the slanderous charges of Hobbism and the unreasonable claims for a non-conformist separation from the established Church, it is evident that he felt he could muster enough 'evidence' to make a credible historical case for an original form of episcopal government in England. This historical argument did not contradict the theorizing on the location of authority in the state, but was a crucial persuasive adjunct to these rational arguments. When Stillingfleet had argued in *Irenicum* that ecclesiastical constitutions were mutable, it cannot have been that he intended to insist that they should be mutable, but simply that Church government had varied with historical and geographical circumstance. By the time of *Origines Britannicae* Stillingfleet felt confident enough in the status of the evidence to display the specific historical circumstances of the original English Church constitution.[39]

---

[38] Stillingfleet, *Irenicum*, 298–9, 385, 386–94, 404.   [39] *Ibid.*, 3.

PETER HEYLYN AND THE DEFENCE OF THE 'ECCLESIA ANGLICAE'

If it had been the brief of Church historians like Stillingfleet or Jones to argue for the jurisdictional competence of the Church of England against Catholic charges of schism, other historians sought to define the legitimacy of the national Church in terms of its institutions: most importantly in terms of the divine right of episcopacy. The occasion of the re-establishment of the Church of England in its full authority, restored to the 'episcopal throne, bearing the keys of the kingdom of Heaven with her, and armed (we hope) with the rod of discipline', was accompanied by a learned volume of historical argument that made the *esse* of the true Church lie in the divine right of its government by bishops rather than the sole jurisdictional competence of the royal supremacy.[40] One of the major polemicists of the Church of England was the High Church man Peter Heylyn, described by his biographer as the 'venerable Bede of our Age'.[41] Heylyn was applauded as a faithful historian who combined good 'Latin, reason and history' in defence of the Anglican establishment. Heylyn was a High Church man of the Laudian genre: outspoken in defence of the Church in the 1630s and suffering the consequences during the 'Egyptian darkness' of the Interregnum. Heylyn had been hounded around the countryside, fleeing from one refuge to another. One of the hiding holes, at Mr Lizard's house in Winchester in which Heylyn took refuge, was a place of concealment usually reserved for papists, 'in which room, instead of a papist, a right protestant doctor, who was a professed enemy both to popery and puritanism'. With the restoration of both Church and monarchy in 1660 peace once again descended upon Israel, and Heylyn became reverenced by the gentry as 'St Jerome was by St Augustine'.[42] Throughout the Interregnum Heylyn had scoured manuscript collections in search for a scholarly vindication of English episcopacy. Even blindness did not terminate his research. Although the bulk of Heylyn's High Church polemic was written prior to 1660 there was still an extensive corpus of works composed in the early years of the Restoration in the stentorian timbre of the *vox clerici*.

[40] G. D. D'Oyly, *The Life of William Sancroft* 2 volumes, (1821), II, 346. See also G. Reedy, 'Mystical Politics: The Imagery of Charles II's Coronation' in P. J. Korshin (ed.), *Studies in Change and Revolution* (Menston, 1972). R. S. Bosher, *The Making of the Restoration Settlement* (1951); I. M. Green, *The Re-Establishment of the Church of England* (Oxford, 1978), especially 22–5. See also for an interesting account of the popular reception of the Restoration, T. Harris, *London Crowds in the Reign of Charles II* (Cambridge, 1987), 36–61. For accounts of the fragmentation of ecclesiastical order in the 1640s and 1650s, see C. Hill, *The World Turned Upside Down* (1975), and *Puritanism and Revolution* (1972); A. L. Morton, *The World of The Ranters* (1975); B. Capp, *The Fifth Monarchy Men* (1967).

[41] Bernard, *Theologicus Historicus* in Heylyn, *Ecclesia Restaurata* (2 volumes, Cambridge, 1849), I, clxxvi.

[42] *Ibid.*, cxiv, cxli, cxlvi, clxxxii.

Ecclesia Restaurata, first published in 1661 and reprinted in 1670 and 1674, defended the clericalist vision of the Reformation. Even after his death in May 1662, Heylyn was identified with the High Church tradition, in particular, due to the posthumous publication of his works. The first publication of major importance was his hagiographical biography of William Laud, *Cyprianus Anglicanus*, published in 1668 and reprinted in 1671 and 1719. The work was not only notable for its unashamed approval of William Laud's life and actions, but also for recommending the possibility of a union with the Church of Rome. His argument was that there were only minor abuses and corruptions which separated the two communions.[43] Richard Baxter, the moderate Presbyterian, was aghast at Heylyn's suggestion, arguing that Heylyn's work was evidence of the vigour and continuity of the Laudian tradition in the 1670s.[44]

The importance of Heylyn's polemic was re-emphasized in *Aerius Redivivus* (1670 two editions, 1672) which anatomized the seditious principles of Presbyterianism. The final monument to Heylyn's centrality as a High Church proponent in the Restoration is the posthumous publication of his historical works *The Historical and Miscellaneous Tracts* in 1681, prefaced with a eulogistic life of the author. This folio work reintroduced Heylyn's most important pre-Restoration polemics. The volume contained *Ecclesia Vindicata, Or the Church of England Justified* (1657), which was itself a combination of earlier tracts on the histories of liturgies, episcopacy and tithes; the *History of the Sabbath*, originally published in 1631 and 1636; *Historia Quinqu-articularis*, first published in 1660; the *Stumbling Block of Disobedience* (1658) and a *Treatise de Jure Paritatis Episcoporum* composed in 1640.[45] In these works Heylyn presented a coherent and extensive defence of clericalism. It is this vision which we will explore.[46]

---

[43] P. Heylyn, *Cyprianus Anglicus* (1668), see 'A Necessary Introduction to the Following Work', 19, 39.

[44] See W. M. Lamont, *Richard Baxter and the Millennium*, 84, 98, 105, 114–15, 131, 183, 243, 249, 251–2, 302–3. Lamont gives an excellent exegesis of Baxter's fusion of the apocalypse with Protestant imperialism: Baxter's ideas of the Christian magistrate and the national Church are crucially distinct from Heylyn's 'Grotian' schemes.

[45] M. A. Goldie, 'John Locke and Anglican Royalism', *Political Studies* 31 (1983) has shown Heylyn's close identification with Filmerite royalism: Algernon Sidney referred to the cleric as the 'master' of Filmer's work. Heylyn has been given credit for arguing for the rights of Convocation to meet in tandem with Parliament in 1661. G. Every in his *The High Church Party*, 35, suggests that Archbishop Lamplugh of York used Heylyn's arguments in 1689 to prove that 'no Parliament ought to be called without a meeting of the clergy at the same time'.

[46] Heylyn's High Church prescriptions were also presented in a more simplistic historical form in his *A Help to English History*; the work was originally published in 1641. It was reprinted three times in the decade following 1671, and finally in 1709. The work was a textbook or handbook of chronological catalogues of the kings, bishops and lords of Church. In this manner the theorizing and detailed narrative of Heylyn's vision of the past was distilled into dates, facts and figures which appeared baldly uncontentious. But as Heylyn wrote, 'these

The premise of Heylyn's history was that religious worship was a necessary component in human society. Heylyn deduced principles for the true model of ecclesiastical and political order from this axiom. All societies had practised religion upon set terms. In the *History of Liturgies* Heylyn set about historically refuting the claims of the Interregnum 'Smectymnians' who had insisted that Jesus and the primitive Christians had not employed strictly prescribed forms of religious worship. Heylyn cited the Pauline injunction of 1 Corinthians 14, xxiii, that all things be done in order, thus avoiding the 'chaos of devotion'. Liturgies originated in one divine 'original mould' rather than 'man's extemporal wit'.[47] Drawing upon historical evidence of both Judaeo-Christian and pagan religion, Heylyn asserted that God had established a transcendent structure for religious worship, consisting of prayer, praise and preaching. He wrote: 'So by the law and light of nature, which was the way whereby he was pleased to manifest himself, and make known his will unto the Gentiles, they were also directed to set forms of worship, though otherwise utterly mistaken in the object of it'.[48] Throughout the work Heylyn made continual citations from Maimonides' work upon the origins of idolatry, intending to use historical examples from other non-Christian religions as evidence of the structural similarity of all religion.[49] For Heylyn the coincidence in the practice of marriage, burial, and priestly vestments, for Judaic, Christian and pagan religions was indicative of divine commendation and prescription of these practices.[50] An examination of the history of 'gentile' religion was necessary,

that we may see how universally all sorts of people have agreed in this, to institute set forms and determinate rites, whereby to order and direct their whole devotions. And having shown out of their most unquestionable records and monuments, with what a general consent they entertained those public formulas which had been recommended to them by the former times; we shall proceed to the affairs of the Christian Church ... And then I hope it will seem reasonable to the indifferent and sober reader, that if a prescribed form of worship hath been admitted in the world, semper, ab omnibus, et ubique, according to the rule of Lyrinensis, at all times formerly, in all places too, and by all sorts of people of what ever sect so ever; it must needs be a most unheard of novelty to reject them now.[51]

following catalogues will make it evident and apparent' that both regal and episcopal government were legitimate.

[47] P. Heylyn, *Of Liturgies, or set forms of publick worship ... in way of an historical narration* in *The Historical Tracts*, 50.

[48] Heylyn, *History of Liturgies*, 51.

[49] Citations of Maimonides at 54, 62, 64, 67, 71. It is interesting to note here that the same work by Maimonides was the foundation of the Dutchman Gerard Vossius' 'Arminianism'. Vossius' translation and commentary on Maimonides, *De Origine et Progressu Idololatriae* was a central influence on Lord Herbert of Cherbury. The latter's *De Religione Gentilium* (1663) was translated in 1705 into English. As I argue below, Cherbury's work is essentially anticlerical, and is a formative influence on such thinkers as Charles Blount and John Toland.

[50] Heylyn, *Histories of Liturgies*, 65–9.   [51] *Ibid.*, 79.

Christ left the pattern of religious worship and ceremony to the determination of the Church. In answer to the denial of the 'Smectymnians' Heylyn then produced evidence of early liturgies of Peter, James and Mark.[52] Heylyn argued that a set pattern of religious worship determined by the Church was a 'natural' state of affairs, at the same time as asserting that there were historical precedents for it.

Heylyn was also to discourse upon the specific case of England. In the *History of Episcopacy* (1657) he illustrated the continuity of a *de jure divino* episcopal hierarchy in Christianity, deduced from the distinct natures of the original twelve Apostles, and the seventy disciples. Heylyn followed the assertions of Cyprian and De Dominis, in arguing that the Apostles were the prototype of episcopal managers.[53] Episcopal authority originated by analogy with the original civil sense of the word which meant 'overseer'; the classical writer Plutarch had referred to the Roman legislator Numa Pompilius as the 'bishop' or guardian of the Vestal Virgins. Heylyn argued, by this historical case, for the subordination of the body of the Church to the hierarchy of the bishops. Although bishops and presbyters shared a common form of *sacerdos* in relation to the laity, in issues of jurisdiction the priest was subject to the bishop. He wrote in explanation, 'inferior presbyters may ... feed the particular flocke committed to them by the word of doctrine, the Bishop may only ... so feed them with the word of doctrine, as that he also rule them with the rode of discipline ... so primitive antiquity did arme the Bishop with a Crozier or pastoral staffe'.[54]

Heylyn analysed episcopal authority along traditional scholastic lines. Authority was divided into two forms, 'potestas ordinis, and potestas jurisdictionis; the power of order and the power of jurisdiction'. Heylyn advanced the bishop to a supereminent authority in the Church. The whole power of ordination was vested in the bishop alone; although presbyters participated in ordination it was rather 'ad honorem Sacerdotii, quam essetiam operis, more for the honour of the priesthood, than for the essence of the worke'. The bishop exercised authority over presbyter and laity alike.[55] Heylyn had thus defined the nature of episcopacy, while documenting its continued existence in England, providing an argument against the claims of papists and Presbyterians alike. Following Cyprian's suggestions that episcopacy was a valid authority in itself, and not reliant on papal Rome, in Part Two of the *History of Episcopacy* Heylyn set out to give a historical defence of English episcopacy. A patriarchal episcopacy was prior

[52] *Ibid.*, 98ff, and following.
[53] Heylyn, *History of Episcopacy*, I, 7–25, 30–2. See N. Malcolm, *De Dominis: Venetian, Anglican, Ecumenist and Relapsed Heretic* (1984) and J. P. Sommerville, *Politics and Ideology in England 1603–1640* (Essex, 1986).
[54] Heylyn, *History of Episcopacy*, I, 56–7, 82.   [55] *Ibid.*, I, 151, 162, 166.

to the arrival of the emissaries of Rome upon British shores.[56] Heylyn produced the testimony of Gildas, 'one of the oldest antiquaries of the British nation' who had insisted that the conversion of Britain had taken place during the reign of Tiberius Caesar.[57] While Heylyn acknowledged that this evidence was not totally authoritative, he insisted that there was definite proof for the establishment of an independent British episcopacy in the time of the first Christian monarch of Britain, King Lucius.[58] He wrote,

and herewithal we have a pregnant and infallible argument, that Britaine being in itself a whole and complete Diocese of the Roman Empire, no way subordinate unto the prefect of the City of Rome, but under the command of its owne Vicarius or Lieutenant Generall; the British Church was also absolute and independent, owing not suit nor service, as we used to say, unto the Patriarch or Primate of the Church of Rome, but only to its own peculiar and immediate primate; as it was elsewhere in the Churches of the other Diocese of the Roman empire.

Heylyn followed the argument of Richard Hooker, who had insisted that the status of Church government necessarily mirrored that of the civil model.[59]

Heylyn's history was ecclesiologically anti-papal: he continually lauded the principles and precedents of Cyprian against the claims of the Pope. Cyprian argued that Christ had instituted the Apostles 'with an equality of power and honour; pari consortio praediti potestas et honoris'.[60] Church government was 'aristocraticall', each patriarch being 'absolute and independent with the bounds and limits of his own jurisdiction'. Arbitration between independent Churches was by mutual correspondence, rather than papal co-ordination. These independent patriarchal rights were documented and confirmed by the sixth canon of the general council of Nicea.[61] This presentation not only undermined papalist claims, but again also elevated the authority of episcopacy.

Heylyn's defence of the independent rights of patriarchal Churches can be seen in his treatment of the history of Constantine. The historical model of the first Christian Roman emperor had been central to the rhetoric of the Reformation. The vision was engraved on the mind of English society via John Foxe's *Acts and Monuments* (1570) which presented the security of the English Church relying upon the protection of the Godly Prince. Although Heylyn referred to Constantine's conversion as a 'blessed sunshine', a Prince 'whom God raised upon purpose ... to become the greatest nursing father

[56] *Ibid.*, II, 41–68. See Heylyn's citation of Cyprian's *De Unitate Ecclesia* and *Epistles*, especially Part II, chapter 3.

[57] Heylyn, *History of Episcopacy*, II, 53.

[58] The pagan temples were converted to Christian Churches, and the hierarchy of bishops and archbishops introduced. Heylyn was not as precise about the number of new bishoprics created from the pagan equivalents, as earlier men such as Francis Goodwin had been, because of the fragmentary nature of the surviving records and the monkish distortions of the Middle Ages. Heylyn *History of Episcopacy* II 62–65.

[59] Heylyn, *History of Episcopacy*, II, 68, 27.   [60] *Ibid.*, II, 403.   [61] *Ibid.*, II, 87.

thereunto, that ever was before him in the Church of Israel, or since him in the Israel of the Church'.[62] He constructed a defence of the Church from a pre-Constantinian period of history. The implication was that the Church held independent existence from the monarchy. Heylyn had insisted that the procedure for settling disputes among the stars of Christendom was 'innate' within each Church, being located within the convocation and assembly of both national and provincial councils. This power was exercised by each Church 'as their own particular' before the protection of Christian emperors was available. Even after the establishment of Christianity under the wing of the civil state, 'that power is not extinguished but directed only'. The model of the pre-Constantinian Church was to be repeatedly invoked by the non-jurors of the 1690s, to uphold their notion that the Church was to be considered as a separate *societas* from the civil state, with its own forms of hierarchy, duty and obligation.[63]

The second historical period that Heylyn concentrated his polemical effort upon was that of the Reformation. It was of crucial importance to the Anglican Church that the Reformation settlement was freed from the Catholic charge of heretical schism. Heylyn defended the Henrician experiment in *Ecclesia Restaurata, Ecclesia Vindicata, Historia Quinqu-Articularis*, and most succinctly in the introduction to *Cyprianus Anglicus*. The first of these works saw Heylyn's explicit defence of the Henrician innovations. The Reformation was a *renovatio* carried out by the clergy under the aegis of the monarchy. The reforming principle was not the Protestant continuity of Foxe's Wycliffe, but a return to the model of the primitive Church. He wrote: 'The superstitions of the Church of Rome [were] entirely abrogated, and all things rectified according to the Word of God and the Primitive practice.'[64] This interpretation of the Reformation was legitimated by the idea of the rights of a national Church, which as the conciliarist Jean Gerson had suggested could reform itself *per partes*, rather than through the operations of a general council. Heylyn's narrative is punctuated with references to clerical dynamic behind the changes; in *Ecclesia Vindicata* this was given a full conceptual treatment. Heylyn noted that the English experience was commonly attacked from two sides, 'by

---

[62] *Ibid.*, II, 470.
[63] *Ibid.*, II, 81. See, for example, T. Brett, *An Account of Church Government and Governors* (1701), 1–7, at 7; 'But why should I trouble myself to collect particular proofs and authorities when it is manifest from all Church history, that the Christian Church before it had any supreme magistrate in its communion for above three centuries, was actually governed by its pastors, and has continued to be so ever since in the greatest part of Christendom.'
[64] Heylyn, *Ecclesia Restaurata* (3rd edition, 1674- CUL Classmark: Pet. 12.21). Please note that in general I have used the 1674 edition of this work (CUL classmark Pet. 12.21), although because of missing pages and faulty pagination, where indicated, I have used other versions.

those of Rome, to have too little of the Pope, and too much of the parliament;
by those of the Genevian Party, to have too little of the people, and too much
of the Prince'.[65]

The Catholic polemicist Thomas Harding had accused the Anglican
settlement of being 'meer Parliamentarian'. Heylyn recognized the detrimental effect such claims could have upon the integrity of his Church; he was
insistent that all alterations and renovations in religion had been instituted,
ordered and created by the clergy. The crucial point for Heylyn was the
nature of the clergy's submission to the statute 25 Henry VIII. Prior to this
act the clergy, 'acted absolutely in their Convocations, of their own authority, the kings assent neither concurring nor required'. The Act of Submission simply restituted to the English monarchy rights which had been
usurped by the papacy. The Reformation was executed, 'by the Clergy in
their Convocations ... the Parliaments of those times contributing very little
towards it, but acquiescing in the wisdom of the sovereign prince, and in the
piety and zeal of the ghostly fathers'. The role of the Parliament was simply
to add the 'temporal sword' to the rulings of the Convocation, to make them
more effective. Heylyn explicitly refuted the accusations of the Catholic
Saunders, who suggested that the Act of Submission had rendered the
authority of the clergy dependent upon the civil power. Episcopal authority
came from no other 'hands than those of Christ and his Apostles'.[66] In reply
Heylyn repeatedly indicted the historical usurpation of monarchical rights by
the papacy, employing the arguments and evidence of such men as diverse as
Jean Gerson the conciliarist, and Paolo Sarpi, the apologist of Venetian
independence.[67] Echoing an earlier sermon of Laud 'Jerusalem is builded as a
City', Heylyn argued that the English Church was as a 'city at Unity in itself'.
Within the structure of this independence the monarchy entertained coercive
authority over the clergy in issues of 'corruptions of manners, or neglect of
the public duties to Almighty God, abuses either in the Government or the
parties governing'. The monarchy, however, had no control over doctrinal
purity; the only arbitrators in this theological area was the whole body of the
clergy 'rightly called and constituted'. The monarch following the pattern of
the biblical kings (Josias, Jehoshaphat and Hezekiah) could aid and facilitate
the restoration of true doctrine, but were incompetent in doctrinal issues
without clerical inspiration.[68] Heylyn denied the monarchy any sacerdotal
power.

[65] Heylyn, *Ecclesia Restaurata*, 123–4; *Ecclesia Vindicata*, v.
[66] Heylyn, *Ecclesia Vindicata*, 1, 2, 3, 5, 18, 12, 20. See also Heylyn, *Cyprianus Anglicus*, 2.
[67] On J. Gerson see B. Tierney, *The Foundations of Conciliar Theory* (Cambridge, 1955), and
Religion, Law and the Growth of Constitutional Thought 1150–1650 (Cambridge, 1982);
L. B. Pascoe, *Jean Gerson: Principles of Church Reform* (Leiden, 1973); on Sarpi see
D. Wootton, *Paolo Sarpi between Renaissance and Enlightenment* (Cambridge, 1983).
[68] Heylyn, *Ecclesia Vindicata*, 29, 39–40.

The image of the Reformation for Heylyn was an action directed by clerical inspiration to expel the illegitimate accretions of popery. *Ecclesia Restaurata* had a further polemical point to score. The pure waters of the Convocation's reform, had been muddied by the impure waters of self-interest and heresy. The 'transmarine' influence of Jean Calvin and Zwingli had attempted 'to reduce this Church into . . . nakedness and simplicity'. The 'pyrates of court' had attempted to enrich themselves under the guise of renovation. The Edwardian reforms, in Heylyn's presentations, saw 'the pillars of the Church removed, the very foundations of it shaken, and the whole fabric of religion so demolished, that scarce one stone there of did seem to stand upon the other'.[69] Contrary to the Protestant tradition of Jewel and Foxe who had treated Edward VI as a second Josiah, Heylyn ignored the Godly Monarch, while the reign of Mary, usually the focus of extended anti-Catholic invective, was treated in detached prose. On the other hand, every opportunity was employed to revile the influence of the 'Frankfort Schismatics' who were repeatedly portrayed as attempting to press the legitimate Reformation beyond its true bounds. Heylyn replaced the popish threat to the English establishment, with that of Continental Protestantism. Calvinist theology was presented as contradictory to the principles of both religious and civil security. The Geneva Bible was reviled as seditious, 'in reference to the civil magistrate and some as scandalous in respect of civil government'.[70] Heylyn hysterically indicted the infiltration of 'Zwinglian Gospellers' into the Church of England.[71]

The Reformation was presented as a necessary institutional exercise; what Heylyn lamented was the self-interested men who had attempted to radicalize the clerical momentum for their own aggrandizement. In the *Stumbling Block of Disobedience* he anatomized the political and theological distortions of Jean Calvins' thought. Turning from this theoretical discussion, Heylyn documented the history of these subversive ideas in *Aerius Redivivus, Or the History of The Presbyterians* (1670). The history extended from the first institution of Presbyterianism in sixteenth-century Geneva, until the

---

[69] Heylyn, *Ecclesia Restaurata*, 95, 101, 191.   [70] *Ibid.*, 234, 230–1.

[71] He wrote, of the reign of Elizabeth: 'But all this while there was no care taken to suppress the practice of another faction, who secretly did as much endeavour the subversion of the English Liturgy, as the Pope seemed willing to confirm it; for whilst the prelates of the Church, and other learned men before remembered, bent all their forces towards the confuting of some Popish errors, another enemy appeared, which seemed openly not to aim at the Churches doctrine, but quarrelled at some rites and extrinsicals of it. Their purpose was to show themselves so expert in the Arts of War, as to take in the outworks of religion first, before they levelled their artillery at the fort itself' (*Ecclesia Restaurata*, 13; note this citation is from the 1661 edition (CUL classmark L*.10.23(c)). See also H. Hickman, *Historia Quinqu Articularis Exarticulata* (1673), who objected vehemently to Heylyn's false indictment of the Reformation: see especially 'Epistle to the Reader' where Hickman argued that Heylyn had catholicized Luther's theology in order to force a breach between the Lutheran and Zwinglian reformations.

time of Charles II. With their claim to a 'pretended purity', the Presbyterians had undermined the English Church. This paralleled the turmoil and strife of the Interregnum; he wrote 'the ensuing story may be parallel'd in our late combustions; actor for actor, part for part, and line for line; there being nothing altered (in a manner) in that tragedy but the stage of theatre'.[72] The Presbyterians were presented as iconoclasts, violent, enthusiastic and seditious. As Heylyn wrote, 'from the principles and practice of these Great Reformers, it hathe ever since been taken up as a ruled case amongst all their followers, that if the Kings and Princes should refuse to reform religion, that the inferior magistrate, or the common people, by the direction of their ministers, may bothe and ought to proceed to a Reformation, and that by force of arms if need so require'.[73] He established from historical principle, that Presbyterianism was contrary to the existence of a stable and religious society.

One of the central components of the historical rhetoric of earlier Anglican apologists was that the English Church had re-established a continuity with a pre-Protestant tradition at the Reformation. To counter the Catholic question 'where was your Church before Luther?' the historical precedents of the Waldenses of France, the Hussites of Bohemia and the trials of John Wycliffe were deployed. This tradition was a commonplace in the Restoration. Henry Care's *History of Popery* (1678–83) lovingly documented in detail the struggles of the proto-Protestants against the deviant usurpations of the papacy. Heylyn did not consider the English Reformation heir to this tradition. In 1627 the youthful Heylyn had argued against Prideaux, the Regius Professor of Divinity at Oxford, who claimed that the visible Church of England was a direct succession from the Wycliffites. Heylyn upheld the continuity of the Church of England from the apostolic succession, even though this meant that the English Church was derived in part from the traditions of Rome. On Wycliffe, Heylyn complained 'yet had his field more tares than wheat; his books more heterodoxies, than sound Catholic doctrine'.[74] The workers of the Reformation followed no such inspiration. The principles of the Reformation were deduced from 'the more pure and sincere christian religion taught in the scriptures; and in the next place to the usages of the primitive Church'. If the English Church did follow any of the Continental reformers it was the moderate pattern of Luther or Melancthon, rather than Calvin or Zwingli. Heylyn was insistent that the English reforms had not intended to deviate any further from the Roman Catholic Church, than the latter had departed from the ceremonial and doctrinal simplicity of the Primitive Church.[75]

---

[72] Heylyn, *Aerius Redividus*, Preface, Sig. A4r.   [73] *Ibid.*, 27.
[74] Heylyn, *Historia Quinqu-Articularis*, II, 8.
[75] *Ibid.*, II, 18, 76.

Thomas Fuller, a man who had made an ideological position out of his 'moderation' was one of Heylyn's prime targets. Fuller's *Church History* (1655) was a hurried production, for the author feared that 'the Church of England be ended before the history there of'. Heylyn did not receive Fuller's massive work with rapturous applause. He pontificated upon the duties of the true historian, and the dangers of partiality. Fuller's work had dangerous implications, Heylyn wrote, '[he] hath intermingled his discourse with some positions of a dangerous nature, which being reduced into practice, as they easily may not only overthrow the whole power of the Church as it stands constituted and established by the laws of the land, but lay a probable foundation for the like disturbances in the civil state'.[76] Fuller's work not only contained 'aberrations from historical truth' but also 'such a continual vein of puritanism, such dangerous grounds for inconformity and sedition to be raised upon, as may easily pervert the unwary reader, whom the facetiousness of the style (like a hook baited with a painted fly) may be apt to work on'. Heylyn identified the seditious principles which lurked beneath the 'moderate' narrative: murdering of kings was avowed 'for necessary prudence', 'the sword extorted from the supreme, and put into the hands of the common people, whensoever the reforming humour shall grow strong amongst them'. Finally Fuller was accused of betraying the 'hierarchy of the Bishops' in favour of the Presbyterian cause, 'whom he chiefly acts for'.[77] Fuller replied to these charges in the *Appeal of Injured Innocence* (1659); he insisted that his work had retained its purity, and was not subject to the 'mercenary embraces' of self-interest.[78] Fuller suggested that it was the very impartiality of his work that was bound to subject it to hostile criticism. He wrote, 'the Independent, being the Benjamin of the parties ... taxeth me for too much fieriness, as the Animadverter ... chargeth me for too much favour unto them'.[79] It was only in old age that Fuller and Heylyn became capable of rational discussion and finally friendship.

Henry Hickman (d. 1692) was the most vocal and persistent objector to

---

[76] Heylyn, *Examen Historicum*, Preface, Sig. A3v–A4r. Heylyn berated Fuller for a paucity of style, for including verses, heraldry and other extraneous material into his history, which was more like a 'Church Romance' than 'a well built ecclesiastical History'. See Heylyn, *Examen Historicum*, Introduction, Sig. B2r.

[77] *Ibid.*, Introduction', Sig. B5r.

[78] Fuller, *Appeal of Injured Innocence*, Dedication: 'to ... George Berkeley'.

[79] *Ibid.*, Part I, 11. In reply to Heylyn's *Examen*, Fuller dealt with each objection point by point in an attempt to maintain the integrity of his position. The problem was of the reaction of the reader to this assertion and counter-assertion; who should be believed? Fuller identified the problem of radical historical incommensurability when he commented, 'Satis pro imperio, MUST is for a King; and seeing the Doctor and I are both Kings alike, I return, he MUST NOT be so understood; as to any judicious and indifferent reader will appear', Fuller *Appeal of Injured Innocence*, Part I, 50 (note the CUL edition used: P.2.14~2, has a faulty pagination, this refers to the second page 50).

Heylyn's history.[80] His works, *Plus Ultra, Or England's Reformation Needing to Be Reformed* (1661) and *Historia Quinqu-Articularis Exarticulata* (1673), dealt with Heylyn's evils. Hickman's central complaint was that any reader of Heylyn's work would 'conclude from the doctors premises, that England's Reformation is sadly defective'.[81] Hickman's complaint was that Heylyn had argued that the first Henrician changes in religion had entirely abrogated the corruptions and superstitions of the Church of Rome. He declared:

> Sir you have dealt very deceitfully with your readers in your History, in jumbling doctrine, Discipline and worship together; as if because there was a Reformation in Doctrine, and that grounded upon the word of God, there must also be a Reformation in the rest too (which was little or not at all) and that grounded on the word also; this deceit runs through your Book: you tell us ever anon of a Reformation according to the word of God and the Primitive practice: but in all your book there are but three instances of the conformity of the Reformation to the rule of the sacred scripture, and they are only in point of doctrine and not in discipline or worship.[82]

According to Hickman's theological perspective valid Reformation innovation had been achieved in the administration of the eucharist in two kinds, clerical marriage, and the Common Prayer being translated into the vernacular. Hickman attacked Heylyn's treatment of the 'Zwinglian Gospellers', and reaffirmed their challenge. He wrote:

> If any learned man of our adversaries to be able to bring one sufficient sentence out of the Holy Scripture, or any one example of a Bishop, minister, or Martyr, either in the time of King Edward VI, viz. Cranmer, Latimer, Ridley, Hooper, Ferrar, Philpot, Bradford, Taylor or any other, or in the time of Queen Elizabeth out of reverend Jewel, who do directly and ex professo plead for, and commend the present liturgy in the frame of it, or that episcopacy is Jure Divino, or for adoration towards the Altar, bowing at the name of Jesus, figuring with the sign of the cross, wearing of caps, and surplices, kneeling at the sacrament, or for the exercise of Church power by lay-chancellors; if you, reverend Sir, or any other be able to produce any such authority or example, contending as you do professedly for these things, the Zwinglian Gospellers will then be content to subscribe.[83]

Hickman viewed the Henrician Reformation as incomplete, and in need of further reform. The Reformation that Heylyn presented as prescriptive was a shoe too tight for Hickman; the misfit was the continued existence of episcopacy. Hickman issued a warning of conscience to Heylyn, 'but Sir, it is good to remember your latter end, you know not that your conscience may be then awakened, and read over this history you have written, and pinch you for the erratas of your zeal'. Hickman demanded the end of *de jure divino*

---

80 Hickman, a stern defender of non-conformity, was ejected from his Fellowship at Magdalen Hall, Oxford at the Restoration. He left England and lived in Leiden for most of the remainder of his life, see *DNB*.
81 H. Hickman, *Plus Ultra* (1661), 'To the Christian Reader', Sig. A2r–v.   82 *Ibid.*, 12.
83 *Ibid.*, 13.

episcopacy, the bishops ought to return to their primitive lustre, and feed their flocks with the milk of scripture, rather than aim for temporal grandeur.[84] In his *Historia Quinqu-Articularis Exarticulata* (1673) Hickman assaulted Heylyn's doctrinal position. The subtitle of his work was a 'History of Arminianism'.[85] The latter was a Dutch theological movement of a liberal tenor; it suggested that man had the competence of will to refuse God's grace. For those blinkered by the lapsarian determinism of Calvinism, this suggestion was a direct assault upon the omnipotence of God, and smacked of popish doctrines of free will which cast God as a debtor to man's good works.[86] Hickman set out to draw the elaborate historical parallel between the conflicts of Pelagius and Augustine, and the division between the Arminians and the Calvinists. His point was to ally himself with the correct pattern of Augustinian theology, while corrupting the integrity of the Arminians with the charge of Pelagianism.[87] Hickman refuted Heylyn's argument that there had been a distinction between the Reformation theologies of Luther and Calvin; he suggested a monolithic predestinarianism for all the reformers. Hickman suggested that Heylyn had attempted to form a bridge with popery at the best, and at the very worst with the Socinians, who upheld the full competence of human reason and will.[88] He objected to the dilution of Protestantism presented in Heylyn's vision of the Reformation: the latter's conception of the era was that of creating a purged continuum with the past, while Hickman saw it as the seedbed of a new order that had only been briefly glimpsed in previous history.

If we briefly examine the later career of Heylyn's histories it is apparent that Hickman thought he was justified in detecting the vestiges of popery in Heylyn's work. Gilbert Burnet had made this specific charge in the preface to his own history of the Reformation.[89] The Catholic convert Peter Manby

---

84 *Ibid.*, 14–16, 24–34, 37–40.

85 Hickman was to employ history to undermine Heylyn's claims; he wrote that there were two methods of fighting anti-Christ: 'The first apodictical, proving the truth, and retelling the errors opposite to it, by evidence of scriptures, and strength of Reason: the second historical confirming truth by the testimonies and authorities of men renowned for learning and piety' (*Historia Quinqu-Articularis Exarticulata*, 2).

86 There is a paucity of work studying the historical meaning and complex usages of the idea of 'Arminianism', see A. J. Harrisson, *Arminianism* (1938); N. Tyacke *Anti-Calvinists: The Rise of English Arminianism c. 1590–1640* (Oxford, 1987).

87 Hickman, *Historia Quinqu-Articularis Exarticulata*, 21–8. On Pelagianism, see J. Passmore, *The Perfectibility of Man* (1974), 1–40.

88 Hickman, *Historia Quinqu-Articularis Exarticulata*, please note the mispagination of the CUL edition: references here are to the faulty pagination: 397, 429–32.

89 See also Burnet to Fulman, 7 September 1680: 'And I shall tell you freely, Dr Heylin is an author whom I have found in many particulars grossly insincere; for I have seen in the Cotton Library many of the vouchers which he wrote from, in which he has with a sort of spite picked out only what might be a reproach to that time, and has left the most considerable things that might represent matters more honorably. I have not enlarged on these discoveries, because I had no mind to expose him more than was necessary; but I give no sort of credit to

preferred to use Heylyn's work against the more Protestant narrative of Burnet's *History*.[90] The most conclusive evidence is the work of one George Touchet, an unregenerate papist. In 1673 he published his *Historical Collections out of several Protestant Historians* to propagandize the Catholic claim to the true faith. Touchet's aim was to negate the value of the 'Protestant' past. Having read these histories he was amazed 'to find in them, that the alteration of Religion here hath been totally carried on by worldly interest'.[91] His aim was to inform the reader 'exactly' how the progress of the Reformation was carried out. Once again a Catholic polemicist recommended Heylyn's work as a valuable resource. Touchet cited Heylyn as insisting that the Reformation had been inspired by Henry VIII's 'politick ends'; self-interest was the motivation for the dissolution of the monasteries.[92] Touchet appreciated Heylyn's account and hostility to the 'Zwinglian Gospellers' and the influence of Continental Calvinism. Heylyn's restrained description of the Marian regime was converted by Touchet into a description of Mary's 'moderation'. The latter part of Touchet's *Collections* was directly lifted from Heylyn's *Aerius Redivivus*, emphasizing the seditious character of the Presbyterian sect. Touchet stated his opinion about the Reformation succinctly: 'For although the Reformation of religion was here pretended; yet it evidently appears by our English History, that nothing but worldly and carnal interests carried on this business.'[93]

Contemporaries recognized the reactionary nature of Heylyn's works. In *King Edward the VIth His own Arguments against the Popes Supremacy* (1682) Edward VI was vindicated from the 'severe and unjust censure' of Heylyn's history. Heylyn had commented in his history of the Reformation that it had not been an infelicity to the Church of England that the young king had died at an early age. The author of the remarks was indignant at Heylyn's aspersions on the Edwardian period: 'He says expressly, that his minority was abused, to many acts of spoil and rapine, even to an high degree of sacrilege.'[94] The author reversed this charge, and insisted that Heylyn's notion of sacrilege was not concerned with an idea of dishonour to God, but 'lies in clipping the wings, and abridging the power of Church men, who were little God almighties in the affairs of the Church'. Heylyn's hysteria and censure of the young king were compared with 'the ravings of

this authority' (N. Pocock (ed.), *The History of the Reformation* (7 volumes, Oxford, 1865), VII, 37).

[90] See below, pp. 84–6.   [91] G. Touchet, *Historical Collections* (1673), Preface, Sig. A2r.

[92] *Ibid.*, 23–4, 77–83.

[93] *Ibid.*, 212–36, 337, 489–90. Note R. Baxter, *The Second Part of the Non-Conformists' Plea for Peace* (1680), Preface, Sig. A4r, complains about the papist tenor of Heylyn's history, and Touchet's use of it. Thanks to J. Marshall for bringing this to my attention.

[94] Anon., *King Edward the VIth*, 99.

one of Baal's priests, when good King Josias defiled the high places where the Priests had burnt incence'.[95]

Peter Heylyn was no Roman Catholic, neither was he a Protestant of the Erastian variety. That men could consciously choose one historical interpretation over another was not merely a preference of scholarship, but was a reflection of the historical needs of their particular ideological beliefs. Heylyn's works can be read within the Restoration context as a restatement of the High Church position against the interference of Parliament in affairs of religion, and the drive for toleration and comprehension. To defend the national Church against the claims of popery was the crucial ideological enterprise which faced all Anglicans whether High or Low Church. Heylyn attempted to justify the autonomous status of the Church of England without falling into the scylla of popery or the charybdis of Presbyterianism. For Heylyn the resolution of this theoretical tension was found in the historical idea of Cyprianic episcopacy. Following Cyprian he defined Christian duty in terms of obedience to episcopal government. *De jure divino* episcopacy provided a cogent antidote to both papalist and Presbyterian claims and rendered the national Church independent. While Heylyn's visions preserved the Church of England from obligation to the papal see, it implicitly argued for the independence and separate estate of the clerical order. Other theorists preferred to defend the national Church with an history of the Royal Supremacy, rather than with a clericalist history of episcopacy. The Church of England was to be justified in terms of the *regnum* rather than the *sacerdotium*. It was from this reopening of the ecclesiological debate of the Reformation that the radical Erastianism of the infidel Freethinkers originated.

FROM BURNET TO TINDAL: VARIETIES OF ERASTIANISM

One of the most significant of Reformation studies that contradicted Heylyn's clericalism (and for that reason strongly recommended to the English Protestant reader by William Nicolson) was Gilbert Burnet's *History of the English Reformation* (1679–1714). Nicolson insisted that Burnet's work was the final statement upon the subject. It was a paradigm of scholarship. Ranke complimented the work for its modernity, and H. Foxcroft echoed this opinion arguing that Burnet's conception of history was 'essentially modern'.[96] The inspiration for Burnet's work was faith rather than pure research: the *History* was designed to combat the papalistic assertions of the French translation of Nicholas Saunder's *De Origine ac Progressu Schismatis Anglicani* (Cologne, 1585; translated Paris, 1676).

---

[95] *Ibid.*, 101, 105–6, 107.
[96] H. Foxcroft, *A Life of Gilbert Burnet*, (Cambridge, 1907), 151.

Burnet started his work between 1677 and 1678: the first volume was completed and published on 23 May 1679. This publication certainly eased the rather arduous process of research for the further volumes. The archiepiscopal hostility of William Sancroft, and the enmity of the Duke of Lauderdale (his former patron), had closed the Cottonian Library to Burnet's investigation. After the first publication its full resources were laid open. Thomas Tenison directed Burnet to many important documents in the collections at Corpus Christi College, Cambridge, while Bishop Turner provided him with the services of two amanuenses. On 11 July 1679 a royal warrant threw open the vaults of the Paper Office. Lord Russell, the Chancellor, sent the historian funds, while Lord Halifax offered him a pension. In the autumn of 1680 the University of Oxford conferred an honorary doctorate upon Burnet. The highest praise was the vote of thanks accorded by both Houses of Parliament in December 1680 and proudly displayed in all future editions of the *History*.[97]

Although the *History of the Reformation* was ultimately the fruit of Burnet's solitary researches, the Scotsman clearly sought and received scholarly aid from others. The Dean of Bangor, William Lloyd, and the Dean of St Paul's, Edward Stillingfleet, were his primary abettors. In a *Letter to the Lord Bishop of Coventry and Litchfield* (1693), written to William Lloyd, refuting the hostile charges of Anthony Harmer, Burnet acknowledged this debt, 'it was you both, that I chiefly depended as to the correction of my work; and all the world knows how exact you are in those matters'.[98] Lloyd had provided Burnet with his own chronological collections, and revised the first draft of the history with 'censorious severity'.[99] Burnet, especially after the High Church and non-juror attacks upon his work, made continual public reference to his helpers in an attempt to shore up his integrity and credit. By the 1690s the *History* was (almost) being presented as a collaborative effort of the most eminent men in the Church. What did the *History* argue which was so crucial to these men?

In the preface to the first volume of the *History* Burnet made his intentions clear: he intended to defend the Henrician and Edwardian reforms. He pointed out that there were many Continental works on the Reformation by such men as Sleiden, Thuanus and Sarpi, but no English equivalent. The

[97] *Ibid.*, 153–66; N. Pocock (ed.), *The History of the Reformation* (7 volumes, Oxford, 1865), VII, 1–25; G. Burnet, *Reflections upon a Pamphlet Entitled Some Discourses* (1696), 80. The most recent account of the *History of the Reformation* is J. E. Drabble, 'Gilbert Burnet and the History of the English Reformation: the Historian and His Milieu', *Journal of Religious History*, 12 (1983) – a superficial piece that contains a number of factual errors. See also A. G. Dickens and J. Tonkin, *The Reformation in Historical Thought* (Oxford, 1985), 108, where Burnet is applauded as a 'major contribution to the emancipation of English history from the annalistic method'.
[98] G. Burnet, *A Letter* (1693), 17 and *Reflections on a Book* (1700), 25.
[99] Burnet, *A Letter* (1693), 2.

papist accusations of Saunder's work against the English schism lay unanswered. John Foxe's work was a commendable, but not comprehensive, attempt; Lord Herbert of Cherbury had spent little time discussing religion in his life of Henry VIII; while Heylyn's attempt was such that one would be fair in thinking either, 'he was very much ill-informed, or very led by his passions ... that one would think he had been secretly set onto it by those of the Church of Rome'.[100] Burnet intended to answer the Catholic charge that the Reformation had been carried on 'by the lusts and passions of King Henry the Eighth, carried on by the ravenousness of the Duke of Somerset, under Edward the Sixth, and confirmed by the policy of Queen Elizabeth and her Council to secure her title'.[101] Burnet conceived his work as a restatement of the principles of Protestantism against the filth and fables of popery.

For Burnet the Reformation was a reaction against both Roman Catholicism, and the dangers of clericalism. The inspiration of John Wycliffe was heralded as the beginning of the Reformation in England. The clergy of the early sixteenth century were worm-eaten with superstition and corruption. They were ignorant and lewd, men who openly attracted the contempt and hatred of the people, 'they had engrossed the greatest part of both the riches and power of christendom, and lived at their ease and in much wealth. And the corruptions of their worship and doctrines were such, that a very small proportion of commonsense, with but an overly looking on the New Testament, discovered them.' The theological necessity for reform had been aided by the monarchical intent to oust the papacy from the British realm. The king had justified his actions by the precedents of the 'fathers, councils, Schoolmen, and Canonists'.[102] All the manuscripts and statutes in defence of this point were duly placed in Burnet's appended collection.

Burnet praised Henry VIII's reassumption of the imperial authority in Church affairs and deployed Reformation arguments in defence of the royal supremacy drawn from both the bishop's and king's books, and Gardiner's *De Vera Obedienta*. The Church of England was competent to reform itself upon the precedents of Cyprian and the tradition of apostolic equality, coupled with lack of scriptural or historical evidence for the supremacy of St Peter. The dynamic of Reformation by royal supremacy was defended by both scriptural and rational argument. The primary example was biblical: the case of Moses and Aaron indicated that in the 'Old Testament they found the Kings of Israel intermeddled in all matters Ecclesiastical'.[103] The examples of Solomon and Abiathar, plus Jehoshaphat, Hezekiah and Josias, were supplemented by the actions of the primitive Christians who rendered obedience unto Caesar. Argument from reason was then subjoined. Burnet wrote, 'that there must be but one supreme; and that the King being supreme

---

[100] Burnet, *History of the Reformation*, I, Preface, Sig. Bv.   [101] *Ibid.*, I, Preface, Sig. B2r.
[102] *Ibid.*, I, 23, 30, 97.   [103] *Ibid.*, I, 138–42.

over all his subjects, clergymen must be included, for they are still subjects. Nor can their being in orders, change their former relation, founded upon the law of nature and nations.' To supplement this argument the historical cases of British kings, Lucius, Canute, Ethelred, Edgar, Edmond, Athelstan, and Ina were all displayed. Monarchical power was dissimilar from papal, since it was bound to be conformable to the laws of God.[104]

In his discussion of the royal supremacy of Henry VIII, Burnet employed the language of *renovatio*. The king had made no claims to new authority, but simply reassumed a lost power. In the preface to the second volume of the *History*, Burnet specifically defended the rights of the royal supremacy. There had been much objection to the Reformation because it had been undertaken without the assent of the majority of the clergy, but simply enacted upon the authority of the king, rather than the whole Church. Burnet again defended the royal supremacy upon scriptural, rational and historical grounds. He wrote, 'that such a Reformation can no more be blasted by being called a Parliament religion, than the Reformation made by the Kings of Israel without or against the majority of the Priests, could be blemished by being call'd the King's religion'.[105] This contradicted Heylyn's vision which argued that the Reformation was necessarily clerically inspired, and merely ratified by the king's authority. For Heylyn the 'true' reforms were undertaken by Convocation authority, the role of the Parliament and the monarchy was to act 'post-fact' in creating the power of the secular sword to defend the spiritual injunctions. Burnet countered this narration. Although he attributed some dynamic in the doctrinal reform to Convocation, the clergy in general were treated as a recalcitrant force, self-interested and attached to the revenues of popery.

For Burnet the threat to the Reformation was an internal one, rather than any Continental movement. The enemy was the clergy of the Church of England, rather than a foreign sect. Thus, in chronicling the reforms of the 1540s, Archbishop Cranmer was represented as pushing for further reformation, while Stephen Gardiner was depicted as launching a popishly inspired conspiracy against him. Burnet validated the dissolution of the monasteries as a legal retrieval of wealth for the monarchy, which by 'secret practises' the monks had gained and encroached from the jurisdiction of the civil state. The dissolution was justified in terms of spiritual purification, rather than private aggrandizement. As Burnet noted with approval, Cranmer intended to use the new wealth to create more efficient bishoprics, 'according to the Scripture and primitive rules'.[106]

Burnet's history was premised upon a particular definition of religion: 'Religion is chiefly for perfecting the nature of man, for improving his

104 *Ibid.*, I, 141–3.   105 *Ibid.*, II, Preface, Sig. B2r.
106 *Ibid.*, I, 180–94; II, 189, 302–44.

faculties, governing his actions, and securing the peace of everyman's conscience, and of the societies of mankind in common.' This was the role of religion in its 'true' and pure form; the passage of time saw accretions to this purpose, usually undertaken in the name of 'interest'. Superstition, idolatry and 'priestly dominion' had been erected upon the pure original of Christianity. Burnet's history presented the Reformation as renovating corrupt religion back to its original purity. For example, he focused upon the history of image worship. The reformers were strict upholders of the second commandment, which plainly forbade all worship of visible objects. Such men as Gardiner, Bonner and Tunstall were presented as considering such Reformation as iconoclasm.[107] Cranmer meanwhile, according to Burnet, advanced the Reformation slowly but securely, trusting in the providence of God: English reformation was the mean way between superstition and irreligion.[108] Burnet's vision of true religion and his soteriological theory indicate his implicit anticlericalism. Salvation was to be achieved by a combination of Christ's intercession and individual conformity to the rules of the Gospel: this reduced the sacerdotal role of the priesthood. His attitude towards the Reformation idea of the Eucharist indicates this sentiment. He wrote:

It is certain there was no part of worship more corrupted than this sacrament was. The first institution was so plain and simple, that except in the words, this is my body, there is nothing which could give colour to the corruptions that were afterwards brought in. The heathens had their mysteries, which the priests concealed with dark and hard words, and dressed up with much pomp; and thereby supported their own esteem with the people.[109]

Originally Christian practice had been simple, but had suffered the corrupting and mystifying influence of the priesthood. The sacrament was extended from its original commemorative function, to become a superstitious vehicle for the advance of the priesthood. The English Reformation was characterized as exiling the last remnants of heathenism.[110] Burnet noted that the dispute over the Eucharist had been a hard fought battle because the priesthood saw it as the last bastion of their *sacerdos*; he wrote, '[they]

---

[107] *Ibid.*, II, Preface, Sig. Ev, (paginated), 9, 25.
[108] One of the most crucial reforms was the publication of vernacular homilies; Burnet explained: 'The chief design in them was to acquaint the people with the method of salvation according to the gospel; in which there are two dangerous extremes at that time which divided the world. The greatest part of the ignorant Commons seemed to consider their priests as a sort of people who had such a secret trick of saving souls, as mountebanks pretend in the curing of diseases ... the other extreme was of some corrupt gospellers, who thought if they magnified Christ much, and depended upon his merits and intercession, they could not perish, which so ever way they led their lives' (*ibid.*, II, 27, 30).
[109] Burnet, *History of the Reformation*, II, 62.
[110] Note the radicals – Charles Blount, John Toland, and, later still, Conyers Middleton – repeatedly attacked the Catholic and 'popish' religions as new systems of paganism.

accounted it as the chief support now left of their falling dominion, which being kept up might in time retrieve all the rest. For while it was believed that their character qualified them for so strange and mighty a performance, they must needs be held in great reverence.'[111]

The Reformation had reinstituted the primitive pastoral role of the clergy. The role of the priest and bishop was to tend to the flock, to catechize children rather than search for worldly advancement. The settlement of the articles of religion was presented as a moderate and latitudinarian action; a return to the primitive simplicity of creeds rather than post-Nicene complexities. The principle of the Reformation was to follow the Melancthonian temper of indifference, rather than scholastical subtlety. The role of the clerical order was to be moral and theological supervisors, rather than sacrificial priests.[112]

In Burnet's third volume of the *History* (1714), the notion of the Reformation as a pastoral purification of priestly dominion is even more pronounced. The work was published in response to the many attacks that had been launched on the *History* in the 1690s and 1700s. Burnet perceived all these attacks as popish, or at least indicative of a new trenchant clericalism. He commented upon his non-juror and High Church opponents:

[They] are taking the very same methods, only a little diversified, that have been perused in Popery, to bring the world into a blind dependence upon the clergy, and to draw the wealth and strength of the nation into their hands. The opinion of the sacraments being an expiatory sacrifice; and of the necessity of secret confession and absolution; and of the Church's authority acting in an independence on the civil powers, were the foundations of popery, and the seminal principles out of which that mass of corruptions was formed.[113]

Burnet's fear for the Church in 1714 was that, 'we are insensibly going off from the Reformation, and framing a new model of the Church, totally different from our former principles'. Burnet noted that his original *History* had been written to combat the perils of the Duke of York's popery; the publication of the third volume was a similar timely injunction. He warned: 'It seemed a proper time to awaken the nation, by showing both what Popery, and what the Reformation was; by shewing the cruelty and falsehood of the former, and what patience and courage of our reformers was; and the work had generally so good an effect then, that if the like danger seemed to revert, it may not seem an improper attempt to try once more to awaken a nation that has perhaps forgotten past danger, and yet may be

---

[111] *Ibid.*, II, 104. The connection between the notion of the Eucharist as a sacrifice, and the power of an independent clerical order was to become a contentious issue in the 1690s with the rise of the Unitarian and Arian theologies, which rejected any priestly *sacerdos*. See next chapter.

[112] *Ibid.*, II, 164–9, 195–202.   [113] *Ibid.*, III, Preface, xii.

nearer than ever.'[114] Burnet saw the obvious parallel between the dangers of the Church of England in the 1680s and the 1700s; his remedy was to fill the debate with historical visions of the Reformation. He was to provide his readership with images, stories and patterns of popish behaviour with which they could analyse the state of contemporary religion.

The key to the publication of the third volume can be seen in his advocation of John Colet's *Sermon ad Cleros* (1511) as an anticlerical tract. More's *Utopia* (1516) was given a similar interpretation. The High Church polemicist Francis Atterbury had made use of Colet's sermon in his *Rights of an English Convocation*, arguing that it legitimated clerical immunity from civil jurisdiction. Burnet insisted that Colet had attacked the secular involvements of the sixteenth-century clergy. Colet had railed against the practices of the clergy, writing that the 'spouse of Christ, the Church whom ye would should be without spot or wrinkle, is made foul and disfavoured'. Colet argued that the Church had transgressed the Pauline injunction, 'be not you conformable to this world'. The Church had become tainted with the sin of devilish pride, carnal concupiscence, worldly covetousness and secular entanglements. It had become a servant of men rather than Christ.[115] Burnet commented in his *Reflections* (1700) that it had been Colet's sermon which had inspired his writing of the *History of the Reformation*. He declared, 'that once I had intended to have published it as a piece that might serve to open the scene, and to shew the state of things at the first beginning of the Reformation; but I was diverted from it by those under whose direction I put that work, they thought that it might have been judged that I had inserted it on design to reflect upon the present, as well as on the past state of things'.[116] This was exactly what Burnet felt necessary in 1714. Like Colet, Burnet insisted that the role of the clergy was to be good, to set a Reformation example, and minister to their flocks.[117] Burnet reintroduced the language of the Reformation; the appeals to primitivism and piety, coupled with an hostility towards 'superstition' and 'popery'. Burnet considered himself a 'watchdog' against the 'mystery of iniquity' that was advancing in the Church of England. For Burnet the 'true' religion (and that embodied in the Reformation) was 'religion in the soul' rather than the *sacerdos* of popery. He defined the difference between his religion, and that of his High Church opponents thus:

[114] *Ibid.*, III, Introduction, viii.
[115] See 'The Sermon of Doctor Colet, Made to the Convocation at Paulis' in J. H. Lupton, *Life of Dean Colet* (1909), 296; note also T. Smith (ed.), *A Sermon of Conforming and Reforming Made to the Convocation at St Paul's Church in London by John Colet DD* (Cambridge, 1661). See also P. I. Kaufman, 'John Colet's Opus de Sacramentis and Clerical Anticlericalism: The Limitation of the "Ordinary Wayes"', *Journal of British Studies* (1982).
[116] Burnet, *Reflections on the Rights, Powers, and Privileges* (1700), 5.
[117] Burnet, *History of the Reformation*, III, 219. For More as an anticlericalist 30–3.

[I] have another notion of the worship of God, than to dress it up as a splendid opera: [I] have a just notion of priesthood, as a function that imports the care of souls, and a solemn performing the public homage we owe to God; but do not invert it into a political piece of craft, by which means men's secrets are to be discovered, and all subdued by a tyranny that reaches to men's souls, as well as to their worldly concerns.[118]

Burnet was not allowed to monopolize the moral authority of the Reformation unhindered. The stock counter-polemic was that the reforms had been executed 'by the power and interest of a few persons for their own advantage.'[119] This can be illustrated from the case of Peter Manby (d. 1697), a Roman Catholic convert and Dean of Derry. On 26 July 1686 he received dispensation from James II to proclaim publicly his conversion to Catholicism while still retaining his clerical office. In 1688 James elevated Manby to the position of Alderman of Derry. Manby's conversion was a calculated public manœuvre. He published an account of his reasons for converting, couched in historical terms, *The Considerations which obliged Peter Manby, Dean of Derry to Embrace the Catholique Religion* published in 1687, in both London and Dublin. William King, the Chancellor of St Patrick's, Dublin, later to be archbishop of the same city, answered Manby's assertions in his *An Answer to the Considerations* (Dublin, 1687). Manby was to reply to this work in the same year in *A Reformed Catechism, in Two Dialogues Concerning the English Reformation*. Manby's original work dealt with the English Reformation. In his examination of the Henrician reforms Manby had convinced himself that the innovations had no true theological mission. He characterized the Reformation as the product of secular and private interests. Manby drew his historical evidence from the work of Peter Heylyn, the High Church Anglican, rather than the more 'Protestant' work of Bishop Burnet.

The introductory pages of Manby's work discussed the relative merits of the two compositions. Surprisingly Manby insisted that Burnet's work was a legitimate description of the Reformation. In his *Reformed Catechism* he printed, opposite the title page, the parliamentary commendations of Burnet's work. The intention was not to commend Burnet's ecclesiological vision but to condemn the Reformation as incompatible with the prescripts of true religion. While Manby asserted that Burnet's narrative was a true description, the description itself was not prescriptive because it showed the Protestant reforms as irreligious. The years of Henry VIII and Edward VI were times of secular aggrandizement. Archbishop Cranmer had executed the 'spirit of Hobbes of Malmesbury' in diminishing the status and authority of the Catholic Church.[120] The Reformation was presented as a parlia-

---

[118] *Ibid.*, III, Introduction, xxii. [119] P. Manby, *A Reformed Catechism*, 'To the Reader'.
[120] Manby, *Considerations*, 'To the Reader', Sig. A4v.

mentary procedure, he wrote: 'The design of this catechism, is to shew ... that the English Reformation was not the act and deed of the National Church or Clergy of England; neither in the days of Henry VIII or Edward VI, nor of Queen Elizabeth; but imposed on the nation by the interest and power of a few persons for their own advantage, viz. the raising of fortunes out of Church lands.'[121]

Manby's work was a catechism of history: there are repeated injunctions and directions to the reader. Manby addressed his audience; 'Good reader, I humbly desire this favour of thee, to set aside prejudice and interest for the space of two or three hours, whilst thou art reading this book, which are but pearls upon both thy eyes that will hinder thy sight.' There are explicit directions to the reader to note particular examples, or parts of the narrative.[122] The final pages of the *Reformed Catechism* are an epitome of the Plutarchian model; the life and characters of Thomas Cranmer, the Archbishop of Canterbury and Manby's *bête noire*, were set side by side with that of the Bishop of Rochester, John Fisher, Manby's hero. Fisher was presented as the martyr who died defending the Church against an 'inundation of sacrilege, schism and confusion'. Manby's directive to the reader was, 'now Reader, (wer't thou to choose thy religion) consider which of these two guides thou wouldst follow'.[123]

William King's reply to Manby's incitements to Catholicism was similarly articulated in historical terms. King's position was that the Reformation was valid because it conformed to the standards of the historical prescription of the rights of national Churches. King's method was to unmask the deviant content of Manby's preference for Heylyn's text. King described Manby's intention:

he gives this character, that Burnet strains all his wit to palliate the doings of the Reformers, and paints them out to advantage; Heylyn represents them honestly for the most part, and in their own colours: whereas in truth the first doth generally lay down naked matter of fact only, and leaves the reader to judge; and the other passes his own censures and gives his own gloss on them.[124]

In his second reply, King suggested that Manby had deliberately manipulated and mis-cited Burnet's work to place it in a bad light.[125] King ridiculed Manby's claim to be an historian; his work contained 'only a history of the

---

121 Manby, *Reformed Catechism*, 7.
122 *Ibid.*, 'To the Reader', iii–iv, 3. 'Note, let the reader observe here', 33, 64, 86.
123 *Ibid.*, 86, 102.
124 W. King, *An Answer to the Considerations which Obliged Peter Manby* ... (Dublin, 1687), 10.
125 W. King, *A Vindication of the Answer to the Considerations* (Dublin, 1688), 8–10, 31; 'I desire therefore the reader to look over the history, and compare those who were for the Reformation with such as opposed it; and let him say in his conscience, which seems of God and religion: and not to take the character from the mangled and broken account Mr. M. gives some of them.'

mistakes, or supposed mistakes of some reformers: which is rather accusation than history; and in as much that a great many things are forged 'tis a libel'.[126] For King the history of the Reformation was a demonstration of the truth of the Protestant faith: this demonstration was premised upon empircal 'matter of fact'. Manby had attempted to present false data. He had asserted that 'almost all the Bishops' in the reign of Edward VI had been expelled from their sees for dissenting from the pattern of innovation. King insisted that in all his researches he could only find five such examples. It was as if, as King wrote, the Catholic religion 'consisted in protestation against matter of fact'.[127]

While the case of Peter Manby's assaults on Burnet's *History* illustrates the ultimate polemical context of historical scholarship, it is also important to examine the more learned attacks upon his account of the Reformation. Unsurprisingly the initial hostilities came from Roman Catholic quarters, and in particular from France. The *History* had been translated into French by M. de Rosemond as *L'Histoire de la réformation de l'église d'Angleterre* (1683–85), and a Latin edition appeared at Geneva in 1682 giving ample opportunity for Continental scholars to appraise Burnet's efforts. The Frenchman Varillas in his history of heresies had undertaken an extensive anatomy of Burnet's historical errors, and as we have seen Burnet spent much time and effort in denying and countering these accusations. Joachim Le Grand in his *Histoire du divorce de Henry VIII Roy d'Angleterre et de la Catharine d'Arragon* (Paris, 1688) proposed to refute Burnet's volumes and restate Saunder's original thesis. Le Grand argued that Burnet's history was riven with 'fautes'. Burnet's research was not history but polemic calculated to appeal to the radical Protestants in their attempted exclusion of the Catholic Duke of York in 1680.[128] This Catholic assault was given even greater prestige in the magisterial work of Jean Bossuet, Bishop of Meaux, *Histoire des variations des églises protestantes* (Paris, 1688). The premise of Bossuet's argument was that any deviation from the Catholic faith was an indication of the falsehood of such opinion: Burnet's history indicted itself. The English Reformation was a schism from the true Church. The idea of a national Church separated from the universal Church was both anathema and premised upon the false dominion of the civil authority over the spiritual. As Bossuet argued: 'A nation, which looks on itself as a complete

---

126 *Ibid.*, 33.
127 King directed a further assault against Manby's work; in appealing to the individual conscience of the reader Manby undermined the Catholic rule of faith (*ibid.*, 4, 6–7, 23).
128 Le Grand commented: 'Bien plus peut-on douter que cet ouvrage n'ait été entrepris pour préparer les espirits des peuples cet changement que voulaient faire au Angleterre au Duc de Mônmout, au Comte de Shaftesbury, au Comte de Salisbury, au Lord Russel, au rests enfin de cette horrible faction de Cromwel toujours opposée a l'autorité Royale, toujours preste a troubler la tranquillité publique, et à ruiner les loix fondamentale de l'état', *Histoire du divorce* (Paris, 1688) 181–6.

body, which regulated its faith, in particular, without regard to what the rest of the Church believes, is a nation which separates itself from the universal Church, and renounces unity of Faith and Sentiment, so much recommended to the Church by Jesus Christ and his Apostles.'[129] This opinion was epitomized, for Bossuet, in Burnet's presentation of the life and works of Thomas Cranmer (1489–1556), Archbishop of Canterbury. Cranmer was 'Mr Burnet's Heroe'.[130] Bossuet set out to both destroy Cranmer's character and undermine Burnet's admiration for the reformer. Cranmer was a hypocrite.[131]

For Bossuet, Cranmer's most heinous crime was his defence of the royal supremacy and the implied subjection of the spiritual order to the civil power. Displaying the infamous 'Cranmer manuscript' proffered by Burnet in his 'Collection of Records'[132] Bossuet insisted that 'Cranmer and his adherents' believed 'that Jesus Christ had instituted Pastors to exercise their power dependently of the Prince in every function; which certainly is the most monstrous and the most scandalous flattery that ever entered into the hearts of men'.[133] These opinions were no fleeting aberration, but a persistent sentiment of both Cranmer and the English Reformation. Rather than deal with the many and various objections to Burnet's *History of the Reformation* this examination will focus upon his treatment of Cranmer and the reception of this treatment.

Burnet was swift to react to these Continental insults: in a *Letter to Mr Thêvenot* (1689) he rebutted the claims of both Le Grand and Bossuet. In reply to Le Grand, Burnet dealt with the mistakes the Frenchman had charged him with. Le Grand's primary error was to 'give Cranmer the worst character that he could make for him'. In the same way Burnet countered Bossuet's arguments and scholarship: the English Reformation was a 'progress' not a 'variation'.[134] Bossuet's portrayal of Cranmer was unnecessarily malignant. According to Burnet the reformer deserved eulogy rather than insult. In his history Burnet had described Cranmer as a learned and moderate divine who followed the pattern of Scripture and the Primitive Fathers. While it is unsurprising that Roman Catholic polemicists should direct venom against a reformer who dismantled the bastions of papalism,

---

[129] J. Bossuet, *History of the Variations of the Protestant Churches* (2 volumes, Antwerp, 1742), I, 325–8, 339.

[130] *Ibid.*, I, 298; Le Grand, *Histoire du Divorce*, 96ff.

[131] 'Here then we have him all at once. A Lutheran, a married man, a concealer of his marriage, an archbishop according to the Roman Pontifical subject to the Pope, whose power he detested in his heart, saying mass which he did not believe in, and giving power to say it; yet nevertheless, if we believe Mr Burnet, a second Athanasius, a second Cyril, one of the most perfect prelates the Church ever had' (Bossuet, *History of the Variations*, I, 303).

[132] Burnet, *History of the Reformation*, I, Book iii, document xxi, 220, and following.

[133] Bossuet, *History of the Variations*, I, 323–5; see also 363–5.

[134] Burnet, *A Letter to Mr Thêvenot*, 11–12, 23.

the assaults by men within the Anglican communion requires detailed and careful explanation. The Catholic convert Peter Manby using the evidence of the 'Cranmer Manuscript' had argued that Cranmer had more of the 'spirit of Hobbes of Malmesbury' than Christ.[135] The Cranmerian Reformation was tainted with the radical Erastianism of Hobbism. The independent authority of the *sacerdos* was incorporated under the aegis of the civil state.[136] This Erastian charge was made first, not by the renegade Catholic Manby, nor the Continental antagonists, but by the High Church apologist Simon Lowth.

Simon Lowth (1630–1720?) appointed Dean of Rochester by James II, refused the Oath after 1690, and opposed all Erastian tenets in his *Of the Subject of Church Power* (1685). Edward Stillingfleet, John Tillotson and Gilbert Burnet were all indicted for their espousal of Cranmer's opinions. Edward Stillingfleet in his *Irenicum* (1661) was one of the first men to deploy the evidence of the 'Cranmer Manuscript' to justify his opinions. Stillingfleet argued in *Irenicum* that there was no definite prescribed model of Church government left by Christ or revealed by God. Church structures and institutions could be 'right' not only if definitely commended, but also if the result of legitimate choice. The legitimate authority to constitute Church government was the civil one. The converse of this position was that 'Church power' was not to be considered of 'any divine institution, but only from positive and ecclesiastical laws made according to the several states and conditions wherein the Church was'.[137] With a most 'impartial survey' Stillingfleet illustrated the notion of the mutability of Church government. His prime evidence was the 'Cranmer Ms' which was 'exactly transcribed out of the Original'.[138] Stillingfleet concentrated upon questions (9)–(16), all of which concerned Church government; both the questions and Cranmer's replies were published. Question (9) had inquired whether the Apostles had made bishops by necessity because they lacked the authority of a higher power, 'or by authority given them of God'.[139] Cranmer's reply asserted that the king had authority over all issues, both civil and spiritual; spiritual ministers were to be considered analogical to civil ministers, neither of which held any authority beyond the king's grant. The diverse 'comly ceremonies and solemnities' used in the admission to office were not of theological necessity, but simply for good order. The ecclesiastical men were considered

---

[135] Manby, *Considerations*, 'To the Reader', Sig. A4v.   [136] Manby, *Catechism* 30–5.
[137] Stillingfleet, *Irenicum*, 374.   [138] *Ibid.*, 386–93.
[139] *Ibid.*, 390. For a modern edition of the Cranmer manuscript, see G. D. Duffield (ed.), *The Work of Thomas Cranmer* (Appleyard, 1964) and J. E. Cox (ed.), *Miscellaneous Writings and Letters of Thomas Cranmer* (Cambridge, 1846). On Cranmer's ecclesiology, see W. D. J. Cargill Thompson, 'The Two Regiments' (unpublished Cambridge PhD., 1960), 247–75; see also J. Marshall, 'The Ecclesiology of the Latitude-Men 1660–1689: Stilling-fleet, Tillotson and "Hobbism"', *Journal of Ecclesiastical History* 36 (1985).

dependent upon the civil authority: this was a challenge to the traditional notion of the royal supremacy that approached the thought of Thomas Hobbes.[140] The orthodox interpretation of the royal supremacy suggested that the civil authority extended over the 'externals' of the Church; Cranmer's view suggested that the Church was a body whose existence solely lay upon the will of the king. In his answers to questions (13)–(14), Cranmer had suggested that the monarch had authority to preach, teach the word and consecrate priests and bishops, in cases of necessity. Stillingfleet noted that Cranmer's clear judgement was testimony that the particular form of Church government was subject to the 'determination of the Supreme magistrate'.[141]

Lowth from his High Church *de jure divino* position regarded Stillingfleet's Erastianism, even in its moderate form, as heresy, for 'all Church power was designed by Christ, and actually left by his Apostles only to Church officers, the order of the Gospel-Priesthood, the Bishops, Presbyters and Deacons, to be separated on purpose and successively, instated is such the jurisdiction and government, by such of themselves that had before received, and were fully invested with it'.[142] Stillingfleet had been wrong to attempt to assimilate Cranmer into his Erastian schemes by employing 'mistaken Mss', which had been incorrectly transcribed. This error was rendered more capital because Stillingfleet had caused such an imperfect record to be printed 'among the records of Dr Burnet's Church History, and abusing the House of Commons to a Publick approbation of it'.[143] According to Lowth, Stillingfleet had passed the manuscript to Burnet from the Cottonian Library. Following John Durell, Dean of Windsor, in his *Sanctas Ecclesia Anglicanae adversus Iniquas ataque Invereindas Schismaticorum Criminationes Vindicae* (1669), Lowth asserted that both Stillingfleet and Burnet had left passages out of the original manuscript. Of particular importance was the omission of Cranmer's approval of *de jure divino* episcopacy noted in his subscription to Dr Leighton's paper which contradicted his earlier deviant opinions.[144] Lowth's general point was that it was unnecessary to print such worthless documents, especially since the opinions contained in them were no part of the legally established Reformation. Therefore any publication of the 'Cranmer Manuscript' had a sinister latitudinarian end of placing the Godly Cranmer in the Erastian camp.

Burnet replied to Lowth's criticisms in two acerbic letters. He denied Lowth's malicious suggestion of a 'designed fraud'; he confessed: 'I printed no record in that collection without comparing the copies exactly with the original, for I thought it too important a thing to trust it to any person whatsoever.'[145] To be precise Burnet had printed the sections mentioned in

---

140 See Hobbes, *Leviathan*, III–IV, and below chapter 6.   141 Stillingfleet, *Irenicum*, 393.
142 S. Lowth, *Of the Subject of Church Power*, (1685), 6.
143 *Ibid.*, Preface, (unpaginated) 12.
144 *Ibid.*, 484–90.   145 G. Burnet, *A Letter to Mr Simon Lowth* (1685), 2.

Durell's work, but he had merely placed them in a more convenient order. To prove this he printed parallel passages from Lowth's work and his own collections.[146] Having defended his scholarly reputation Burnet defended his original assertions: Cranmer was a man of moderation and piety. The manuscript contained Cranmer's private and transient opinions which held no bearing upon the theological tenor of the Reformation. Burnet defended a moderate Erastian interpretation of the royal supremacy, although this was certainly radical enough to offend the High Churchmen. This Erastianism did not extend itself with complete Hobbesian rigour. In his *Reflections on the Relation of the English Reformation* (1689), an examination of Abraham Woodhead's *Church Government Part Five* (1687), Burnet made his point clearly. The royal supremacy was an architectonic device: the king was an overseer, the supremacy was an issue of prerogative rather than sacrament. Citing Twysden, Burnet argued that the Reformation had merely restored rights to the civil sovereign which had been usurped by the papacy. Civil authority had the power to command anything that was 'just and lawful': the Reformation was a legitimate and moral effect of this power.[147] For all these moderate definitions and denials Burnet and Cranmer were reviled by the High Church for the logical radicalism of their position.

The opinion that the authority of the Church lay solely in the arbitration of the civil power was what the 'high spirited Bishops' of the 1690s despised.[148] Henry Dodwell writing in the context of the deprivation of the bishops, after their refusal to take the Oath in 1689, spoke out for the 'independence of the sacred, on the civil authority'.[149] He insisted that the Church should not be bound by a pattern of the Reformation which threatened its own power. The times of Henry VIII were when 'the invasions of the sacred power were most manifest'. This opinion was justified by making reference to the 'Cranmer Ms'. Dodwell argued that Henry had advanced Cranmer simply because he was willing to betray his clerical function. Dodwell commented, 'so far he proceeded in his flattery of the Civil magistrate, that he allowed no more gifts of the Holy Ghost in the laying on of hands of the Presbytery, than in the collation of any Civil office'.[150] Burnet was criticized for treating as a hero a man who 'wholly resolves all obligation of conscience into civil empire'. Cranmer could not be considered as the leader of the 'true' Reformation since he had attempted to destroy the

---

146 *Ibid.*, 3–4, reprinting, Lowth, *Of Church Power*, 485, and Burnet, *History of the Reformation*, I, Collection of Records, III, 227.
147 G. Burnet, *Reflection on the Reformation*, 19, 20–1, 25–6.
148 See Tindal, *Rights of the Christian Church*, 257, citing Sarpi's dictum that the Church of England would become priest-ridden because of episcopal pretensions.
149 H. Dodwell, *Doctrine of the Church of England*, (1694), v.   150 *Ibid.*, xi–xii, xiii.

Church as a separate society: this same Cranmerian spirit was evident in the deprivations of 1690.[151]

If we now turn to deal directly with the replies to Burnet's publication of the third volume of the *History* it becomes apparent how the battle over the nature of the past intermixed with issues of the present. The 1700s saw the High Church extending their vociferous objections to the nature of the Revolution Church settlement into the streets of Westminster. The crucial issue was whether the Church was to be considered as an appendage of the state, or an independent organization with its authority derivative from Christ alone. Burnet had restated his pastoral vision of the Reformation. Three works explicitly renounced Burnet's accusations: *Speculum Salisburianum* (1714) by Philoclerus, *A Preface to the B...p of S..r..m's Introduction* (1713) by Jonathan Swift under the name of 'Gregory Misosarum', and George Sewell's *An Introduction to the Life* ... (1714). The latter argued that Burnet's definition of popery as any independence of the Church from the state was meaningless, for the independence of the Church was one of the necessities of true religion. He wrote,

for my Lord if the Church be dependent on the state, and religion that can obtain the sanction of the civil authority, has all that is required, and that is necessary for the truth of religion. It is the creature of the state, which is direct Hobbism, as ever was propagated, and will serve the turn of the Pope and Mahomet, as well as the true and uncorrupted faith.[152]

Sewell argued for the independence of the Church from the model of the pre-Constantinian Church, proving that the Church had competence of discipline and jurisdiction prior to the architectonic role of monarchy. The use of this model was also deployed by Dodwell, Lowth, Brett and Leslie: it was directly contrary to the imperial model of the Foxian Reformation.

The High Church replies to Burnet's work elided his anticlericalism with the principles of the Freethinkers. Swift noted that Burnet used the word 'clergyman' with such distaste it was if he were 'not of that number'.[153] Swift feared more from clergymen of Burnet's tenor, than the encroachments of popery.[154] Philoclerus maintained that the realms of the Church and state were separate aspects of the world with mutually exclusive terrains. The fault of men of Burnet's temper was that they wished to reduce the morality or 'truth' of religion to the determination of the state. Christianity and its

---

[151] A similar approach was assumed by Jeremy Collier in his *Ecclesiastical History* (1707–10) who condemned the Cranmerian reforms as 'Erastian tenets' and insisted that God had given the clergy a commission independent of the state (II 89, 93, 198).

[152] G. Sewell, *An Introduction*, 62.

[153] Swift, *A Preface*, 31; see also Philoclerus, *Speculum Salisburianum*, 18–19, where the author suggests Burnet's colleagues are Toland and Collins.

[154] Swift, *A Preface*, 16–17, 53–4; Philoclerus, *Speculum Salisburianum*, 17, 33.

Church, for the High Church man, was a transcendent principle not subject to the mutability of civil prudence.[155]

The difference between an Erastian and a sacerdotal vision of the Church became more pronounced after the 1660s. This debate between a defence of the Church in terms of the sacerdotal authority of episcopacy or the jurisdictional competence of a reforming monarchy provided the conceptual language of the later radical attacks upon the authority of the Church. The latent anticlericalism of Erastian arguments was apparent in early works like Sir Roger Twysden's *Historical Vindication of the Church of England* first published in 1657 and republished in 1675. Twysden, a collaborator with John Selden on the *Historia Anglicanae Decem* (1652) and admirer of the Venetian anti-papalist Paolo Sarpi, took the encroachment of the papacy upon a pristine British independence as his central theme. The work instanced when, where and how the papacy had erected its illegal authority; the intention was to vindicate the Reformation in its expulsion of these encroachments. The essence of Twysden's position lay in the argument that the papacy had no theological claims to exercise authority over the British Church, thus any powers that were gained must have evolved from the authority of human laws. The latter were revocable by the same authority that created them in the first place.[156] Papal authority had been admitted into England on the basis of 'custom' and was regulated according to stipulations and contracts. Twysden was certain that the English monarchy was not subject *de jure divino* to the papacy. The historical premise of this argument was that Christianity was planted in England by non-papal sources. The English Church had different ceremonial practices (Easter and baptism) from the Church of Rome, which indicated Eastern rather than European origins. Twysden documented the increase of papal power in England during the era of the Saxons and the Normans. The first great promoter of this illegal incursion was Anselm, who was thwarted by Henry I's firm defence of his rights. Twysden continued to catalogue the infiltration of papal legates, palls, and other apparatus of iniquitous jurisdiction. The papacy had facilitated its claims by corrupting the dependence of the British episcopacy on the monarchy, and replacing it with an obligation upon Rome.[157] Twysden had shown that if there had been any correspondence between the Church of England and the Church of Rome, this had been based upon love rather than duty. The popes could rather 'consulere than imperare'. Twysden

---

[155] *Ibid.*, 50, 69–70, 72.
[156] R. Twysden, *Historical Vindication* (1675), 4–5. On Twysden and Sarpi, see J. L. Lievsay, *Venetian Phoenix: Paolo Sarpi and Some of his English Friends 1606–1700* (Kansas, 1973), 45–6, 87–9.
[157] Twysden, *Historical Vindication*, 6–26.

in his chronological narration documented the achievement of papal power in England, which was gained 'as I have showed, by little and little, voluntarily submitted unto'. The rights of the papacy in England were rather *jure humano* than *jure divino*.[158]

In discussing the monarch's capability and authority in ecclesiastical affairs Twysden deployed the familiar scholastic definitions of 'authority' and 'power'. The distinction was between the ideas of 'ordinis' and 'jurisdictionis'. The former was the capacity to administer the sacraments. The latter was subdivided into 'internal, where the divines by persuasions, wholesome instructions, ghostly councell, and the like so convince the inward conscience, as it is wholly obedient to his dictates . . . and external, where the Church in foro exteriori compels the Christians obedience'. The king had no sacerdotal potential, but concerned himself with the outward policy of the Church.[159] The texture of Twysden's argument worked in the following manner: first he stated that kings, by logical definition, were competent to exercise complete ecclesiastical authority; secondly that this authority had been ratified by custom and usage; thirdly this gave the monarch 'authority' to reclaim such power if lost. The actions of the Henrician Reformation were justified in this framework; as Twysden commented on Henry VIII's titular capacity as the head of the Church, '[it] added nothing new to him but a title; for he and his successor after it, did never exercise any authority in causes ecclesiastick, not warranted by the practice of former kings of the nation'.[160]

Twysden finished his work with a discussion of the historical evolution of the attitude towards the treatment of heretics. Following Sarpi he argued that the Primitive Church did very little against such men, but left them to the devices of God. Princes had very rarely proceeded to blood unless the heretic had entertained subversive intentions. Issues of theological defiance were treated with tolerance, because men's various capacities might easily lead them to different opinions and perceptions. Twysden described the gradual control grasped by the popish clergy over the definition and persecution of heresy. Innocent III was the first to erect the Inquisition in 1216; from this point on the practice spread like wildfire. Originally there had been no persecution of heretics because the only offence was against God who alone could effect punishment. Later heresy became defined as an offence against the practices of men and their institutions; persecution became a form of clerical self-interest. Twysden's argument was similar to Sarpi's *History of*

---

[158] *Ibid.*, 68, 72.
[159] *Ibid.*, 93. The example of Gallicanism was also deployed., Twysden cited (94–5, 105) Charles Le Faye who displayed many historical precedents which showed that 'la police extérieure sur l'église' was in the control of emperors, kings and princes.
[160] *Ibid.*, 107, 117.

the Inquisition and also gesticulated towards Thomas Hobbes' treatise upon the history of heresy.[161]

In Twysden's work there was a latent anticlericalism drawn from his admiration for the primitive model of Church government proposed by Paolo Sarpi. This evolution of the idea of the royal supremacy as an instrument of anticlericalism was made more explicit in the work of William Denton (1605–91), a theorist who combined Sarpi's histories with Hobbes' Erastianism. In 1680 he translated Sarpi's *A Treatise of Matters Beneficiary*, a work that informed his own *Jus Caesaris et Ecclesia vera Dictae* (1681). Denton set out to defend the 'just rights and powers of princes, and civil magistrates': to calumniate these rights was to offend Christ.[162] The *Jus Caesaris* was directed against all those who argued that the authority of the Church was independent from the civil authority. Both Pope and presbyter were indicted.[163] The subject of Denton's discourse was not the 'mystical Church' of Christ but its visible manifestation. In this manner the Church was to be considered as a society of men, rather than a gathering of believers. The Church was to be considered as a corporation, as 'an union by laws and statutes; or else they were not more significant than so many men meeting at a play or a Whitsun Ale, quod non est aliquid formatum, non est aliquid vere unum; that which hath no set form or fashion can have no true real identity; for it is the form of everything which giveth it a distinct entity of unity'. Denton used this corporationalist notion to explain the relationship between the national and parochial Churches. As in the civil sphere each corporation was derivative from the authority of the 'power paramount' of the king, so each parish Church was dependent upon the national. The obligation of the particular to the general was premised upon the 'publick power of all societies being above every soul contained in the same fraternities'. To allow independence of decision within a society would be to take away 'all possibility of sociable life in the world'.[164]

Denton legitimated the concept of national Churches from the scriptural models of Jerusalem, Ephesus and Corinth. Prior to the Constantinian

---

[161] *Ibid.*, 142–3, 148–52. There needs to be separate research on both Twysden's relationship with Sarpi's works (see Lievsay, 87–92, who suggests Twysden may have been preparing a critical edition of Sarpi's *History of Trent*) and the connections between Sarpi's and Hobbes' works on the origin of the Inquisition and the idea of heresy. Interestingly, although Twysden's *Historical Vindication* is riddled with citations from the 'Wise Venetian', on the specific origins of the Inquisition at the Lateran Council, Twysden cited a rather curious source, Ludovico Paramo's *De Origine et Progressu Officii Sanctor Inquisitionis* (Matriti, 1598). Paramo was the Sicilian inquisitor who had argued that the Jews should not be persecuted to death because this would compromise the salvation of the world. See E. Burman, *The Inquisition* (Wellingborough, 1984), 76, 192; H. Kamen, *Inquisition and Society in Spain in the Sixteenth and Seventeenth Centuries* (Indiana, 1985), 48.

[162] W. Denton, *Jus Caesaris et Ecclesia vera Dictae* (1681), 'To the Reader' Sig. A2r.

[163] *Ibid.*, 31, 33, 36, 39.

[164] *Ibid.*, 10, 11, 12, 15.

establishment of the Church, each particular society had been under the particular authority of the Apostles and their successors. Denton followed Sarpi's analysis in arguing that the original form of Christian disciplines had rested upon the injunction 'to love one another as yourself'. This original simplicity and innocence had been corroded by the craft and subtlety of the clergy, thus Christian discipline became 'meer worldly forms set up for meer worldly self ends and interests'. To support this point Denton gave continual reference to Sarpi's *Treatise of Benefices*. The idea of the historical degeneration of Christianity and the expansion of popery was the central tool of Denton's condemnation of contemporary deviance. He wrote that originally bishops had been by custom and consent employed in matters of Church discipline, 'which in process of time soon degenerated into a usurpation by the artifices of the priests or Bishops, of which Rome in full time taking hold, made great use to the abusing of the power of the brethren, and to incroach upon the principles of the body of the Church'. The present Church was merely an institution that operated for the 'grandeur, benefit, and domination of Ecclesiastics only'.[165]

Denton insisted that the Church had to be understood outside of this narrow hierocratic caste. The Church of Christ was an invisible and spiritual society, governed only by Christ who 'knoweth the hearts of men'. After the ascension of Christ there remained a visible government by teachers, prophets and apostles. Christ had instituted a priesthood that was 'touching the application of the authority to the person' dependent upon the body of the Church.[166] The clergy could derive no power from Scripture, but were servants of the body of the Church, with only the authoritative qualities of exhortation, reproval and rebuke. Denton's argument was premised upon a belief that God had given the body of the Church 'power over itself'. Following both Sarpi and Hobbes, Denton insisted that the clergy had usurped power over this body, by restricting the notion of the Church to 'noe but clergy and clergymen'. Combining this principle with the right to excommunication the clergy had established a false dominion.[167] In reality the whole body of the Church, just as in the civil state, had 'the power to make laws and ordain punishments for any of its members'. Denton echoed Hobbes when he described the historical transition of the government of the Church from democracy to monarchy. He wrote that in the beginning the Churches had been governed by a type of 'common council', but that the clergy had established a 'monarchical regiment'. This usurpation had been effected through custom rather than right.[168]

Denton thus argued against the 'independency' of the parish, by using the

---

[165] *Ibid.*, 17, 18–19, 20, 21, 23. [166] *Ibid.*, 24.
[167] *Ibid.*, 82–103, citing Sarpi, *Treatise of Matters Beneficiary*.
[168] Denton, *Jus Caesaris*, 24, 26–7. See Hobbes, *Leviathan*, IV and below 135n.

notion of the 'independence' of the national Church as a corporation. The illegal 'independence' of the Presbyterians and Independents was also vilified as an encroachment upon the civil power. This was to create a 'regnum in regno'. The claim to a separate sacerdotal authority smacked of popery. Denton was to define 'priesthood' in a broad manner in order to exclude such spiritual claims. The capacity of the priest was simply to know the truth: ordination was not necessary to create this didactic competence. There was a general right and duty which all Christians had to study for each other's good. He wrote, 'to save souls every man is or ought to be a priest, the command is universal 19 Lev. 17 thou shalt not hate thy brother in thine heart thou shalt in any wise rebuke the brother and not suffer sin upon him'.[169]

Denton suggested that the false independence of the clergy had been facilitated by the force that custom wielded over men's minds. He conceived of the role of the civil sovereign as a restraint upon malevolent interests within society. The only effective way the civil power could operate was if it was authoritative. He wrote, 'that the supreme power ought to be intire and undivided, and cannot else be sufficient for the protection of all, if it do not extend over all, without any other equal power to control or diminish it; and that therefore the supreme temporal magistrate ought to command Ecclesiastical persons as well as Civil'.[170] The prince had the duty to preach Christian fundamentals to the body of the people, so to effect this he had to have control of the mechanism that supervised the dissemination of this doctrine. Just as it was a monstrous body that had two heads, so those who attempted to elevate the authority of the Pope or presbyter were attempting to create an unnatural condition.[171]

In Denton's view an established liturgy was a necessity for the well-being of the state. He cited Cicero's dictum that the prosperity of Rome fluctuated with the purity of its religion, and wrote that 'nothing but religion can maintain Humane society; without it all manner of wickedness, and savage cruelties would abound; religion only doth bridle, and keep in order Commonwealths'. If religion was such an important component of society then it must necessarily fall under the direction of the civil magistrate. Since the duty of the magistrate was to keep the body of the people secure, any group that assaulted the efficacy of this action threatened the good of the people, and were thus illegitimate. Just as in a civil context the body of the people would be unhappy with a ruler who advanced his own interest over the majority's, so a spiritual guide who intended to establish his own self gain would find authority and obligation withdrawn from him. The intention of

---

[169] Denton, *Jus Caesaris*, 31, 39, 48–9, 50.   [170] *Ibid.*, 62.

[171] Once again Denton used Sarpi to justify his denial of the notion of two societies of the civil and spiritual. Denton, like Hobbes, attacked the thought of Robert Bellarmine who had strongly argued for the distinction. Denton, *Jus Caesaris*, 107–11. See Hobbes on monstrous bodies politic *Leviathan*, 173–4.

Denton's text was to undermine illegitimate clerical power, and defend the rights of civil sovereignty.[172]

High Church theologians were always ready to point out the irreligious dangers of their clerical opponents. One of the common accusations made by the non-jurors against Burnet's vision of the relationship between Church and state was to associate his scheme with that of Matthew Tindal's *Rights of the Christian Church* (1706). That the High Church men could make such a polemical connection between Burnet's latitudinarian Reformation and the radical Erastianism, of Tindal's *Rights of the Christian Church* is testimony to the ambiguity of the Erastian legacy of the Reformation. Tindal's *Rights of the Christian Church* was published within the context of the Convocation controversy. In its assault upon the rejuvenated High Churchmanship of the 1690s, its negation of the idea of clerical *sacerdos* and its defence of a tolerance within the parameters of a national Church (all called for in the name of Reformation), this work can be seen as a bridging text between the radical Erastian implications of Reformation ecclesiology and Enlightenment notions of civil religion. Tindal presented his arguments in historical terms: in particular in terms of an historical exegesis of the Reformation. The tenor of this history was a radical assault upon the very notion of a clerical order. In face of this challenge Tindal's work was burnt by the common hangman in March 1710 and became the focus of much clerical excoriation.

Tindal's text is a skilful and learned blend of anthropological study, ecclesiastical and juristic history, and studies in comparative religion, all combined to argue for the popular origins and administration of the Church. Citing authorities as diverse as Edward Stillingfleet, John Selden, Paolo Sarpi, Samuel Pufendorf and James Harrington, Tindal denied the clergy any independent authority, sacerdotal, ecclesiastical or legal, from the laity. Tindal united the claims of a national Church with the rights of the private conscience. To justify this argument he presented the history of the Reformation. In particular he argued in defence of the 'Cranmerian heresy'. The Cranmerian Reformation, as Tindal presented it, was anticlerical in intent. Cranmer had uprooted and undercut the very notion of an 'independent'

---

[172] Denton, *Jus Caesaris*, 191, 195–206. Denton's thought is a complex mixture of orthodoxy and unorthodoxy. In particular his use of Paolo Sarpi is problematic. D. Wootton, *Paolo Sarpi between Renaissance and Enlightenment* (Cambridge, 1983), passim, has argued that Sarpi's approval of the primitive pattern of the Christian Church was a subtle ploy to attack the general foundations of clericism. He also suggests that Sarpi conceived of religion as an instrumental mechanism to create social stability, as a form of Platonic or Averroeistic medicine for the body politic. We can see that Denton is widely appreciative of Sarpi's thought, and that he was explicitly anticlerical. How far this hostility to hierocracy extends is difficult to determine. His later work, *Some Remarks Recommended unto Ecclesiasticks* (1690), was profoundly anticlerical. It indicted the High Church 'linsey-wolsey Divines' who by perverting Scripture set all 'squinting towards Aribtrary Power'. See *Some Remarks*, 1, 3, 4–5, 7.

clergy. Once again the 'Cranmer Ms' was cited as evidence. In his *Defence of the Rights of the Christian Church In Two Parts* (1709) Tindal again reaffirmed that his original point was to defend the fundamental gains of the Reformation against priestly reaction. In Tindal's thought the Erastianism of the Reformation mutated into a notion of religion that, as the following chapters will show, was constitutive of the English Enlightenment.[173]

---

[173] See Tindal, *Rights of the Christian Church*, citation of Selden (*De Synedriis*), 42, 70, 107; of Sarpi (*Letters in English*, and *A Treatise of Benefits*) 257, 310–11, 359, 360–1, 362; of Harrington, (*The Prerogative of Popular Government*) 170, 357; for references to Cranmer see pages 126–8, 144, 178 and passim. See below, chapter 6, 'Civil Theology', for an extended discussion of this issue.

———————————— ❧ 4 ❧ ————————————

'Historia monotheistica'

JUDAISM, ISLAM AND CHRISTIANITY: UNITARIAN POLEMIC, 1671–1718

Clerical historians, as the previous chapter has discussed, engaged each other in disputations about whether one form of ecclesiastical government (by bishops) or another (by presbyters) was the legitimate model. Although there were manifest disagreements about the precise identity of the true Church, these debates were matters of form rather than substance. Writers like Heylyn and Burnet, although rivals in their precise interpretations of theology and government, were united in the insistence that there was a true and identifiable Christian religion that excluded other religions as heresy or heathenism. In the act of excluding the other religions this consensus invested the Christian priesthood (in either a high or low form) as the legitimate legislators and teachers of a true Christian society. Commonly it has been argued that the radicals who aimed at undermining the clerical monopoly of power in the Restoration did so by evangelizing the claims of reason. Deconstructing the power of Christian belief was achieved merely by elevating the rationality of the human intellect (so John Locke's *Essay Concerning Human Understanding* (1690) is embraced as the epistemological eclipse of religion), in combination with the political and liberal constitutional achievements of the Glorious Revolution of 1689. In this interpretation, nurtured by the liberties of the so-called Toleration Act, a group of Freethinking rationalists in the 1690s set about unpicking the propositional components of Christian belief especially in their denial of the existence of God. As the following chapters intend to show, this view of the radical assault is both misguided and optimistic. To argue that the struggles between priest and Freethinker were conducted in terms of an individual assault upon belief is anachronistic; the suggestion being that Christian belief was simply a set of incorrect propositions that once corrected would give way to rational belief.

Individuals in the late seventeenth century were Christians not merely

99

upon misguided logical grounds: that is not just because they believed that a transcendent God existed, but as the previous chapters have argued, because they absorbed convictions about the historical truth of Christianity from other sources. This form of belief or prejudice was not predisposed to capitulate to the logical assertion that God's existence could not be proved. The radicals thus set about revising the exclusivity of Christian history and belief not by denying God but rewriting the history of religion. If clerical historians had been concerned to authorize Christian matters of fact, radicals like Charles Blount and John Toland sidestepped propositional debates about the existence of God, and proposed alternative histories of the Christian past. The intention was to fragment the narrow Christocentric view of the past.

That the radical attack eschewed the merely propositional arguments against Christianity can be seen in the debates of the 1690s about belief in the Trinity. The turbulent waters of ecclesiological dispute were not quietened by the Church settlement of 1689. The Toleration Act had redrawn the Church of England as merely established rather than national, but more importantly it had reaffirmed statutory protection to the fundamental Trinitarianism of orthodox belief.[1] During the 1690s it was this broadly Protestant doctrine that became the focus of repeated attacks. Catholic exegetes like Richard Simon had undermined the scriptural justification for the Trinity by insisting that crucial passages were interpolations and forgeries. The Trinitarian controversy produced conflicts between Anglicans over how exactly the mystery was to be understood and discussed. For example Robert South (1634–1716) accused William Sherlock (1641?–1707) of polytheism for his unorthodox explanation of the doctrine. Charles Leslie, the cleverest of non-jurors, complained of the anti-Trinitarian tinctures in Archbishop Tillotson's latitudinarian moralism. Many apparently orthodox Anglicans were found to have anti-Trinitarian leanings: Isaac Newton's clandestine scriptural investigations led him to a closet Arianism, while his pupil William Whiston professed his opposition to the Trinity openly and was rewarded by clerical persecution. Edward Stillingfleet engaged in an intense and long-running polemic with John Locke over the supposed Socinianism of the *Essay Concerning Human Understanding* (1690).[2]

---

[1] The ideological significance of the Trinity is much ignored in studies of Church politics in the seventeenth century. The assaults of the 1640s and 1650s were treated as profoundly irreligious: see B. Worden, 'Toleration and the Cromwellian Protectorate' in W. J. Sheils (ed.), *Persecution and Toleration: Studies in Church History* 21 (Oxford, 1984).

[2] See, for example, J. E. Force, *William Whiston: Honest Newtonian* (Cambridge, 1985). See also J. E. Force and R. H. Popkin, *Essays on the Context, Nature, and Influence of Isaac Newton's Theology* (The Netherlands, 1990), in particular the chapter by Popkin, 'Newton as a Bible Scholar'.

The challenges of anti-Trinitarianism (varieties of Arianism, Socinianism and Unitarianism) were serious and potentially revolutionary. Traditional examinations of anti-Trinitarianism have treated it as a significant but ultimately unimportant event in the history of the period. Such studies have been too internalist, simply committed to narrating the complexity of the theological positions and counter-positions between Trinitarian and anti-Trinitarian. Such theological complexity has reinforced the historiographical irrelevance of the Socinian contribution to the political thought of the period. In contradiction to this neglect I should like to suggest that the Socinian or Unitarian polemic of the 1690s was a crucial movement in the development of the Enlightenment idea of religion. H. R. Trevor-Roper in a seminal essay on the religious origins of the Enlightenment in *Religion, the Reformation and Social Change* (1967) argued that Socinianism, as an Erasmian hermeneutical enterprise, was a central tributary of the Enlightenment. In describing Socinianism as the heir of Erasmus, Trevor-Roper delivered two historiographical blows: the first, that Socinianism not Calvinism was dynamic in the process of modernity, and second, that this movement was politically non-radical or conservative.[3] Accepting J. G. A. Pocock's point that the roots of the English Enlightenment drew from a soil fertile in the language of religion, the suggestion is that Socinianism should be examined, not just as a scriptural method, but also for the radical non-orthodox historical dimensions and models proposed in its polemic. In stepping outside of the Judaeo-Christian *saeculum* and appealing to other religious pasts, Socinianism opened the door to a radical religious position epitomized in the attempt by John Toland to syncretize the claims of the Old Testament, the New Testament, and the Koran in his *Nazarenus* (1718). From the Socinian and Unitarian insistence on the value of a history of monotheism developed the radical interest in other religions. Onto the investigation of the comparative structures of different religions men like Stubbe and John Toland grafted the classical idea of civil religion.[4]

[3] H. R. Trevor-Roper, *Religion, the Reformation, and Social Change* (1967), 193–237. See M. Walzer, *The Revolution of the Saints* (Harvard, 1982) for the most cogent assertion of Calvinist radicalism. It is interesting to note that Skinner's investigation into the scholastic origins of Calvinist theories of revolution argues explicitly against Walzer's thesis. H. Davis, *Worship and Theology in England from Andrewes to Baxter and Fox 1603–1690* (Princeton, 1975) and J. Redwood, *Reason, Ridicule, and Religion: the Age of Enlightenment in England 1660–1750* (1976), 156–76 and passim are typical of the encyclopaedic history of theological debate. See also G. Reedy, *The Bible and Reason: Anglicans and Scripture in late Seventeenth-Century England* (Philadelphia, 1985); Clark, *English Society*, 280–2.

[4] J. G. A. Pocock, 'Post-Puritan England and the Problem of the Enlightenment' in P. Zagorin (ed.), *Culture and Politics from Puritanism to the Enlightenment* (1980), 104–5. For a general discussion of the tradition of civil theology see R. I. Boss, 'The Development of Social Religion: A Contradiction of French Freethought', *JHI* 33 (1973); C. M. Sheroner, 'Rousseau's Civil Religion', *Interpretation* 8 (1979).

ORIENTALISM: IMAGES OF ISLAM 1660–1730

One of the historical pasts displayed by the Socinians was that of monotheistic Islam. Charles Leslie, the principal non-juror polemicist, argued against the Socinians in his *Socinian Controversy Discussed* (1708); 'Mahomet is much more Christian than these, and an express unitarian, but these are not so well in the world as Mahomet is, therefore you would not own Mahomet to be of your party, lest the people should stone you, for they all have a great aversion to Mahomet.'[5] For Leslie it was a straightforward and effective polemical method to indict Socinian theology with Islamic paganism. It is the framework of this polemic to which we now turn.

There had been a perennial interest in Islam since the foundation of the religion. The seventeenth century saw a renaissance of scholarly research into the realities of Moslem religion, society and history, concerned more with establishing facts than scoring theological victories. This academic interest provided the backcloth to the Islamic polemic. Traditional trading links with Spain had occasioned the dissemination of Arabic culture. Prior to the seventeenth century, knowledge gained from the East had been overwhelmingly mathematical, medical and scientific rather than theological. In particular classical culture and texts had been regained for the West via Arabic translations and editions. The Reformation interest in achieving an uncorrupted biblical text turned to Hebraic and Arabic languages as critical philological tools.[6] The patrons of orientalism in the early seventeenth century were the High Church divines Lancelot Andrewes and Archbishop Laud. The latter was the prime mover in the creation of a Chair in Arabic Studies in his own University of Oxford. In Cambridge, the Chair was

5 Leslie, *Theological Works*, II, 313–14.
6 See D. A. Paulin, *Attitudes to Other Religions* (Manchester, 1984) chapter 6, 81–103; 'The Treatment of Islam'; J. J. Saunders, 'Mohamed in Europe: A Note on Western Interpretations of the Life of the Prophet', *History* 39 (1954); J. Kritzeck, 'Moslem–Christian Understanding in Medieval Times', *Comparative Studies in Society and History* 4 (1961–2); G. L. Van Roosbroeke, *Persian Letters Before Montesquieu* (1932); B. P. Smith, *Islam in English Literature* (Lebanon, 1939); E. Renan, *Averroes et Averroisme* (Paris, 1852); P. M. Holt, *Studies in the History of the Near East* (1973), chapters 1–3, and 'Seventeenth-Century Arabic Studies' (unpublished D.Phil. Oxford, 1955); N. Daniel, *The West and Islam* (Edinburgh, 1980); also R. Southern, *The Western View of Islam* (Harvard 1962); S. Chew, *The Crescent and the Rose* (1958). For a more recent analysis, see E. Said, *Orientalism* (1978), 1–80; A. Hamilton, *William Bedwell and the Arabists 1563–1632* (Leiden, 1985); N. O'Brown, 'The Prophetic Tradition', *Studies in Romanticism* 21 (1982). On the importance of travel literature, see R. W. Franz, *The English Traveller and the Movement of Ideas 1660–1732* (New York, 1968); W. G. Rice, 'Early English Travellers to Greece and the Levant' in *Essays and Studies* (Michigan, 1939); E. K. Shaw, 'The Double-Veil: Travellers' Views of the Ottoman Empire, Sixteenth through Eighteenth Centuries' in E. K. Shaw and C. J. Heywood (eds.), *English and Continental Views of the Ottoman Empire 1500–1800* (Los Angeles, 1972). For important primary sources see Lancelot Addison, Simon Ockley and Joseph Pitts.

created with the finance and under the influence of a merchant, Thomas Adams.[7] The academic side of oriental studies is exemplied in the life and works of Edward Pococke (1604–91). Pococke was chosen to be preacher to the trading post at Aleppo, returning to England in 1636. The following year he set out to Constantinople in the company of another cleric, John Greaves (1602–52), the famous mathematician and astronomer. In 1641 Pococke returned to Oxford via Paris; en route he met the Continental scholars Suonita and Grotius, men with extensive oriental interests. Pococke, with the financial encouragement of Robert Boyle, made an Arabic translation of Grotius' work *De Veritate Religione Christianae* (1660), plus versions of the Book of Common Prayer and the Anglican liturgy. Both Pococke and Archbishop Ussher had agents or associates in various Moslem ports to collect Arabic texts and manuscripts.[8]

Edward Pococke's research was learned and erudite; an examination of later work upon Islamic religion and society reveals that many English writers were indebted to Pococke's studies. His *Specimen Historia Arabum* (1648) was a source for both orientalist and polemicist. Once Arabic texts were released from their native language into more comprehensible Latin, particularly when accompanied by detailed explicatory notes, they encouraged both disinterested curiosity and polemical manipulation of the history of Islam. Early in Pococke's career one astute politican recognized the possibilities of orientalism as a challenge to theological orthodoxy. John Selden, during a period when Pococke's pre-civil war Laudian connections could have caused both political and financial embarrassment, gave the scholar ideological credit by patronizing his researches into the chronicles of Patriarch Eutychius of Alexandria. Selden's aid was not disinterested: in researching the foundations of the Alexandrian Church he hoped to gain material for the refutation of the episcopal model lauded by the clerics.[9] Simon Ockley, Professor of Arabic in Cambridge, commented in the introduction to the second volume of his *History of the Saracens* on the life 'of our great doctor Pococke, who could have unlocked the treasures of the East'. Pococke was placed in the humanist tradition of Erasmus and Bude.[10] Ockley reserved his scorn for Selden's manipulation of Pococke's scholarly prowess, 'purely to gratify his own vanity ... to raise an argument of the equality of Bishops and presbyters ... and sneer upon our established

[7] B. Lewis, *British Contributions to Arabic Studies* (1937); A. J. Arberry, *The Cambridge School of Arabic* (Cambridge, 1948); H. R. Trevor-Roper, *William Laud* (1965), 273–4.

[8] The cases of Lancelot Addison, Joseph Morgan and Joseph Pitts suggest that there was first-hand knowledge of Islam through trade and pastoral endeavours. See also A. Hamilton, *William Bedwell*, 94.

[9] Matthew Tindal, in his *Rights of the Christian Church* (1706), 328, was to use Pococke's research into this text for exactly this purpose.

[10] S. Ockley, *History of Saracens*, 32, 33. See A. Kararah, 'Simon Ockley' (unpublished Ph.D., Cambridge, 1955).

episcopal Church and clergy'. Ockley himself attempted to follow the impartial task of orientalism, but his researches were put to infidel uses by William Whiston and he himself published *The Improvement of Human Reason* (1708), a translation of an eleventh-century Islamic text, with additions and commentary in answer to the claims of the 'enthusiastics'.[11]

During the medieval period most of the invective directed against the Moslem religion was based upon false and manipulated information. Islam was treated as a Christian heresy, and the intention of Western works was conversion. The medieval canon was to persist in the popular mind until the Unitarian arguments of the late seventeenth century.[12] It is worth examining this canon to illustrate the preconceptions with which the Unitarian applause for Islam was received. The quintessential statement of this older tradition can be found in the work of a master of Southampton Grammar School, Alexander Ross, in his 1649 translation of Du Ryer's French edition of the Koran. As Ross noted, 'it may happily startle thee to find him so to speak English, as if he had made some conquest of the nation'. As the work was unpopular with the 'higher authorities' when it was published, (they considered it would exacerbate the Interregnum tendency to heresy), Ross annexed *A Needful Caveat or Admonition*. Importantly, the complete work was reissued in 1688 when the *Caveat* must have had greater relevance.

Ross justified his translation in terms of comparing the heretical Eastern religion with the truth of Christianity. The 'sweet evangelical manna' could be contrasted with the 'poysonable quails' of Islamic doctrine.[13] The Koran was a collection of blasphemies, lies and fables. Ross insisted upon the traditional assessment of the work (as an admixture of Judaism, paganism

---

[11] On Whiston's use of Ockley's research, see Hearne, *Remarks and Collections*, III, 57, 485. Ockley's academic work is best exemplified in his *History of the Saracens* (2 volumes, 1708 and 1718), a magisterial work ignored now, but much applauded by Gibbon. *The Improvement of Human Reason* (1708) is an interesting work which needs separate and extensive examination. The work was originally translated into Latin by Edward Pococke, son of the great Arabist, in 1671. This was followed by the first English translation by the Quaker George Keith in 1674. Interestingly, Henry More commended George Keith as a man 'of a good witt and quick apprehension ... very philosophically and platonically given'. More, the Cambridge Platonist, exchanged his own *Enchiridion Metaphysicum* for Keith's edition of the *Oriental Philosophy*. See M. H. Nicolson (ed.), *The Conway Letters* (Yale, 1930), 391–2. A further edition and translation was made by the non-juror George Ashwell in 1688. For a general history of the work, see A. S. Fulton, *The History of Hayy Ibn Yockdan* (1929). See also L. Kontler, 'The Idea of Toleration and the Image of Islam in Early Enlightenment English Thought' in E. H. Balazs (ed.), *Sous le signe des lumières* (Budapest, 1987).

[12] See William Bedwell's *Mohamedis Imposturae* (1616 and 1624). This work was reported to be a true Muslim text. Its contents belie this claim. See also Isaac Barrow, 'Of the Impiety and Imposture of Paganism and Mahometanism' in A. Napier (ed.), *The Theological Works of Isaac Barrow* (9 volumes, Cambridge, 1859), V, 411–26.

[13] A. Ross (trans.), *Du Ryer's Koran* (1688), 'A Needful Caveat', Sig. D2r.

and Christianity) retelling the tale of the Nestorian heretic Sergius who was supposed to have helped Mahomet compose the Alkoran. In the brief sketch of Mahomet's life, the emphasis was upon his cunning and intuition in adapting a theology to the requirements of the Arabians, in the name of temporal dominance. Mahomet's conversation with the Archangel Gabriel had been fabricated to cover up his epileptic fits in front of his wife. The fabulous tale of the prophet's training a pigeon to eat grain out of his ear, suggesting that it was really delivering the message of God, was retold. Similar to this was the emphasis on the prodigious sensuality of the prophet, and his adaption of revelation to allow himself free sexual licence. The central ideas of Ross' commentary were the combination of Mahomet's religion being an human imposture designed to erect temporal authority 'under pretence of reformation of religion', and that of his success being due to the wrath of God providentially punishing Christianity for its spiritual laxity.[14]

Islam was not a religion of conscience but established upon the power of the sword, or because of its 'easiness'. If the Arabians accepted the religion freely it was because 'it was friend to their thievery and lechery'. Ross also deployed the other characteristic of the medieval canon: just as gold might be found in dung so there was some good in the Koran, particularly the Koranic acceptance of the Christian Gospel as 'full, right, a light, and a guide to salvation'. Ross acknowledged that although Mahomet accepted the Gospel his reading of it was heretical for, 'he endeavoureth to overthrow Christ's divinity with Arius and Nestorius, and the Jews his ghostly fathers'.[15] At the end of his work Ross gave a prophetic pronouncement concerning this 'unhallowed piece'. He commented that as men were like bees which can 'suck honey even out of henbane, there might be no danger in reading the Alcoran, but most men are like spiders ... and ... suck ... poyson out of even the sweetest Roses'. Recalling the Christian variety of the Interregnum, Ross restated the warning that the rise of Mahomet had been encouraged and facilitated by the rents in 'the seamless coat of the Church' in Heraclitus' day. He feared the advance of a seventeenth-century 'Mahometan darknesse, which God may justly inflict upon us'. The later reprinting of this translation and commentary can in face of the nascent Trinitarian controversy hardly have been unconsidered.[16]

[14] Ibid., 'The Life of Mahomet', vii.
[15] Ibid., 'A Needful Caveat', Sigs. C7v, D2v; 'The Life of Mahomet', i–xviii.
[16] Ibid., 'A Caveat', Sigs. D8r–v; 'Life of Mahomet', ii; for a later translation of the Koran, see G. Sale, The Qu'ran (1734), the Preliminary Discourse of the work is pro-Unitarian. See also A. Arberry, The Koran Interpreted (2 volumes, 1955) who points out that Sale introduced 'carefully italicized supplies' in his translation which were intentionally reminiscent of the authorized version of the Bible.

UNITARIANISM, ISLAM AND THE HISTORY OF THE TRINITY

The roots of the polemical usage of Islam lie in the assault of the Socinians (or Unitarians) on the Anglican establishment.[17] English Socinianism had its roots in the early seventeenth century, linked closely with the Dutch Remonstrant movement and Polish Socinianism. Socinian texts were persistently shipped into England from Lowland ports, so much so that Laud introduced in 1637 measures to restrict the entrance of books from Holland. The *Racovian Catechism*, which elevated the claims of rationality over revelation, and stated the unipersonality of God and as a corollary the humanity of Christ, was first published in England in 1609 dedicated to James I. It was publicly burnt. The 1640 Laudian Canons had intended to introduce anti-Socinian restraints. The impact of the Laudian demise was to encourage the publication of Socinian tracts. The leviathan of the movement was John Biddle, who in 1652 published an English translation of the *Racovian Catechism* which Francis Chennell referred to as that 'Racovian Alcoran'. It is important to note that although Biddle died in 1662 after a disease contracted while imprisoned by the Restoration authorities, his Interregnum works were republished in the 1690s in the double-columned Unitarian tracts financed by Thomas Firmin. Even during the relative laxity of religious surveillance of the Interregnum the Socinians had been subject to persecution under the draconian Blasphemy Act of 1648.[18]

---

[17] Throughout this chapter, I intend to use the terms 'Socinian' and 'Unitarian' as interchangeable. Both groups stressed the necessity of reason in the evaluation of Scripture, and insisted upon the unity of God undermining the deification of Christ. Stephen Nye in his *Brief History of the Unitarians, also called Socinians* (1687) pointed out that since the term 'Socinian' had become pejorative he preferred the name 'Unitarian'. For a simple definition of the theological distinction between Orthodox, Socinian and Arian, see D. Williams, *A Vindication of the Sermons of His Grace John Archbishop of Canterbury, concerning the Divinity and Incarnation of our B. Saviour* (1695), 2:

> The Orthodox hold, that Christ the Word and only begotten of the Father, was truly and really God from all eternity, God by participation of the Divine nature and happiness together with the Father, and by way of derivation from him, as light from the sun; that he made all creatures, and so could no more be a creature, than it is possible for a creature to make itself ... The Arians conceive, that sometime before the world was made, God generated the Son after an ineffable manner, to be his instrument and minister in making the World. And this Son is called God in Scripture, not in the most perfect sense, but with respect to the creature whom he made ... Socinus held, that the Son was not in being till he was the Son of the Virgin; and that therefore he was a God, not in nature, but by way of office, mission, or representation, as Moses, and others are called God in Scripture.

[18] H. J. McLachlan, *Socinianism in Seventeenth-Century England* (Oxford, 1951), 18; E. Wilbur, *History of Unitarianism in Transylvania, England and America* (Harvard, 1952), 167–92, 193–5. On J. Biddle, see F. Kenworthy, 'The Toleration Act of 1689', *Transactions of the Unitarian Historical Society* 7 (1939–42). On Freke, see *DNB* and L. W. Levy, *Treason Against God* (New York 1981), 321–2. R. Wallace, *Antitrinitarian Biography* (3 vols., 1850). A. Gordon, *Heads of Unitarian History* (1856). R. M. Mongomery, 'A Note on the Acts of Parliament Dealing with the Denial of the Trinity', *Transactions of the Unitarian*

During the Restoration Socinianism appears to have extended its influence to the highest levels. The coterie surrounding the philanthropist Thomas Firmin included Locke, Tillotson the future Archbishop of Canterbury, and minor members of the Anglican Church, such as Stephen Nye (1648–1719) and Henry Hedworth (1626–1705). Indeed, it was the latter who used the term Unitarian for the first time in print in *The Spirit of the Quakers Tried* (1672). Such was the ubiquity of the movement that Andrew Marvell was able to comment in the same year that 'the Socinian books are tolerated and sell as openly as the Bible'. By 1676 there were at least three Socinian meeting houses in London. The religious settlement of 1689 saw Socinians classed with Roman Catholics in being placed beyond the comfort of toleration. The Socinians were to achieve liberty of worship in 1813. Persecution descended upon such men as Arthur Bury (1624–1713), rector of Exeter College, Oxford, for the publication of his *Naked Gospel* (1690). The author was excommunicated, deprived and fined £500, while his book was burnt. William Freke unwittingly sent his *Brief but Clear Confutation of the Doctrine of the Trinity* to both Houses of Parliament in 1694. The result was that the work was condemned and burnt by the public hangman, while Freke was forced to recantation and fined. Thomas Aikenhead, a student of Edinburgh University, was condemned as an heretic for his Socinian opinions and hanged in 1697. In 1698 the 'Act for the more effectual Suppression of Blasphemy and Profaneness' attempted to proscribe all discussion of the Trinitarian controversy, imposing for a second conviction denial of all civil rights and three years imprisonment. The act was reinforced by royal command in 1714.[19]

Historical Society 6 (1935–8). R. E. Florida, 'British Law and Socinianism in the Seventeenth and Eighteenth Centuries' in L. Szczucki (ed.), *Socinianism* (Warsaw, 1983).

[19] H. J. McLachlan, 'Links between Transylvania and British Unitarians from the Seventeenth Century Onwards', *Transactions of the Unitarian Historical Society* 17 (1979–82); W. Whittaker, 'The Open Trust Myth', *Transactions of the Unitarian Historical Society* 1 (1917–18). See C. Leslie, 'Of the Socinian Controversy' in *Works*, II, 14, for reports of free distribution of Unitarian tracts. Leslie wrote of the Unitarians: 'They have arrived to that pitch of assurance, as to set up public meetings in our halls in London, where some preach in them who have been spewed out even by the Presbyterians for their Socinianism.' Wilbur, *Unitarianism*, 198–9, 212–14; McLachlan, *Seventeenth-Century Socinianism*, 285; on Aikenhead, see Levy, *Treason Against God*, 325–7. Note that Aikenhead was accused of preferring the Islamic scheme over the Christian, in particular he was charged with rejecting the canonicity of Scripture and reading atheistical texts. See T. B. Howell, (ed.), *A Complete Collection of State Trials* (1812), XIII, 918–39. The best account of the Aikenhead affair is the essay by M. Hunter, 'Aikenhead the Atheist: The Context and Consequences of Articulate Irreligion in the Late Seventeenth Century' in Hunter and Wooton, *Atheism*. On general background, see Redwood, *Reason, Ridicule and Religion*, 27–42. On Firmin, see S. Nye, *Life of Firmin* (1698 and reprinted 1791); H. W. Stephenson, 'Thomas Firmin 1632–1697' (3 volumes, D.Phil. Oxford, 1949); for a hostile contemporary account, see Luke Milbourne, *A False Faith not Justified by Care For the Poor Prov'd in a Sermon*, 28 August 1698. See also Hearne, *Remarks and Collections*, I, 102; 'Tho. Firmin ... a rank

One of the suggestions of Arthur Bury's work the *Naked Gospel* (1690), which contributed to the virulent Anglican reaction, was his treatment of the Islamic theme. Bury inverted the traditional theme of Mahomet's rise as a product of divine providence. The commonplace argument for the veracity of Christianity, following Augustine, had been that Christ's teachings had been established by their own merits alone. Christ, the son of a carpenter, joined by a vagabond group of illiterate fishermen, had confounded philosophers and risen above kings, eschewing temporal force. The orthodox use of this argument had been to compare these Christian origins with the worldly advance of Islam by the sword. This not only revealed its human origins, but also classified it as a scourge of God. Bury insisted that the same argument could be used in favour of that 'lewd Impostor' Mahomet. He continued: 'so the victories of the Alcoran over the Gospel must be evidence, that as the religion of Moses was better than that of the Canaanites, and the religion of Christ better than that of Moses; so must the religion of Mahomet be better than that of Christ.'[20] Bury noted that to suggest the rise of Islam was not the product of divine providence was in effect to deny the existence of a divine guide. Bury did not unequivocably applaud Mahomet's actions, for many additions were included in his scheme 'most suitable to his Lusts'. Mahomet was 'not an apostate, but a reformer': his task was one of purification. The Islamic prophet was cast in the mould of Christian reformer, professing Christian and monotheistic articles of belief. Bury continued, 'so from the prosperity of the Alcoran, we have an Argument for the Divinity of the Gospel, as invincible against all power but what was derived from itself'. The justice of God's providence was to ensure that the truths of Christianity did not go undefended. Bury's analysis was a clever piece of insinuation.[21] Christianity in the East had become corrupt through the manipulation of the Gospel; it was Mahomet's good fortune to re-institute the true gospel, which in Bury's view was Unitarian. In opposition to Ross' providential scheme which presented Islam as a scourge and deformed image of pristine Christianity, Bury considered Islam within its own terms. Islam was not a misshapen mirror image of Christianity, but an object of commendation. Bury called for the purification of Christian Scripture, following the pattern of the Corinthians. The result of this would be that, rather than the mysteries of faith which he considered the product of the historical rise of priestcraft after the post-Nicene Athanasian Creed, the simple dogma of the Gospel in its largest edition would be 'repent and believe'. This attack upon 'mystery'

Socinian was a great man with Dr Tillotson Archbp. of Cant. and others of the same leaven promoted by K. William to some of the best dignities and preferments.'

20   A. Bury, *Naked Gospel* (1690), Preface, Sig. A3r. Note, it is interesting that Bury's work was published in a double columned format – a style typical of, and identified with, the Unitarian publications such as Firmin financed *The Faith of One God* (1691).

21   Bury, *Naked Gospel*, Preface, Sig. A3v.

in religion was to pre-empt the suggestions of Toland in his *Christianity Not Mysterious* (1696).[22]

William Freke (1662–1744) who suffered at the hands of Parliament in 1694 for his anti-Trinitarian beliefs, emphasized the connection between the Unitarian insistence on the unity of God and Islamic monotheism. Freke, who later renounced his Unitarian convictions to prophesy the 'great Elijah', argued in his *Vindication of the Unitarians* (1690) a 'short and sinewy' text, that the Trinity was the 'stumbling block in Christianity'. Freke noted that he had fallen into 'Arianisme' while searching the New Testament for scriptural evidence for the Trinity. Adopting a commonplace Unitarian argument, he insisted that there was as just a case for the truth of the Trinity as there was for the absurd Catholic mystery of transubstantiation. The notion of a triple Godhead offended all 'Jews, Turks, and Pagans': it was the ground on which Mahomet had based his division from Christianity. As Freke noted, the Koran contained 'above a hundred' indictments of the dogma. One of the central historical arguments was that the Trinity had only become part of Christian creed some three hundred years after Christ's death.[23] This stock Unitarian argument was made even more emphatically by Stephen Nye (1648–1719), the rector of Little Hormead, Hertfordshire, close associate of Thomas Firmin and major Unitarian controversialist.

In his *Brief History of the Unitarians, called also Socinians* dedicated to Firmin and Henry Hedworth, first published in 1687 and republished in 1691 (in the collection financed by Firmin) *The Faith of One God*, Nye insisted that Socinianism was heir to pristine monotheistic Christianity. He invoked the pattern of the Nazarenes, an early Judaeo-Christian sect, as the legitimate ancestors of the Unitarian movement. The translators of the Old Testament from Hebrew to Greek, Theodotian and Symachus, the Early Fathers Paul of Samosatus, Lucianus and Photinus, Bishop of Antioch, were all professing Nazarenes. As early as A.D. 194 Pope Victor had commenced the obliteration of the true Unitarian doctrine 'that god is One'. The Arians had introduced the first errors of doctrinal corruption which had laid the path clear for the Trinitarian ascendancy achieved at the Council of Nicea in A.D. 325. The Nazarene faith had only survived in the 'Turkish and other Mahometan and Pagan Dominions'.[24] The historical model of pre-Nicene Unitarianism, and its links with Islam, was reiterated and reinforced by Nye in his *Letter of Resolution Concerning the Doctrines of the Trinity and Incarnation* (1695). Trinitarian Christianity could claim no ancient tradition but was 'Novelties, corruptions, and depravations of genuine Christianity'. The Apostles' Creed and the Nazarene faith were both the most ancient

---

[22] *Ibid.*, 8.   [23] W. Freke, *Vindication of the Unitarians* (1690), 6, 26, 27.
[24] S. Nye, *Brief History of the Unitarians, Called also Socinians*, 10–11, in *The Faith of One God* (1691).

beliefs and 'the very doctrines that are now called Socinian'. The Athanasian Trinity established at Nicea was the historical font of all Christian corruption. The supremacy of the papacy, worship of the Virgin Mary, saints, images, the mystery of transubstantiation, the authority of Church tradition, papal indulgences and the theology of Christ's satisfaction, were all doctrinal accretions grown out of the corrupt Trinitarian Christology. Arguing against Ralph Cudworth's *True Intellectual System of the Universe* (1678), which proposed that the truth of the Trinity could be traced to a Mosaic 'theology of Divine original', Nye insisted that Trinitarianism was a corruption of heathen Platonism which confused 'properties of the Divine nature for persons, or willfully and affectedly allegoris'd them into persons'. The doctrines of the Trinity and Incarnation, according to Nye, were the main obstacles between Christianity and Islam and Judaism. As 'divers historians' had noted, Mahomet had 'no other design in pretending himself to be a prophet, but to restore the belief of the Unity of God'. Mahomet proclaimed himself disciple of the 'Messias or Christ' aiming to restore the Unitarian 'true intent of the Christian religion'. Mahomet's success in converting Asia, Africa and part of Europe was not to be attributed to the force of arms but to 'that one truth in the Alkoran, the unity of God'.[25]

As will be shown below, the historical connection between the Nazarenes and Islam was to form the central theme in the work of both Henry Stubbe and John Toland. While the work of Arthur Bury, William Freke and Stephen Nye displays no reluctance to identify Unitarianism with monotheistic Islam, the most radical case of Unitarian–Islam syncretism to be found in the enigmatic *Epistle Dedicatory to his Illustrious Excellency Ameth Ben Ameth* (1682). In early January 1682 Ahmet Ben Ahmet, Moroccan ambassador, presented Charles II with two lions as a gift of peace from his master the Sultan. Ahmet Ben Ahmet's diplomatic mission was concerned with the rights of possession of the fortress port of Tangiers ceded to the English sovereign as part of Catharine of Braganza's dowry. This was the scene for an interesting episode in Unitarian history. A 'cabal of Socinians in London' took the opportunity to attempt to present the Moroccan ambassador with an address of theological unity. They intended to give Ahmet Ben Ahmet a collection of four works: the introductory *Epistle* which concerns us, the *Epistola Ameth Benandala Mahumetani*, an account of a conference between Ahmet Ben Abdalla a Spanish Moor, Maurice of Orange, and Eugene of Portugal that purportedly took place in 1612, the *Animadversiones in Pracedentem Epistolam*, and *Theognis Irenaeus Christiano Lectori*

25 S. Nye, *Letter of Resolution Concerning the Doctrines of the Trinity and Incarnation* (1695), 11, 12–14, 15–17, 17–18. It is interesting to note that Cudworth's Mosaic thesis was echoed by Charles Leslie in his *Socinian Controversy Discussed* (1708) in the second dialogue. On Nye's authorship of the *Letter of Resolution*, see H. McLachlan, 'Seventeenth-Century Unitarian Tracts', *Transactions of the Unitarian Historical Society* 2 (1919–22), 152–6.

Salutem, an anti-Trinitarian polemic written under the name of Theognis, Arian Bishop of Nicea. The dedicatory *Epistle*, which Charles Leslie republished in his *Socinian Controversy Discussed* (1708), is a succinct account of the perceived links between the theologies of Islam and the Unitarians.

The 'two philosophers' who composed the *Epistle* addressed Ahmet Ben Ahmet as a representative of the 'fellow worshippers of that sole supreme Deity of the Almighty Father and Creator'. Although the *Epistle* admitted that there were differences between Unitarianism and Islam the work insisted that they shared the necessary common truth in accepting 'the religion of an only one Godhead' which brought them to a closer fraternity with each other than with Trinitarian Christianity. The defence of one God 'without personalities or pluralities' was a pristine and original tradition that included, 'not only all the patriarchs down from Adam until Moses, not only all the Jews under the written law and the Old Testament to this very day, were still worshippers of an only one God (without a Trinity of persons), but that also all the Primitive Christians, in and after Christ and his Apostles' time'. In distinction from the post-Constantinian 'backsliding Christians' who believed in 'three co-equal and self subsisting persons, whereof every one is an absolute and infinite God' original Unitarians like Paul of Samosatus and Marcellus Bishop of Ancyra upheld a monotheism that was maintained by Mahomet.[26]

THE ANGLICAN COUNTER-POLEMIC: ISLAM AS HERESY IN THE 1690S

John Edwards, as bigoted an adversary as his father Thomas Edwards, attacked the *Letter of Resolution* in his *Socinian Creed* (1697). The Socinians were allying themselves with the Jews and the Mahometans, magnifying the Koran in considering it reconcilable with the Gospel if the doctrine of the Trinity was laid aside. The Socinians were in 'mere complacency with those infidels'. Indeed Edwards in his *Socinianism Unmasked* (1696) had confronted John Locke, the author of the *Reasonableness of Christianity* (1695), firstly as a Socinian, and then by implication as a Moslem. He wrote with obvious malevolence, 'it is likely I shall further exasperate this author when I desire the reader to observe that this lank faith of his is in a manner no other than the faith of a Turk'. Edwards objected to Locke's assertion that there was only one necessary defining credal belief in Christianity accessible to all understandings, i.e. that Jesus was the Messiah. Edwards slyly commented that Locke 'seems to have consulted the Mahometan bible'. We know that

---

[26] Anon, 'An Epistle Dedicatory to his Illustrious Excellency Ameth Ben Ameth', reprinted in C. Leslie, *Theological Works*, II, 18–20, 22, 22–23, 23–24.

Locke possessed an edition of the Koran.[27] The complicity between Locke and Islam according to Edwards was the notion of the nature and divinity of Christ; the Koran treated Christ purely as a prophet, 'as a great man, one commissioned by God, and sent by him into the world. This is of the like import with our good Ottoman writer the Vindicator saith of our saviour, and this he holds is the sum of all that is necessary to be believed concerning him'. Edwards insisted that Locke was 'confounding Turky with Christendom'.[28]

The Anglican counter-polemic was not only strengthened by the identification of Socinian theology with Islamic, but also by their complicity as human impostures. If Socinian theological endeavour led to heretical Islamic statements about the divinity of Christ, then their interpretive methodology was similarly deformed, resting upon the depraved human intellect. Francis Fullwood, originally a non-juror, but now anxious to illustrate his orthodoxy, entered the controversy with *A Parallel: Wherein it Appears that the Socinian agrees with the Papist* (1693). His central charge was that Socinians manipulated scriptural texts by their 'own private sense (if not their Wit and Phansie)', rather than the tradition of patristic interpretations. Fullwood extended his notion into a fully fledged definition of fanaticism; he wrote, 'modern fanaticism and enthusiasm, I reckon to be nothing else, but a religion (if it deserves that name) that hath no foundation, either in the word of God, or sound reason, but is founded in dreams or Phantasies, or pretended inspiration or divine revelation besides and other than the Holy Scriptures'. Fullwood's logic from this point was incisive; Mahomet's religion as all Christians acknowledged could be termed 'fanatical and enthusiastical'. The conclusion was inevitable 'is not Socinianism, as truly phanatical and enthusiastical, as the Papacy; not to say Mahometanism?'[29]

---

[27] See J. Harrison and P. Laslett, *The Library of John Locke* (Oxford, 1971), 70, which shows that Locke possessed the 1649 French translation of the Koran. See D. D. Wallace, 'Socinianism, Justification by Faith, and the Sources of John Locke's *The Reasonableness of Christianity*', *JHI* (1984). See de Beer, *Correspondence of Locke*, V, 86–7, 96, 135–42, 145–7, 172, 207–29, where Locke corresponded with Firmin, Furley and Limborch (himself another suspected Socinian), about the case of a Dutch 'damsel' who had converted to Judaism because of her opposition to the Trinity. The current research of both J. Marshall and R. Iliffe into the theologies of John Locke and Isaac Newton would suggest that Edward's accusations were broadly correct.

[28] J. Edwards, *Socinianism Unmasked* (1696), 53–4; Edwards also attacked *The Letter of Resolution* in the same terms in *Socinian Creed* (1697), 227–8.

[29] F. Fullwood, *A Parallel*, 19, 23, 25. To reinforce this connection it is worth noting that Peter Browne in his *Letter in answer to ... Christianity Not Mysterious* (1697) commented upon John Toland's attempts, 'certainly by all these promises of so much new light in the world which hath lived in darkness so many hundred years, we can't guess he designs to be no more than head of an ordinary sect, but to be as famous an imposture as Mahomet'. See also R. South, *Sermons* (3 volumes, 1698), Dedication to Peter Browne, 'But on the contrary amongst [them], when a certain *Mahometan Christian* (no new thing of late – notorious for his blasphemous denial of ye *'Mysteries'* of our religion, and his insufferable virulence

The Unitarian *Epistle* of 1682, although never presented to Ahmet Ben Ahmet, became the focus of anti-Socinian polemic in the 1690s. In 1694 and 1697 Charles Leslie composed letters attacking such Islamic preferences which are published in his *Socinian Controversy Discussed* (1708) along with a transcription of the *Epistle*. Leslie treated the Unitarians 'as scouts amongst us for Mahomet'. The Unitarians could 'in no propriety be called Christians; that they are more Mahometans than Christians and far greater enemies to Christianity than the Mahometans'. Leslie insisted that Islam was less corrosive of Trinitarian Christianity than the English challenge. The Unitarians were reviled for representing the 'Mahometans as the true Christians, and our Christianity as mere paganism and Heathenism'. Contrary to the Unitarian interpretation, where Mahomet was applauded for re-establishing a primitive and pure Christianity, Leslie suggested that the 'Alkoran is a system of Arianism' and therefore 'vile heresy'. The only traditions Unitarians could appeal to were heresies.[30] In the fourth dialogue of the main body of *Socinian Controversy Discussed* Leslie presented a more specific dissection of the Nazarene–Islamic model found in Nye's *Brief History of the Unitarians* (1687) and *Letter of Resolution* (1695). His strategy was simple: the ancient traditions of monotheism were heresy. Simon Magus, the magician, was the creator of Nazarene doctrine. The Nazarenes were a 'sort of Christians who affected that name rather than to be named after Christ or Jesus'. Leslie pondered how many modest Socinians would be both amazed and scandalized to learn the heretical wellsprings of their faith. This polemic was reinforced by Leslie's ironic argument that Mahomet was a more orthodox ancestor than the Nazarenes or Ebionites. The Alkoran certainly applauded Christ as Messiah, but the Socinians overstated this applause, 'as Mahomet improved Arianism, so the Socinians have exceeded even the Alkoran in their contempt of Christ'.[31]

The prescriptions of sacred history were crucial in Leslie's view: it was the arena where theological and political dispute could be resolved. He wrote, 'all controverted points in divinity, either as doctrine or discipline; for everyone of them must be determined by matters of fact.' Many like the Socinians claimed the commodious privilege of prescription from histories which were little more than heresy. Comparative religious history was fraught with heterodoxy. In a *Short and Easy Method with the Deists* (1704)

against the whole *Christian Priesthood*', (note by Toland BL. Birch 4465, folio 58). See also Toland's answer to Browne's accusation in the same note: 'The Reason for this odd compliment I am yet to learn, unless it be that I can't drink wine enough to pass for orthodoxy with some doctors: for I am by no means for propagating Religion by Force, in which respect the Doctor is a very good Mahometan, how ill a Christian so ever he may be' (Birch 4465, folios 63r, 64).

30 Leslie, *Theological Works*, II 39, 34, 36, 38, 53–4.
31 *Ibid.*, II, 295–6, 303, 304, 310–11, 314.

Leslie, in warning his readership against the dangers of Charles Blount's 'parallel' between Christ and Apollonius of Tyre, also pointed out the dangers of the Unitarian elision of Mahomet and Christ: many 'say that there is no greater ground to believe in Christ than Mahomet'. In Leslie's opinion a truthful examination of the historical 'matter of fact' should 'demonstrate the truth of the Christian religion, and at the same time distinguish it from the impostures of Mahomet and the whole Pagan world'. A cursory examination of the history of the foundation of Islam revealed a history of fable, imposition and corruption. In face of the display of the histories of Judaism, Islam and paganism as comparable to Christian history it became incumbent upon Anglican controversialists to neutralize the moral value of such pasts.[32]

One of the first and most successful anti-Islamic histories was *The First State of Mahumedism; or an Account of the Author and Doctrines of that Imposture* (1679) written by Lancelot Addison (1632–1703), Dean of Litchfield. Addison had been chaplain at Tangiers and was author of a sociological study, *West Barbary, or a Short Narrative of the Kingdom of Fez and Morocco* (Oxford, 1671), which gave an account of the sacred, civil, and domestic customs of the country. In the *First State of Mahumedism* Addison was concerned to give an account of the progress of Mahomet's empire to awaken 'all Christian magistrates into a timely suppression of False teachers, though never so despicable in their first appearance, lest (like Mahumed) they second heresy with force, and propagate enthusiasm with conquest'. Mahomet succeeded in establishing his imposture with 'craft and management'. Using the pretence of revelation he constructed a faith suitable to the desires of the people. The Koran written by the Nestorian Bahira and a Jewish renegade 'Abdalla Calen' was in effect a 'hodge-podge of Judaism, Gentilism, and Christianism'. The decay, heterodoxy and contention of Eastern Christianity had created the conditions for Mahomet to establish an empire under pretence of religious reformation, 'he was a prophet in show, but a tyrant in project'.[33] The historical interpretation of Islam as a triumph of empire was given extended treatment in Humphrey Prideaux's *The True Nature of Imposture Fully Displayed in the Life of Mahomet* (1697) which addressed the Unitarian assaults upon Trinitarianism of the 1690s. The work sold two editions in the first year of publication, and a tenth edition was on sale by 1722 indicating its popularity as the staple and ubiquitous Anglican defence against the infidels.[34]

32 C. Leslie, *Dissertation Concerning the Use and Authority of Ecclesiastical History* in *Theological Works*, I, 412, and *A Short and Easy Method with the Deists* in *Theological Works*, I, 3–8, 9, 10–12, 28–38.
33 L. Addison, *The First State of Mahumedism* (1679), 'To the Right Honorable Sir Joseph Williamson', Sig. A2r–v, 26–30, 32, 41, 63, 67, 84, 119, 126–37.
34 See *The Letters of Humphrey Prideaux*, 185–7, on the extensive demand for his work.

Prideaux drew an easy parallel between the sectarianism of the 1650s and 1690s, which in turn mirrored the confusion and disunity evident in the Eastern Church at the time of Mahomet. The warning was to beware that God might 'raise up some Mahomet against us for our utter confusion'. Although Prideaux employed many modern scholarly translations and commentaries upon Islamic texts to deny some of the more fabulous anti-Islamic Christian fictions, the *True Nature of Imposture* condemned Mahomet and Islam without respite. As Addison had insisted, Mahomet had established a political empire on the foundations of religious imposture. Pretending to revive the old religion of Adam, Abraham and Ishmael, Mahomet presented himself as a reformer of idolatry. His real motives were ambition and lust. The Islamic legislator co-ordinated the principles of his religion to suit the desires of the debauched Arabs. The Koran was composed by two heretical Christians at Medina, a Persian Jew Abdia Ben Salom, and the Nestorian Sergius: Mahomet was illiterate. To disguise his epileptic fits Mahomet had fabricated visions of the angel Gabriel. Employing the full range of the 'art of insinuation' Mahomet had adapted heathen ritual and doctrine to the needs of his reformation: the Caab at Mecca became the centre of his worship as it had been for the pagan.[35] In his appended *A Discourse for the Vindication of Christianity from the Charge of Imposture* Prideaux made his hostility to the infidels, both Islamic and Unitarian, perfectly apparent. The anti-Trinitarians implied that contemporary Christianity, rather than Islam, was human imposture. Prideaux wrote that the central problem was, 'whether the Christian religion be a truth really given unto us by Divine Revelation from God our Creator, or else a mere humane invention, continued by the first propagators of it, to impose a cheat upon mankind'. According to Prideaux's classification, religious imposture involved the quest for secular advancement established by 'craft and fraud' and backed by force and violence. Christ had intended no civil advancement, but had even redefined the Jewish idea of the temporal Messiah into a purely spiritual authority. Islam and Mahomet could only be defined in terms of the pursit of empire. The New Testament established a message of 'mortification, repentance, and self-denial' while the Koran promoted 'fighting, bloodshed, and conquest'. Islam had only triumphed by the force of arms and the sword. Christ had simply employed the prerogatives of truth and faith. As Islam was imposture, so was the Unitarian economy.[36]

A later work to plough the same polemical furrow in linking the Islamic and Unitarian heresies was the anonymous *Historical and Critical Reflec-*

[35] H. Prideaux, *The True Nature of Imposture* (1697), xiii, 34, 16, 18–19, 137, 21, 36, 40–7, 14–15, 93, 114–16. For Prideaux's use of orientalist scholarship, see his appended *An Account of the Authors Quoted in this Book*, 153–80.

[36] H. Prideaux, *A Discourse for the Vindication of Christianity* (1697), 5, 7, 16–24, 27, 45–7, 131.

tions upon Mahometanism and Socinianism (1712). The treatise was one of a collection published as *Four Treatises concerning the Doctrine, Discipline, and Worship of the Mahometans* (1712). The four works included in this collection illustrate the tension between the impartial investigation of Islam, and the employment of this scholarship in theological debate. The first work, *The Life and Actions of Mahomet*, although it employed the latest Arabic translations 'Abulfaragius, Abul Feda, Elmacinus, Septencastiensis, Hottinger, Busbequius, Pocock etc.', presented an identical interpretation of the Prophet's life to Prideaux's *True Nature of Imposture*. The next text, *Of the Mahometan Theology*, a work of profound and impartial scholarship by Adrian Reland, Professor of Oriental Tongues at the University of Utrecht, was concerned to give a short system of Islamic theology translated from Arabic sources and illustrated with Reland's own notes. The work rejected the traditional unthinking hostility towards Islam, and simply presented the tenets of Islam without recommendation or condemnation. The third treatise, A. Bobovius' *A Treatise concerning the Turkish Liturgy*, was similarly scholarly and impartial.

The *Historical and Critical Reflections* was a hostile work par excellence. It employed the scholarly researches of Reland, Pocock, *et al.*, to establish with greater authority the heterodoxy of both Islam and Socinianism. Citing Reland's *Of the Mahometan Theology* the author noted that Mahomet's central doctrinal position was the 'unity of God' which was merely a revival of the ancient anti-Trinitarian heresy of Paul of Samosatus, Theodotian and Photinus. The Mahometans insisted upon calling themselves 'Unitarians' in opposition to orthodox Christians whom they termed 'Associants'. The Socinians and Mahometans collaborated in insisting upon the corruptions and forgeries in Scripture upon which the Trinity was erected. The radical Unitarian Francis David in his polemics of the 1590s had repeatedly cited the Alkoran against the Trinity. The *Racovian Catechism* used identical definitions of the unity of God to the Koran. The early heretic Ebionites had fled into Syria to become the first Mahometan converts. The crucial charge against both Unitarian and Mahometan, echoing Prideaux's condemnation, was that they were Pelagian heresies or human theologies, 'more like the moral philosophy of the Pagans, than the doctrine of our Lord and Saviour Jesus Christ'.[37]

THE TRINITY, CHRIST'S SATISFACTION AND ANTICLERICALISM

It is apparent that orthodox Anglican theologians agreed in identifying the Islamic tenor of Unitarian theology. It is also apparent that Unitarians such as Arthur Bury, Stephen Nye and William Freke willingly acknowledged the

[37] Anon, *Historical and Critical Reflections* (1712), 156, 157, 171, 172–4, 189, 206.

prescriptive value of Mahomet's reformation. At the centre of this debate lay the crucial doctrine of the 'unity of God' and the clash between a monotheistic or tritheistic explanation of God. We must examine the political implications of these rival theologies. What were the challenges and issues that the Islamic rhetoric masked? Socinian argument rejected the Christian status of the Anglican establishment, considering it a corruption from the veridical model of pre-Nicene Christianity. Contemporary Christianity in the Unitarians' view conflated the ritual and worship of the person of Christ with the practice of religion. The Unitarians demanded a reform of the ecclesiastical establishment to the pattern of primitive morality.[38]

The controversialists of the 1690s acclaimed the authority of personal rationality, insisting that the application of reason to Scripture could produce only a Unitarian theology. What they demanded was not a new vision of ecclesiastical government, but reformation of the existing system. It must be noted that such writers as Stephen Nye and Arthur Bury retained their livings in the Church, although critical of its theology. Unitarians railed against doctrines of persecution and forcing of conscience. Criticism of the Anglican Church was not *qua* ecclesiastical form but theological content. What they demanded was an alteration in faith to satisfy divine prescriptions. A typical example of this reformism was the system of Primitive Christianity propounded from within the Anglican establishment by William Whiston, and particularly Samuel Clarke's attempted revision of the Prayer Book.[39]

The orthodox overreacted. Their perception was that the Unitarians not only proposed a new theology, but that this revision was a threat to the very basis of ecclesiastical authority. This focused upon Unitarian Christology. Edward Stillingfleet in a sermon preached at St Laurence-Jewry, London, in 1691, *The Mysteries of the Christian Faith Asserted and Vindicated*, briefly stated the crux of the Trinitarian dispute while discoursing upon the text 'that Christ came into the world to save sinners'. The dispute centred upon the two opposite conceptions of Christ's soteriological efficacy, 'by the

[38] An interesting case of a later Unitarian espousal of Islam is that of Edward Elwall (1676–1744); see *DNB*. Elwall, a Wolverhampton weaver and colleague of the poet John Byrom, was vociferous in his defence of Unitarianism. He suffered trial and persecution at the hands of his Anglican adversaries. His public profession was for the Ebionite faith, and he adopted a blue mantle: 'a Turkish Habit out of respect to the Unitarian Faith of the Mahometans'. Joseph Priestly, the late eighteenth-century Unitarian, publicized Elwall's struggles. See *The Memoirs of Edward Elwall* (Liverpool, 1817); E. Elwall, *Idolatry Discovered and Detected* (1744), and *Dagon Fallen Before the Ark of God, Or the Inventions of Men Not Able to Stand before the First Commandment Thou Shall Have No Other Gods But Me* (1741); J. Priestly, *The Triumph of Truth* (1775).

[39] See R. Howard, *A Twofold Vindication* (1696), 47–8; 'I am certainly informed that the Unitarians in England have no ministry at all; they do not separate from the Church on account of their different opinion from the Church: they never separated in England from the common assemblies to worship; which in my opinion, is pious, charitable and prudent.'

doctrine and examples of the man Jesus Christ, by the power he attained through his sufferings; or, by the eternal son of God's assuming our nature, and suffering in our stead in order to the reconciling of God to us and making a propitiation for our sins'. Christ is either an example or a sacrifice. The Anglican position argued that Christ was the 'high priest' of the Church. Christ as the son of God was endowed with, and exercised, a sacerdotal power in his sacrifice, which was a complete satisfaction for man's sin. This Christology required that *sacerdos* was to be present in the temporal Church, identified in the priesthood. Elevating the competence of human reason to perceive the example of Christ and follow its precepts undermined the Trinitarian distinction between *sacerdos* and laity. The conception of Christ's sacrifice as a total propitiation of sins elevated the Church on earth to ministrators of this divinity: to undermine the sacrifice of Christ was to undercut the authority of the human priesthood. Francis Fullwood commented astutely in his *Socinian Controversy* (1693) on Socinian authors, 'who with subtlety and spight enough endeavour to ruine our ecclesiastical as well as spiritual state'. Edwards had pointed out in his *Socinian Creed* that the *Racovian Catechism* hinted that the Eucharist might be administered 'by the hands of private Christians and such as are not devoted to the ministry.' This was literally to 'subvert Christianity'.[40]

Edward Stillingfleet noted the potentially dangerous incoherence in the logic of the Unitarian position. The Unitarian argued that the Anglican Church, by its Trinitarianism, elevated a man to the status of deity thus falling into idolatry or polytheism. Stillingfleet insisted that if it was a duty and a sin to worship any other than the true God with proper divine worship, and Christ was to be considered a mere mortal, surely it was idolatrous to worship a creature? This was to ignore the distinctions the Unitarians introduced into the varying levels of worship. However, as Fullwood noted in his *Parallel*, many only worshipped Christ to 'avoid the scandal of dishonouring our Lord, and offending other Christians'. Some Unitarians when faced with the charge of idolatry for worshipping a mere creature, followed the example of Socinus' countryman Francis David, who denied the validity of worshipping Christ. These men were in Fullwood's phrase 'desperate enemies of our Lord and Saviour'. The natural consequence of

---

40 E. Stillingfleet, *Mysteries of the Christian Faith Asserted*, 333–4, appended to Stillingfleet, *A Discourse Concerning Christ's Satisfaction* (1696; CUL classmark G.13.2), xx; Fullwood, *Socinian Controversy* (1693), 23; Edwards, *Socinian Creed*, 179, and *Socinianism Unmasked*, 107. See Leslie, Dialogue VI: 'Of the Satisfaction Made by Christ for Our Sins' in 'Of the Socinian Controversy', *Theological Works*, II, 346–400, and *An Answer to the Last Examination of the Last Dialogue Relating to the Satisfaction of Jesus Christ* in *Theological Works*, II, 441–502. See also L. Milbourne, *Mysteries of Religion Vindicated* (1692), 'Or the Filation, Deity, and Satisfaction of Our Saviour Asserted, against Socinians and Others', especially 639–784, 'Our Lord's Satisfaction Asserted'. On Islamic notions of the role of Christ in the Koran, see G. Parrinder, *Jesus in the Qu'ran* (1965).

Unitarian theology was indifference in religion and ultimately atheism.[41] The issue of Christ's satisfaction was dealt with by Charles Leslie in the voluminous *Socinian Dialogues*. He stated, with uncharacteristic succinctness, that the crux of the debate was 'no less whether what we worship is God or a creature, whether we adore the true or false God, and are the grossest Idolaters in the world'. In *Dialogue V*, 'Of the satisfaction of Christ made for our sins', Leslie dissected the subversive implications of Unitarianism. The doctrine of full satisfaction was the foundation of the Christian religion. The Socinian in his *Dialogue* replied with the antinomian assertion that 'it is a great hindrance to piety; for if Christ has paid the whole debt, what need we do any more?' The Unitarian position was that while the death of Christ on the cross was a necessity for salvation, it was not the cause. It was an historical action, a necessary condition, but not universally and synchronically efficacious. For the Unitarian, Christ's sacrifice was necessary because it indicated God's willingness to accommodate mankind, but having opened the door to salvation it offered no other benefit. The Unitarian soteriology rested upon individual conformity to the pattern of Christ's life and teachings.[42] The author of the *Historical and Critical Reflections* made an astute comment when he noted that Unitarian doctrine was a direct descendant of the Pelagian tradition. For the Unitarian, religion was the comforter of social harmony, 'to reform the manners of men, to restrain human nature from falsehood and treachery, from sedition and rebellion ... Better it were there were no revealed religion than to be acted by a religion that is continually supplanting government, and undermining the welfare of mankind'. Leslie answered, that 'this may be perhaps like a politician, but not very like a Christian'. His complaint was that this reduced all to morality: if Christian behaviour was given such a wide circumference then it could include anyone who acted in a virtuous manner. Leslie pointed out, 'so that if a Mahometan, Jew or Pagan, leads a good moral life, he has the very essence of a Christian, and then no doubt is a Christian, let his system of faith be what it will'. This was the high road to subversion and atheism.[43]

[41] Stillingfleet, *Mysteries of the Christian Faith Asserted*, 363; Fullwood, *A Parallel*, 10–11. See Toland, *Collections*, II, 307 commenting on Jacobite accusations of witchcraft and heresy; 'Well; if magic won't do, heresy must. I am a dangerous anti-trinitarian, for having often publickly declared that I could as soon digest a wooden, or breaden deity, as adore a created spirit or a dignified man. This Socinianism and Arianism are, one would think, very orthodox.'

[42] Leslie, *Socinian Dialogues* in *Theological Works*, II, 14, 361; Nye, *Brief History of the Unitarians*, 33.

[43] Leslie, *Theological Works*, II, 377, 492; Edwards, *Socinian Creed*, 185; *Historical and Critical Reflections*, 157; for a similar analysis of the political implications of non-Trinitarian theologies, see E. Leach and A. Alcock, *Structuralist Interpretations of Biblical Myth* (Cambridge, 1983), 'Melchisedech: Icons of Subversion and Orthodoxy', 67–89. In particular page 75 on the implications of the distinction between Christ as Incarnation, and Christ as Crucified.

So far this chapter has been concerned to examine the Unitarian–Anglican debate over the value and meaning of the sacred history of Islam. Radical as the anticlerical implications of the Unitarian Christology were, the intention of such men as Stephen Nye and Arthur Bury was not to overthrow Christianity but to reform its deviant Trinitarianism. There was a more radical enterprise which, in appealing to the history of Mahomet, suggested not just an end to Trinitarian theology but also to the very idea of a 'Christian' society. In *Mahomet No Impostor* (1720), written under the assumed Arabic name of Abdulla Mahumed Omar, the Anglican denigration of Mahomet epitomized in Prideaux's *True Nature of Imposture* (1697) was subject to radical analysis. As Abdalla Mahumed Omar wrote to his fictional Moslem correspondent in Mecca commenting on Prideaux's work, 'it is no new matter to find a Christian author railing at the Great Prophet, and heaping together a company of false and scandalous reflections, to render him and his religion odious to their own people'. According to Omar, Mahomet had re-established an economy based upon faith in 'one eternal God, the Creator of all things'. Opposed to this the Christians were more intent upon upholding heathenish dogmatism, and promoting idolatry rather than establishing 'moral institutions'. The Islamic faith could be reduced to two central doctrines, the unity of God and 'the moral duties that are to regulate our actions towards one another'. The binary choice presented by Omar was between a conception of religion which was primarily ceremonial, or one which established a system of social duties and harmony.[44] A much later work, Count Boulainvilliers' *Life of Mahomet* (1731), written originally in French, echoed this interpretation. As Ishmael had restored the simple natural religion, so had Mahomet renovated Judaeo–Christian corruption. Boulainvilliers commended Mahomet's deliberate construction of a theology calculated to establish social morality and political order, following the ancient tradition of the politic legislator Numa Pompilius. This tradition of treating Mahomet as a civil theologian had its genesis in two earlier English works written by Henry Stubbe and John Toland.[45]

STUBBE AND TOLAND: TOWARDS A CIVIL THEOLOGY,
1671–1718

The two most important radical texts employing the Islamic prototype were the manuscript work of Henry Stubbe (1632–76), *An Account of the Rise and Progress of Mahometanism*, composed in 1671, but with an extensive

---

[44] (Abdulla Mahumed Omar) *Mahomet No Impostor* in T. Killigrew (ed.), *Miscellanea Aurea: Or the Golden Medley* (1720), 164, 172, 174, 176, 179.
[45] H. Boulainvilliers, *Life of Mahomet* (1731), 30, passim.

covert circulation in the early decades of the eighteenth century, and John Toland's *Nazarenus or, Jewish, Gentile, and Mahometan Christianity* (1718). This work was written as a contribution to the controversy inspired by Benjamin Hoadly's attack on the clericalist state. In examining Stubbe's text I intend to place it within the broad context of the Unitarian–Islamic syncretism I have already described. This will extend the treatment already suggested by J. R. Jacob in his *Henry Stubbe, Radical Protestantism and the Early Enlightenment* (1983) and argue that the Stubbe manuscript was a direct influence upon Toland's *Nazarenus* (1718). Both works set out to present an unbiased view of Islam, rejecting the slanders of the medieval canon identified in Prideaux's work. It must be remembered that especially when Toland's work was published it was into a public arena which had perceived Islam through the distorting lens of Prideaux's polemic.[46] The extent of the influence of Stubbe's manuscript is uncertain. We know that Charles Blount plagiarized a section in his *Oracles of Reason* (1693) and also that he sent Rochester extracts of the *Account*.[47] An unnoticed influence can be found in Sir John Finch's correspondence with Lord Conway between 4 and 14th February 1675. These letters give a 'politic' account of the growth of Islam including a presentation of the Islamic notion of the unipersonality of God, and the importance of Alexandrian Judaism. Mahomet is referred to as both a wise prince and legislator. There also may be the possibility that William Temple read and adopted Stubbe's work.[48]

The historical scheme, of both texts, is the dynamic between true religion and superstition, rather than the Anglican conception of a line of true succession from the apostolic age. Both Stubbe and Toland accepted the Islamic conception of the sacred past. The Islamic notion, put simply, is that there has always been one true religion: the prophets in lineage from Adam, through Noah, Moses, Christ, and finally the seal of all prophets, Mohammed have all been expounders of this one truth.[49] Both Noah and Christ can be called 'Muslims' or 'Believers'. The Islamic conception of the prophetic past argues that each succeeding prophet was sent by God to re-establish the true tenets of religion after it had become (almost inevitably) corrupted. Each

[46] H. Stubbe, *An Account of the Rise and Progress of Mahometanism*, ed. H. M. Khan Shairani (Lahore, 1954). See also the appendix of the latter, 'Containing Early Christian Legends and Notions Concerning Islam', 209–254. On Stubbe, see J. R. Jacob, *Henry Stubbe, Radical Protestantism and the Early Enlightenment* (Cambridge, 1983), and 'The Authorship of An Account of the Rise and Progress of Mahometanism' in *Notes and Queries* 26 (1975), 10–11; C. Hill, *The Experience of Defeat* (1984); L. Kontler, 'The Idea of Toleration and the Image of Islam in Early Enlightenment English Thought' in E. H. Balazs (ed.), *Sous le signe des lumières* (Budapest, 1987).

[47] See J. Treglown (ed.), *The Letters of Rochester* (Oxford, 1980).

[48] See B.L. Add. 23215 f. 77v–82v, 'Muslim Reports'; W. Temple, 'Of Heroick Virtue', *Complete Works*, I, 220–6, where he applauds Mahomet's fabrication of a theology to promote virtue, and framed to Arian inclinations.

[49] Stubbe, *An Account*, 86–104.

successive prophetic system replaced its predecessor in complicity with the doctrines of the true religion. Stubbe and Toland can thus be seen to place the historical past of Judaism, Christianity, and Islam into a Polybian framework.

The unifying theme throughout both works is the foundation of all religious truth on the premises of the unity of God. As Christianity was a reformation of the corruption of Mosaic law so Islam was a regeneration of post-Constantinian Christianity. Stubbe in particular concentrated on the pre-Moslem state of Eastern Christianity. Applying notions of Machiavellian causality he presented Mahomet as an oriental version of Cesare Borgia: as Christ's renovation had been assisted by the fortunate collaboration of circumstance (the oppression of Judaism by the Romans, and the general expectation of a Messiah) so Mahomet happily perceived the opportunity in Christian division to re-establish true religion and abolish idolatry. Mahomet, convinced of the unity of God, 'accomplish'd himself in civil and military prudence' through his travels and converse, and erected a 'new religion and empire' amidst the decay and debauchery of Eastern Christianity. Stubbe continued to note that the theology Mahomet established was compatible with original Nazarene and Arian Christianity.[50]

Mahomet used what Stubbe termed 'policy' to establish his renovation and outmanœuvre his enemies. Mahomet manipulated the superstitious Arabians from idolatry to the true religion. For example, Mahomet retained the Caab for religious worship, and the pilgrimage to Mecca, as ingrained within the Arabic character. Stubbe wrote, 'and did ingeniously accommodate to his ends those superstitious usages which were imprinted in the breasts of the Ismaelites', towards the worship of one God. The Koran was the embodiment of 'rational belief', and Mahomet commended for 'on the one hand not clogging men's faith with the necessity of believing a number of abstruse notions which they cannot comprehend, and which are often contrary to the dictates of reason and commonsense; nor on the other hand loading them with the performance of many troublesome, expensive and superstitious ceremonies'. Stubbe insisted that concomitant with the advance of true theology came the institution of civil virtue. Mahomet is assimilated into the tradition of Lycurgus, Numa and Solon for the introduction of moral

---

[50] Stubbe, *An Account*, 76–87, 153–5, see 153: 'For my part I believe that he was a convert to the judaising Christians and formed his religion as far as possible in resemblance of theirs.' For an earlier and hostile interpretation of Mahomet as a 'politic' legislator, see Francis Osborne *Political Reflections upon the Government of the Turks* (Oxford, 1662, 3rd edition) and Sir Paul Rycaut's *The Present State of the Ottoman Empire* (1668). See C. J. Heywood, 'Sir Paul Rycaut, a Seventeenth-Century Observer of the Ottoman State: Note for a Study' in E. K. Shaw, and C. J. Heywood (eds.), *English and Continental Views* (Los Angeles, 1972), 33–59.

imperatives under the guise of religious duty.[51] One of the most radical components of Stubbe's polemic against the established clerical order can be found in the opening section of his manuscript which gives an account of the state of Judaism and Christianity from the time of Christ to Mahomet. This concerned itself with the early history of Christian doctrine and belief. Unitarian historians like Stephen Nye had argued that the theological character of primitive Christianity was anti-Trinitarian, citing the rather vague precedent of the Nazarene Christians. Stubbe was to present a full blown historical narrative of the Jewish origins of Christianity: it was this historical thesis which was the premise of Toland's *Nazarenus*.

Stubbe insisted that Christianity was a Jewish heresy. Originally the 'Nazarens' or 'Judaising Christians' received Christ as a temporal Messiah according to Judaic notions of the Messiah. He wrote;

They did never believe Christ to be a natural son of God, by eternal generation, or any tenets depending thereon, or prayed unto him, or believed the Holy Ghost, or the Trinity of Persons in one Deity, is as evident as 'tis that the Jews and they did expect no such Messiah, and the introducing such doctrines would have been capital among them as tending to blasphemy and Polytheism.

Citing Selden's *De Synedriis* (1650–3) Stubbe argued that Christianity 'was but a Reformation of Judaism'.[52] For Stubbe the whole constitution of the Primitive Church followed the pattern of the Jewish synagogue, 'no temples, no Altars, no sacrifices were known in those days, nor was the name of Priest then heard of'.[53] Stubbe argued that as the Judaic Christians retained many of their Mosaic rituals and laws, so Gentile proselytes encouraged by St Paul retained their pagan ceremonies and beliefs. He wrote; 'Thus Pantemus and Clemens Alexandrinus mixed Stoicism with Christianity, Origen and others Platonism and Peripateticism and I have read of Cynical and Epicurean Christians.' It was from these pagan and 'Ethnick' sources that Christ's deification originated. Christological notions evolved from that of a tempo-

---

[51] Stubbe, *An Account*, 93, 101–2, 168, 177, 164, 180–3. It is interesting to note that Boulainvilliers' later work *Life of Mahomet* (1731) applauded Mahomet unreservedly as a Machiavellian legislator. As I have noted above, this text was translated into English in 1731. The introductory remarks commented on Boulainvilliers' effort, 'he has wiped of the aspersion that deformed his [Mahomet's] character; set him in the fairest point of light; and described this hero, and this orator, with an eloquence equal to his own'. *Life of Mahomet* (1731), Sig. A2v. Montesquieu used the *Life of Mahomet* when he applauded Mahomet's institution of polygamy and abstention from pork as laudable civil policy adapted to the conditions of the East. See R. Shackleton, *Montesquieu: A Critical Biography* (Oxford, 1961); P. Kra, 'Religion in Montesquieu's Lettres Persanes', *SVEC* 52 (1970). For a later manifestation of this tradition, see E. S. Shaffer, *Kubla Khan and the Fall of Jerusalem* (Cambridge, 1975), 56–8.

[52] Stubbe, *An Account*, 16, 26–7. Note also that Toland makes explicit reference to Selden's work in *Nazarenus* (1718), 30. He wrote, Selden 'has asserted Christianity to be no more than Reformed Judaism'.

[53] Stubbe, *An Account*, 20.

ral to a 'spiritual Messiah'. It was from these foundations, combined with an admixture of theological speculation and imperial manipulation, that Christian theology abandoned its Judaic heritage and embraced the absurd and abstruse doctrine of Trinitarianism.[54] Sectarianism, superstition and clerical self-advancement was the state of Christianity against which Mahomet was to introduce his renovation.

For Stubbe all religions ought to have had a common foundation in Noachic natural law. Beyond this groundbed the outward formula of religion was irrelevant, as long as it did not contravene the precepts of rationality. He noted that the Moslem worshipped the true God and if there was any error it was 'rather in the manner than the object of their devotion'. The outward form of religion is considered heuristically; any practice may be legitimated as long as it advances true practical piety. Stubbe ended his tract with a controversial point in vindicating the Moslems from erecting Islam upon force of the sword. He did not deny Moslem violence, but justified its employment in the extirpation of idolatry.[55]

While Stubbe had asserted the Nazarene origins of Christianity, John Toland was to argue a powerful scholarly case. Following the promptings of Hobbes' *Leviathan* (chapter 33), Toland early in his career was interested in the monuments of early Christianity, in particular the origins of the scriptural canon. While Hobbes had thrown doubt on the authenticity of certain Old Testament texts, Toland turned to the New Testament. His earliest statements were in *Amyntor: or a defence of Milton's Life* (1699). Here Toland quite casually displayed a catalogue of New Testament material, orthodox, apocryphal and downright fictitious. Toland's factual catalogue was an obvious irritant to the orthodox.[56] Toland's general historical point was that the present canon had only been established as late

---

[54] Stubbe, *An Account*, 29, 33, 35–48. For anti-Pauline notions, see also Toland, *Nazarenus* 23–4, 25 on St Paul as an 'apostate from the law'. On Nazarenes, see H. Conzelmann, *History of the Primitive Church* (1973) (trans. J. Steely), 134–9, Chapter 13 'Jewish Christianity after the Jewish War'; H. Chadwick, *The Early Church* (1968), 9–32; J. W. C. Wand, *A History of the Early Church* (1937); see S. Pines, 'The Jewish Christians of the Early Centuries of Christianity According to a New Source', *Proceedings of the Israel Academy of Sciences and Humanities* 2 (1968); R. A. Pritz, 'The Jewish Christian Sect of the Nazarenes' (Ph.D., Hebrew University, 1981).

[55] Stubbe, *An Account*, 164, 192–205.

[56] See Toland, *Amyntor* (1699), 20 ff., note at 40; Toland points out that the Gospel of Barnabas is lost; see also *Collections*, I, 350–403, where Toland updates this earlier catalogue. In this later work Toland proudly (at 355–6) noted that his work was well received by Continental scholars like Fabricius and Pfassius. The intention of the later update was to defend the original discussion from the more orthodox rebuttals like S. Nye, *An Historical Account. A Defence of the Canon of the New Testament* (1700) and J. Richardson, *The Canon of the New Testament Vindicated* (1699) (note that I have used the 3rd edition of 1719). Interestingly, both Nye and Richardson objected to Toland's aside (*Amyntor* 64) that the 'Nazarenes or Ebionites' were the 'oldest Christians'.

as the council of Laodicae in A.D. 360.[57] In *Amyntor* Toland had made two casual references that, amplified, became the basis of his important *Nazarenus*. He discussed the lost Gospel of Barnabas, and described the Nazarenes as the founders of Christianity.

Toland had first been interested in the Nazarenes while under the tuition of Frederic Spanheim, at the University of Leiden. Although the latter was responsible for directing Toland to material on the Nazarenes, as Toland noted, his own opinions 'differ widely from my master in this point'. Toland had begun work on his *Nazarenus* in 1710, based on the discovery of a manuscript copy of the Gospel of Barnabas.[58] Toland had discovered the manuscript Gospel on his travels through Amsterdam in 1709. We know for certain that the work ended up in the possession of Prince Eugene in Vienna. Toland's contacts with Eugene and the Baron d'Hohendorf perhaps provide an explanation of Toland's knowlege of the work. Toland was introduced to the work by Jean Frederic Cramer, counsellor to the Prussian King Frederick I, and his ambassador at Amsterdam. Cramer was a learned scholar with distinct anti-Trinitarian leanings. He had edited the Socinian works of Giovanni Michele Bruto in 1698.[59] The manuscript of the Gospel of St Barnabas is of mysterious origins. Western biblical scholarship has long dismissed the work as a mid- to late-medieval forgery.[60] The reception of the Gospel in Muslim scholarship has not seen such an unequivocal assault upon its veracity: the majority of Islamic theologians insist that the Gospel is the only true and uncorrupted Christian text. The work purports to be a true account of the life of Jesus by Barnabas against the false teaching of St Paul who had elevated Christ into a divinity. The work is broadly based upon the New Testament, the Koran, and other unidentifiable interpolations. The most recent and detailed analysis of the manuscript argues that although the work does contain late Islamic and Christian additions it is based upon a

---

[57] See *Amyntor*, 57–8. Note that Toland was up to his old tricks again in citing the High Church Dodwell in favour of this argument (see *Amyntor*, 69–78, where Toland cites and translates Dodwell, *Dissertationes Irenicum*, paragraphs 38–9). Dodwell was forced to rebut the association in an appended letter to Richardson's attack on Toland.

[58] See *Nazarenus*, iii; Carabelli *Tolandiana*, 207–9. Rumours of Toland's discovery were rife; note the alarm occasioned by Francis Hare in 1713; 'as if a new Gospel were to be foisted, I know not how, into the room of the four old ones', *Nazarenus*, xxv.

[59] J. Cramer (ed.), *Opera Varia Selecta De G. M. Bruto* (Berlin, 1698). See L. Cirillo and M. Fremaux *L'Evangile de Barnabé: recherches sur la composition et l'origine* (Paris, 1977), 50–1, where it is suggested that Bruto 'Grand dénicheur des manuscrits anciens' may have been responsible for the dissemination or conservation of the Gospel of Barnabas. Bruto was Historiographer Royal to King Etienne Bathary of Transylvania.

[60] See L. L. Ragg, *The Gospel of Barnabas* (Oxford, 1907); W. E. A. Axon, 'On the Mohamedan Gospel of Barnabas' in *The Journal of Theological Studies* 3 (1901–2), 441–51; L. L. Ragg, 'The Mohamedan Gospel of Barnabas', *The Journal of Theological Studies* 6 (1904–5), 424–33; J. Fletcher, 'The Spanish Gospel of Barnabas', *Novum Testamentum* 18 (1976); J. Slomp, 'The Gospel in Dispute', *Islamochristiana* 4 (1978); D. Sox, *The Gospel of Barnabas* (1984).

substratum of an original gnostic Gospel.[61] The most notable characteristic of the work is its denial of the Passion and Resurrection of Christ arguing that it was Judas who was crucified (itself a Koranic assertion) and that Christ foretold the advent of Mahomet. Toland readily employed this text as evidence, following Stubbe's argument, of the continuity of Judaic, Christian and Islamic theology.[62]

The intention of *Nazarenus* was to give 'a clearer account, than is commonly to be met, of the Mahometan sentiments with relation to Jesus and the Gospel; insomuch that it is not without sufficient ground that I have represented them as a sort of Christian, and not the worst sort either, tho' far from being the best'. The existence and veracity of the Barnabas Gospel was highly contentious. The rector of St Nicholas', Thomas Mangey, in his *Remarks upon Nazarenus* (1718), charged Toland with deliberate fraud as an oblique means of undermining the canonicity of Scripture. Toland persisted in refuting the orthodox charge that the Koran was the work of the Nestorian heretic Sergius, suggesting instead that it had its origins in 'the earliest monuments of the Christian religion'. He continued; 'Mahomet is named in this book of Barnabas, as the designed accomplisher of God's economy towards man. Tis in short the ancient Ebionite or Nazarene system, as to the making of Jesus a mere man ... and agrees in everything almost with the scheme of our modern Unitarians.' As did Stubbe, Toland deployed the Islamic notion of the succession of the prophets as the authors of new institutions each increasingly perfect, 'tho' in substance it still be one and the same religion'. Toland accepted the Islamic charge that Jesus' prophecy of Mahomet, that he would come 'to complete or perfect all things,' had been erased from Scripture by the priests.[63]

In reply to Toland's assertions Thomas Mangey not only rejected his opinion of the nature of Barnabas' Gospel but also denied Toland's suggestion that the Nazarene sect was the primitive Christian model. Mangey's philology indicated that the term 'Nazarene' had been used pejoratively of early Christian heretics. Mangey continued to postulate that Toland's Nazarenes were in fact the followers of Ebion, a disciple of Simon

61 See L. Cirillo and M. Fremaux, *L'Evangile de Barnabé*, passim.
62 See *Nazarenus*, 16, 17–18.
63 Toland, *Nazarenus*, iii, 5, 6, 9, 13; for a similar analysis of the role of the Gospel of Barnabas, see G. Sale 'Preliminary Discourse' in his translation of the *Qu'ran* of 1734. See BL. Birch 4465 folio 20. Letter to Toland dated 20 June 1720 from Martin Eagle 'a true Ebionite' of Silver Street Cambridge (possibly a lecturer in oriental languages), which complimented Toland on the excellence and 'heroick spirit' of *Nazarenus*. The impact of Toland's work on the Gospel of Barnabas can perhaps be best considered by comparison with the twentieth-century reception of the work of M. Baigent, R. Leigh and H. Lincoln, *The Holy Blood and the Holy Grail* (1982), and the recent (1987) *The Messianic Legacy*. Interestingly, the first part of the most recent work deals in detail with early Nazarene Christianity, suggesting Islamic connections, echoing Toland's arguments, see 132–60.

Magus and Cerinthus. In this manner Mangey attempted to taint not only Toland's primitive model, but also by implication the Moslems, for they drew not upon an orthodox Christian heritage but 'nothing but Arianism or Nestorianism'. Mangey in a general reference to Toland's work wrote, 'his expression of the Mahometan Christianity is the only passage in this book which I do not condemn, provided he would mean by it not the Muselmans on the other side of the water, but the Socinians here. These may truely and properly be termed Mahometan Christians'.[64]

Both Stubbe and Toland turned to a history of Islam to describe their visions of civil religion and to assault Trinitarian Christianity. The connection between the two texts is a moot issue. Thomas Mangey in his critical reply to Toland made reference to Stubbe's work (which he had seen). Mangey was surprised that 'among the many unbelieving books that have been lately published, this should escape'.[65] The idea of a 'Mahometan Christianity' is common to both works, as is the assertion (borrowed from Selden) of the Judaic origins of Christianity, and a devout hostility towards Pauline theology. Both Toland and Stubbe agree that Noachic and universal natural principles are the foundation of all true religion.[66] There is, however, a distinction between the works, both in argument and content. The main thrust of Stubbe's work is historical: Mahomet is advanced as a polemical model of the politic legislator who employed the façade of religious inspiration to create a rational civil theology. Toland's enterprise was on a grander scale. Although Toland employed the same historical framework of the succession of reforming prophets (from Adam to Mahomet) renovating corrupt theological systems back to a groundbed of natural law, his concern was to examine the relations between the three great dispensations (Judaism, Christianity and Islam) and of these to the general idea of religion. Toland's work is also a more pronounced work of scholarship. In his discussion of Islam he was able to draw upon a *corpus* of oriental study that was unused

---

64 T. Mangey, *Remarks upon Nazarenus* (1718), 46, 47. See J. Richardson, *The Canon of the New Testament Vindicated*, 71–8; also the hostile remarks appended to Toland's *Collections*, II, 'Critical Remarks upon ... Nazarenus', which attacked Toland's use of patristic sources, in particular his manipulations of Irenaeus and Epiphanius. Toland defended himself in *Mangoneutes: Being a Defence of Nazarenus* (1720): again he noted that scholars of the class of Fabricius had acknowledged his work, (at 141, he notes that Fabricius, *Apocryphal Code of the New Testament*, 3rd volume, 387–94, 'inserted the whole historical part of Nazarenus without altering or omitting a word').

65 Mangey, *Remarks Upon Nazarenus*, 43. Toland (BL. Birch 4465 folios 63–64) compiled a collection of passages to show 'that I am not the first who put *Christian* and *Mahometan* together'.

66 Stubbe and Toland both discuss the paraclete-John 16.7 as either Isa or the comforter (Stubbe, *An Account*, 172–4, and Toland, *Nazarenus*, 13). Both use Epiphanius and Irenaeus (Stubbe, *An Account*, 18, and Toland, *Nazarenus*, 78–9). Both have anti-Pauline passages (Stubbe, *An Account*, 57–61, and Toland, *Nazarenus*, 25–36). Perhaps Stubbe is more radically Islamic in referring to Jesus throughout his work as Isa – the Qu'ranic phrase.

by, or unavailable to, Stubbe. Reland's *De Religione Mahomedica Libri Duo* (Utrecht, 1705) is repeatedly cited, as are the works of Levinus Warner, Ludovico Marracci and Gabriel Sionita. On the history of Judaism he supplemented Selden's *De Synedriis* with Jacob Rhenferd's *De Fictis Judaeorum et Judaizantium*, Stephen Curcelleus' *Diatriba de Iesu Sanguinis* (Amsterdam, 1659) and Christian Becmannes' *Execitationes Theologica* (Amsterdam, 1643), as well as repeated citations of Grotius, Salmasius and Vossius. Toland importantly also made his own innovative contributions to biblical criticism in his speculations on the Nazarene Gospel of the Hebrews and the Gospel of Barnabas.[67]

Toland's hermeneutical enterprise was grander than mere discussions about the canon: he wished to establish an 'accord' between the economies of the Old and New Testaments, in order to reconcile the disputes between Peter and Paul on circumcision, and Paul and James on faith and works.[68] This scriptural criticism indicates the 'religious' or 'spiritual' premises from which the deist movement extended, rather than being founded in the name of secularization. The general consideration of Toland's work was to focus upon the historical transition from Judaism to Christianity: if the relationship between these two economies could be comprehended then the 'original plan of Christianity' would be displayed. Echoing Selden, the broad theme of Toland's thesis was that Christianity was no more than 'reformed Judaism'. This argument held certain implications for the status of Jewish law. If, as Toland argued, early Christianity was a Judaic institution, did this imply that Christians were bound by the divine Mosaic ceremony and ritual, or could there be a more political explanation of these practices? The biblical context was the dispute between Paul and Peter over the ritual of circumcision: were gentile Christians obliged or exempt (Galatians II, verses 1–9). Paul, as the 'Apostle of the Uncircumcision', contended that Gentiles were exempt not only from circumcision but the whole of the Mosaic law because of the liberty established by the Gospel. In the case of gentile Christians Toland assented to this argument, but when dealing with the Nazarenes of Jewish Christians he insisted the law of Moses was still in force. The distinction between Jewish and gentile Christian was to remain in the Church for ever.

---

67 See D. Patrick, 'Two English Forerunners of the Tübingen School: Thomas Morgan and John Toland', *Theological Review* 14 (1877). See also Graf Reventlow, 'Judaism and Jewish Christianity in the Works of John Toland', *Proceedings of the Sixth World Congress of Jewish Studies* 3 (1977); M.Wiener, 'John Toland and Judaism', *Hebrew Union College Annual* 16 (Cincinnati, 1941); R. S. Wolper, 'Circumcision as Polemic in the Jew Bill of 1753', *Eighteenth Century Life* 7 (1982); for Toland's later influence, see Moses Mendelssohn (1729–86) in A. Jospe (ed.), *Jerusalem and other Jewish Writings* (New York, 1969), 124–6; and M. Pelli, 'The Impact of Deism on the Hebrew Literature of the Enlightenment in Germany' *Eighteenth Century Studies* 6 (1972–3).
68 Toland, *Nazarenus*, Preface, vii–viii.

Christ himself had merely perfected the Levitical law, and was bound to follow Judaic ritual.[69] This thesis was contrary to the orthodoxy. Thomas Mangey countered Toland's claims: Christ had repealed and abrogated Mosaic law as insufficient for salvation. The ceremonial law was merely a type and shadow of Christ who had fulfilled it as the Messiah.[70] All Christians *qua* Christians were in a state of liberty from previous divine injunction. Archbishop Tillotson echoed this general principle in his sermons on Matthew that 'Christianity doth not destroy but perfect the law'. Once again the law was the shadow of faith. The Jewish dispensation was insufficient for man's sanctification and justification, which was only possible through Christ's sacrifice.[71] Toland's premise was different: both Christians and Jews were bound by moral and natural law which Christ had simply republished. This moral, natural or Noachic law was fundamental to all true religion, 'which being one and the same substance from the beginning, tho' in circumstances the institutions of it at different times be different, and consequently more or less perfect'. The Jewish ceremony and ritual was to be considered, 'no less national and political, than religious and sacred: that is to say, the expressions of the history of their peculiar nation'.[72] Here was heresy indeed. Toland implied ultimately that all ceremonial manifestations of religion were no more than mere political and historical device. In the appendix to *Nazarenus* Toland indicated the radical possibilities of this argument placing it in the context of his much understudied earlier work *Origines Judicae* (The Hague, 1709). In the appendix he posed two 'problems, Historical, Political, and Theological, concerning the Jewish nation'. The primary and most interesting question was how had the Jews preserved themselves as a 'distinct people' since the time of Moses and their dispersion? While leaving the interrogative tantalizingly open, Toland displayed his admiration for the *Republica Mosaica*, 'which I admire infinitely, above all forms of government that ever existed. Whether at any time in actual exercise, as those of the Spartans and Romans of old, and now that of the Venetians; or subsisting only in idea, as the Atlantis of Plato, Sir Thomas More's Utopia and such

---

[69] *Ibid.*, 31–6, 37–40.   [70] Mangey, *Remarks upon Nazarenus*, 64, 71, 73–84, 95.
[71] J. Tillotson, *Sermons* (4 volumes, 1704), IV, 85ff., 113ff.
[72] Toland, *Nazarenus*, 30, 38, 65–7. Toland's political analysis of Jewish law formed the basis for his liberal arguments for naturalizing the Jews in his *Reasons for Naturalising the Jews in Great Britain and Ireland* (1714). It is to be noted here that Toland was echoing the proposition of his Republican mentor Harrington who argued in *Oceana* that the Jews should be allowed to resettle Ireland while retaining their own religion and rituals. S. B. Liljegren in 'Harrington and the Jews', *K. Humanisticka Vetenskapssam* 4 (1931–2), argues that this was indicative of Harrington's liberal tolerationist ideals. The recent work of D. Katz, *Philo-Semitism and the Re-admission of the Jews to England* (Oxford, 1982) in discussing the millennarian and conversionist schemes of the 1650s portrays Harrington as arguing for readmission on economic grounds (31, 240). Harrington's deliberate eschewal of converting the Jewish nation seems to fit uneasily with Pocock's millennarian interpretation.

like'.[73] Toland complimented Moses as the paradigm of the politic legislator, 'far superior to Saleus, Charondas, Solon, Lycurgus, Romulus, Numa, or any other legislator'.[74] While Stubbe presented Mahomet as the archetype of the civil theologian, Toland insisted upon Moses' pre-eminence. This was inherently subversive. To the orthodox the Mosaic institutions were the direct product of God; Toland characterized them as the product of human politics.

Toland's brief correspondence with the anonymous S*** R*** neatly indicates the heresy in his *Nazarenus*. The letter was composed in reply to the questions posed in Toland's appendix to *Nazarenus*. If Toland wanted non-providential and non-miraculous explanations for the historical unity of the Jewish nation he would find adequate answer in Spinoza's *Treatise Partly Theological and Partly Political* (English translation 1689).[75] As S*** R*** pointed out, Spinoza argued that the Jewish nation had retained their common identity because of the ceremonial law in general, and in particular because of the ritual of circumcision. As the anonymous author succinctly commented, 'the foundation of the whole seems to be circumcision'.[76]

Spinoza's *Treatise Partly Theological and Partly Political* was reviled for its innovative biblical criticism by all orthodoxy. Its propositions formed some of the central premises of Toland's *Nazarenus*. The Old Testament account of the Jewish nation had been interpreted by Spinoza as a straightforward political and historical narration. The Mosaic state was rather a political than religious institution.[77] Spinoza suggested political ends for the Mosaic ceremony: this argument was accepted and adopted by Toland.[78] Moses was a legislator who introduced religious ceremony into his commonwealth not due to divine inspiration but for 'the temporary prosperity of government.'[79] Mosaic institutions like circumcision had been instruments to preserve the nation and government: for the Jew the love of nation became an act of piety.[80] If Toland's Spinozist borrowings were not completely

73 Toland, *Nazarenus*, Appendix 1; see also Toland, *Collections*, II, 392, Toland to Leibnitz, 14 February 1710, on Toland's intention to write a large study of the *Republica Mosaica*; and Toland, *Hodegus* (1720) as an extract of this larger work.
74 Toland, *Nazarenus*, Appendix 8. Note that Harrington placed Moses firmly in the same tradition of politic legislators, and saw nothing wrong in doing so: see Toland *Works of Harrington* (1700), 178, 407. For Harrington human prudence was at the same time both natural and divine. Note that this was contrary to orthodox Hebraic scholarship such as Peter Cunaeus, *Of the Commonwealth of the Hebrews* (1653) – a work which Harrington had read – which insists, at pages 2–3, 'that the Greek Legislators, compared to Moses are but of yesterday'. Importantly Rousseau in the *Social Contract*, II, chapter 7, 'The Legislator', recommends the model of Moses to the 'true political theorist', at 197.
75 Toland, *Collections*, II, (S*** R*** to Toland, 10 July 1720), 448–52. Note the passage S*** R*** recommends Chapter 3 of Spinoza's work.
76 Toland, *Collection*, II, 452.
77 B. Spinoza, *Treatise Partly Theological and Partly Political* (1689), chapter 3, 64–6.
78 *Ibid.*, chapter 5, 104–5.   79 *Ibid.*, 103, 105, 115–17.
80 *Ibid.*, 357, 382. Spinoza commented (79–80) 'that only the sign of circumcision may be able to perpetuate the nation'. See J. Schwartz, 'Liberalism and the Jewish Connection: A Study of

evident in *Nazarenus* they were well displayed in his *Origines Judicae* (The Hague, 1709), described by William Warburton as a 'senseless dissertation'.[81] *Origines Judicae*, published in Latin to hide its infidel arguments from the vulgar, is an epitome of Toland's heretical hermeneutic. Toland interpreted the Old Testament account of Moses by the application of ancient pagan texts. The crucial classical work was Strabo's narrative of Moses as a legislator learned in the Egyptian arcana in the *Geography* (volume VII, pp. 283–9). Toland's one-hundred-page dissertation was simply an extended commentary and justification of Strabo's text. As Toland's correspondence with Leibnitz indicates, this interpretative strategy was unacceptable. Leibnitz wrote: 'Strabon est un auteur grave, mais lors qu'il parle de Moyse, il paroist qu'il prend les actions et les sentimens de ce legislator selon les pretentions et les chimeras des Grècs.'[82] In a later letter Leibnitz reaffirmed this point after Toland had rebutted his challenge to Strabo's authority.[83] Toland rather arrogantly replied; 'I shan't make the least alteration in either Adeisdaemon or the Origines Judicae since the attempts to answer or censure them appear to be as impotent as they were malicious, and therefore have confirm'd others no less than myself in the truth of my allegations.'[84]

Toland argued, along with Strabo, that Moses was in the same tradition as Minos, Lycurgus and Zamolxis. Moses was originally an Egyptian priest educated in the hidden secrets of the *prisca theologia* which resembled a Spinozist pantheism rather than the orthodox Judaeo-Christian theologies. As Toland explained, again following Strabo;

Mosem enivero fuisse Pantheistam, sive, ut cum recentioribus loquar, Spinosistam, incunctanter affirmat in isto Loco Strabo: eum namque exhibet docentam, nullam dari Numen a materia et compage mundi hujus distinctum, ipsaque Naturam, sive rerum universitatem, unicum esse et supremum Deum; cujus partes singulas creaturas dicas, et totum, si velis, creatorem.[85]

Another favourite classical source, Diodorus Siculus, was cited to supplement this point. Moses learned in 'omni sapientia Aegyptiorum' calculated a civil theology to lead the Jewish nation to social harmony. The Jews after the exodus from Egypt had been riven with idolatry and superstition, accustomed to corrupt Egyptian practices.[86] While Moses privately enter-

Spinoza and the Young Marx', *Political Theory* 13 (1985); P. Slyomovics, 'Spinoza: Liberal Democratic Religion', *Journal of the History of Philosophy* 23 (1985).

[81] W. Warburton, *Divine Legation of Moses* (4 vols., 4th edition, 1765), II, 219.

[82] Toland, *Collections*, II, (Leibnitz to Toland, April 30 1709) 383.

[83] *Ibid.*, II, 401.   [84] *Ibid.*, II, 390, Toland to Leibnitz, 14 February 1710.

[85] J. Toland, *Origines Judicae* (The Hague, 1709), 104, 117. For a general discussion, see D. B. Sailor, 'Moses and Atomism', *JHI* 25 (1964).

[86] Toland, *Origines Judicae* 140, 146–7 citing Tacitus, *Histories*, V, which is also used in C. Blount's *Oracles of Reason* (1693), 'Letter to Major A Concerning the Origins of the Jews', 129–32.

tained true pantheistical beliefs he established a popular system of ceremony and ritual to accommodate vulgar Jewish inclinations.[87] Such argument was explicitly contrary to orthodox appreciation of Moses as a divinely inspired messenger of God. Instead of a providential explanation of the Jewish religion Toland suggested, as had Stubbe with the history of Islam, that Moses was a man informed by human wisdom alone.

While the Unitarians and their opponents were willing to deploy the history of Islam as a prescriptive or proscriptive model of true religion, this historical pattern was taken one step further in the work of Stubbe and Toland. The step was taken towards such heretical arguments like those contained in the clandestine *Traité des Trois Imposteurs*, which suggested that Moses, Christ and Mahomet had all been politic legislators employing the façade of divine inspiration for civil ends. For Stubbe and Toland, Mahomet and Moses were legislators founding their principles upon true monotheistic roots. In these early histories of religion, the classical idea of the legislator combined with the notion that religion should be employed for social purposes to become one of the primary roots of civil theology. How such histories of monotheism evolved into fully fledged histories of religion, forming the foundations for the radical idea of civil religion, will be the subject of the rest of this book.[88]

[87] Toland, *Origines Judicae*, 155.
[88] There is a later development of this radical interpretation of Islam which needs further treatment elsewhere. The important works are: J. Morgan, *Mahometanism Fully Explain'd ... Written in Spanish and Arabick in the Years MDCIII for the Instruction of Moriscoes in Spain* (2 volumes, 1723–5). This purported to be a literal translation of a manuscript composed by Mahomet Rabadan and deposited in Harley's collection. It is most likely a forgery. The list of subscribers includes Anthony Collins and Barnham Goode. The first volume was perceived by the public as a 'burlesque upon Scripture'. Morgan also composed a two-volume history of Algiers (1728). Other important works are 'Zelim Musulman' (A. Radicati), *A Parallel Between Mahumed and Sosem* (1732) and *Reflections on Mohamedism, and the Conduct of Mohamed* (1735). Note that J. S. Mill in *On Liberty* in M. Warnock (ed.), *Utilitarianism* (1979), 177–8, applauds the moral precepts of the Koran over the New Testament. See for a later discussion J. Rendell, 'Scottish Orientalism from Robertson to James Mill', *HJ* 25 (1982).

'Prisca theologia'

NATURAL RELIGION AND THE HISTORY OF PRIESTCRAFT, 1660–1722

'Let us detest all priestcraft' was the rallying cry of the early English enlightenment.[1] The achievement of the Republican Freethinkers was to separate the idea of 'true religion' from the sociological example of seventeenth-century Christianity. This enterprise was fundamental to the Enlightenment, but (as we shall see) although presented with the rhetoric of liberty of reason, it was conducted in the name of true religion. Such a claim was the premise for David Hume's *Natural History of Religion* (1758) and the more vociferous anticlericalism of Voltaire and d'Holbach. Echoing Paolo Rossi's work, *The Dark Abyss of Time*, which has disinterred the pre-history of Vico's *New Science*, this chapter will explore the texts that enabled Hume to write such a work. Contrary to popular belief Hume's *Natural History of Religion* was no innovative landmark in the history of the sociology of religion. The elements of this work (the tension between monotheism and polytheism, the corrosive influence of the priesthood, and the parallelism of pagan with Christian superstition) were all forged in the seventeenth century by such scholars and critics as Herbert of Cherbury,

---

[1] The intention is to stress the English Republican contribution to the Enlightenment (see following chapters); this can be most readily identified in the adoption of Harringtonian civil theologies by such thinkers and actors as Rousseau and Robespierre: for a general discussion see N. Hampson, *Will and Circumstance* (1983). On this theme Engels has some illuminating comments, see *Socialism: Utopian and Scientific*, 386–7, 395, in Marx and Engels, *Selected Works* (Moscow, 1968). See also F. Manuel, *The Eighteenth Century Confronts the Gods* (Cambridge, 1959), and *The Changing of the Gods*, (Hanover, 1983), especially chapter 2, 'Deists on True and False Gods'; P. Hazard, *The European Mind 1680–1715* (1973); C. J. Betts, *Early Deism in France* (The Hague, 1984); D. C. Allen, *Doubt's Boundless Sea: Scepticism and Faith in the Renaissance* (Baltimore, 1964); N. L. Torry, *Voltaire and the English Deists* (Yale, 1967); D. P. Walker, *The Decline of Hell* (1964); I. O. Wade, *The Intellectual Origins of the French Enlightenment* (Princeton, 1971); L. Althusser, *Politics and History: Montesquieu, Rousseau, Marx* (1982).

Charles Blount, John Toland and John Spencer.[2] Rather than treating religious belief, ceremony and ritual as transcendent principles, these men cultivated an idea of religion as a social and historical institution, a tradition that could be traced back through Machiavelli to the classical analysis of Cicero in *De Natura Deorum*. In treating religion as a manifestation of social and political structures, as the product both of human psychology and priestly manipulation, the radicals were committed to an historical investigation of its causes and effects. With these historical enquiries such men as Blount and Toland developed their civil theologies as necessary adjuncts to their social and political prescriptions. These historical scrutinies drew upon a wide variety of polemic and scholarship. The most visible manifestation of this approach was inspired by an anticlerical tradition rooted in the ambivalent rhetoric of Reformation humanism and which can be most easily identified in the thought of Thomas Hobbes.[3] The study of Hobbes has suffered from a tendency to secularize his thought. His theological unorthodoxy has been too often read as an indication of a distaste for all things religious (rather than all things popish) and proof of his modernity. Hobbes, the anticlerical deconstructor of priestly fraud, was a crucial instrument in the development of a radical history of religion that laid the foundation for the Enlightenment. The radicals were not inspired by the absolutist Hobbes of Books I and II of *Leviathan* (1651) but the anticlericalist of the little studied second half of the work. The Freethinkers anathematized Hobbist principles of absolute sovereignty, preferring a neo-Harringtonian analysis

[2] See D. Hume, *The Natural History of Religion*, (ed.), A. W. Colver (Oxford, 1976); P. Rossi, *The Dark Abyss of Time* (Chicago, 1985); D. A. Paulin, *Attitudes to Other Religions* (Manchester, 1984); on Hume, see for example J. C. A. Gaskin, *Hume's Philosophy of Religion* (1978), at 146:

> Although the authorities and evidence which Hume produced for his conclusions in the N[atural] H[istory of] R[eligion] are almost all drawn from the observations of ancient authors, the problem which he discusses – the psychological and anthropological causes and origins of religious belief and its effects – is, as Mossner observes, essentially modern, and to Hume should go the credit for being the first great modern to treat of it systematically. From it arises much modern thinking on the subject.

Gaskin continues to describe the *Natural History of Religion* as the 'first move in what might now be called the sociology of religion'. For a fine destruction of such Whiggish notions in the history of anthropology, see J. A. Boon, *Other Tribes, Other Scribes* (Cambridge, 1982). The origin of different attitudes to religion has been usefully explored by J. S. Preus in his recent *Explaining Religion: Criticism and Theory from Bodin to Freud* (Yale, 1987). This work is a sound study, based on the premise that (at x), 'it is not necessary to believe in order to understand, indeed that suspension of belief is probably a condition for understanding'. While the general argument of his case is persuasive, Preus prefers to emphasize the French contribution over the English, suggesting that the English investigation was essentially epistemological (following Herbert of Cherbury) while the French was sociological. This chapter intends to investigate the sociological dimensions of the English tradition.

[3] For an important study of the legacy of the Reformation see H. Graf Reventlow, *The Authority of the Bible and the Rise of the Modern World* (1984) in particular Parts II and III. For the most recent and persuasive account of Hobbes' religious thought, see R. Tuck, 'The Christian Atheism of Thomas Hobbes' in Hunter and Wootton (eds.), *Atheism*.

of political authority. Men such as Charles Blount, John Trenchard, and Thomas Gordon consistently applauded Hobbes' deconstruction of priestly fraud.[4] In Books III and IV of *Leviathan* Hobbes had argued for a rigorous Erastianism. The clergy were subject to the jurisdiction of the civil sovereign and could claim no independent authority. In his notions of 'personation' and an unorthodox reading of the Trinity Hobbes devalued the social and political role of the clerical order. Repeatedly citing Christ's dictum that his kingdom is not of this world, Hobbes argued that the priesthood were only adept as promoters of morality.[5] Throughout the second half of *Leviathan* Hobbes combined theological commentary, sacred hermeneutics and historical narrative to arraign the misdeeds of the 'unpleasing priests' who had usurped the authority of true religion for their own temporal ends. He narrated the tying of the three knots on Christian liberty and applauded the theological freedom of the Interregnum.[6] While the second half of *Leviathan*

[4] To give an exhaustive bibliographical footnote on the state of scholarship on the thought of Hobbes is impossible here. The fault with all the works detailed here is a failure to examine the explicit and implied anticlericalism of Hobbes' thought. See L. Strauss, *The Political Philosophy of Hobbes*, (Oxford, 1936); A. E. Taylor, 'The Ethical Doctrine of Hobbes' in K. Brown (ed.), *Hobbes Studies* (Oxford, 1965); M. Oakeshott, 'Introduction' to *Leviathan* (Oxford, 1946); H. Warrender, *The Political Philosophy of Hobbes* (Oxford, 1957); C. B. Macpherson, *The Political Theory of Possessive Individualism Hobbes to Locke* (Oxford, 1962); K. Thomas, 'The Social Origins of Hobbes Political Thought' in K. Brown, (ed.), *Hobbes Studies*; F. C. Hood, *The Divine Politics of Thomas Hobbes* (Oxford, 1964); M. M. Goldsmith, *Hobbes' Science of Politics* (1966); F. McNeilly, *The Anatomy of Leviathan* (1968); D. P. Gauthier, *The Logic of Leviathan* (Oxford, 1969); Q. Skinner, 'History and Ideology in the English Revolution', *HJ* 8 (1965), and 'Conquest and Consent: Thomas Hobbes and the Engagement Controversy' in G. E. Aylmer (ed.), *The Interregnum* (1972).
[5] Hobbes, *Leviathan*, III, chapter 41, 'Of the Office of our Blessed Saviour' at 512–21. See J. G. A. Pocock, 'Time, History, and Eschatology in Thomas Hobbes' in *Politics, Language and Time* (1972); P. Springborg, 'Leviathan, the Christian Commonwealth Incorporated', *Political Studies* 24 (1976), 171–83; L. Strauss, *Spinoza's Critique of Religion* (New York, 1965), 86–104. Recently there has been new interest in Hobbes' religious thought, for example, E. J. Eisenach, 'Hobbes on Church, State, and Religion', *History of Political Thought* 3 (1982), 215–44, and D. Johnston, *The Rhetoric of Leviathan. Thomas Hobbes and the Politics of Cultural Transformation* (Princeton, 1986), 114–15, 117, 134, 147–50, 183. It is interesting to note that the study of Hobbes' religious thought is currently flourishing in the Soviet Union: see J. Thrower, *The Marxist–Leninist Scientific Atheism* (Berlin, 1983), especially chapter 6, 'The History of Atheism, Freethinking, and Humanism' at 288–308, which gives a detailed bibliography of Soviet studies, plus a list of university courses on Hobbes' anticlericalism (404, 468).
[6] See Hobbes' *Leviathan*, IV, chapter 47, 385:

First, the power of the Popes was dissolved totally by Queen Elizabeth; and before the Bishops, who before exercised their functions in right of the Pope, did afterwards exercise the same right of the Queen and her successours ... And so was untied the first knot. After this the Presbyterians lately in England obtained the putting down of Episcopacy: And so was the second knot dissolved: and almost at the same time, the power was taken also from the Presbyterians: and so we are reduced to the Independency of the Primitive Christians to follow Paul, or Cephas, or Apollos, every man as he liketh best: Which if it be without contention, and without measuring the doctrine of Christ, by our affection to the Person of

is an important anticlerical tract, its hostility towards the ghostly estate is muted by the sheer length and complexity of the arraignment. A far more accessible source for Hobbes' anticlerical tenets is his poetic history *A True Ecclesiastical History from Moses to the Time of Martin Luther*, originally published in Latin in 1688, and translated and prefaced by Thomas Rymer in 1722.[7]

In this work Hobbes provided a simplified historical treatment of the decline of religion and the rise of priestcraft. Primitive Christianity is a simplistic and natural religion intent upon establishing morality rather than worldly advancement. Christ's yoke was easy and innocent of persecution. From this pristine original the priesthood with the corrupt apparatus of pagan philosophy and scholastic 'jargon' turned religion into a trade. False miracles, idolatry, ghosts and goblins created a priestly empire over the minds of the laity. The clergy 'deified their dreams'. In this manner the sacerdotal order set up an independent interest, creating a double kingdom upon which they forged a tyranny that extended to civil affairs. It was this triple analysis (of an original primitive natural religion, of priestly corruption and priestly tyranny) that was to form the backbone of the Freethinking impeachment of the Church.[8]

One of the most articulate promoters of Freethought and religious toleration of the 1690s was Matthew Tindal of All Saints College, Oxford. In his *Rights of the Christian Church Asserted* (1706) he resisted the High Church claims of such men as Francis Atterbury and Charles Leslie.[9] Tindal,

his Minister, (the fault which the Apostle reprehended in the Corinthians) is perhaps the best.

[7] This work has gone largely unnoticed in commentaries upon Hobbes. See H. Macdonald and M. Hargreaves, *Thomas Hobbes: A Bibliography* (1952), 75. See also J. Aubrey's reference to the work in *Remaines of Gentilism and Judaisme* in J. Buchanan-Brown (ed.), *Three Prose Works of John Aubrey* (Sussex, 1972), 13–137, citing Hobbes, *Historia Ecclesiastica*, 62. Aubrey, particularly in his *Brief Lives* (2 volumes edited by A. Clarke, Oxford, 1898), stresses the anticlerical Hobbes: see Aubrey *Brief Lives*, I, 338–9, 358, 364, 382, where he makes reference to the *Ecclesiastical History* in commenting on Hobbes' fear of episcopal retribution in the Restoration. He wrote: 'Which he fearing that his papers might be search't by their order, and he told me he had burnt part of them; among other things a poeme, in Latin hexameter and pentameter, of the encroachment of the clergie (both Roman and Reformed) on the Civil power.'

[8] T. Hobbes, *A True Ecclesiastical History* (1722), 34–6, 89–90, 94–5, 105–6, 110–14, 150. For one example of the later influence of Books III–IV of *Leviathan*, see M. Tindal, *Rights of the Christian Church* (1706), especially chapter 6, 190–232, which indicts the 'labyrinth of words' and 'transcendent metaphysics' created by the priestly manipulation of Aristotelian 'jargon'.

[9] It has been suggested that this work was an adaption of a Dutch Spinozist work, *De jure Ecclesiasticorum* published in Amsterdam 1665. See R. S. Colie, 'Spinoza and the Early English Deists', *JHI* 20 (1959), and 'Spinoza in England 1665–1730', *Transactions of the American Philosophical Society* 107 (1963). Contemporary reaction to Tindal's reputation can be gauged from the treatment of F. Littleton, Fellow of All Souls, who was refused his MA because it was known he favoured the *Rights*. See Hearne, *Remarks and Collections*, II, 94.

following Harrington's analysis, considered the Church as a democratic society. The clergy could only have authority based on the consent of the members of this Church. Clerical authority was an exact analogue of civil authority, both being premised on the consent of society.[10] The clergy could claim no *sacerdos* from the apostolic succession, but only a character based upon their perceived ability to effect honour to God, and good for mankind. As soon as these conditions were violated their legitimacy crumbled.[11] Since the Church of England was the epitome of persecution and intolerance, Tindal needed to provide some account of when, why and how the ecclesiastical establishment had deviated from the legitimate mean.

Tindal, as Hobbes before him, turned to an historical investigation to illustrate the passage and causes of corruption. He pointed to the history of heathen religion and argued that the priestly creation of mystery and ceremony had resulted in a malformed conception of religion. The High Church Anglican clergy were the inheritors of this manipulative tradition. He wrote: 'Nothing would expose Priestcraft more, than an Historical account, how, and upon what motives the clergy vary'd in their notions and practices concerning thy Lord's Supper: at first, how they made it a mystery in the Heathenish sense of that word and for Heathenish reasons that they might have the same power as the priests of the idols had.'[12]

While Hobbes and Tindal presented general historical argument as an indictment of priestly manipulation there was a vast *corpus* of knowledge, historical, anthropological and hermeneutical, which presented more specific assaults on clerical deviance and corrupt religion. Many of these learned investigations were conducted in terms of examinations of pre-Christian and heathen religions. Although many writers denied their researches intended any covert assault upon the true religion, hostile implications were often very apparent. By analogy an indictment of heathenism insinuated against the status of all religion. A popular vulgarization of this polemic, and one which will locate the parameters of this tradition, was Sir Robert Howard's *A History of Religion* (1694).

A POPULAR HISTORY OF RELIGION

Robert Howard, dramatist, brother-in-law to Dryden, staunch Whig and Privy Councillor was described by John Evelyn as, 'a gentleman pretending to all manner of Arts and Sciences'.[13] In the *History of Religion* (1694) he exhibited both his wide variety of reading and his inherent distaste for

---

[10] 'All things relating to Religion are either Means or ends; the last as carrying real worth with'em, are to be embraced on their own Account: but the first as having no such Excellency are obligatory for the sake of the last only; and consequently are to be continued or chang'd, as serves best to promote these Ends for which they were instituted' (Tindal, *Rights*, 122, 80).

[11] *Ibid.*, 123, 84.   [12] *Ibid.*, 43, 98, 101.   [13] J. Evelyn, *Diary*, II, 215.

priestcraft. The original subtitle of the work, 'The History of Religion, as it has been abused by Priestcraft' indicated his anticlericalism.[14] The premise of the work was that while all societies had some form of religious institution (it was this that distinguished man from beast) in many cases a variety of folly had been substituted for a correct pattern of theology.[15] Howard suggested that religion (almost from the beginning) had been corrupted by priestly artifice, mystery and metaphysical obscurity.[16] This was illustrated by a series of historical case studies. Arguing for a euhemeristic interpretation of the origin of religion (that is that the heathen gods were originally deified men) Howard presented the reader with a collection of pagan examples of *penates* or 'household gods'. The pagan priests had fabricated gods to serve their own purposes. The point was extended into a Christian context by Howard's repeated parallel of pagan worship with Catholic equivalents. The pagan Hades was the Catholic purgatory, heathen demonology was the pattern for Christian worship of saints, and gentile sacrifices were a model for Christian practice.[17] Priests of all types had employed the two instruments of 'mystery' and 'persecution' to establish their false dominion. Drawing a comparison between contemporary practice and the Egyptian temple of Isis and the god of silence, Harpocrates, Howard followed Grotius in insisting that theological mystery was the essential 'art' of deviant religion.[18] The *History of Religion* argued for the continuity of heathen and Christian priestcraft.

Howard was insistent that his text was only directed at the modern paganism evident in the Roman Catholic Church. Both the work and its reception belie this claim.[19] Although reviling popish priests in particular, Howard made the general point that all priests tended to create doctrinal obscurity to ensure their own interpretative monopoly. The priesthood alone was to be the interpreter of the 'dark subtilties' of religion. This was a contemporary issue, he explained, 'the learned now a days have for their obscure writings, and dark gibberish even to keep the (prophane) vulgar from daring to use their own understandings about matters which they do see to be so perplex'd and intricate'.[20] The prime example was the doctrine of the Trinity. Francis Atterbury pounced upon these subversive implications in a sermon before Queen Mary at Whitehall, *The Scorner Incapable of True Wisdom* (1694). He rebutted Howard's 'pretended histories of religion' arguing that he was 'so possess'd with the notion of priestcraft, and pious frauds, as to apply it indifferently to all religions, and to everything in religion'.[21] Charles Leslie in his *Charge of Socinianism against Dr Tillotson*

[14] R. Howard, *A Twofold Vindication of the Late Archbishop of Canterbury and the Author of the History of Religion* (1696), 27.
[15] R. Howard, *History of Religion* (1694), 1–2.   [16] *Ibid.*, Preface, iv; text, 22, 43.
[17] *Ibid.*, 52, 28–9, 35–6.
[18] *Ibid.*, 53–4, 56.   [19] *Ibid.*, Preface, vii.   [20] *Ibid.*, 80, Preface, xii–xiii.
[21] F. Atterbury, *The Scorner Incapable of True Wisdom* (1694), 10, 16.

Considered (1695) echoed this complaint, 'he ridicules all reveal'd religion, and turns it into what he calls priestcraft'. According to Leslie, Howard implicated not only popish doctrines like transubstantiation but also true doctrine like 'the Trinity, Incarnation, Divinity, and Sacrifice of Christ'. Importantly, Leslie suggested that Howard had plagiarized his arguments from the infidel Charles Blount who, in his Great is Diana (1680), had ridiculed the Christian priesthood under the 'cobweb veil' of the heathen priests. In his account of the original of sacrifices and idolatry Howard followed Blount.[22] Leslie noted that both men reduced religious action to the level of 'inward repentance' and morality.

Although Howard had reviled contemporary Christianity in his History of Religion he did not deny the value of religious experience but prescribed a model for reformation. Citing with approval the example of Archbishop Tillotson, he argued that Christ had established 'a religion which consults not only the eternal salvation of mens souls; but their temporal peace and security, their comfort and happiness in this world'. Howard proposed a theology of practice rather than proposition. The nature of religion necessarily linked it to 'moral righteousness' and could be resolved into the social injunction to do 'as we would be done by'.[23] In his Twofold Vindication (1696) Howard re-emphasized these points. His concern was to promote the 'moral religion' and the 'moral Gospel' of Christ. Morality and revelation were much the same thing, simply 'diverse names, under which the same things are denoted'. Christianity was a 'perfect system of all the laws of nature'. With the corruption of the Mosaic law Christ had been sent to restore the 'old moral religion'.[24] Importantly in this defence Howard acknowledged some of the works which had formed the foundations of his own. Charles Blount was an influence, although Howard pointed out that he hoped his own research was presented in a more temperate and respectable manner. The other named text was John Spencer's De Legibus Hebraeorum (1685), a massive work of erudition comparing pagan and Judaic ritual. Spencer's work was employed by Howard to argue that sacrifices were no part of divine religion, 'the true religion which is acceptable to God on its own account dwells in the mind, exerts itself in praises of, and prayers to God, in acts of temperance, justice, and mercy, this needs not multitudes of pompous rites to recommend it'.[25]

Howard's work is important not as original research but because it acts as a neat summary of previous polemic and erudition. Without being directly

---

[22] Leslie, Charge of Socinianism, 'A Supplement', in Theological Works, 635–8. Note that Leslie pointed out that there was some discrepancy in the work of the two infidels, in particular over whether the priesthood or civil tyranny was the ultimate cause of idolatry. See Blount, Great is Diana, 7, and Howard, History of Religion, 6.

[23] Ibid., xx–xxii, 64, 102.   [24] Howard, Twofold Vindication, 159, 162–4.

[25] Ibid., 113–19, 122, 122–4.

plagiaristic it relies heavily on an extensive *corpus* of prior investigation of which Blount's *Great is Diana* and Spencer's *De Legibus Hebraeorum* are notable examples. It is to this bulk of infidel scholarship which we will now turn.

HEATHEN RELIGION AND PRIESTCRAFT: HERBERT TO TOLAND

Lord Edward Herbert of Cherbury (1583–1648) and his *De Religione Gentilium* (published posthumously by Isaac Vossius at Amsterdam in 1663) are of particular importance in the development of this deistical history of religion. A second Latin edition of this work was published in 1700, and an English translation made by William Lewis in 1705. The *Antient Religion of the Gentiles* (1705) and the later *Dialogue between a Tutor and His Pupil* (1768) firmly identify Herbert's relationship with deism.[26] Herbert's *Antient Religion of the Gentiles* was premised upon the epistemological assertions of his two earlier works *De Veritate* (Paris, 1624) and *De Religione Laici* (1645). In both these works Herbert had evolved and expanded his idea of five fundamental and common notions which contained the natural premises of religion. These were the perception of a supreme God, the existence of rewards and punishments in a future estate, the injunction to worship God by virtuous action, and the importance of repentance.[27] In the *Antient Religion* Herbert set out to examine the complicity of pagan religion with this universal scheme.

The crucial premise of the *Antient Religion* was Herbert's conception of a 'just' deity. A just God could take no pleasure in 'the eternal reprobation of those to whom he never afforded any means of salvation'. Thus even though

---

[26] On Herbert, see D. P. Walker, *The Ancient Theology* (1972). It will be implicit in my argument that Walker's thesis that Herbert was an espouser of an ancient astral worship is misguided: to counter this argument I would suggest Herbert's anticlericalism is a much more fruitful tradition to explore. See also B. Willey, *The Seventeenth-Century Background* (1979), 111–23; C. J. Webb, *Studies in the History of Natural Theology* (Oxford, 1915), 344–59; R. Bedford, *The Defence of Truth* (Manchester, 1979), 258–9, has a useful discussion about whether Herbert is to be considered a man of the Renaissance or of eighteenth-century deism; note that Bedford (178–9) rejects Walker's astral thesis, but overemphasizes the epistemological, rather than anticlerical, polemics of Herbert's work. See H. R. Hutcheson (ed.), *Lord Herbert of Cherbury's De Religione Laici* (Yale, 1944); D. A. Paulin 'Herbert of Cherbury and the Deists', *The Expository Times* 94 (April 1983). Note that the traditional argument that Herbert was the founding father of deism is found in John Leland's *A View of the Principle Deistical Writers* (1764). See D. A. Paulin, *Attitudes to Other Religions* (Manchester, 1984), which argues this point. Paulin does not, however, stress the anticlerical content and intention of Herbert's work. See also E. J. Sharpe, *Comparative Religion: A History* (1975), especially 2–5 and 15–20; and L. Salvatorelli, 'From Locke to Reitzenstein: The Historical Investigation of the Origins of Christianity', *The Harvard Theological Review* 22 (1929); A. J. Kuhn 'English Deism, and the Development of Romantic Mythological Syncretism', *PMLA* 71 (1956).

[27] Herbert *Antient Religion* 3.

the pagans had no specific divine revelation, 'universal divine providence' implied that they must have had some natural access to true religion.[28] Traditional Christian thought had treated all heathen religion as an epitome of diabolical superstition, idolatry and irreligion. Herbert, with a typical Erasmian optimism, argued that all non Judaeo-Christian societies had some form of true religious worship because human nature had an innate tendency to worship the supreme deity without the commodious aid of revelation. Although admitting that paganism had become corrupt Herbert wondered whether 'amongst those heaps of Ethical Superstitions, a thread of truth might be found'. By historical investigation he set out to examine the origins of religion. This was ultimately to be located in the yearning of man's noble mind to find a state of eternal repose, 'for God inspiring all men with a desire of an eternal and more happy state, he tacitly discovered himself, who is eternal life, and perfectly happy'. This natural recognition of the deity was translated into an adoration of the stars which in their constancy and order resembled the permanence of the supreme god.[29] This 'Deus Optimus Maximus' was identified with the Christian God. From this minimalistic premise Herbert displayed the multiplicity of pagan adoration of the stars, planets and lesser deities. In order to defend the merits of heathen religion Herbert presented the distinction between *cultus symbolicus* and *cultus proprius* borrowed from Gerard Vossius' magisterial *De Origine ac Progressu Idololatriae* (Amsterdam, 1641) a work which provided the *Antient Religion* with a vital and comprehensive source account of heathen religious worship.[30] Herbert explained the distinction between a proper and symbolic worship; 'Proper worship is, the adoration of the Supreme God, the Sun, the Moon, Heaven, or the whole world, particularly and respectively in themselves: Symbolical, is the worshipping the Supreme God in the Sun, Heaven, or World.'[31] Proper worship was due to God alone. Symbolical worship which epitomized the heathen practice was acceptable because *au fond* it was a pious adoration of the true God. For example, Herbert pointed out that pagan worship of the sun was valuable because it terminated in the proper worship of God: the sun was appreciated as 'that noble emblem of the Supreme God'.[32]

Herbert's appraisal of the history of pagan religion did not simply consist

[28] *Ibid.*, 5–6.   [29] *Ibid.*, 3, 8, 9, 79.

[30] Vossius' work is cited throughout Herbert's work on at least forty-two occasions, in places *in extenso*. It is important to note that Cherbury manipulated Vossius' distinction. It had been the Dutch scholar's argument that the pagans had worshipped the stars as *cultus proprius* not *cultus symbolicus*. Cherbury's insistence on the symbolic nature of astral worship rather undermines Walker's point about his supposedly hermetic religion. On Vossius, see J. N. Wickenden, 'Early Modern Historiography as Illustrated by the work of G. J. Vossius 1577–1649' (2 volumes, unpublished Ph.D., Cambridge, 1963), and C. S. M. Rademaker, *The Life and Works of Gerardus Joannes Vossius 1577–1649* (Assen, 1981).

[31] Herbert *Antient Religion*, 295.   [32] *Ibid.*, 44.

of straightforward commendation. In Chapter 16 'A censure of the religion of the Heathens and the occasion of it' he expanded on a theme that runs throughout the whole work: that superstition and idolatry had often corrupted true worship due to the ambitious manipulations of the priesthood. Religious ceremony was necessary only to 'lay a more strict obligation on men, to do that which they were oblig'd before to do voluntarily'. The priesthood rather than corroborate these natural instincts did 'debilitate and enervate these truths'.[33] The 'crafty priests' created a plurality of divinities, ceremonies and mysteries to further their own power. By creating specious theologies and systems of sacrifice, expiation and penance, the priesthood established a monopoly over religion. By deceitful tricks and forgery of revelation the heathen priest imposed an implicit faith upon the laity to seduce them from true worship to a false sacerdotal alternative. The natural inclination to repentance was changed into a collection of 'dark rites and ceremonies' calculated to elevate the authority of the priest.[34] Ceremony and ritual was thus the product of priestcraft. The originally pure symbolic worship was corrupted by the figments of clerical imagination.[35] The implications of this historical argument were unorthodox. Herbert argued that religion in its original and uncorrupt form was both a natural and moral action which could be conducted without the mediating caste of an hierocratic order between man and God. Although religious ceremony could be employed to facilitate this natural worship the most rational and true form was to be found in a 'pure mind and a Holy life'. The sound parts of heathen religion, their 'virtue, faith, hope and love', should be commended by all Christians for, 'the Antients agree with us, who allow no means of salvation can benefit or advantage us without the mind, virtue, piety and faith'.[36] This description of the origins and decline of heathen religion, and the radical implications of this model were adapted and adopted by many later infidel writers but primarily by Charles Blount (1654–93), a professed disciple.

Blount is a much vilified and underestimated theorist. Rather than lay emphasis upon his plagiarism, his poor style and unoriginality, it would be more fruitful to consider his work as crucial polemics in the formation and dissemination of Enlightenment perceptions of religion. Throughout the entire corpus of his published works, from the *Anima Mundi* (1679) to the *Oracles of Reason* (1693), Blount intentionally publicized the widest variety of unorthodox thinkers ranging from ancient texts (men like Cicero, Seneca and Tacitus), through the Renaissance (Vanini, Cardan and Pomponazzi), to the atheistical moderns (Hobbes and Spinoza). It is thus as a publicist rather than a plagiarist that Blount should be appreciated, and in this guise as a

33 *Ibid.*, 366–8.   34 *Ibid.*, 274–82, 282–90, 316–20.   35 *Ibid.*, 12–16, 31, 138.
36 *Ibid.*, 11, 299, 316–18.

wellspring of the Enlightenment. Blount's transmission of Herbert's thought was crucial to this enterprise.[37] Blount's indebtedness to Herbert is *in tandem* both easy to recognize and difficult to assess. He openly acknowledged his admiration for Herbert's notions. In his *Religio Laici* (1683), an adapted and partially translated version of Herbert's *De Religione Laici* (1645) Blount noted that he often 'made use of, and grounded the chief of my discourse upon his five Catholick or Universal principles'.[38] Certainly in his 'Summary Account of the Deists Religion' and 'Of Natural Religion', both short essays in the *Oracles of Reason* (1693), Blount openly referred to Herbert's five notions, the historical universality of natural religion, and the proscription of images, sacrifices and priestly mediators from the practice of true religion, which was identified with morality and the rule of right reason rather than priestly mystery. Blount stressed the anticlerical tenor of Herbert's work. In *Religio Laici* (1683), following Herbert's third notion that, 'vertue, goodness, and piety, accompanied with faith in, and love to God, are the best ways of worshipping him' Blount rejected all 'rites, mysteries and sacras'.[39] Supplementary testimony to Blount's borrowings from Herbert has been traditionally adduced in the suggestion that a Herbert manuscript (which was published in Herbert's name as *A Dialogue between a Tutor and His Pupil* in 1768) was used by Blount in his footnoted edition of Philostratus' *Life of Apollonius Tyaneus* (1680). Pierre Bayle was the first to make the claim in his entry on Apollonius in the *General and Historical Dictionary*, and this assertion has become a scholarly commonplace. H. R. Hutcheson in his edition of Herbert's *De Religione Laici* has been the most forceful and recent proponent of this thesis.[40] It is apparent from Hutcheson's language that he held a certain distaste for both Blount's character and his work. He

[37] Blount's dissemination of Renaissance anticlericalism and the English reception of the thought of such men as Vanini and Pomponazzi is understudied. For general accounts, see P. O. Kristeller, 'The Myth of Renaissance Atheism and French Freethought', *Journal of the History of Philosophy* 6 (1968); C. B. Schmitt, 'Renaissance Averroism Studied through the Venetian editions of Aristotle-Averroes', *Atti Dei Convegni Lincei* 40 (1979), 121–42; E. Cassirer, P. O. Kristeller and J. H. Randall (eds.), *The Renaissance Philosophy of Man* (Chicago, 1948); W. B. Fleischmann, *Lucretius and English Literature 1580–1740* (Paris, 1964); J. Owens, *Sceptics of the Italian Renaissance* (New York, 1893); P. O. Kristeller, *Eight Philosophers of the Italian Renaissance* (California, 1964), chapter 5 on Pomponazzi; Anon. *The Life of Lucilio Vanini ... with an Abstract of His Writings* (1730). See J. A. Redwood, 'Charles Blount, Deism, and English Freethought', *JHI* (1976), and *Reason, Ridicule, and Religion* (1979); Mysticus, *Charles Blount, gent: His Life and Opinions* (1917); U. Bonante, *Charles Blount: Libertismo e Deismo nel Seicento Inglese* (Florence, 1972); P. Villey, 'L'Influence de Montaigne sur Charles Blount et sur les deistes anglaises', *Revue du Seizième Siècle* 1 (1913).
[38] Blount, *Religio Laici* (1683), Epistle Dedicatory, Sig. A8v–A9r.   [39] *Ibid.*, 48, 52–4.
[40] H. R. Hutcheson (ed.), *Lord Herbert of Cherbury's De Religione Laici* (Yale, 1944), 48, 71–4. Note that Bedford, *Defence of Truth*, 189, points out that the earlier Italian scholar Rossi also doubted the authenticity of Herbert's authorship of the *Dialogue*.

commented that 'Blount has received altogether too much credit from the historians of deism'. On the charges of plagiarism he noted 'that such charges acquire a definiteness which is at first startling and soon monotonous'. Blount's 'thefts' from Herbert are established with both 'certainty and boredom'. This portrayal is opposite to that presented in the *Biographia Britannicae* which insisted that Blount was a man of 'wit, learning, and zeal'. Although Hutcheson allows for the possibility that Blount may have been the author of the *Dialogue between a Tutor and his Pupil* (1768), he is firmly convinced by a textual comparison of Blount's *Life of Apollonius* (1680) and the *Oracles of Reason* (1693) with the *Dialogue* not only that Blount borrowed from this source, but that the dialogue was the fruit of Herbert's pen.

There is no direct material evidence to suggest a definitive attribution of the authorship of the *Dialogue* to either Blount or Herbert. It is certain that the work was constructed within a Herbertian framework of the five common notions of natural religion.[41] The Tutor and the Pupil set out to discuss the varying status of different revelations in terms of a distinction between the 'serious part' of religion depending on 'notions written in our Souls' and 'the religious manners, forms, and rites ... depending ... on tradition, apparition, pretended revelation, mysteries and the like, which grew up in latter times, and for the most part were but the inventions of priests'.[42] The text echoes Herbert's insistence that, 'before religion (i.e.) rites, ceremonies, pretended revelations and the like were invented, there was no worship of God but in a rational way'. The prescriptive model was the ancient unsacerdotal pattern. The *Dialogue* is certainly indebted to Herbert's *Antient Religion*: apart from general argument there are passages directly transcribed from the earlier work, for example the discussion of the priestly manipulation of repentance.[43] Even with the acknowledgement that the *Dialogue* was composed with Herbert's *Antient Religion* as a source, and accepting that there are some direct (although scattered and disordered) textual links between Blount's work and the dialogue, my suggestion is that there are textual references and arguments in the later work which simply were not available to Herbert. These references can be attributed to Blount's eclectic anticlericalism.

The structure of the *Dialogue* is between a Tutor and a Pupil. The former is more learned and restrained (Blount's characterization of Herbert's thought), while the latter is hot-headed and vehement in his indictment of the priesthood, almost always presenting the most extreme anticlerical implications of the Tutor's theses (Blount's self-characterization). The general theme of the work is an extended history of how the five common notions of

---

[41] *A Dialogue*, 7–8.   [42] *Ibid.*, 27.
[43] *Ibid.*, 27, 42, 53, 73; 187–8 follows Herbert, *Antient Religion*, 316–20.

natural religion became corrupted by priestcraft. For each topic under consideration a wide variety of illustration is mustered: this eclecticism smacks rather of Blount's digressive style, than the more ponderous prose of Herbert. Unlike Herbert's *Antient Religion* the hostility of the *Dialogue* against the clerical order is extended from a purely pagan context into an explicit condemnation of the 'modern priests'.[44] The dialogue also contains a considerable body of biblical criticism that was simply unavailable to Herbert. For example, the discussion of the Mosaic account of the Creation, which the *Dialogue* argued that Judaic legislator had recounted from ancient tradition.[45] More importantly the dialogue notes that Moses' writings were destroyed during the Babylonian captivity and that the Pentateuch had been retranscribed from memory by the prophet Esdras. This hermeneutic claim had been first made by Isaac La Peyrère and Spinoza in publications after Herbert's death.[46]

The *Dialogue* contains extensive reference to the historical pattern of Islam: it appears that the text borrows directly from Henry Stubbe's manuscript account of Mahomet when discussing the politic proscription of eating swine's flesh in order to prevent leprosy. Once again this argument would have been unavailable to Herbert (Stubbe's text was written *c.* 1671) while we know that Blount copied passages of the manuscript to send to Rochester which were also published in the *Oracles of Reason*.[47] There is yet further evidence that the bulk of the *Dialogue* was composed after Herbert's death. The *Dialogue* contains extensive discussion of pagan oracles which could most likely have been drawn from Bernard Fontenelle's *History of Oracles* (1688). The text echoes precisely Fontenelle's argument which suggested the persistence of oracles three hundred years after Christ, and that the Primitive Church Fathers employed 'officious lies' and oracular prophecy to facilitate the reception of Christ among the pagans.[48] The last piece of evidence against Herbert's authorship is the references to the gentile origins of the Jewish dispensation contained in the *Dialogue*. In the *Antient Religion* Herbert had dismissed the issue. He wrote, 'nor will it be much material, if according to ancient writers, they had many of their religious rites from the Egyptians'. The *Dialogue* is replete with references asserting the Egyptian origins of the Mosaic law. Abraham and Moses had learned their religious

---

[44] *A Dialogue*, 99–100, 102.

[45] *A Dialogue*, 17–18. Note that the first extended presentation of this thesis was by Thomas Burnet in his *Archaeologiae Philosophicae*, a text which Blount translated and defended in his *Oracles of Reason* (1693).

[46] See R. H. Popkin, *Isaac La Peyrère 1576–1676* (Brill, 1987).

[47] *A Dialogue*, 68, 70; see H. Stubbe, *An Account of Mahomet*, 76, 153–5, 167–9. Note that this passage was also employed by Boulainvilliers in his *Life of Mahomet* (1731), and that the *Biographia Britannicae* notes Blount's design, 'of writing the life of Mohammed, the Turkish Prophet'.

[48] *A Dialogue*, 130–4.

opinions in Egypt. Christ himself had travelled to the East in search of knowledge. The general point was that the Mosaic institution was raised upon gentile and Egyptian foundations. From this premise the author insisted that Judaic obligations continued in force during the early years of Christianity, and that many 'modern Christians' held ceremonial practices in common with the ancient Jews and Egyptians.[49] Although there may have been classical sources from which Herbert might have derived such arguments it seems that Blount is the more likely candidate for the authorship of these passages. The evidence is circumstantial but twofold. The argument of the *Dialogue* is a condensed version of the grand thesis proposed by John Spencer in his *De Legibus Hebraeorum* (1685): no one before this work had presented such a convincing case for the Egyptian origins of Jewish ritual. Blount certainly read this work, and himself discussed the issue in print. In a letter to 'Major A' printed in the *Oracles of Reason* Blount presented Moses as a man learned in Egyptian religion and philosophy. Tutored in Eastern arcana, 'Moses and the Jews took diverse of their customs from the Egyptians; as for instance, their circumcision'. Again following Spencer (and perhaps John Aubrey) Blount asserted that the 'ancient Jews, and Modern Christians, have many rites and ceremonies common with the Gentiles'.[50]

This evidence redresses the authorship of the *Dialogue* in favour of Blount. The *Dialogue* is still testimony to Blount's indebtedness to Herbert's work: but it betrays also Blount's radicalization of Herbert's originally eirenic intentions. Blount extended Herbert's original thesis on the value of heathenism into a full blooded indictment of established religion. This radical anticlericalism was evident in Blount's own works *Anima Mundi* (1679) and *Great is Diana* (1680). The premise of both these works was that true religion consisted of rational unpriestly worship and that theological and ceremonial superstructures were usually unnecessary and frequently corrupt. In *Anima Mundi; or an historical Narration of the Opinion of the Ancients concerning Mans Soul after this life* (1679) Blount conducted an historical examination of the generation and function of the idea of the soul's immortality. Blount rather feebly denied that his work held any implications for Christian doctrine. The idea of a future state was a natural inclination, 'implanted in everyman's heart'. From this innate premise many doctrines had been created by philosophers and priests. Some argued that the soul was separate from the body, others that they were in necessary unity. Some suggested upon death the soul returned to the soul of the world, others that it perished with the body.[51] Blount insisted that many, both priests and

---

[49] Herbert, *Antient Religion*, 23–4; *A Dialogue*, 15, 29, 67–8, 247–8.
[50] Blount, *Oracles of Reason*, 133–5; also Blount, *Great is Diana*, 38–9, on Spencer's accommodation thesis. See also J. Aubrey, 'Remaines of Gentilisme and Judaisme' in *Three Prose Works*, 131–309.
[51] Blount, *Anima Mundi*, 11, 14, 17–37.

legislators, had played upon this belief and man's natural fear of the unknown to create systems of fable to keep the vulgar in social order. For example the Islamic idea of paradise had been constructed to induce the Arabs to the new religion.[52] Blount's polemical purpose became more evident when he dealt with Seneca and Pomponazzi who had denied any future state but still proposed a life of virtue. Such men maintained the existence of a supreme God, and a belief in providence in earthly affairs if not in an afterlife.[53] Men could lead religious lives without a belief in the immortal soul, although in many cases such a doctrine even if not true could induce men to religious virtue. The same point was reiterated in a letter published in the *Oracles of Reason* 'To Strephon concerning the Immortal Soul'. The letter was an extended commentary upon Blount's favourite Senecan dictum 'Post mortem nihil est, ipsaque mors nihil'. Blount argued here in favour of the death of the soul citing both classical authors like Pliny and scriptural passages. The idea of an immortal soul could only be defended in heuristic terms: some men could follow the pattern of true religion unaided, most needed to be encouraged. Following Plato and Averroes, Blount justified the opinion as a necessary fiction, from the 'absolute necessity and convenience that it should be so'.[54]

In *Great is Diana of the Ephesians* (1680) Blount expanded his historical investigation into a general consideration of the origins and causes of idolatry, in particular of religious sacrifices. While acknowledging that the only true form of sacrifice was 'sit pura mente colendus: a pure undefiled spirit' Blount narrated the priestly corruption of this original. Relying upon an euhemeristic interpretation Blount argued that worship and sacrifice stemmed from the adoration of dead heroes and princes. Ninus had worshipped Nimrod as 'Bel' or 'Belus', that is God. The initial innocent veneration for a prince and his posterity developed with the collaboration of the civil and spiritual estates into a fabricated theology. As these theologies expanded so did the power and authority of the priesthood. Blount commented, 'the original of sacrifices, seems to be as ancient as religion itself; for no sooner had man found out there was a God, but a priest stept up and said, that this God had taught them in what manner he should be worshipped'.[55] The priesthood, exploiting the innate insecurity and fear of humanity, constructed a suitable system of superstition to enthral the vulgar. By ritual and prayer, setting these ceremonies in dark thick groves, the spirit of devotion was naturalized into the people.[56]

Blount's history of religion was, as we have seen, ultimately indebted to Herbert's arguments: this indebtedness was not slavish. Through Blount's

---

[52] *Ibid.*, 36–7, 46–50, 64, 85.   [53] *Ibid.*, 94, 97–9, 100, 104, 105–9.
[54] Blount, *Oracles of Reason*, 118, 121, 124–6.
[55] Blount, *Great is Diana*, 6, 14.   [56] *Ibid.*, 41ff.

reworking of Herbert's research the history of pagan religion became a far more radical tool directed against the Christian priesthood. While the tenor of Herbert's *Antient Religion* was to defend the possibility of heathen virtue, and only by implication to indict the priesthood, Blount's work is directed specifically at the corruptions of the seventeenth-century Christian priests. Blount's intention was not only to defend the merits of pagan virtue but to recommend the pattern of virtue as a replacement for idolatry. This same radical redefinition of religion was displayed in the work of John Toland.

Toland's most important contribution was his *Letters to Serena* (1704) where he discussed both the origins of idolatry, and the history of the soul's immortality. Toland was indebted to both Herbert and Blount: but this was not mere plagiarism. Although Toland borrowed phrases, examples, and illustrations from the two earlier thinkers his writings have an eloquence and erudition that is entirely original. While in Blount's work it is often difficult to discern the author's own beliefs in the deliberate morass of different and conflicting positions presented, in Toland's work his opinion is unequivocally clear.

In the 'History of the Souls Immortality among the Heathens' Toland made explicit Blount's theme of treating the soul as 'an opinion' that 'had a beginning at a certain time, or from a certain author'. Toland gave a brief résumé of the history of Greek materialism. Following Aristotle, he argued that the Greeks originally did not believe in any 'principle or actuating spirit in the Universe itself . . . but explain'd all the phænomena of nature by matter and local motion, levity and gravity, or the like'. For Thales, Anaximander and Anaximenes the universe was infinite and matter eternal. It was Anaxagoras who was the first philosopher among the Greeks to determine the separate idea of 'mind' which was the 'mover and disposer of matter'. From this premise Phercydes and his disciple Pythagoras argued for the immortality of human souls, a doctrine which was greedily embraced by Plato and his followers.[57] Toland followed this unorthodoxy with an even more irreligious claim: Anaxagoras 'borrow'd' his invention from earlier Egyptian tradition. Citing Macrobius and Diodorus Siculus, Toland argued that ancient Egypt was the 'mother of all sciences'. Denying the traditional thesis that all Egyptian learning was gained from the Patriarch Abraham, Toland insisted that the doctrine originated in the theologies of Persian magi and Egyptian priests. It was from this source that Moses gained his knowledge, and similar resonances could be found in ancient British druidical tradition.[58]

---

[57] Toland, *Letters to Serena*, 21–3, 28–9.
[58] *Ibid.*, 29–30, 33–8, 40, 42–3. Note that in referring to the druidical tradition Toland was borrowing directly from Blount's *Great is Diana*, 10–12. It is important to note that Toland was to conduct his own original researches into the history of the druids.

The Egyptians had framed their opinions from funeral rites and 'their historical method of preserving the memory of deserving persons'. Following Diodorus Siculus, Toland displayed the euhemeristic account of religion: from the commemoration of the dead the idea of an afterlife, the Elysian fields and the reward of good and punishment of evil was evolved.[59] The originally pure system of commemoration was perverted into a corrupt theology by priestly manipulation of man's natural desire 'to continue their existence beyond the grave'. Such notions soon became part of 'all men's education'. Wise legislators had recognized the value of the doctrine as a means of social discipline, as Timus Locrus noted, 'we keep the minds of men in order by false reasons, if they will not be governed by true ones'. As Blount did, so too did Toland accept the immortality of the soul as a 'beneficial or convenient' device. Citing both Seneca and Pliny (as Blount had done) Toland argued that tales of hell and an afterlife might only be 'senseless tales and empty words', but if used correctly were valuable.[60]

In the 'Origin of Idolatry' Toland, as Blount and Herbert had done, turned to a more general account of superstition and the corruption of religion. This letter followed Herbert's *Antient Religion* in many details, although this was combined with material from the classical writers on religion such as Cicero's *De Natura Deorum*, Plutarch on superstition, and Diodurus Siculus' histories.[61] Unlike Herbert, Toland directed his criticism at all priests, both ancient and modern. He applauded the euhemeristic explanation of the origins of religion, and accepted Herbert's symbolical interpretation of the ancient theologies but reserved the full force of his venom to indict the corrupt priesthood who had perverted this practice into useless superstition. While legislators attempted to restrain the barbarities of the populace, the priest duped their reason to establish a spiritual tyranny which became the foundation for civil tyranny. The modern example of the papacy and the idea of a *de jure divino* monarchy was testimony to the continuity of 'ancient and modern Heathenism'.[62] The Christian priesthood followed the same corrupt practices of antiquity: for example the 'new idolatry of the Christians', the worship of saints, was grounded upon the same principles as the heathen worship of the dead.

Underlying this polemic was the distinction between the injunctions of the law of nature and 'all positive institutions', and a model of historical change

---

[59] Toland, *Letters to Serena*, 45–52, 95.
[60] *Ibid.*, 53, 55, 58, 60, 67. Note that Toland uses Blount's favourite passages from Seneca ('Post mortem nihil est, ipsaque mors nihil') and Pliny (*Letters to Serena*, 63–6 is the same passage of Pliny as Blount, *Oracles of Reason*, 121–3).
[61] On Toland's borrowing from Herbert are *Letters to Serena*, 78ff. (on Egyptian Astrology), 93ff. (on the Philosophical worship of the four elements), 109ff. (on the 'Dii majorem gentilium, Dii Minorum gentilium').
[62] Toland, *Letters to Serena*, 84, 86, 91–2, 98–102, 123, 127.

in which an originally pristine theology is corrupted, and then renovated by politic and learned legislators. As with the earlier thinkers true worship was identified with the practice of virtue and the rule of right reason and found in the historical example of the *prisca theologia* of Egyptian religion. As Toland explained: 'The most ancient Egyptians, Persians, and Romans, the first Patriarchs of the Hebrews with several other Nations and sects, had no sacred images or Statues, no peculiar places or costly fashions of worship; the plain easiness of their religion being the most agreeable to the simplicity of the divine nature.'[63] Toland's interest in the works of Giordano Bruno, proponent of the Egyptian *prisca theologia*, is particularly interesting.

It has been an historical commonplace that John Toland was deeply involved in the propagation, translation and circulation of many subversive manuscripts.[64] One of his most accomplished clandestine achievements was the dissemination of an account of the life and works of Giordano Bruno, the late-sixteenth century magus, philosopher and religious reformer. In 1698 Toland purchased a number of Bruno's works from the library of Francis Bernard: bound with copies of *De La Causa, Principo et Uno*, and *Le Cena de la Cenari* was a copy of Bruno's *Spaccio della Bestia Trionfante* (London, 1584).[65] It is commonly accepted that Toland circulated covert manuscript works on Bruno's life and thought, both in England and on the Continent, such as the *Life of Bruno*, a translation of Bruno's *Asse* and *Bruno's Sermon*.[66]

I wish to focus upon Toland's dealings with the *Spaccio* in particular. Toland certainly possessed a copy of this work.[67] This same copy may have been presented to the Electress Sophia of Hanover.[68] Toland was publicly associated with the publication of the translated edition in 1713.[69] The

---

[63] Toland, *Letters to Serena*, 19, 71; see Herbert, *Antient Religion*, 314, 'the most ancient temples amongst the Egyptians, were without Statues or images'.

[64] See BL Add. 4295, folio 43:

> Manuscripts of Mine abroad – 'Horroke ***. Life of Jordanus Bruno / Mr Laney Revelation no Rule / Mr Robinson Piece of Ye Roman Education / Mr Hewet History of the Canon [this entry is crossed out – presumably the work had been returned] / Mr(s) Lane A Letter about Error / Mr Wrottesley A piece of Dr Chamberlain's / Mr Hewet Revelation No Rule / Lord Castleton The Cloud & Pillar [crossed out] / Mr Jonvine Toland's perigrinans / Mr Hewet Translation of Bruno's Assera Dialogues / Mr Lord The Creed no Apostolick / My Lord Molesworth Specimen of Ye History of Ye Druids / Mr Hewet Specimen of Ye History of Ye Druids / Ld Castleton Shaftesbury's Letters [crossed out] / Lady Carmine Part of Ye History of Ye Druids [crossed out] / Rd Aylmer Bruno Sermon [crossed out].

[65] See Jacob, *Newtonians*, 228; and BL Add. 12062, 12063.

[66] See Jacob, *Newtonians*, 246; BL Add. 4295 f. 43; F. H. Heinemann, 'Prolegomena to a Toland Bibliography' in *Notes and Queries* 185 (1943), 184.

[67] It may have been Elizabeth I's own copy. See Daniel, *Toland*, 3, 10.

[68] See Jacob, *Newtonians*, 231.

[69] See Jacob, *Newtonians*, 245; A. D. Imerti (ed.), *The Expulsion of the Triumphant Beast* (Rutgers, 1964), 22.

authorship of this translation is obscure: the British Museum catalogue attributes the translation to one William Morehead, 'half brother of John Toland'. Margaret Jacob supports this suggestion, and argues that the translation was originally undertaken for the private use of the Freethinker and colleague of Toland, Anthony Collins.[70] Toland has been accused of stealing this manuscript from Collin's library.[71] With our knowledge of Toland's penchant for purloining manuscripts, and his mischievous ability to claim other people's original scholarship for his own, it might seem likely that Morehead was indeed the translator. I should like to present evidence that may redress the balance in Toland's favour: it certainly suggests his deep involvement in the publication of the *Spaccio*. The evidence is an undated letter 'To Mr ***'. The work was probably written between 1705 and 1708, and was printed in both posthumous collections of Toland's work and correspondence. Despite its availability the piece, rather curiously, has gone unnoticed.[72] The opening sentence of the letter is the telling point in favour of Toland's role as translator. Toland argued that the piece that has so excited 'Dr Morelli' was no contrivance of his own, but that he was the 'Master' of it.[73] This has two implications: first that Toland does acknowl-

---

[70] Jacob, *Newtonians*, 245; see D. W. Singer, *Bruno, His Life* (New York, 1950), 192n. There is a large corpus of Italian literature on Toland and in particular on his relationship with Bruno. The primary Italian work is the indispensible bibliography by Carabelli, but see also G. Aquilecchia, 'Schedu Bruniana: la traduzione 'Tolandiana' dello Spaccio' in *Gionarle Storico della Letteratura Italiano*, 152 (1975); G. Carabelli (ed.), 'John Toland e G. W. Leibnitz: otto lettere', *Rivista Critica di Storia della Filosophia* 29 (1974); and C. Giuntini, 'Toland e Bruno: ermetismo rivoluzionario', *Rivista di Filosofia* 66 (1975). Carabelli *Tolandiana* (1975), 170–1 presents the evidence for William Morehead (1637–92) as translator. There are two arguments against Morehead. The first is that from the only biographical details we have of any William Morehead (in the *DNB*) he seems an unlikely character even to have associated with Anthony Collins, or to have translated such a subversive work. The second argument is that the ascription of Morehead's authorship comes from the testimony of a bookseller, Samuel Paterson (1728–1802), who makes the claim in a sale catalogue of 1750. Without further supporting testimony Paterson's account appears to be based on mere speculation.

[71] Worden, *Ludlow*, 24: see S. Paterson (ed.), *Bibliotheca Westiana* (1773), 44; flyleaf of James Martineau's copy of this translation in Manchester College, Oxford; R. Watt (ed.), *Bibliotheca Britannica* (4 volumes, Edinburgh, 1824), I, 162.

[72] See Toland, *Collections*, II, 376–81. Carabelli, the most assiduous bibliographer of Toland's works, makes no concrete reference to this letter, although he does to a close version of the piece in citing the publication of a Toland letter of 1710 in *A General Dictionary, Historical and Critical* (1735), III, 622–3; see the article on 'Brunus, Jordanus'. A version of the same is employed in F. H. Heinemann, 'John Toland and the Age of Enlightenment' (Oxford, 1949). Here Heinemann makes use of a 'Lettre de Mr Toland sur le Spaccio della Bestia Trionfante, Paris 1584' which was printed in *Nova Bibliotheca Lubencesis* VII (Lubucae, 1756), 158–62. This piece bears a close resemblance to the letter under consideration: although they share common passages they also diverge from each other in elements of composition.

[73] Biographical details of the mysterious Dr Morelli are sparse. R. H. Popkin has established that Morelli was a close friend of Spinoza's. It is clear that Morelli left Holland in the 1670s and moved in the libertine circle of St Evremond in England. That Toland knew Morelli is

edge his role in the production of the work, but that he does not attempt to claim it as an original composition. Secondly we can deduce that Dr Morelli thought the work was typical of Toland's work, so much so that he had accused him of deliberate fabrication. Although this evidence is somewhat speculative, I suggest that in combination with the rest of the letter it does point to Toland's authorship. The letter clearly indicates Toland's interest and knowledge of the genesis and composition of the *Spaccio*.

The bulk of the letter is a precis and synopsis of Bruno's original work. This condensed version could be the substance of the short dissertation that Toland sent to his colleagues on the Continent, such as Georg Leibnitz. He wrote to the latter: 'I confess something more particular ought to have been said concerning the *Spaccio*, which of a printed work, is I believe the rarest in the world but on the other hand it is not a secret to be communicated to everybody.'[74] The dissertation Toland sent to Leibnitz contained a 'most circumstantial account of the Book itself, and secondly a specimen of it, containing three articles out of forty eight'. It seems likely that this letter to Leibnitz was accompanied by a version of Toland's description of the *Spaccio*.

Toland's letter is a succinct description of the content and importance of Bruno's *Spaccio*. The work is presented as an extended dissertation upon the corruption of ancient religion, and of the need to reform it to the prescriptions of the 'intelligible, useful, necessary, and unalterable Law of Nature'. Bruno's work is presented as an injunction to replace vice with virtue, by reforming the symbolic meanings of astral worship. One obvious question which must be addressed is how far this description of the *Spaccio* is accurate. Bruno's work was written as part of a quest for moral reformation.[75] In place of vice, imposture and crime, truth, prudence and order must be established.[76] In the third dialogue Bruno explored the shape of true religious worship, defending unpopular Egyptian ritual as prescriptive.[77] The Egyptians ascended to a true worship of God 'through nature'; they worshipped 'Divinity' in natural objects, rather than the objects themselves

perhaps a significant influence upon the former's Spinozism. See J. Hayward (ed.), *The Letters of Saint Evremond* (1930) 322–4; R. H. Popkin, 'Serendipity at the Clark: Spinoza and the Prince of Condé', *The Clark Newsletter* 10 (1986); R. T. Gunther, *Early Science in Oxford* 14 (Oxford, 1945); Edward Llwyd to Mr John Lloyd (3 March 1691) on Morelli as an anatomist, at 135–6. Importantly the sale-catalogue of Morelli's library survives, *Bibliotheca Morelliana* (1715) (BL SC.292(7)).

[74] Toland, *Collections*, II, 395. The letter was probably composed after 1710.

[75] See Pierre Bayle in *Nova Bibliotheca Lubecensis*, II, 149. 'Ce livre de Bruno est une traite de morale bizarrement dirige: car on y expose la nature des vices et des vertues sous l'embleme des constellations celestes chasses du firmament pour faire place a de nouveaux astres, mais qui represent la verite, la bonte'; Bruno in Imerti (ed.), *The Expulsion*, 115; 'We must purify ourselves internally and externally', see also 74–89.

[76] See Imerti, *The Expulsion*, 139–45.   [77] *Ibid.*, 204, 236–48.

as divine.[78] Bruno insisted that modern theology was a corruption of this pantheistic original.[79] Throughout the *Spaccio* there is one persistent and simple theme: that religion must be employed to further morality and the temperant injunctions of nature. Bruno gestures to the legislator tradition of Numa, who employed religion to civilize the barbarian Romans. The corruptions of modern theology must be replaced by 'industry, military training, and military art, through which the Peace and authority of the Fatherland may be maintained, barbarians be fought, beaten and converted to civilised life and human society, and inhuman, porcine, savage and bestial cults, religions, sacrifices, and laws be annihiliated'.[80] Modern theology was nothing but 'useless and pernicious fable' which ought to be replaced by 'righteous simplicity and the moral Fable'.[81] Bruno in the *Spaccio* presented a version of the Egyption *prisca theologia* as his prescription for a civil theology.

Margaret Jacob has been the most recent commentator on Bruno's influence on Toland.[82] She argues that 'Bruno's thought remains the main source for the development of Toland's philosophy'. While not wishing to underestimate the value and integrity of Jacob's work, I suggest this is an overstated claim.[83] For example, Jacob argues that Bruno is the major influence upon Toland's most cogent work, *Letters to Serena* (1704); Toland himself ascribed the central influence and inspiration to Cicero's *De Legibus*.[84] The general tenor of Jacob's argument is that Bruno provided Toland with his conceptions of natural philosophy. The *Spaccio* informed Toland's notions of the constant motion of matter, the world and the infinite universe. Bruno is characterized as giving Toland a natural philosophy suited to the development of his pantheism.[85] My objection to this thesis is that Jacob has confined her assessment of Bruno's influence on Toland to too narrow an area in only exploring issues of natural philosophy. The religious context, I suggest, is a far more illuminating concern to illustrate Bruno's value to Toland.[86] Toland's central claim for the value of the *Spaccio* is that it is a superb

[78] *Ibid.*, 235, 'Natura est Deus in rebus'.
[79] *Ibid.*, 242ff.; consider, for example, Bruno's assault upon the Trinity, where he argues that Orion/Christ was maleficent in maintaining a bifurcation and contrariety between divinity and nature.
[80] *Ibid.*, 149–50, 257–8. There seems to be a Machiavellian element in these statements.
[81] *Ibid.*, 270ff.; Bruno continued: 'From where the altar stands let superstition, Faithlessness and impiety depart; and there let religion, which is not vain, Faith which is not foolish, and true and sincere Piety soujourn.'
[82] See Jacob, *Newtonians*, 205, 226–9, 232–4, 245–6 and *Radical Enlightenment*, 35–40, 41, 47, 61, 87, 202.
[83] As I argue above, the crucial influence on Toland's thought was the work of Cicero and the Stoics. Perhaps there is a similar case to be made for the influences of antiquity upon Bruno.
[84] Jacob, *Newtonians*, 234; on Toland's claim see BL Add. 4465 f. 7 and § 10 of *Letters to Serena*.
[85] Jacob, *Newtonians*, 233–8.
[86] It is interesting to note that in both letters concerning Bruno's *Spaccio*, Toland makes no reference to notions of natural philosophy.

device for exploding the machinery of priestcraft and superstition. He wrote: 'In one continu'd thread and contexture it contains the whole doctrine of the sphere, the learning and history of the antient Superstition, the confutation of modern imposture, and a compleat system of Ethicks.' Toland noted that many had misinterpreted the purpose of Bruno's work: the *Spaccio* was not a singular assault upon the papacy, for the triumphant beast was not analogous to the notion of the pope as antichrist. He explained:

Au lieu que par la bête il entend toute religion revelée en general, de quelque nature qu'elle sôit et de quelque maniere que se foit qu'elle triomphe dans le monde. Sôit la religion Päienne, sôit la judaique, ou la chretienne, il les attaque, les tourne en ridicule, et les rejette egalement sans aucune cérémonie et sans exception.[87]

In Toland's perspective, Bruno was considered first and foremost as an advocate of anticlericalism, he assaulted the malformed consequences of hierocratic and corrupted religion.

The classical allusions, the councils of gods and astral reformation all had great appeal for Toland given his favourable disposition towards the civil theologies of antiquity. Bruno was cited because of his approval of the moral value of heathen religion over the vice of modern superstition: 'Mais ce qui lui fait le plus de peine, c'est que leurs successeurs sont mille fois pires, les anciens heros etant infiniment preferable aux saints modernes, et la nouvelle superstition bien moins supportable que l'ancienne.'[88] Toland applauded Bruno's scheme for astral reformation because he believed it was a valuable method of inculcating morality in the masses. It was in effect a popular theology. In this manner the *Spaccio* was understood in terms of Toland's espousal of the distinction between esoteric and exoteric philosophy. The *Spaccio* was the result of 'private conferences' where everything was discussed 'freely and without a veil, being secure from the censures or mistakes of the prophane vulgar'.[89] Toland chose to appreciate Bruno, not simply as Jacob's natural philosopher, but more importantly as a civil theologian. Toland's interest in Giordano Bruno's *Spaccio*, and approval of a pre-Judaeo-Christian pattern of religious worship, illustrates the radical attempt to undermine the historical traditions of orthodox religion.[90]

The strategy of Herbert, Blount and Toland was to indict contemporary

---

[87] *Nova Bibliotheca*, 159.　　[88] *Ibid.*, 160.

[89] One is reminded of Toland's descriptions of his Socratic club in *Pantheisticon* (1720).

[90] For a discussion of the history of philosophy, and the idea of the Egyptian origins of the *philosophia perennis* in the Renaissance, see: C. A. Patrides, *The Cambridge Platonists* (Cambridge, 1969), 1–42; G. Aspelin, 'Ralph Cudworth's Interpretation of Greek Philosophy', *Götesborgs Hogkolas Årsskirft* 49 (1943). For an interesting and influential contemporary text, see Thomas Stanley's *History of Philosophy* (1655–62). See also J. Godwin, *Athanasius Kircher: A Renaissance Man and the Quest for Lost Knowledge* (1979); E. Iverson, *The Myth of Egypt and Its Hieroglyphs in European Tradition* (Copenhagen, 1961); and L. Dieckmann, *Hieroglyphs: The History of a Literary Symbol* (Washington and St Louis, 1970).

religion by presenting histories of heathenism. To have launched a direct polemical assault upon sacred history would have been a foolhardy attempt. John Spencer (1630–93), Dean of Ely and Master of Corpus Christi, Cambridge, in his *De Legibus Hebraeorum* (1685) made just this challenge against the Mosaic dispensation, although carefully disguised under a weighty volume of erudition and innovative scholarship. Spencer was foremost an Hebraist of distinction. In 1669 he published at Cambridge his *Dissertatio de Urim et Thummim* which argued that Jewish methods of prophecy were derived from earlier Egyptian auguries. This simple theme, of the continuity of Egyptian and Jewish ceremony, was to form the backbone of his massive later work. *De Legibus Hebraeorum* has been justly applauded as the founding text in the study of comparative religions: its theses were still academically acceptable to early twentieth-century scholarship. It consisted of three parts: the first two books gave the rational, moral and ethical grounds for Moses' ceremonial and sacrificial prescriptions. In general Moses established such ritual to ward the Jewish nation from the idolatrous practices of such peoples as the Zabians. According to Diodorus Siculus and Herodotus the ritual of circumcision originated in ancient Egyptian tradition, 'ideoque gentibus illis, ex antiqua traditione in usu est, ut circumcidant statim a purtu, pueros, ritu ab Aegyptii derivato'.[91] It was in the assertions of Book III 'qua generalius agitur de ritibus et gentium moribus in legem translatis' that Spencer revealed his inherent unorthodoxy. Focusing upon the expansion of Semitic ritual after the original and minimal patriarchal prescription, Spencer argued that the priesthood had encouraged superstitious and idolatrous practice for their own ends. It was Moses' intention to lead the ignorant Israelites away from such corrupt ritual. Spencer argued that the Jewish people through continual correspondence with the idolatrous Gentiles by the process of acculturation had become accustomed to many of their religious habits. Moses accommodated these superstitious inclinations in the creation of his law. Spencer illustrated the correspondence and affinity between Egyptian and Jewish ritual, arguing that the superiority of Egyptian civilization made it unlikely that they should model their theologies upon the actions of the barbarous and itinerant Jews.[92] Sacrifices, communion, temples, festivals, lustrations, priestly vest-

[91] J. Spencer, *De Legibus Hebraeorum*, I, chapter 4, sections iii–vi, 45–59, at 48. See W. Robertson Smith, *The Religion of the Semites* (3rd edition 1927), xiv, and H. P. Smith, *Essays in Biblical Interpretation* (1921). M. Bernal, *Black Athena: The Afro-Asiatic Roots of Classical Civilisation* (1987) discusses at length what he terms the 'ancient model' of the history of philosophy and religion which (as he shows convincingly) argued for the primacy of the Egyptians. Although the work is ambitious in both its arguments and its evidence, it is surprising to note that Bernal makes no reference to either Spencer or Marsham, two of Egypt's most scholarly defenders.
[92] Spencer, *De Legibus Hebraeorum* 519–20, 521–30, 531–3. Note that Newton in 'The Philosophical Origins of Gentile Religion' (Yahuda 17.3) wrote that Spencer's *De Legibus*

ments and tithes had all been borrowed from Egyptian sources. To justify this accommodation thesis Spencer displayed a variety of authorities including such ubiquitous classical authors as Herodotus, Diodorus Siculus and Plutarch, Church fathers like Eusebius and Josephus, but most importantly the Jewish writer Maimonides who in his *More Nevechim* (a section of the *Guide to the Perplexed*) advanced this very thesis. William Warburton pointed out that *De Legibus Hebraeorum* was 'no other than paraphrase and comment on' Maimonides' work.[93]

Spencer's work received an hostile reception. The general opinion was succinctly summed up in the description of it as 'a very learned, but a very dangerous work'.[94] While the first published assaults are to be found in Continental reviews, the *Nouvelles de la Republique des Lettres* (April 1686) was untypical in giving the work extensive and impartial applause, describing it as 'un magazin d'érudition sacrée et profane'. The review speculated that Spencer had composed the work to argue against the 'fanatiques' in England who refused to join the Anglican settlement, 'sous pretexte qu'elle mêle dans le service Divin plusieurs cérémonies d'invention humaine'.[95] The subversive implications of Spencer's work which argued that the Mosaic law was devised for political reasons rather than divine inspiration was identified, and taken up in the more hostile treatment in the *Bibliotheque Universelle*. Here the reviews contradicted Spencer: the Mosaic dispensation was of divine origins calculated against all the corruptions of Egyptian idolatry. Any complicity between the rituals was because the idolaters had used the divine Judaic pattern for their own purposes. Jewish law was necessarily a divine original since it was a type or 'shadow' of Christianity. Spencer had been led into error by incorrect hermeneutical principle in relying too much on the corrupt authority of classical sources. As the review pointed out: to undermine the divinity of Moses was to threaten Christ himself.[96]

These criticisms were reflected in the English reception of *De Legibus Hebraeorum*. John Edwards, in his *Complete History or Survey of all the Dispensations and Methods of Religion* (1699), refuted Spencer's argument

Hebraeorum 'amply shows … that the Mosaic rituals were drawn from the Egyptians'. Many thanks to R. Iliffe, who is currently working on similar themes in Newton's thought, for this reference.

93 W. Warburton, *Divine Legation of Moses*, (4 volumes, 4th edition, 1765), IV, 25. See also *Bibliotheque Universelle* 25 (1693), 432–3, which makes the same point. Spencer acknowledges this debt in *De Legibus Hebraeorum*, III, 527, where he cites the crucial passage (Maimonides, *The Guide to the Perplexed* (Chicago, 1963), III, chapter 32, 526). See also, J. Townley, *The Reasons of the Laws of Moses* (1827).

94 W. Orme, *Bibliotheca Biblica* (1824), 417.

95 *Nouvelles de la Republique des Lettres* 5 (April, 1686), 438, 444.

96 *Bibliotheque Universelle* 24 (1693) (2nd edition, Amsterdam, 1699), 288, 291–5, 297–8, 300.

with simple counter-assertion. The thesis that God had to comply with the errors of human nature and indulge the Jews in 'pagan folly' was contradictory. As Edwards explained: 'Is it to be credited that God forbad and abhorred the Gentile practices, and yet at the same time appointed his people several rites which the Gentile used, yea because they were Gentile rites, and practic'd by the Idolatrous nations, as this author expressly asserts?'[97] A more erudite, but still hostile, appreciation of Spencer's work was made by John Woodward (1665–1728), a correspondent of Edwards, in a manuscript work 'Of the Wisdom of the Ancient Egyptians' which was eventually published in *Archaeologia* (1777), but was in circulation in the early 1700s.[98] Woodward noted with disgust the stir Spencer's work had created: 'No sooner did this work come out but it pleased and took mightily with some, in so much that it became a fashion to ridicule the Jews, slight the Mosaic oeconomy, and represent it as only moulded after the pattern of the Gentiles.' While agreeing that Spencer's work was an epitome of learning, 'he has with infinite industry made a most accurate collation of the Jewish and Pagan constitutions' he denied that *De Legibus Hebraeorum* was little more use than an handbook because, 'when he comes to apply the collation he has made with all that pain and exactness, he falls into the greatest and most erroneous paradox that a man well could, and runs it quite through his whole undertaking. Because of this consent and affinity, he infers that the Jews had those parts of their laws and rites, in which the two nations agree, from the Egyptians'.[99] Woodward denied that Moses was of the same politic lineage as Mahomet, Apollonius Tyaneus, and other 'politicians'. Spencer's thesis of the priority and superiority of Egyptian civilization was rebutted in a long and detailed description of the superstitious practices of these ancients which 'was undoubtedly the wildest and most fantastic that the sun ever saw'. While Moses had been born, bred and educated in Egypt this merely confirmed his revulsion for such a ridiculous worship: this aversion displayed itself in the Mosaic law calculated by God to revile the gentile pattern.[100]

The issues at debate here were a crucible in which the Enlightenment idea of religion, as a natural foundation with a political superstructure, was forged. While orthodox Christians were content to consider Judaism as a type or precursor of Christianity, men of Spencer's and Toland's ilk

---

[97] J. Edwards, *Complete History of Religion* (2 volumes, 1699), I, 250, see also 247–9.
[98] See Holmes and Jones, *The London Diaries*, 271, entry for 5 January 1705, where Nicolson describes dining at Woodward's and perusing his manuscript where 'he takes occasion to run down the Egyptians, as mistaken masters of ancient learning'. See also Anon. to Woodward 12 July (?), CUL Add. 7647.145.
[99] J. Woodward, 'Of the Wisdom of the Ancient Egyptians', *Archaeologia* 4 (1777) 271, 280–1.
[100] *Ibid.*, 238–260, 262, 264–8, 282.

(following Spinoza) took one step back from this tradition and treated Old Testament Judaism not as part of a faith but as a specific historical manifestation of 'religion' set in particular cultural and political circumstances. Woodward had complained that to undermine the Jewish religion was a direct threat to the Christian establishment. While Spencer had confined himself to a consideration of the historical transition from gentilism to Judaism, Bernard Fontenelle undertook to examine the translation from Judaism and paganism to Christianity. Bernard Fontenelle's *The History of Oracles and the Cheats of Pagan Priests* was translated into English in 1688 by Aphra Behn, friend of Charles Blount, Rochester and Buckingham. Fontenelle's work was a popularization of a Dutch work by the anabaptist A. Vandale, *De Oraculis Ethicarum*. He commented on his edition: 'In fine, I have new cast and modelled the whole work.' The work was answered two decades later in 1709 in *An Answer to Mr De Fontenelle's History of Oracles* 'By a priest of the Church of England' and prefaced by a letter of the non-juror George Hickes. Fontenelle's work (with wit, charm and style) refuted the Anglican position 'that the ancient Oracles were delivered by Daemons, and that they ceased wholly at the coming of Jesus Christ'.[101] George Hickes argued that the silencing of the oracles was 'one of the most eminent Miracles that attended the propagation of Christianity'.[102]

Fontenelle's work involved not only an analysis of the nature of the transition from heathen religion to Christian, but also scurrilous reflections upon the conduct of the early Church Fathers. Fontenelle suggested that the Christian polemicists had been willing to accept the existence of daemoniacal oracles because the argument was commodious to their supernatural conception of the deity. It was easier to posit a God more powerful supernaturally than the pagan daemons, than to attempt directly to undermine pagan beliefs. Fontenelle wrote:

So, that to gain a little upon the pagans, there was a necessity of yielding to them what they maintained with so much obstinacy, and to let them see, that tho' there might be something supernatural in the Oracles, yet there was no reason to say, that there was a true divinity concerned in them; and so Daemons were to be brought upon the stage.[103]

The crux of the debate was whether or not pagan religion was merely human imposture, or a supernaturally inspired form of irreligion. Fontenelle's position was that the oracles and ceremonial content of heathen religion

---

[101] Fontenelle, *The History of Oracles*, Preface, Sigs. A6r, A7v. Aphra Behn also translated Fontenelle's *Plurality of Worlds*. Note that Toland in *Letters to Serena* also referred to the Dutch scholar's works with admiration.

[102] Anon. *An Answer to Fontenelle*, 'A Letter written by Dr George Hickes', Sig. A3r.

[103] Fontenelle, *The History of Oracles*, 82–3.

were the product of priestly imposture. In this framework the historical demise of paganism and the rise of Christianity were not causatively and supernaturally linked. Oracles were the product of priestly artifice imposing on a credulous populace. The demise of this imposture was due to human action; i.e. the exposure of priestcraft and the extirpation of heathenism by the Christian emperors.[104]

Fontenelle rebutted the orthodox claim that the oracles had ceased with the advent of Christ due to some supernatural/magical quality. He catalogued the persistence of oracles after the birth of Christ: Julian the Apostate was able to consult the oracle of Delphi about his Persian expedition.[105] Fontenelle gave sociological or political explanations, rather than prophetic, for the decline of heathenism. Thus Fontenelle's apparently uncontentious research into the historical pattern of heathenism had distinctly subversive implications for the nature of the Christian religion. The author of the *Answer* dealt with the charge that the demise of oracles had been due to 'a method intirely Human and natural, and that nothing is to be found in it which ought to be attributed to the power of Christ'. According to the author Fontenelle had been less than fair when he asserted that the Christian tradition maintained that the demise of the oracles had occurred immediately at the birth of Christ. The Anglican position was that silence was rendered 'little by little, as he made himself known to Men, and as the world was inlightened by the bright Beams of the Gospel'.[106] The oracles were created and influenced by daemons. These daemons were banished by the supernatural legacy of Christ and invocation of his name. The very presence of Christians by some spiritual means 'bid the oracles to silence, and drove the devils out of them'. This quasi-magical power remained in the Christian Church: the miraculous story of Prudentius who, by his very presence, hindered Julian the Apostate's attempted daemoniacal sacrifice, was retold.[107]

The author of the *Answer* suggested that this magical power was implicit within all Christians, 'this power always has and always will subsist in the Church; 'tis a mark whereby she is distinguished from all sects of Hereticks'.[108] Fontenelle's portrayal of the Christian Church was essentially de-spiritualized, a body of doctrine rather than a *corpus mysticum*. All claims to supernatural power in Fontenelle's work were the achievements of imposture. The reply to his work was to insist upon a conception of the

104 *Ibid.*, 112, 161–95, 223.
105 *Ibid.*, 173, 194. The last efforts of paganism were terminated under the reigns of the Emperors Valentinian, Theodosius and Arcadius.
106 Anon. *An Answer to Fontenelle*, 159, 169.
107 *Ibid.*, 71, 78, 186. This very theme was to form the subject of a work written by William Warburton in the mid-eighteenth century to justify the authority of the Church.
108 *Ibid.*, 195.

world as a battle between divine and impious supernatural forces, with the Christian Church as the bastion of religion.

THE PSYCHOLOGY OF PRIESTCRAFT

The radical critique examined the progress and decline of heathen religion, describing the dynamic of this process as the result of priestly manipulation. This critique was essentially historical: but it was supplemented by an analysis of the 'origins' of religion not in a temporal sense, but in terms of human psychology. These explications were phrased in sociological and epistemological terms. The importance of this analysis was that the writers made generalized statements about the nature of society, human psychology and the generation of belief systems. Although ostensibly the commentaries were passed upon historical structures they clearly had relevance for contemporary society, and were a reflection upon similar manifestations in that culture.

An anonymous and enigmatic text *Averroeana* (1695), containing the medical opinions of Averroes and the religious opinions of Pythagoras epitomizes the analysis of the radical critique, 'tradition and vain customs rule over most nations; and men are so highly graduated in them, that most of them will not only kill others for not observing their customs, and believing in their prophets; but they will die themselves, rather than leave an evil custom to embrace a good one'.[109] Thomas Hobbes in chapter 12 'Of Religion' in *Leviathan* argued that fear, the essential psychological engine of human motivation, was the root of religious belief. Man's prying desire for knowledge of the future and 'anxiety of the time to come' was the foundation of religion. This facet of existence led to a fear of the power of invisible things.[110] These fears and beliefs could be generated and manipulated by men in authority (usually priests and kings) for their own interests. This stoic psychology was the premise of the radical critique of established religion. Spinoza laid similar emphasis upon fear as part of the human condition and an explanatory cause in the origin of superstition and political authority.[111]

John Trenchard in his *Natural History of Superstition* (1709) gave the Hobbist theme extended treatment. He wrote that 'there is something innate in our constitution made us easily to be susceptible of wrong impressions, subject to panick fears, and prone to Superstition and Error, and therefore it is incumbent upon us, first of all to examine into the frame and constitution

---

[109] Anon. *Averroeana* (1695), 102.
[110] Hobbes, *Leviathan*, 168–9, 172–3. On Hobbes' psychological notions see M. V. Deporte, *Nightmares and Hobbyhorses, Swift, Sterne and Augustan Ideas of Madness* (San Marino, 1974).
[111] Spinoza, *Treatise Partly Theological*, 2–6.

of our own bodies, and search into the causes of our passions and infirmities'.[112] Trenchard continued, echoing Hobbes:

I take this wholly to proceed from our ignorance of causes, and yet curiosity to know them, it being impossible for any man to go far to divest himself of concern for his own happiness, as not to endeavour to promote it, and consequently to avoid what he thinks may hurt him; and since there must be causes in nature for everything that does or will happen, either here or hereafter, it is hard to avoid solicitude till we think we know them.[113]

The origin of causes is mostly hidden from our view, thus there are three alternatives that face man: to abandon the enquiry; to substitute for the true causes ideas of our own, 'Such ... as our own imaginations or prejudices suggest to us', or to rely on other people whom we think more competent. All three alternatives offer grave problems. Man could not exist happily without such enquiry and was thus forced into the arms either of his own imagination or someone else's. To rely on one's own senses and imagination within a context of their infallibility could often result in religious enthusiasm. The alternative posed the problems of fraudulent manipulation by the clergy.[114]

Premised on the idea that people have to arrive at some conceptual scheme in order to understand their existence and the telos of their lives, the radical critique made the connection between 'interest' and 'opinion' resulting in the idea of 'prejudice'. The production of an individual's ideas, beliefs or opinions was determined socially. The executive in this social determination of ideas was attributed to the clergy. One of the most lucid texts in articulating this proposition was John Toland's 'The Origin and Force of Prejudices' in *Letters to Serena* (1704).

Toland's central point, citing Cicero's *De Legibus*, was that 'Neither parents ... or Nurse, or Schoolmaster, or Poet, or Playhouse depraves our senses nor can the Consent of the Multitude mislead them; But all sorts of traps are laid to seduce our understandings ... by those whom I just now mentioned, who when they receive us tender and ignorant, infect and bend us as they please.' The determination and moulding of an individual's ideas commenced as soon as he entered the world, if not before, 'the foundation of our prejudices is very strongly laid before we are born' i.e. in the womb. Trenchard had also commented that 'the Frights and longings of Women with Child stamp images and impressions, of the things feared or desired, on the faetus's, which last long after they are born, and sometimes as long as they exist'.[115] The influence of priestcraft was present at birth, 'we no sooner see the light, but the grand cheat begins to delude us from every quarter. The

---

[112] Trenchard, *Natural History of Superstition*, 9; Howard, *A History of Religion* (1696); Blount, *The Life of Apollonius* (1680), 23, 30, 151. Note that d'Holbach translated portions of the *Natural History* as *La Contagion sacrée* (1767), II, chapters 12–13.
[113] Trenchard, *Natural History of Superstition*, 9–10.   [114] *Ibid.*, 10, 12–14, 16.
[115] Toland, *Letters to Serena*, Preface, Sig. B4r, 2; Trenchard, *Natural History* 25.

very midwife hands us into the world with superstitious ceremonies.' Childhood sees the nurse weaning the understanding on to a diet of superstition. These fables were originally affected to 'keep children under government': the effects continued into adulthood. They 'lay a large foundation for future Credulity, insensibly acquiring a disposition for hearing things rare and wonderful, to imagine we believe what we only dread or desire, to think that we are but puzzl'd that we are convinc'd, and to swallow what we cannot comprehend'. This process was continued throughout school and university 'the most fertile nursery of prejudices'. Prejudice is then reinforced by whatever activity the individual undertakes, 'hence not only every profession, but also every rank of men, have their particular language, which is thought by others to contain very extraordinary matters, much above the common capacity or comprehension'.[116]

Toland described a vision of society permeated with webs of conflicting value systems. The overburdening directors of these systems of 'false' ideas were the clergy. Charles Blount in *Religio Laici* (1683) pinpointed the issue of the social formation of ideas. He wrote: 'We denominate good and evil only from our particular interest; so that perhaps our vertues may prove but false money, of no intrinsick value, although it bear the stamp of our approbation on it'. Men are guided by 'the primary appetite of nature' to establish their own well-being; the perception of this well-being is directed by 'judgement'. This faculty is a product of 'the temper of our brain, & our education' and thus beyond individual control. Blount commented on these factors, 'all which (it is manifest) are not in our own power, but proceeds from the temper of our parents, the diet, climate and customs of our country, with diversity of occurrents and conjunctures of the times'. In this way the patterns of ideas created by the priests for their own interest, in complicity with what Blount called 'this tribunal in the minds of men' (the security seeking psychology of human nature) became traditions and customs.[117]

The Freethinker's theory of knowledge restructured traditional sceptical epistemology into what could be termed political or cultural epistemology. Their scepticism was to concentrate on the notion of a 'commonsense philosophy'. They argued that this process of creating morally certain knowledge was fraught with the distorting idols of interest, prejudice and the burden of custom. This socially generated knowledge (reified into custom) was what the radicals attempted to undermine. Fontenelle acknowledged the difficulty of someone attempting to step out of the streams of custom 'for we have need of strength to resist a torrent, but we need not to follow it'. Trenchard commented upon the entrenched nature of beliefs that determined world views for 'when men have imbibed strong prejudices, which serve their

---

[116] Toland, *Letters to Serena*, 2–3, 6, 7, 11.
[117] Blount, *Religio Laici*, 58–9; and *Great is Diana*, 22.

present interest, or strike forcibly upon their hopes and fears, everything in nature shall be made to contribute to their system'. Blount was still more scathing over how the majority of people came to have opinions: 'Most men (like Carrier Horses) follow one another in a track, where if the fore-horse goes wrong, all the rest succeed him in his errour: not considering that he who comes behind, may take an advantage to avoid that pit, which those that went before are fallen into.' For Toland the majority of people were martyrs to habit, rather than any religious truth.[118]

The manipulation of Scripture, according to the Freethinking critique, was one of the most effective promoters of priestcraft.[119] The analysis focused upon two interrelated issues, about the type of knowledge proposed in the Bible, and to what purpose it was to be used. The second point was that the clergy by abusing the sanctity of Scripture, for their own interests, had falsely represented it. The Anglican accepted Scriptural accounts as 'true' representations of historical reality. The Bible was the oldest history in the world, recounting in specific, 'true' detail the exact chronology of the historical

[118] Blount, *Life of Apollonius*, 19, 22; Fontenelle, *Oracles*, 77; Trenchard, *Natural History*, 33; Toland, *Serena*, 12–13. One of the 'prejudices' that received attention was the belief in miracles. Blount's work *Miracles No Violation of the Laws of Nature* (1683) is of especial interest as it represents a confluence of the thought of Thomas Hobbes, Spinoza and Thomas Burnet. The work was a combination of extracts from Spinoza's *Treatise Partly Theological* and Hobbes' *Leviathan*, with a preface lifted from Burnet's *Telluris Theoria Sacra*. Blount's Anglican adversary, Thomas Browne, replied in the same year with his *Miracles Works Above and Contrary to Nature* deriding the work as a proponent of deism and atheism. See also J. Spink, *French Freethought from Gassendi to Voltaire* (1961) for a discussion of Pierre Bayle's *Pensées sur la comete* (1683) which proposes a similar analysis.

[119] The history of the origins of seventeenth-century biblical hermeneutics is sparse, and there are many areas that need detailed investigation. The reception and usage of the French work of Richard Simon is in need of examination. General works are H. Graf Reventlow, *The Authority of the Bible and the Rise of the Modern World* (1984); W. G. Kummel, *The New Testament: The History of the Investigation of its Problems* (Nashville, 1972) and G. Reedy, *The Bible and Reason: Anglicans and Scripture in Late Seventeenth-Century England* (Philadelphia, 1985). There are interesting accounts of radical biblical criticism in L. Strauss, *Spinoza's Critique of Religion* (New York, 1965), in particular 66–77 on Isaac La Peyrère, and 251–68, and 311–27 on Spinoza's sources. See also R. H. Popkin, 'The Development of Religious Scepticism and the Influences of Isaac La Peyrère's Pre-Adamism and Bible Criticism' in R. R. Bolgar (ed.), *Classical Influences on European Culture AD 1500–1700* (Cambridge, 1976), and 'Some New Light on the Roots of Spinoza's Science of Bible Study' in M. Grene (ed.), *Spinoza and the Sciences*, Boston Studies in the Philosophy of Science 91 (1986). Toland's research on the canon in *The Life of John Milton* (1698) and *Amyntor: Or a Defence of Milton's Life* (1699), especially 25–78, was received with great hostility by the Anglican orthodoxy. A similar reaction was directed against the Arian conclusion of William Whiston's research, which argued that the *Apostolic Constitutions* was the oldest Christian document, see *Primitive Christianity Reviv'd* (5 volumes, 1711). On Whiston, see O. C. Krabbe, *The Apostolic Constitutions* (New York, 1848); E. Duffy, 'Whiston's Affair: The trial of a Primitive Christian 1709–1714', *Journal of Ecclesiastical History* (1976); J. E. Force, *William Whiston: Honest Newtonian* (Cambridge, 1985). Further study should focus upon John Mill's edition of the New Testament of 1707 and its hostile reception. See Hearne, *Remarks and Collections*, I, 22, 28 and II, 20, 25, 186; and A. Fox, *John Mill and Richard Bentley* (Oxford, 1954).

creation and evolution of the world. Writing upon the Mosaic account of the creation Dr John Woodward commented that 'his historical relations are . . . exact; everywhere clear strong and simple'. Woodward's attitude was that if Moses' account was untrue physiologically 'we could with no reason or security have relied upon him in matters historical, moral, or religious . . . And all know how great a superstructure is raised upon his foundation which would assuredly have been in a very shaken and tottering condition, had his accounts of nature proved erroneous.'[120]

The most relevant and influential statements made by opponents of the ecclesiastical establishment were Spinoza's *Treatise Partly Theological* (1689), in particular chapters 1–2 'Of Prophecy' and 'Of Prophets', and Thomas Burnet's *Archaeologiae Philosophicae* (1692). The Burnet tract originally written in Latin was in part translated into English in the year of its publication. The following year saw Charles Blount in his *Oracles of Reason* (1693) publish a defence of Burnet's work, coupled with the republication of the first two chapters of the 1692 English translation of the *Archaeologiae*. Spinoza and Burnet share the same premise. Spinoza argued that when God revealed knowledge to his prophets it was according to their capacities and imaginations. Prophets were individuals who 'had some particular extraordinary Vertue above other men, and were persons very eminent for their constant Piety'. The prophets had no internalized ability of prophesying.[121] Spinoza separated philosophy and theology. Statements in Scripture did not have an epistemological truth value, they were hypothetical constructs to achieve the extension of the divine message. He insisted that God adapted revelations to the understandings and opinions of the prophets, and that in matters of theory (without bearing on charity or morality) the prophets could be, and in fact were, ignorant. It was with this analysis that Spinoza rejected the 'real' existence of miracles. The account of miraculous occurrences in the sacred history were not true physical accounts but designed to appeal to human imagination to inculcate divine doctrine and produce devotion. Thus the accounts were not 'so much to convince our reason, as to affect and possess our minds, and our Imaginations'. Scripture was a fiction calculated to induce men to morality. The value of Holy Writ was not so much the very words and phrases of Scripture, but the intended injunction to virtue.[122]

Thomas Burnet, Master of Charterhouse, followed the Spinozist hermeneutic in his *Archaeologiae Philosophicae* (1692). Burnet concentrated upon the Mosaic account of the creation of the world and the narrative of Adam's fall. Burnet's central theme was that the Mosaic hexameron was not a true philosophical discourse upon the origin of the world (he considered

---

[120] Woodward, 'Egyptians', 262, 277.   [121] Spinoza, *Treatise Partly Theological*, 23.
[122] *Ibid.*, 30, 34, 40–1, 53, 55, 140–4.

that this had been effected in his *Sacred Theory*). Moses in his account had followed the 'popular system' in order to gain acceptance for his divine precepts. He wrote 'that it was not this Sacred author's design to represent the beginning of the world, exactly according to the physical truth; (which would have been no use to the common people who were incapable of being philosophers) but to expound the first originals of things after such a method, as might breed in the minds of men Piety, and a worshipping of the true God'. Moses' intention was not to explain the origin of the universe but to give an explanation adapted to the capacities of the people 'that he might the better help the imagination of the people, to comprehend the first original of things'.[123]

Burnet executed a similar interpretation of Genesis suggesting that, as a physical account, it was fundamentally absurd. Moses' discourse was 'artifically figurative' in order to explain the degenerate nature of man 'as also the Paradisiac State of infant Nature'. The notion of the Garden of Eden was created 'because it was more suitable to the genius and understanding of the Vulgar, to conceive a pleasant Garden or a single field, than that the whole globe of the Earth should put on a new face and new nature, entirely different from what we now enjoy'. In a similar fashion the notion that Eve was created from Adam's spare rib has no physiological truth but was suggested by Moses 'to breed mutual love between sexes & also render efficacious his institution of marriage'. Man's expulsion from this symbolic paradise for the small crime of eating an apple was described by Moses 'only to the end he might procure the greater deference and authority to his own Laws'.[124] Spinoza himself considered the history of the first man as a 'parable' rather than a 'plain and Simple narration'.[125]

How did the Freethinkers' treatment of Revelation interlock with their critique of priestcraft? They argued that Scripture had been composed in terms of an exoteric philosophy or popular theology. This originally accessible knowledge had been veiled and masked by the corrupt influence of the priesthood into 'mystery'. The Freethinkers described the history of this division of knowledge into two social forms: the exoteric and esoteric in

---

[123] T. Burnet, *Archaeologiae Philosophicae*, 41–2. [124] *Ibid.*, 5–7, 8–9, 11, 23.
[125] Spinoza, *Treatise Partly Theological*, 99. William Whiston, in his *Discourse Concerning the Nature, Stile and Extent of the Mosaick History of the Creation* which prefaced his *New Theory of the Earth* (1696), took issue with Burnet's notion. He considered those who have 'been so sensible of the wildness and unreasonableness of That (Scripture), that they have ventured to exclude it from any just sense at all; asserting it to be a meer Popular, Parabolick, or Mythological relation; in which the plain letter is no more to be accounted for or believ'd, than the fabulous representations of Aesop, or at best the Mistical Parables of our Saviour', were executing a mischievous design. Whiston's argument with Burnet's interpretation of Scripture is convoluted and in some ways contradictory.

order to indict priestly manipulation.[126] The most articulate and popular
history of 'mystery' was John Toland's *Christianity Not Mysterious* (1696).
In this work he documented in detail the priestly construction of mystery into
a self-interested theology. Scripture contained nothing mysterious in itself.
True religion had been rendered enigmatic by the priesthood who encum-
bered pure religion with cabbalism and ritual.[127] We must examine the
abstract underpinnings of this popular polemic.

The Freethinkers argued that the clergy had made a claim to be the
possessors of a hidden true knowledge when in fact they had erected a false
system to promote their own self-interest. Charles Blount appealed to the
patterns of pagan antiquity and wrote that in the 'First Ages ... all things
were full of Fables, Aenigmas, Parables, and Similies of all sorts, whereby
they sought to teach and expound knowledge to the Vulgar'. Tales of fortune
and mystery were created to 'induce us to Virtue, piety, and Religion, [such]
as the wonderful pleasures of the Elesian Fields'. John Toland in *Letters to
Serena* (1704) appealed to the original of Pythagoras suggesting that the
philosopher's notion of the transmigration of souls was in effect the veneer of
his 'internal or secret Doctrine' of 'the eternal Revolution of Forms in
matter'. Toland generalized, 'for most of the Philosophers ... had two sorts
of Doctrine, the one internal and the other external, or the one private and
the other publick; the latter to be indifferently communicated to all the
world, and the former only very cautiously to their best friends'. A work
which may have been composed by Toland, *Two Essays sent in a Letter from
Oxford to a Nobleman in London* (1695) probed the origins of such activity.
Fiction was originally mixed with truth in Egypt; the 'mythological' works of
Aesop, Homer, Hesiod or Orpheus had its generation in the 'Romantick
vein' of communication prevalent in Egypt. These seeds of fiction, transplan-
ted into Greece, found the soil very fertile and luxuriant. The Greeks
'addicted to Poetry and Invention, ran upon all figures, Fables and Parable'.
The importation of ideas and methods had been facilitated by the fact that
both Plato and Pythagoras had visited Egypt and received tuition from
Eastern priests. Sacred authors complied with this 'Humour of Parables and
fiction, the Holy Scripture being altogether Mysterious, Allegorical and
Enigmatical; and our Saviour Himself gave his precepts under this veil'.[128]
The letter continues to decry how this division was put to the employ of
self-interested monks and the clerical order.

Cherbury's study of heathen religion was founded on the premise of a
popular/philosophical distinction. The theme of the work had been that the

126 For a similar analysis of the notion of the 'expert', but in the area of scientific knowledge,
    see. S. Schaffer, 'The Political Theology of Seventeenth-Century Natural Science' in *Ideas
    and Production* (1983).
127 Toland, *CNM*, 11, 68–9, 72–3, 158–70.
128 Blount, *Life of Apollonius*, 64; Toland, *Serena* 56, 57, and *Two Essays* (1695), 30, 31, 37.

religious worship of the pagans had been 'symbolical'; the stars were fables of divinities, and ceremonies had been *cultus symbolicus* rather than *cultus proprius*. This was to say that the populace had been unable to conceive of true divinity so they had worshipped it indirectly; that when the stars were worshipped it was not for themselves but for them as a representation of the supreme being. Cherbury wrote that it was necessary 'always to observe that many things which we call Superstitions, were intended by them only to signifie the mystical and occult Adoration of some unknown Deity; and others we esteem Idolatrous, were a Symbolical way of worshipping the Supream God'. Cherbury cited Varro, who determined that there were 'three kinds of theology'. The triple division was 'Mystical, Natural, and Civil'. The mystical part of theology was composed of poets' attributions of qualities of the immortal Gods; the second part was natural philosophy; the third was that which 'the citizens and Priests especially, ought to understand and perform; this contains what sacrifices are to be performed by everyone'. Cherbury asserted that this third sort of theology which ought to have been accommodated 'to the city' had become the 'inventions of Priests'. The rites and ceremonies 'tended more to external Pageantry than the honour of the Supream God, they debauched the Minds of men from the internal Worship of God, sometimes to a magnificent Pomp, and at others to meer empty Ceremonies, to the overthrow of True and Sound Religion'.[129] In *Archaeologiae Philosophicae* Burnet employed an identical Varroistic analysis of the three-fold theology. To justify his treatment of Genesis he had asserted 'who if they will but with me consider the usage and Genius of the Primitive Ages, more especially among the Oriental nations (whose custom it was to deliver their decrees and doctrine by Symbols, Similitudes, and Parables) if they do not conceive with, will yet at least not be prejudiced against those who explain Ancient things after this manner'. As with Cherbury, Burnet cited Varro's analysis; he divided the 'antient Theology into three parts, the fabulous, Civil, and Philosophical. This last was useless to the common people; and the fabulous hurtful; therefore they instituted a middle sort ... for the benefit of the common people, and advantage of human life'.[130]

In 1720 John Toland published his *Clidophorus, Or Of the Exoteric and Esoteric Philosophy*; the subtitle indicates the intention of the work 'That is of the External and Internal Doctrine of the Ancients: The one open and

---

129 Cherbury, *Antient Religion*, 381, 382, 384–5. M. Terentius Varro (116–27 BC), described by Augustine as 'the greatest of Roman scholars, the weightiest authority', was a writer of enormous output, most of which is now lost. Varro's notions were, however, available via Augustine's commentary on his thought in *The City of God*; see D. Knowles (ed.), Book, VI, 229–35.

130 Burnet, *Archaeologiae*, vii, 24, 61, 63–5, 72–4, 74–5. C. Ginsburg, 'High and Low Knowledge in the Sixteenth and Seventeenth Centuries', *PP* 73 (1976), 28–41; Walker, *Ancient Theology*, 186–8.

Publick, accommodated to popular prejudices and the religions established by law; the other private and secret, wherein, to the few capable and discrete, was taught the real truth stript of all disguises'. Toland discussed the notion of Isis in Egyptian theology, pointing out that while the vulgar conceived of a fabulous queen the natural meaning was concerned with 'the nature of all things', that is, the notion of the universe as God. The 'double manner of teaching' was employed throughout the oriental nations: the Ethiopians, Babylonians, Syrians and Persians who were instructed by Zoroaster. A similar tradition was continued with the Gaulish and British Druids.[131] Toland cited Strabo, Parmenides, Pythagoras and the ubiquitous Varro to uphold his thesis that there must be variant forms of knowledge according to the capacities of those concerned. Toland, however, was more explicit in cataloguing the result of this dual system of truth. While acknowledging that this system might have been useful when employed to legitimate ends 'whereby to keep in order the Silly part of mankind', Toland wished to maintain that it had ultimately proved detrimental. He wrote: 'but granting that Supersition had at any time proved beneficial to the public, yet at other times without number, and in things of incomparably greater importance, it will be found detrimental, destructive, and utterly pernicious; nor advantageous to any, excepting Priests or Princes, who dextrously turn it to their own interest.'

Toland described a dynamic where the priests in tandem with a tyrannous secular authority managed to create a 'mystery' to influence the populace for their own ends. Toland upheld the use of metaphor and symbol in explaining and discussing the divine nature and attibutes, indeed in regard to the latter it was 'even absolutely necessary'. The clergy rejected any assault upon their usurped position and thus employed force to prevent that being told 'which shows the multitude to be ridiculous, or their guides Impostors'. Toland objected that what had originated as a pragmatic device of administration had been converted into a tool of interest by the clergy. It was now the philosophers who suffered at the hands of the priests for attempting to search after the truth. Toland's tract finished with an impassioned plea for the uninhibited exposition of the truth, with the eirenic and subversive suggest-

---

[131] On the 'history' of Druids, see Toland's *A Critical History of the Celtic Religion and Learning*, published in his *Collections*, but originally written in letter form to Robert Molesworth. See also Toland's relationship with John Aubrey and the 'history' of Druids in M. Hunter, *John Aubrey and the Realm of Learning* (1975), 59, 205n, 212; and S. Piggott, *The Druids* (1974), 120, 124, 127, 134, 157. J. M. S. Tomkins, 'In Yonder Grave a Druid Lies', *The Review of English Studies* 22 (1946), 1–16; A. L. Owen, *The Famous Druids. A Survey of Three Centuries of English Literature on Druids* (Oxford, 1962), 108–9, 112–17, 121. See also BL Add. 4295, folio 27. A letter from J. Chamberlayne to Toland 21 June 1718; 'I saw my Lord Chanc. yesterday, who among other papers gave me your project of a History of the Druids, which he told me he did not understand, but which he suspected to be level'd agst Christian Priests.'

ion that the division of religions was the product of the priests and the ignorance of the people, while in reality 'all wise men are of the same religion'.[132] One of the major facets of the distinction between the esoteric and exoteric philosophy was that the Freethinkers considered the practice legitimate if it was to effect the public good. If the process was to establish the rule of virtue then it was valid. This argument involved a redefinition of the nature of religion and its relationship with society. The Freethinkers, although they considered religion as a form of morality, did not treat it simply as a politic device. They attempted to reunite the heavenly and earthly cities.

[132] Toland, *Clidophorus*, 68, 71, 72, 82, 88, 94–5, 96. See Toland, the history of *Hypatia* (1720) and Toland, *Pantheisticon* (1751), 93–110, 'Of a Twofold Philosophy of the Pantheists'. It is important to note that the eso/exoteric distinction also informs Toland's *Letters to Serena*.

6

Civil theology

THE HISTORY OF ROMAN RELIGION: HARRINGTON TO MOYLE

Between the 1680s and the 1720s, the Church of England was attacked by writers, as the High Church scholar Thomas Hearne noted, of 'Deistical Republican Principles'. The hierocratic form of religion was rejected: ritual and dogma were replaced by injunctions to virtue. This historical link between religious scepticism and Republican political theory is under-explored. Historians of ideas have tended to view the two categories as mutually exclusive concerns. But to separate religion from politics in this period is a false move. Writers like Toland, Walter Moyle and John Trenchard were both anticlerical and Republican.[1] Modern scholarship has identified these theorists as operating within a secular idiom.[2] The argument of this *corpus* is sophisticated but straightforward. The Republicans were a collection of disaffected men who, though variant in their particular applications and refinements of models of *political* government, shared a collective homogeneity in employing the resources of the *secular* thought of antiquity. These men, disenchanted with the monarchical form of government, turned

[1] Hearne, *Remarks and Collections*, II, 94. One work which has gestured towards the connection between hostility towards the Church of England, and political radicalism is F. Venturi's excellent *Utopia and Reform in the Enlightenment* (Cambridge, 1971), 1–70; also his *Italy and the Enlightenment* (1972), chapter 3, 'Radicati's Exile in England and Holland', 63–103; M. A. Goldie, 'The Civil Religion of James Harrington' in A. Pagden (ed.), *Languages of Political Theory in Early Modern Europe* (Cambridge, 1987).

[2] The canonical texts are Z. Fink, *The Classical Republicans* (Evanston, 1945); C. Robbins, *The Eighteenth-Century Commonwealthsmen* (Harvard, 1959), and (ed.), *Two English Republican Tracts* (Cambridge, 1969); J. G. A. Pocock, *The Machiavellian Moment* (Princeton, 1975), chapters 9–10, and his 'Introduction' to *The Works of Harrington* (Cambridge, 1977). See also B. Worden, 'Classical Republicanism and the Puritan Revolution' in A. Lloyd-Jones, V. Pearl and B. Worden (eds.), *History and Imagination* (1981): here, importantly, Worden does address the relationship between religion and politics in Republican thought during the Interregnum (see especially 193–5). As Worden notes (at 195): 'A fuller study of the classical republicans would dwell on the limits, as well as on the extent, of their rationalism.' This book, in dealing with the Republicanism of the late seventeenth century intends to do just this. The most recent discussion is J. Scott, *Algernon Sidney and the English Republic 1623–1677* (Cambridge, 1988).

to the heritage of classical Greece and Rome (presented either in their original form, or distilled through the alembic of Florentine humanism), and adapted the language and programmes of the pagan past to the pragmatic needs of the times. In stressing their debt to the 'classical republican tradition' the radicals' preoccupation with religious affairs has been side-stepped.

It might be assumed that with such a large body of excellent scholarship there would be little room for further commentary. In particular, the relationship between Republicanism and classical traditions has generated much investigation. Studies on James Harrington, on Henry Neville, on neo-Harringtonianism and on the 'Country' ideologies, have exhumed the influences of Polybius, Cicero and the general relevance of 'Ancient Prudence'. Coupled with this there has been extensive commentary on the political strategies of late seventeenth- and eighteenth-century Republicanism; the desire for a mixed and balanced constitution, the hostility to parliamentary corruption, the objections to the centralizing tendencies of the Bank of England, and the standing army debate have all been thoroughly documented. Let us consider just one such piece of Republican argument.

In 1700 John Toland, the pantheist, published a complete edition of the works of James Harrington, the Republican. Many churchmen reacted to this publication as a 'seditious attempt against the very being of monarchy, and that there's a pernicious design on foot of speedily introducing a Republican form of government into the Brittanic Islands'. Toland and others denied this revolutionary intent. As Pocock has pointed out, Republicanism was a language rather than a programme. While the polemics of Toland, Moyle, Trenchard and Gordon applauded the Harringtonian hostility to tyrannical and arbitrary government, they prescribed no model of legitimate political authority other than 'free government' and liberty. Toland, in defining the principles of a 'commonwealthsman' insisted that he was not against monarchy, merely its abuse. He wrote: 'Commonwealth (which is the common weal or good) whenever we use it about our own government, we take it only in this sense; just as the word *Respublica* in Latin is a general word for all free governments.' The intent of the commonwealthsmen was not to eliminate the monarchy but rescue both the king and country from the 'devouring jaws of arbitrary power'. Toland deployed Harrington's works as an injunction to settle the monarchy, 'under such wise regulations as are most likely to continue it for ever, consisting of such excellent laws as indeed set bounds to the will of the king, but that render him thereby the more safe, equally binding up his and the subjects hands from unjustly seizing one another's prescribed rights or privileges'.[3] This denial,

---

[3] Toland, *State-Anatomy* (1717), 10; Toland (ed.), *Oceana of James Harrington and His Other Works*, cited as *The Works of Harrington* (1700), Preface, vii. See also Toland, *Vindicius*

by the neo-Harringtonians of the 1690s and 1700s, of theoretical and institutional Republicanism poses a serious historiographical problem. The root of this problem lies in the secularist premise of current work. If such men as Toland, Moyle and Trenchard, in rearticulating Harrington's thought, had abandoned the momentum for institutional and political revolution, to what form of change (political, social or religious) were they committed? In its Whiggish way modern scholarship has examined the Republicans as politicians of secularism, a strategy which ignores the practical intent of their intended reforms which were presented in a religious idiom.[4] The emphasis upon the political is, I suspect, a legacy of Victorian scholarship. It is easy for the 'modern' mind to grasp the 'realities', the 'public' nature of politics with its creeds, programmes, dogma and mundane character. 'Religion' for the rational mind, has become marginalized into the internal tabernacle of private belief, without the implications of a public profile.[5]

Liberius (1702), 128; 'I declare by the word commonwealth no pure democracy, nor any particular form of government, but an independent community where the commonweal or good of all indifferently is design'd and pursu'd, let the form be what it will.' Note, in *State-Anatomy* Toland rejected the title of 'democratick Commonwealthsman' which he identified with 'licentiousness': Toland insisted he upheld 'liberty' and a 'government of laws enacted for the common good of all the people', 12–14. Toland, *Anglia Libera*, 92; Toland, *The Art of Governing by Parties*, 31; and Robert Molesworth's translation of Francis Hotman's French treatise *Francogallia* (1721), i–viii. See Toland's comments (*Collections*, II, 339) on the biased reception of his editions of Harrington and Milton: 'This was reckon'd a public service, but rewarded only with the public applauses of such as approv'd the undertaking; while the other side had the most specious pretext imaginable to represent me, what yet in their sense I was not, a most violent republican.' Note, in general Toland's motivation was not simply political – as his biographer wrote in the 'Abstract of the Life of John Toland' in Toland's *Critical History of the Celtic Religion and Learning* (1820), 42, that it was his purpose, 'to render civil government consistent with the inalienable rights of mankind; and to reduce Christianity to that pure, simple, and unpompous system, which Christ and his Apostles established'.

[4] The term 'secularists' was not coined until the 1840s: see *OED* entry. Robbins described the 'Republicans' as 'anticlerical and freethinking', *Two Republican Tracts*, 49. J. G. A. Pocock comments: 'It is part of the intellectual transformation of the age that Toland the anticlerical and quasi-Republican was also Toland the Deist and secularist, systematic foe of the Christian prophetic structure on which typology and apocalyptic depended. The connections between deism, republicanism, and millenarianism at the beginning of the eighteenth century are complex and await unravelling' (*Works of Harrington*, 143).

[5] The crucial issue in contention here is the interpretation of religious belief. Modern writers have tended to draw a conceptual distinction between what they would term theology and ideology; 'ideologies' deal exclusively with secular activities, while theology remains cloistered in multi-various private languages. Religion may have been defused in modern Western society as a coherent and dynamic force, but this is no excuse for treating it as such an anaemic quantity in past societies. Our conception of religious belief today is determined by the notion of subjectivity; religious belief is a form of private self-expression, at worst a mere hobby. Religion for the early modern period was not a question of 'belief', with its implications in modern usage as something peculiar to the individual. Religion was not an isolated opinion about the corporality of Christ, the manifestation of the Holy Spirit, or the nature of ordination; it was a culturally dominant language, a co-ordinating matrix in which ideas about social reality were conceived and debated. See F. Jameson, 'Religion and Ideology' in F. Barker et al. (eds.), *1642: Literature and Power in the Seventeenth Century* (Essex, 1981).

The secularist analysis has posed a further scholarly lacuna. We have become comfortable with the obviousness of the connection between deism and Republicanism: men of Harrington, Moyle and Toland's ilk were anticlerical, secular and 'modern'. But the evasion of a serious examination of the relationship between deism and Republicanism renders the theorists of the 1690s and 1700s incoherent. How are we to explain the fact that Harrington and Toland, the apparently modern secularist tolerationists, consistently justify the necessary maintenance of a nationally established Church. The *locus classicus* of this problem is Harrington's *Oceana* (1656), to some the original text of modern political science, written with a 'total lack of spiritual content'.[6] However, in his utopian prescription Harrington was committed to a national Church establishment, a theme echoed in Toland and Shaftesbury almost verbatim.[7] In order to unravel this paradox we must examine the meaning of Republican anticlericalism. In this way both problems (the abandonment of programmatic Republicanism and the insistence upon a national Church) can be resolved. The general theme of my argument will be that the Republicans extended the parameters of traditional ecclesiological debate from discussing the rival claims of conflicting *imperium* and *sacerdotium* to a fusion of the state and religion, embodied in the classical idea of *religio* or civil religion.

POLITICAL ANTICLERICALISM: PRIESTS AND DIVINE RIGHT TYRANNY

The major radical objection levelled against the Church was the link between civil and spiritual tyranny. As Matthew Tindal commented, the slavery of the body and the mind were inseparable. A hierocratic society entailed a

---

[6] See G. P. Gooch and H. Laski, *English Democratic Ideas in the Seventeenth Century* (Cambridge, 1954), 249, 'a markedly secular spirit may be noticed throughout his works'; C. Blitzer, *An Immortal Commonwealth* (Yale, 1970), 166, applauds 'the substantial correctness of Gooch's characterisations: His [Harrington's] interests, his convictions, and his habits of thought were all essentially secular. Surely the fact that these writings on religion are so extensive can no more be taken as evidence of their author's alleged spirituality than can the fact that Hobbes devoted almost half of his *Leviathan* to the same subject'; J. Shklar, 'Ideology Hunting: The Case of James Harrington', *American Political Science Review* 53 (1959), 684. See also F. Raab, *The English Face of Machiavelli* (1964), 204: 'The theme of this whole work has been the retreat from God in the realm of politics ... a totally secular analysis of history and politics.'

[7] See Harrington, *Works* (1700), 58–9 on the notion of private and public religion. These phrases are cited in John Toland's *State Anatomy* (1717), 27–8 'for as the conviction of a mans private conscience, produces his private religion, so the conviction of the national conscience, or of the majority, must everywhere produce a National religion'. See also Toland, *Vindicius Liberius* (1702), 107–15 and *Anglia Libera*, 94; and the third Earl of Shaftesbury, *A Letter Concerning Enthusiasm*, 16–17, in *Characteristicks*. See also C. Hill, *Puritanism and Revolution* (1972), chapter 10, 'James Harrington and the People', 289–303.

tyrannical one.[8] Although religion was essential to the state, it could also become a corrupting factor. There was a powerful tradition of objections to clerical influence in affairs of state, epitomized in the thought of Thomas Hobbes, a resource which the Republicans drew upon while objecting to his idea of sovereignty. Hobbes attacked the 'ghostly' authority for challenging the civil power, 'working on mens minds, with words and distinctions, that of them selves signifie nothing'.[9] There was also a Republican anticlericalism found in Harrington's work. Henry Ferne, Archdeacon of Leicester, suggested that Harrington's *Oceana* followed the anti-Christian model of Hobbes' work. Harrington argued for a radical Erastianism. The church was created by the consent of the people. In his narration of ecclesiastical history Harrington took cause to indict the clergy for usurping this popular right. By scriptural manipulation, in particular the self-interested mistranslation of the words 'ordination' and 'church' the clergy had turned religion into a trade. It was in this context that Harrington was the first person to use the word 'priestcraft' in print.[10]

One of the severest recriminations against the clerical order was its fostering of civil tyranny. The clergy, by false 'metaphysics' and the creation of a *de jure divino* defence of the monarchy, had elevated tyranny into a type of divinity. This association of the clergy with the ideological defence of civil tyranny was central to the Republican indictment of contemporary religion. One of the most popular and effective discussions can be found in the collaborative work of John Trenchard (1662–1723) and Thomas Gordon (d. 1750), *The Independent Whig* (20 Jan 1720 to 18 June 1721) and *Cato's Letters* (5 November 1720 to 27 July 1723). Commentary on these works has dealt with the Machiavellian and neo-Harringtonian analyses of corruption and liberty. Indeed both works addressed contemporary political and economic issues such as the Peerage Bill and the commercial fideism of the South Sea Bubble, but there is also a more general anticlerical

---

Note page 298, where Hill points out that Harrington wished to combine toleration with a national Church establishment.

[8] Tindal, *Rights of the Christian Church*, 268, 275.

[9] Hobbes, *Leviathan*, 370. See also William Temple, 'Of Health and Long Life' in *The Complete Works* (2 volumes, 1720), I, 278: 'Now 'tis certain, that as nothing damps or depresses the spirits like great subjection or slavery, either of body or mind; so nothing nourishes, revives and fortifies them like great liberty.' For general discussions of *de jure divino* notions of kingship, see J. N. Figgis, *The Divine Right of Kings* (New York, 1965), and Sommerville, *Politics and Ideology*.

[10] See *Pian Piano* in Pocock, *Works of Harrington*, 372. Note that M. Tindal, *Rights of The Church*, Henry Neville, *Plato Redivivus*, and J. Toland, *The Primitive Constitution of the Christian Church* employ both Harrington's Erastian model of the primitive Church and his philological criticism. Harrington's works are scattered with ironic anticlerical remarks: see, for example, 'an ounce of wisdom is worth a pound of clergy', Pocock, *Works* (*Oceana*), 308–9, the same remark is in *Pian Piano*, 381, See also Pocock, *Works*, 382: 'shake the yoke of the priest' and 438, 530.

dimension.[11] The authors of the *Independent Whig* and *Cato's Letters* agreed with Hobbes 'that religion, or the worship of a deity is natural to man', indeed religion was necessary for good government.[12] The priesthood by claiming the existence of a fairy dominion had corrupted this natural inclination. The authors countered the clergy's insistence that 'speculative atheism' was corrosive of civil society, with the charge that the institutional-ized 'practical atheism' of the clerical estate was that which both 'spoil'd mens morals and made them bad subjects'.[13] The recurrent theme of both these works was that the clergy by their mysteries, dogma and theologies undermined all principles of reason, liberty and morality.

In Thomas Gordon's important later work, the prefatory discourses to his translation of Tacitus' histories (1728–34), the link between a deviant clergy and a malfunctioning civil government became more visible.[14] The issue was 'the principle of God's appointing and protecting Tyrants'. The complicity between the *de jure divino* claims of the monarchy and the clergy provoked Gordon's ire. He wrote: 'It is impossible for the hearts of men to contrive a principle more absurd and wicked, than that of annexing divine and everlasting vengeance to the resisting of the most flagrant mischief which can possibly befall the sons of men; yet it has found inventors and vouchers.' Commenting upon the Roman experience, Gordon insisted that the decline of virtue and prosperity was only complete with the deification of the Emperor Augustus, who became an engine of tyranny promoting super-stition and 'public slavery'. Implicit within the religious devotion paid to a monarchy was the enforcement of civil servitude, 'for superstition enslaves as effectually as real power, and therefore confers it; nor is tyranny ever so complete as when the chief magistrate is chief pontiff, as were the soldats of Egypt and Bagdad'.[15] Only in a state of 'liberty' could life, property and religion be secure. The idea of religious worship, unless coupled with toleration of belief, could be

[11] J. G. A. Pocock does allude to the anticlerical tenor of these works. See *Machiavellian Moment*, 475–6 for a discussion of the links between Puritanism, Republicanism, and deism. My work intends to give this speculation a fuller treatment.

[12] Trenchard and Gordon, *Independent Whig* (1721), 321–2 citing Hobbes, *Leviathan*, chapter 12.

[13] Trenchard and Gordon, *Independent Whig*, 84–6, 324, 333.

[14] These prefatory discourses were translated into French in 1794. The *Independent Whig* was also translated into French by the materialist Baron d'Holbach in 1767. Gordon's anticler-icalism is also evident in his manuscript history of England, see BL Add, 20780. For a general discussion of Gordon, see J. M. Bullock, *Thomas Gordon the Independent Whig* (Aberdeen, 1918); J. A. W. Gunn, *Beyond Liberty and Property* (Montreal, 1983), 7–42 has an interesting discussion of Gordon and Trenchard's work in relation to Tacitus, but eschews the anticlerical elements in their polemics. See also O. Ranum, 'D'Alembert, Tacitus, and the Political Sociology of Despotism', *Transactions of the Fifth International Congress of the Enlightenment* 2 (Oxford, 1981), and J. N. Shklar, 'Jean D'Alembert and the Rehabilitation of History', *JHI* 42 (1981).

[15] T. Gordon, *The Works of Tacitus* (4 volumes, 1737), I, 100, 104, 133, 178.

converted into an apparent engine of tyranny and delusion, into a manifest market and commodity for deluders, who whilst they are openly engaging in nothing but gain, and fraud and domineering, and the like very selfish pursuits, all very worldly, have the conscience to preach up self denial, to preach against the world, and to claim successorship to the poor, wandering, holy and disinterested Apostles.

Gordon's theme was that the clergy had managed to usurp a power over the minds of men, and that civil servitude was founded upon this premise.[16]

Gordon was not isolated in maintaining these thoughts. John Toland in his *Anglia Libera* (1701) argued that while it was 'natural' for every government to have some form of 'public and orderly way' of worshipping God, that this was to be placed under the inspection of the civil magistrate. Toland proclaimed with the 'stentorian voice' of liberty, that tyranny had inevitably used religion for devious purposes. The Stuart monarchy was the most recent example: 'they found out a new device to persuade the people by the most awful impressions of religion, and under no less a penalty than eternal damnation, to a non-resistance and passive obedience to the Prince's commands of whatever nature soever.'[17] In his *Art of Governing by Parties* (1701) Toland continued the theme of the potentially divisive role of religion. The clergy were a persuasive institution and an effective means for the dissemination of authority, 'their being posted more commodiously than any army, one at least in every parish all over the Kingdom'.[18] Toland's complaint was that the Stuart monarchy had erected the principle of 'party' as a means to create and reinforce monarchical absolutism. Particularly effective had been the exploitation of religious differences, 'because it enters more or less into all our other divisions, and has been not only the chiefest, but also the most successful machine of the conspirators against our government, well knowing with what fury men oppose one another when they imagine they are fighting for God, and hazarding the salvation of their souls'.[19] Toland argued that divine right of kings 'was set up at first by a few aspiring clergymen, to ingratiate themselves with weak princes, who had designs inconsistent with the laws'. To conduct government upon such principle was to construct a world of 'chimeras and inconsistence'. Toland suggested that the clergy's claim to establish 'religion' was false, he explained: 'I am satisfied ... that a religion which diminishes the wealth or the power of any nation, which injures their bodies or inslaves their conscience, is not the most likely to make the best provision for their souls,

---

[16] *Ibid.*, III, 6, 220. Note also that Harrington defined 'absolute monarchy' in religious terms, see Toland, *Works of Harrington*, 507.

[17] Toland, *Anglia Libera*, 95, 181–3. Note that Toland (*Anglia Libera*, 26) inverted the *de jure divino* rhetoric by insisting that popular approbation was 'the only divine right of all magistracy, for the voice of the people is the voice of God'.

[18] J. Toland, *Art of Governing*, 24. Note that this is to the CUL classmark Syn. 7.76.24.[11]

[19] *Ibid.*, 19.

and to procure their eternal happiness.'[20] The direct conceptual links between the motors of civil tyranny and deviant religion were forged, a religion which encouraged or provided the foundations for secular discomfort was in Toland's view by definition no religion at all.

The critic, playwright and radical polemicist John Dennis (1657–1734) refuted the claims of the High Church Henry Sacheverell in a similar manner. Sacheverell had argued for a 'political Union' of the *de jure divino* authorities of the monarchy and the clerical order. Dennis noted in his *Danger of Priestcraft* (1702) that 'the arbitrary and tyrannical power of the Prince depends upon the illegal impious power of the Priesthood'.[21] Dennis argued that since all government was both 'for and from the people', who had entered into civil society for the defence of their 'rights', that the question must be asked by what means had the people come to give up these rights and subject themselves to the arbitrary will of their rulers. The latter condition was contrary to the purpose of government, and probably a worse condition than the state of nature. The answer was straightforward. The tyrannous power of the king had prevailed upon the 'corrupt part of the clergy to trump up those wretched abominable doctrines of the Jus Divinium, non-resistance, and passive obedience upon the people'.[22]

Dennis' point was that the current practices and beliefs of the clergy were directly contrary to the principles of good government. They simultaneously usurped false rights to the sovereign, while grasping deviant authority to themselves. He exclaimed: 'They support a power in their Kings of cutting the throats of the people, they reserve to themselves the privilege of cutting the throats of their Kings.'[23] In theological terms Dennis suggested that the rule of priestcraft, with its implicit hostility to the principles of liberty and true government, was the rule of Antichrist. In *Priestcraft Distinguished from Christianity* (1715) Dennis made distinct the 'Priest of God from a Priest of Baal'.[24] His thesis was premised upon the great persuasive authority the clergy had; he explained, 'that the doctrines which the clergy teach to the people, and the examples they give them, have an extraordinary influence upon their thoughts and actions, is evident from experience and from the very reason of the institution of the order'.[25] Dennis' complaint was that the present clergy neither propagated the tenets of Christianity, nor any form of morality. The role of Christian institutions was to establish the rule of Christ, which was that of reason, law and liberty. The rule of Antichrist was

---

20 Toland, *State-Anatomy*, 11, 20.
21 Dennis, *Danger of Priestcraft*, 16. On Dennis see the introduction to his *Works* (Baltimore, 1950); H. G. Paul, *John Dennis, His Life and Criticism* (New York, 1911); J. Wood Krutch, *Comedy and Conscience after the Restoration* (New York, 1949).
22 Dennis, *Danger of Priestcraft*, 16.   23 *Ibid.*, 17.
24 Dennis, *Priestcraft Distinguished*, Preface, Sig. Av.
25 *Ibid.*, Sig. Ar.

opposite to these tenets, and established the 'empire of passion and will'. Rather than following the Christian injunction of charity, the modern priests pursued the principles of self-love and spiritual pride. Thus 'spiritual tyranny' was implicitly integrated with 'temporal tyranny' to create a 'blind and impious obedience' in the people.[26]

As Dennis was certain of the necessary connection between spiritual and civil tyranny, Robert Molesworth in his influential *Account of Denmark* (1694) presented a similar sociological interpretation. Arbitrary authority invested in the Danish king had been facilitated by the influence the clergy held over the consciences of the people. The clergy and the monarchy had made a mutual 'contract' for their own benefit.[27] He commented: 'The clergy, who always make sure bargains, were the only gainers in this point ... as the instruments that first promoted, and now keep the people in a due temper of slavery; the passive obedience principle riding triumphant in this unhappy Kingdom'.[28] Molesworth pointed out that although clerical dominance was traditionally a facet of 'popery', the Church of England also had the potential capacity to create a 'blind obedience' for deviant purposes.

The point should now be apparent. Men such as Toland, Dennis, Molesworth, Trenchard and Gordon were emphatic that secular tyranny was forged in the arena of 'religion'. The notions of *de jure divino* authority, whether in a secular monarch, or in the clerical order, were mutually reinforcing in their falsity. The Republicans directed their hostility against civil disorder via an assault upon the clerical manipulation of 'religion'. The intention was twofold. The primary assertion was to maintain that arbitrary government was incompatible with 'true religion'.[29] The secondary implication was that any religion which existed under an arbitrary government was deviant. What the clergy of the Church of England upheld as 'Christianity', the Republicans considered as a 'deadly engine in the hands of a tyrant to rivet his subjects in chains'.[30]

Anticlericalism was a crucial part of the radical analysis of the problems of civil government. Modern commentators have usually deduced from this the simplest of equations: that anticlericalism implied irreligion. By attacking the priesthood, men like Dennis, Toland, and Gordon (in the modern and contemporary Anglican interpretation) assaulted all religious principle. John Dennis clearly rebutted such suggestions in drawing a fundamental distinc-

26 *Ibid.*, 4, 5, 19, 23.   27 R. Molesworth, *Account of Denmark*, 55, passim.
28 *Ibid.*, 74.
29 See Trenchard and Gordon, *Cato's Letters*, II, 290–303.
30 Trenchard and Gordon, *Cato's Letters*, II, 265. Religion under the rule of tyranny was the epitome of superstition, it was 'wild whimsies, delusive phantoms, and ridiculous dreams'. The human soul under such a system was degraded and defaced with 'slavish and unmanly fears; to render it a proper object of fraud, grimace, and imposition; and to make mankind the ready dupes of gloomy impostors, and the tame slaves of raging tyrants. For, servitude established in the mind is best established' (*Cato's Letters*, II, 291).

tion between the natures of 'priestcraft' and 'religion'. He objected strongly to those men who attacked religion *qua* religion. Even though the attempt of such men was to rid society and religion of priestcraft (which was a just design), they made no plans 'to establish any other religion in the room of that which they would destroy'. All nations and societies needed religion, 'for the religion of every country in which the natives and their forefathers have been educated, and which is antecedent or coeval to most of its laws and customs; whether true or false, is certainly the basis of that country's constitution'. It did not matter whether a national religion was true or false as long as the public doctrine and worship was established for the 'welfare and good government' of the nation.[31] John Toland similarly asserted the integrity of his own religious beliefs. He declared: 'in all the books I ever wrote, there is not one word against religion; but on the contrary, several vindications of its purity and excellency from the superstitious practices and worldly usurpations with which it has been often deform'd, but chiefly by priests'.[32] Toland's only crime was an inveterate hatred of 'priestcraft'. Toland admitted that he held certain unorthodox notions about religious issues, but saw no contradiction in claiming this theological heterodoxy, publicly professed, with a similar public confession of his membership of the established Church.[33] For the modern commentator this appears rather confusing; both Dennis and Toland acknowledged public and established religion, while insisting that it was not necessarily 'true'. Toland could do so while maintaining his opposition to many of its tenets, while Dennis could declare that it was unnecessary whether the public religion was 'true or false'.

FROM ERASTIANISM TO CIVIL THEOLOGY: THE ROMAN EXAMPLE

As an antidote to the modern marginalization of the Republicans' religious opinions it is necessary to explore how they adopted and adapted the traditional language of Erastianism in creating an idea of the national Church as a civil religion. The Reformation debate between the claims of the civil and spiritual powers can be identified in the ambiguity of the idea of the royal supremacy which placed the supervision of external ecclesiastical affairs in civil hands, but still made provision for an independent and *de jure divino* spiritual *ordo*. While non-jurors like George Hickes and Charles

---

[31] Dennis, *Vice and Luxury Publick Mischiefs*, 78, 103. See also Harrington, *A System of Politics*: 'As not this language, nor that language, but some language; so not this religion, nor that religion, yet some religion is natural to every nation' (Pocock, *Works of Harrington*, 838).

[32] Toland, *State-Anatomy*, 21.

[33] *Ibid.*, 22–3; see also *Anglia Libera*, 99. For Toland's credo see *Collections*, II, 302. See also Toland's definition of 'faith', 'which is the internal participation of the divine nature, irradiating the soul; and externally benefiting in beneficence, justice, sanctity, and those other virtues by which we resemble God, who is himself all goodness' (*Nazarenus*, v–vi).

Leslie premised their clericalist vision on a defence of an independent and superior *sacerdotium*, the radicals extended the originally mild language of the royal supremacy into a fully blown denial of *sacerdos* and the absorption of the clerical body into the civil state.

As Hobbes argued, the logic of sovereignty entailed that all authority, both civil and sacerdotal, extended solely from the fount of civil power. Harrington, using different principles, insisted that religious authority could only originate, as did civil authority, in the consent and acclamation of the body of the people. The Republicans acknowledged Hobbes' position that religious authority originated in the lay power, but applauded Harrington's 'democratic' analysis of the nature of this power. Since religion was an issue of personal conviction and conscience, religious authority could only derive from the consent or acknowledgement of the congregation.[34] Harrington had suggested the extreme 'Erastian' position following Cranmer, that the election of officers of the Church was an action similar to the election of civil ministers.[35] As the authors of *The Independent Whig* argued against those who maintained the divine right of the clergy, 'your Church is a creature of the constitution, and you are creatures of the law'. The idea of *sacerdos* was a priestly fiction.[36] For these men there was no colour or pretence for the chimerical distinction of ecclesiastical and civil, 'in any other sense than the words, maritime and military' are used to denote different branches of the executive power.[37] These radical arguments were presented with the veneer of Reformation Erastianism.

To the orthodox Anglican this extreme Erastianism implied a cynical manipulation of religion: it was simply a tool of the civil state employed in the needs of prudence and pragmatism, rather than to tend the transcendental 'spiritual' needs of the soul. The 'clergy' were to be merely state servants selected by merit rather than sacerdotal vocation. The religious chalice was

---

34 See Harrington, *Pian Piano* (1657), and Part II of *The Prerogative of Popular Government* (1658): for a discussion of this debate, see Pocock, 'Introduction', *Works of Harrington* 67–90. See also Tindal's *Rights*, passim.

35 Pocock, *Works of Harrington*, 519: 'And why is not ordination in the Church or Commonwealth of Christ as well a political thing as it was in the Churches or Commonwealths of the Jews or of the Heathens? Why is not the election of officers in the Church as well a political thing as election of officers in the State?'

36 Trenchard and Gordon, *Independent Whig*, xxix, 43, 45. The authors of *The Independent Whig* were vociferous in their Erastianism, citing Erastus at length:

> that every state had the same authority of modelling their ecclesiastical as civil government; that the Gospel gave no preheminance, or authority to Christians over one another, but that everyman alike (who had suitable abilities) was qualified to execute all the duties and offices of their most Holy religion; and that it is a matter of prudence and convenience to appoint particular persons to officiate for the rest, with proper rewards and encouragements, which persons would be intitled to no more power than they themselves gave them. (*Independent Whig*, I, 91)

37 *Ibid.*, 105–6.

drained of its divine draughts, and refilled with the new wine of secular rationalization. While it is true that the Republicans launched an assault upon the clerical order, on its wealth, on its political entanglements and corruption, and ultimately upon the very idea of a separate caste of religious experts, all this was done in the name of 'religion'. The religious nature of this enterprise has been rejected by both Anglicans and modern scholarship. The arguments of both the defenders of hierocracy and of modern commentators have been premised upon the mutually exclusive natures and claims of 'religion' and 'policy'. The position was, as Henry Fletcher suggested, how could 'policy and piety both lie in a bed, and yet not touch one another?'[38]

The religious policy of the Republicans has usually been condemned as 'politick religion' in an attempt to taint their schemes with the dylogistic model of Machiavelli. The orthodox usage of the word 'religion' during this period held certain incantations: primarily it gestured towards the tenets and institutions of Christianity. The 'truth' of Christianity hegemonized the value of the word 'religion'; the social implications of this usage were the propagation of a set of divine principles by a clerical body. Implicit in the use of the word was the apparatus of sacerdotalism: religion implied priest. In its orthodox construction the meaning of religion was collapsed into the tenets of Christianity; the beliefs of the latter were based upon a notion of the 'other world', upon truths defined not in terms of the world, or society, but by a spiritual determinant. In order to appreciate the Republican meaning of the word 'religion' we have to recognize that there was (and is) no necessary connection between the persuasive content of the term 'religion' and the claims for the veracity of Christianity. It was the commonplace assumption of the complete coincidence of the meanings of the terms 'religion' and 'Christianity' that the Republicans attempted to dissolve. In a similar manner, we as modern observers have to shed our hostility to the usage of the word 'religion' within a temporal and social context.[39]

One of the best illuminations of the Republican idea of the value and function of religion can be found in the traditions, both intellectual and historical, which they promoted. Antiquity and the canons of ancient prudence provided not only political ideas, but also beliefs about religion.

---

[38] Raab, *The English Face of Machiavelli*, 79.
[39] It should be made clear that someone like Toland or Dennis believed in the truth of religion, and (to some extent) in the truth of Christianity, but that the criteria for truth was very different from orthodox descriptions of Christian truth. As argued in chapter 4, Toland's notion of true religion was broad enough to encompass Judaism, Islam and Christianity. One suspects that, for example, people like Toland and Stillingfleet used the words 'truth' and 'Christianity' in radically incommensurable ways. The issue over whether the radicals were 'atheistic' is to some extent an anachronism: for the Anglican hierarchy they most certainly were, while for the modern historian to attempt to assess the 'truth' value of past religious belief is both methodologically naive and unacceptable. The task is to understand, not to indict or arbitrate.

Men such as Toland, Neville, Harrington, Molesworth and Moyle all insisted upon the importance of reading the classical works Hobbes had proscribed in *Leviathan*. The 'classics' were ubiquitous in the education of the literate of the period. Editions of the works of antiquity were available in both original languages and competent translations; the works of Cicero, Aristotle, Polybius, Plutarch, Tacitus and Plato were commonplace.[40] Robert Molesworth commented:

The books that are left us of the ancients (from whence as fountains, we draw all that we are now masters of) are full of doctrines, sentences, and examples exhorting to the conservation or recovery of the public liberty, which was once valued above life. The heroes there celebrated are for the most part such as had destroyed or expelled tyrants; and though Brutus be generally declaimed against by modern school boys, he was then esteemed the true pattern and model of exact vertue.[41]

Molesworth complained that the modern educators, the priests, were too concerned with elegance and style, rather 'than the matters contained within them'. He considered the education of the youth as the very foundation 'stones of the publick liberty'. To allow education to be manipulated by a caste whose interest was opposed to the public benefit was detrimental. The immediate necessity was for education to follow the ancient pattern and to be administered by the philosophers rather than the clergy.[42] John Toland reinforced this notion in his *Cicero Illustratus* (1712). He adduced 'that the whole, or at least the greatest part of the progress we make in eloquence and politicks, is owing to the Greek and Latin authors, whose manners in their

---

[40] See E. Sandys, *A History of Classical Scholarship* (3 volumes, Oxford, 1930); H. S. Bennett, *English Books and their Readership 1603–1640* (Cambridge, 1970), 133–4. The appeal of classical antiquity to the Republicans could be viewed as a further strand of the 1690s dispute between the ancients and the moderns, inspired by Fontenelle: see W. Temple, *Essay Upon Ancient and Modern Learning* (1692), who firmly applauds the lessons of ancient prudence: 'For political institutions, that tend to the preservation of Mankind, by civil governments; 'tis enough to mention those of Cyrus, Theseus, Licurgus, Solon, Zalencus, Charondas, Romulus, Numa Pompilius, besides the more ancient institutions of the Assyrian and Aegyptian governments and laws, wherein it may be observed such a reach of thought, such depth of wisdom, and such force of genius, as the presumption, and flattery itself of our age, will hardly pretend to parallel, by any of our modern institutions' (*Complete Works*, I, 302). Temple was so enamoured with the principles of ancient prudence that he even applauded non-Western models such as Chinese and Peruvian legislators who 'in practice ... excell the very speculation of other men, and all those imaginary schemes of the European wit, the institutions of Xenophon, the Republic of Plato, the Utopians, or Oceanas of our modern writers' (see 'Of Heroick Virtue', *Complete Works*, I, 204–10); arguing against Temple, see W. Wotton, *Reflections Upon Ancient and Modern Learning* (1694); for a useful and witty summary of the dispute, see J. Swift, *A Full and True Account of the Battle Fought Last Friday between the Antient and Modern Books in St James Library* (1704).
[41] Molesworth *An Account of Denmark*, Preface, xxvi.
[42] *Ibid.*, xx-xxv. See also Tindal, *Rights*, 84–5, 128, 268, 295–6, on the superiority of Greek education. See also *Independent Whig*, 'Of Education', 215–30; Toland, *State-Anatomy*, 'Of Universities and Pulpits', 69–70; and 'Letter Concerning the Roman Education' in Toland, *Collections*, II, 1–17.

books (as it were speaking from their tombs) did formerly and do still give the universe inimitable lessons of refin'd speaking of the Art of government, and of the most polished as well as the most virtuous Regulations of manners, all illustrated and confirmed by an infinite number of examples'.[43] Toland's work attempted to raise a subscription to aid his intended publication of Cicero's complete works with a critical apparatus suitable for the general reader. He feared that the way Cicero was taught in school meant he was ill-appreciated. Toland excoriated, 'that preposterous method of putting the works of Cicero at random into the hands of raw schoolboys [which] may be counted among the reasons why many men conceive such false notion of this divine author, and almost tremble at his name remembering the many lashes they have received from their dull pedagogues upon his account'.[44]

Walter Moyle, appreciated by both Montesquieu and Edward Gibbon for his knowledge of antiquity, lauded the lessons of the classical writers. He wrote in 1698: 'I study nothing but the Roman history and the constitution of their government.' Herodotus, Thucydides and Xenophon were amongst the myriad of ancient writers commended for their 'wonderful sense of religion'. Moyle had read the entire corpus of classical literature in the original tongues, but had refused to study any literature after the fourth century. The stories of ancient Greece and Rome contained 'useful treasures' to be put to contemporary use.[45] The bulk of Moyle's work was either in the form of translations from, or dissertations upon, the classics; his work *An Essay Upon the Roman Government* is characteristic. He also translated Xenophon's discourse upon the revenue of Lacedaemon as a direct commentary upon the fiscal policies of the 1690s. The satirical works of Lucian were published as an assault upon superstition, manifest in both the absurd ceremonies of pagan religion, and such contentious Christian dogmas as the Trinity.[46]

One of the men of antiquity most consistently applauded by the Freethinkers and Republicans was Marcus Tullius Cicero.[47] Montesquieu wrote in

43 Toland, *Cicero Illustratus* (1712), a portion of which was translated and published in the preface to Cicero, *Tusculan Disputations* (1715), xii–xiii.
44 Toland, *Cicero Illustratus* in Cicero, *Tusculan Disputations* (1715), xviii.
45 W. Moyle, *Works* (1727/Hammond, ed.) 17, 10–11, 33, 245.
46 See W. Moyle, *An Essay on the Lacedaemonian Government*, (1698). Also *Translations from Lucian* for satires on the clergy, idolatry and ritual in 'Of Sacrifices', 'Dialogue with Hesiod' and 'A Dissertation upon the Age of the Philopatris, A Dialogue commonly attributed to Lucian'. See also Thomas Gordon's (d. 1750) important editions of Tacitus' *Annals* and *Histories* (1728–34) which were accompanied by valuable introductory discourses.
47 For the most recent discussion of Ciceronianism, see R. Browning, *The Political and Constitutional Ideas of the Court Whigs* (Louisiana, 1982). Browning suggests that Ciceronianism was a Court Whig development to counter the radical Catonic ideology of the

his *Discours sur Cicéron* (1716): 'Cicéron est, de tous les anciens, celui qui a eu le plus de merité personnel, et a qui j'aimerois mieux ressembler.' The desire to identify oneself with the orator of Rome was prevalent amongst the Republicans. Walter Moyle suggested that Andrew Fletcher was the 'Cicero' of the Country Party.[48] John Toland, writing to his patron Robert Molesworth on his decision not to serve in Parliament any longer, compared Molesworth's retirement to the seven years' inactivity of Cicero. Toland hoped that just as Cicero's seclusion from political activity had resulted in all those 'incomparable books' that 'in the like manner, my Lord, that excellent work, wherein you have made such progress, and which seems to resemble so nearly Cicero's De Republica, will be a nobler task, and more useful to mankind, than any senatorial efforts'.[49] Locke had recommended Cicero's *De Inventore* and *De Officiis* in his treatise on education as essential to the study of ethics and oratory. Cicero was honoured in the pantheon constructed by Anthony Collins in his *Discourse on Freethinking* (1713). Indeed Collins had prepared his own translations of *De Natura Deorum* and *De Divinatione*. Cicero's membership of the society of Freethinkers was not uncontended. While Collins attempted to assert that Cicero held no belief in the immortality of the soul, the more orthodox men of the time, the clerics Samuel Clarke, Richard Bentley and Bishop Berkeley, attempted to integrate Cicero within a Christian framework.[50] The ancient past was not just

Republicans. My suggestion is that within a religious context there was already a radical usage of Cicero.

48 Montesquieu, 'Discours sur Cicéron' in *Œuvres complètes* (3 volumes, Paris, 1950), III, 15. Moyle, *Works* (1727/Hammond, ed.), 284.

49 Toland, *Collections*, II, 492. Toland had also referred to John Locke as a modern Cicero, (*Life of Milton* (1761), 136).

50 The same debate, and attempted assimilation, was continued between Samuel Clarke and the 'apostle' of deism, Matthew Tindal. Clarke insisted that Cicero, although confident of the existence of a natural religion, had pointed out the necessity of revelation. Tindal on the contrary held that Cicero's philosophy indicated the sufficiency of natural religion to lead men to perfection. The apotheosis of Cicero worship can be found in Conyers Middleton's *History of the Life of Marcus Tullius Cicero* (1741). The work was a popular success, having over 3,000 subscribers. Middleton, the Keeper of the University Library at Cambridge, argued that the role of history was to be both entertaining and instructive. Middleton's complaint was that too many of the Lives published concentrated upon military heroes, rather than the 'pacific and civil character'. His remedy was to supply the public with the Life of Cicero. The latter was virtue embodied; the *De Officiis* was an almost perfect moral system. Middleton cited Erasmus who considered that Cicero was inspired by the deity. Middleton, *The Life of Cicero*, I, Preface, xv–xvii and II, 560. For a further discussion of Cicero's influence see: M. E. Neilson, 'Cicero's *De Officiis* in Christian thought 300–1300' in *Essays and Studies in English and Comparative Literature* (Michigan, 1933); G. Gawlick, 'Cicero and the Enlightenment', 657–82 in *SVEC* 25 (1963); G. A. Burnett, 'The Reputation of Cicero among the English Deists 1660–1776', (unpublished Ph.D., California, 1947). Cicero's influence can be best appreciated from examining the *Wing Catalogue*. The editions of his works are countless. For example, *Opera quae extant Omnia* (1681); *De Officiis* (1648–95), eleven editions; *Tully's Offices* (1680), five editions. On Collins, see J. O'Higgins, *Anthony Collins the Man and His Work* (The Hague, 1970) at 35, which shows that

considered as an academic influence, but as a living seedbed of moral authority.

In *De Natura Deorum* Cicero subjected Roman religion to careful analysis presenting the various Epicurean and Stoic arguments about the nature and function of religion. One of the crucial distinctions made in the work was between the notions of *religio* and *superstitio*. Both were forms of religious worship. *Superstitio* was the formalistic worship premised upon the 'vain fear of the Gods', *religio* was devotion which resulted from a pious adoration of God.[51] The former was rejected because it performed no useful function for society, while *religio* was premised upon principles that supported the unity of society. During the discussion of the variant doctrines, and explanations of the gods of the Roman Republic, Cotta the Sceptic had suggested, 'totam de Diis immortalibus opinionem fictam esse ab hominibus sapientibus Republicae casa: ut quos ratio non posset eos ad officium religio duceret'.[52] The implication was that Roman theology was a fictive system, calculated to wield an influence over those who could not be restrained from doing ill through the simple exercise of reason: *religio* was an invention of the politicians.

While Cicero in *De Divinatione* revealed a more explicit disbelief in the ceremonies of Roman religion, this did not imply that he argued for the end of such ritual. The work dealt at length with Roman divination and augury. Cicero acting as a critic of these practices nevertheless warned against the danger of falling either into 'blasphemous impiety', or 'old women's superstition'.[53] In Cicero's opinion divination could have no basis either in art or nature. The practices were 'mere superstitious practices, wisely invented to impose on the ignorant'.[54] Cicero defended the institution of the diviners 'for the sake of their influence on the minds of the common people', and the interests of the state.[55] He argued that whilst one might criticize the science

---

Collins had seventy-four entries in his library catalogue under Cicero which included three copies of *De Divinatione* and nine of *De Natura Deorum*.

[51] See C. D. Yonge (ed.), *The Treatise of Marcus Tullius Cicero* (1853) in *De Natura Deorum*, I, xlii.41. Hereafter all references to Cicero's works are contained in this volume, unless otherwise stated. For a general discussion of Roman religion and its relationship with the state see: A. Wardman, *Religion and Statecraft among the Romans* (1982); Numa Denis Fustel de Coulanges, *The Ancient City* (Baltimore, 1980); R. J. Goar, *Cicero and the State Religion* (Amsterdam, 1972); for more detailed discussions see: D. Grodynski, 'Superstitio' in *REA* 76 (1974), especially 40–3; G. Szemler, 'Religio, Priesthood, and Magistrates in the Roman Republic' in *Numen* 18 (1971), especially 121, 123, 126–7; T. A. Dorey (ed.), *Cicero* (1965), 135–214; Myrto Dragona-Monachou, *The Stoic Arguments and the Providence of the Gods* (Athens, 1976). See also J. Thrower, *The Alternative Tradition: Religion and the Rejection of Religion in the Ancient World* (The Hague, 1980), 203–31.

[52] Cicero, *De Natura Deorum*, I, xliii.41.   [53] Cicero, *De Divinatione*, I, iv.145.

[54] *Ibid.*, I, xlvii.188.

[55] *Ibid.*, II, xxviii-v.229–31.

of soothsaying in private 'the interest of religion and the state' required them to be publicly acknowledged.[56]

This Ciceronian notion of a civil theology or *religio* was consciously employed by the Republican theorists. The radical Anthony Collins had made personal translations of both works. The founder of seventeenth-century Republicanism, James Harrington, had applauded the Roman's works. In *Oceana*, Cicero's 'most excellent Book De Natura Deorum' is commended, even though it overthrew the validity of the national religion.[57] Harrington commended the Ciceronian model of religion above the 'modern prudence' of the clergy, which resembled more the 'shrieking of the lapwing' than the voice of truth. Cicero's work upon divination was also applauded by Harrington. He commented:

By the way it has been a maxim with legislators not to give check to the present superstition, but to make the best use of it as that which is always the most powerful with the people; otherwise tho' Plutarch was interested in the cause, there is nothing plainer than Cicero in his book *De Divinatione* has made it, that there was never anything such as an Oracle, except in the cunning of Priests.[58]

It is important to note that the legislator Archeon of *Oceana* is explicitly modelled upon the pattern of the ancient legislators Numa Pompilius, Lycurgus and Solon (who were lauded by Cicero), with the implication that religion in *Oceana* was to have the same functional characteristics as *religio* in the ancient states.[59]

WALTER MOYLE, NEO-HARRINGTONIANISM AND NUMA
POMPILIUS

The most extensive and coherent commentary applauding the Roman model of religion was Walter Moyle's (1672–1721) *Essay on The Roman Govern-ment*, a work written and circulated in manuscript form in the late 1690s and first published posthumously in the 1726 collection of his unpublished works

56 *Ibid.*, II, xii.211.
57 Toland, *Works of Harrington (Oceana)*, 211. See also Toland, *Serena*, 117; M. Tindal, *Christianity as Old as the Creation* (1731), iv.
58 Toland, *Works of Harrington (Oceana)*, 209.
59 Cicero was not the only source for the history of classical civil religion: for example one of the most frequently cited works was Polybius' (206–124 BC) *Histories*. Editions of the work had been translated in 1634 by Edward Grimeston, and in 1698 by Henry Sheeres. The crucial passage, cited, for example, by Walter Moyle, Conyers Middleton and the *Traité des trois imposteurs*, discussed the role of religion in the Roman Republic. See Moyle in Robbins, *Two Republican Tracts*, 212; C. Middleton, *Life*, II, 552; *Traité des trois imposteurs*, BL Sloane 2039, folio 64r. It was popular civil theology that preserved the Roman Republic. Since the populace were 'fickle and full of ill managed passions; as likewise easie to be worked into heats and animosities' the legislators constructed, 'specious dreads, and these sorts of fictions' to restrain them (Polybius, *Histories* translated H. Sheeres, 72–3; see F. W. Walbank *Polybius* (1972), 59).

edited by Thomas Sergeant.[60] Moyle was educated at Exeter College, Oxford although he did not sit for his degree. Between 1695 and 1698 he represented Saltash in the Commons. As a parliamentarian Moyle was identified as an 'Old Whig' being vocal upon such issues as the Place Bills, the Standing Army debates, issues on public welfare and the state of the Royal Navy. His political radicalism can be identified in his collaboration with John Trenchard on the polemical *An Argument against Standing Armies* (1698). Moyle, a frequenter of diverse coffee houses such as Maynwaring's in Fleet Street, the Grecian at the Temple, and Will's in Covent Garden, associated with such radicals as John Dennis, John Trenchard, Anthony Fletcher and Henry Neville, as well as the dramatists William Congreve and John Dryden. It was in this coffee house company that Moyle picked up his disgust of the clergy. Although Moyle was a staunch parliamentarian who held the liberty of his country close to his heart, he was acknowledged by his peers first and foremost as a man of extensive erudition.

From an examination of Moyle's extant correspondence it is apparent that his scholarly interests were many and varied. While he corresponded upon 'dramatical criticism' with John Dennis, or runic inscriptions, ancient monuments, Roman medals, druidical stones, ornithology and meteorological phenomena, his main interest and passion was the study of ancient history. As his friend Anthony Hammond declared: 'His thoughts were rather turned upon making the best advantages by reading, especially in history, from which he collected the forms, constitutions, and the laws of government.'[61] Moyle's reading was focused upon the history of antiquity, although later in his life he became fascinated with the history of early Christianity.[62] Although Moyle completed excellent and important translations and commentaries upon various classical themes and issues, his most important work for its commentary upon the role of religion in Republican thought is the *Essay on Roman Government*.[63]

[60] It is important to note that a manuscript copy of the first part of the *Essay* exists in the Shaftesbury Papers in the PRO reference PRO/30/24/47/4. Fox-Bourne in his two-volume Life of Locke mistakenly attributed the work to Locke. H. R. Russell-Smith rightly argued that the work came from Moyle's pen. This still leaves unresolved the genesis and authorship of the particular manuscript in the Shaftesbury collection. It is apparent from examination of the text that the handwriting is *not* John Locke's. The connection between Locke and the manuscript is not entirely shattered as the handwriting is almost certainly that of Locke's amanuensis, Sylvanus Brownover. Many thanks to J. Marshall for identifying the latter's script.

[61] Moyle, *Works* (1727/Hammond, ed.), 'Some account of Mr Moyle and his writings', 28, and passim.

[62] See, in particular, his controversy with Humphrey Prideaux over the issue of the Thundering Legion in *Works* (1726/Sergeant, ed.), II, 1–390, and with Mr Naylor and William Whiston on the origin of Christian Churches in *Works* (1726/Sergeant, ed.), I, 376–98.

[63] For example his dissertation upon the origins of the *Philopatris* in *Works* (1726/Sergeant, ed.), I, 285–364, *An Essay on the Lacedaemonian Government* in *Works* (1727/Hammond, ed.), 47–77, and various translations of Lucian in *Works* (1727/Hammond, ed.).

Moyle has been classified as part of the neo-Harringtonian resurgence of the 1690s. The *Essay on Roman Government* has been noted as an important work for the transmission of 'a continuing classical tradition' to the eighteenth century.[64] Little attempt, however, has been made to examine the *Essay* in any detail, and in particular the nature and tenor of the Harringtonianism contained in the work.[65]

The *Essay*, composed in two unequal parts, was written by 1699. The context of the work is clearly Harringtonian, being concerned to discuss the causes and alterations in the Roman state from limited monarchy to oligarchy. The conceptual tool employed in this narrative was the Harringtonian notion that the balance of empire followed the balance of property. While accepting the validity of this interpretation, I wish to suggest that there was a further Harringtonian dimension contained in the *Essay* which deals specifically with the role of religion in the state. This discussion is found in Moyle's exposition of the actions of the legislator Numa Pompilius. This commendatory presentation of Roman state religion informs us in detail of the role religion and anticlericalism play in Republican thought.

Moyle had been encouraged in his hostility towards the clerical order by such men as Neville and Trenchard. In his *Essay upon the Lacedaemonian Government* (1698) he blamed infringements upon liberty on clerical manipulation, he wrote: 'I must tell you plainly, that the clergy have for a great number of years contributed chiefly to perplex the notions and muddle the brains of the people about our English constitution'.[66] In the work upon the Roman government he expanded his hostility into a fully fledged indictment of the 'modern policy' which allowed the hierocratic caste to usurp a 'supremacy, or at least an independency on the civil power over half of Europe'.[67] Moyle had referred to specifically Harringtonian vocabulary to discuss issues of religion. For the Romans, religion 'was a part of their policy, so their clergy likewise were a part of their laity, and interwoven into the general interest of the State; not a separate independent body from the rest of the community, nor any considerable balance of the civil government; but settled upon such an institution, as they could have neither interest nor power to act against the public good'. It was Moyle's purpose in Part I of the *Essay* to elucidate and recommend this ancient prudence.

It was the great genius of Numa Pompilius (715–673 BC) to construct a religious institution that was the 'wisest and most politic system' ever created in its efficacy and influence over the morals of the people and its application

---

[64] See Robbins, *Two Republican Tracts*. This is the edition employed in general, although I have compared it with the first printed edition of 1726 and the manuscript referred to above.

[65] M. A. Goldie, 'The Civil Religion of James Harrington' has dealt with some of the religious dimensions of Harrington's work; he omits, however, any consideration of the influence of *Oceana* on later Harringtonians such as Toland and especially Moyle.

[66] Moyle, *Works* (1727/Hammond, ed.), 62.   [67] Robbins, *Tracts*, 216.

to 'all the ends of civil society'.[68] Numa was able to combine a nationally established Church that was reliant upon the civil state with a liberty of individual belief and worship. For Moyle, Numa's creation was an example of the benefits of a complete Erastianism. The Senate held sway over all affairs of religion.[69] Moyle cited Cicero, one of his favourite authorities after that of Dionysius of Halicarnassus, 'cujus est summa potestas omnium rerum'. The priesthood was not separate from the laity, 'they were by their original constitution all chosen out of the nobility, and afterwards out of the richest and greatest men of the commonwealth: and consequently had such an interest in the civil state, as they would not sacrifice to their particular order.'[70]

One of the crucial benefits of this Erastian scheme was the provision of tolerance for diverse beliefs. Although Numa was cautious of introducing new rites and forms into the national religion this did not imply that private beliefs were to be supervised. Indeed, anyone who asked the Senate for permission might 'celebrate the mysteries in private'. There was a 'universal liberty in religion'; persecution was non-existent. This was the pattern of religion Moyle applauded and wished to see inform the practices of the Church in his day. As Moyle pointed out, the tolerance of Numa's regime had encouraged the expansion of his empire.[71]

Moyle's recommendation was of a national religion calculated to be part of state policy and 'subservient to all the great ends of government and society' with enough latitude to tolerate a diversity of *privately* articulated theological opinions and rites. Moyle not only presented Numa's ecclesiological prescriptions, but also applauded his theology. Numa proposed a simple and rational civil theology: it was the very simplicity of the creed that led it to be a unifying force in society rather than a divisive one. As Moyle commented: 'the common principles of religion all mankind agree in; and the belief of these doctrines a lawgiver may venture to enjoin; but he must go no further if he means to preserve a uniformity in religion.' Numa enjoined belief in no follies, absurdities or contradictions which might ultimately be the cause of schism and sedition. He instituted two simple articles of belief; '1st that the Gods were authors of all good to mankind. 2nd, that to obtain this good the gods were to be worshipped; in which worship, the chief of all was to be innocent, good and just.'[72]

In Moyle's presentation of Numa's credal minimalism we can see a direct commentary upon the theological distractions of the 1690s about the nature of the Trinity. Moyle, following the distinction between an esoteric and

---

[68] *Ibid.*, 215, 209–10.
[69] *Ibid.*, 214: 'All innovations in the National worship, such as the adoption of new gods, and the institution of new forms and ceremonies in religion, were appointed by the authority of the Senate.'
[70] *Ibid.*, 216.   [71] *Ibid.*, 213.   [72] *Ibid.*, 210–11.

exoteric philosophy, argued that there was a dual conception of the nature of God (a popular and a philosophical one). It was only to conform to the 'popular opinion' that men spoke of the godhead as a plurality. The notion of the 'absolute and perfect unity of the Godhead' was too refined for the people who had become accustomed to polytheistic notions due to the 'interest of priests'. For Numa and Moyle the idea of the immortality of the soul was regarded rather as a 'problem of philosophy than an article of divinity', although (citing Polybius) Moyle argued that popular belief ought to be encouraged for its usefulness to the state. The intention of Numa's civil theology was not abstruse speculation but the promotion of virtue, justice and the love of the nation.[73]

Moyle recommended Numa's civil theology to advance the prerogatives of a civil religion against the clericalist alternative of the Church of England. It is my claim that this advocacy of a civil theology is directly indebted to James Harrington's suggestions in *Oceana* (1656), *Pian Piano* (1657) and the *Prerogatives of Popular Government* (1658). As I have already noted, Moyle's *Essay* was composed within the parameters of a specifically Harringtonian enterprise: to explain the transition from limited monarchy to oligarchy. The causal explanation for this shift in the type of government was in terms of a structural alteration in the distribution of property. This is straightforward Harringtonianism. The specific cause of this transition was, according to Moyle, the rise of priestcraft. Implicit in this description of priestcraft was the advance of the clerical order to a state of independent wealth and dominion.[74]

Moyle followed Harrington explicitly in his analysis of 'power'. He wrote: 'Power is of two kinds, imaginary or real. Imaginary power is authority founded upon opinion. Real power is founded upon dominion and property.'[75] Moyle's point was that the Roman clergy (and by implication any Church establishment) should have little 'imaginary power' and no 'real power'. It was Moyle's use of the Harringtonian notion of 'power' based upon opinion which was to be his crucial weapon in the arraignment of priestcraft. Moyle denied any supernatural warrant for the clerical order; the authority of the priest was usually erected upon 'opinion' and 'a persuasion in the people of their divine mission and designation; or from a reverence to their mystic ceremonies and institutions; or for their pretended empire over the consciences of mankind'. Moyle thus proscribed any independent *sacerdos* from the mechanics of his civil religion. Moyle also denied the clergy any right to possession of 'real power'. He explained; 'Authority founded on dominion, results to the clergy either from a right of supremacy

---

[73] *Ibid.*, 212.
[74] For a similar Harringtonian analysis, see Shaftesbury, *Characteristicks*, III, 42–60 of a 'landed hierarchy' swallowing the civil state in the ancient Egyptian and Hebrew states.
[75] Robbins, *Tracts*, 217.

over the Church, or a legal jurisdiction and coercive power over the actions, the lives, and the conduct of the laity.'[76] But the case of the Roman Church clearly argued against clerical possession of property. Citing Cicero's *De Divinatione*, Moyle argued that the Roman clergy were originally from the higher social orders lest the dignity and authority of religion might be prostituted to mercenary ends. Initially the clergy were not even supported by voluntary oblations. As Moyle commented: 'It may seem strange to our age, where the appearance of Godliness is such a great gain, that the Roman clergy should serve their gods for nought.'[77] It was with the subversion of the commonwealth that the clergy became salaried, this being part of imperial policy to undermine liberty. Moyle noted that tyranny and priestcraft seemed to go hand in hand.

In the *Essay on Roman Government* Moyle rearticulated the Harringtonian recommendation of the civil theology of ancient Rome, proposed in *Oceana* (1656). It was in the development of the idea of civil theology that such men as Moyle, Toland and Tindal could syncretize the claims of a national Church with the rights of the individual conscience. The vision Moyle distilled from the patterns of ancient prudence was an extreme Erastianism: the Church was simply an instrument of the civil state employed to facilitate a rational and moral society.

Montesquieu thought Walter Moyle had understood Roman religion perfectly. In his *Dissertation sur la politique des Romains dans la religion* presented at the Bordeaux Academy in 1716 he echoed Moyle's work with precision. He wrote: 'Ce ne fut ni la crainte ni la piété qui établit la religion chez les Romains, mais la nécessité ou font toutes les sociétés d'en avoir une.'[78] For Montesquieu the difference between the Romans and other peoples was that 'que les Romains firent la religion pour L'état, et les autres L'état pour la religion'. Legislators such as Numa, Romulus and Tatius, 'asservirent les dieux à la politique'. The Romans established toleration as a foundation stone of civil security.[79] The appeal to the exemplar of Roman

---

[76] *Ibid.*, 217–18.   [77] *Ibid.*, 220–3.

[78] Montesquieu, *Dissertation sur la politique des Romains dans la religion* in *Œuvres*, III, 38; On Montesquieu, see R. Shackleton, *Montesquieu* (Oxford, 1960); L. Althusser, *Politics and History: Montesquieu, Rousseau, and Marx* (1982); P. Kra, 'Religion in Montesquieu's *Lettres Persanes*', SVEC 52 (1970); R. Oake, '*Montesquieu's Religious Ideas*', JHI 14 (1953); G. L. Van Roosbroecke, *Persian Letters before Montesquieu* (1932).

[79] Montesquieu, *Dissertation sur la politique des Romains dans la religion*, 45. In his *Reflections upon the Causes of the Grandeur and Declension of the Romans*, translated into English in 1734, the religious theme was again prominent. Montesquieu ascribed one of the major causes of Rome's decline to the corruption of the civil theology of the city. With the subversion of the ancient altars came the collapse of the Roman state. First Stoicism, then Christianity, undermined the coherence of the original establishment. The end of toleration and Justinian's attempt to establish a religious uniformity weakened the foundations of the state. Montesquieu argued that the Christian theology was incompatible with the requirements of virtue and justice. With the advance of monkish religion, the rage of disputation and

religion was ubiquitous as a means to undermine the claims of the modern priesthood. The simple coda of the argument was that 'religion' was only valuable in the service of the state.

Classical notions of religion and its function were both a source and a determinant of Republican ideas about the role of religion in society. The idea of civil theology was based upon the distinction between the commonly accepted popular religion, and the 'true' set of propositions which only a community of wise men could comprehend. The truth or falsity of the state religion was to be determined not by the rectitude of its doctrines, but by its efficacy in creating a certain type of society. Supplementary to this was the attack upon superstition and priestcraft. Religion employed in the correct manner was valid regardless of its content; however religion which became the tool of private interest, either of civil or priestly tyranny, was anathema. The other side of Republican civil religion was the private worship of true pantheism neatly displayed in John Toland's personal religion.[80]

Toland was, and still is, an elusive figure; the extensive range of his work, both printed and covert manuscripts, presents bewilderment to many of his commentators. Many historians have attempted to categorize him, to assign him a particular ideology, to present a coherent description of his work. The majority have simply relapsed into asserting he was a hired hack, a pragmatist, a man intrigued by his own brilliance in search of profit and place.[81] Toland's infatuation with Cicero provides a powerful insight into his character and intentions. Throughout his work Toland makes constant reference to and citation of Cicero; extracts directly quoted form pivotal passages in many of his works. Toland's use of Cicero extends beyond the acknowledgement of intellectual influence, to a fervent evangelism to spread his mentor's philosophy. In *Clito* (1700), Toland, following Cicero *De*

---

the hydra of controversy dissolved the unity of the state. This degenerate model was compared with the virtue of the Roman priesthood of the earlier empire; see Montesquieu, *Reflections on the Causes of the Grandeur and Declension of the Romans*, 95, 200, 221, 229, 237, 242–3, 247, 252.

[80] Note that Rousseau also made a distinction between private truth and public fable; he wrote in an early draft of the *Social Contract*: 'The social virtues of pure souls, which constitute the true cult that God desires from us, will never be those of the multitude. It will always believe in Gods as senseless as itself' (cited in N. Hampson, *Will and Circumstance* (1983), 34).

[81] The classic denigration of Toland is seen in L. Stephens, *English Thought in the Eighteenth Century* (2 volumes, 1949). B. Worden in his *Edmund Ludlow: A Voyce from the Watchtower* (Camden Society, 1978) also treats Toland with distaste. More recent sympathetic studies have been executed by M. Jacob in her *Radical Enlightenment*, and by R. Sullivan in *John Toland and the Deist Controversy* (Harvard, 1982). The latter, in particular, is a detailed and useful work. Contemporaries, too, found it difficult to classify Toland's thought: see A. Boyer, *The Political State of Great Britain*, XXIII (1722), 340, 'as for religion . . . it is more easy to guess what he was not, than to tell what he was! 'Tis certain, he was neither Jew, nor Mahometan: but whether he was a Christian, a Deist, a Pantheist, an Hobbist, or a Spinozist, is the question?'

Oratore (II.9), extolled the role of the orator and the power of language to reinstate reason in the public sphere.[82]

In his *Pantheisticon* (1720), one of his most unguarded works published originally in Latin, but translated into English posthumously, the ideas and words of Cicero provide the main theme of the work. Biblical text was replaced with extended citation of sacred Ciceronian scripture.[83] The Ciceronian distinction between *religio* and *superstitio*, and of the necessity for a popular religion, formed the central framework of John Toland's religious thought. The title page of *Adeisdaemon* (The Hague, 1709) was a citation of *De Divinatione* (II.57) 'Ut religio propaganda etiam, quae est juncta cum cognitione naturae; sic superstitionis omne ejiciendae' declarative of Toland's intent to promote the cause of true religion and uproot superstition. In *Origines Judicae* a similar intention had been pronounced, again using Cicero as a source. The latter work saw Toland explicitly applauding the Ciceronian description of a state religion, he wrote; 'Errabat enim (ut alibi scribit Cicero) multis in res antiquas, quam vel usu Iam, vel doctrina, vel vetustate, immortatum videmus; retinetur autem et ad opinionem vulgi, et ad magnes utilitates Reipublicae, nos, religios, disciplina, jus augurum, collegi autoritas.'[84] The paramount tribute Toland paid to the memory of Cicero was in his *Cicero Illustratus* (1712) where the author insisted that he held Cicero in the same regard, as the latter did Plato. The work was an attempt to encourage popular interest in Cicero's thought; the obfuscations of scholarly texts were to be transcended by a vernacular translation replete with detailed biographical and explanatory notes.[85]

Toland in *Clidophorus* (1720) and *Pantheisticon* (1720) gave a succinct account of the classical idea of the distinction between a popular and a philosophical religion. Following Varro, Plutarch and Cicero, Toland maintained that for different levels of intelligence there were different types of

[82] See Toland, *Collections*, II, 325–6, on the 'divine volumes of Cicero', and Cicero as 'the most eminent philosopher, politician, and orator in the world'.

[83] See Toland, *Pantheisticon* (1751), citations from Cicero, *Tusculan Disputations*, To the Reader, 43, 72; *De Divinatione*, To the Reader, 67, 71, 86–7; *De Natura Deorum*, 97–8; *De Republica*, 85; *De Legibus*, 102–8. Note (page 80) that prayers are offered to Socrates, Plato, Cato and Cicero. Other classical figures so honoured are Selomo, Thales, Anaximander, Xenophanes, Theano, Ocellus, Democratus, Parmenides, Dicaearchus, Confucius, Cleobulina, Pamphila and Hypatia. See also Toland, *Adeisdaemon Sive Titus Livius a Superstitione Vindicatus ... Annaxae sunt ejusdem Origines Judicae* (The Hague, 1709), passim. Note that Elisha Smith sent Thomas Hearne a manuscript copy of Toland's *Adeisdaemon* in 1707. See Hearne, *Remarks and Collections*, I, 319: note that Smith rather mistakenly thought Toland to be a 'man of Religion, & of ye faith of ye Church of Eng[lan]d'. Hearne was to complete and publish his own edition of Livy in 1708. See also Carabelli, *Tolandiana*, 140.

[84] Toland, *Origines Judicae*, 101–2.

[85] Note the potential ambivalence of the use and relevance of classical literature for scholarship and polemic. Thomas Hearne, the High Church academic who haunted Oxford, made similar proposals for a complete edition of Cicero's works. See Hearne, *Remarks and Collections*, II, 128–9, 186, 192, 207, 269–70.

knowledge. The mass of the people could only be instructed by the use of myth and fable; the wise alone could comprehend the pure reason of philosophy. Although he feared the potential manipulation of the priests Toland insisted upon the necessity of a public and civil religion. In *Pantheisticon* he presented the world with his private religion. He wrote, 'we must talk with the people, and think with the philosophers'.[86] If the public religion was overtly corrupted the wise must retire in secret to practise their worship away from the eyes of the masses.[87] The injunction of Toland's society was 'let us detest all priestcraft', the participants were to reject the popular absurdities and 'the inventions of crafty knaves' and turn to philosophy as a guide to life.[88] Cicero was cited incessantly on this point for, as Toland acknowledged, the society was completely indebted to his thought.[89] Cicero's *De Officiis* provided the society with a 'distinct, and exact idea of the best and most accomplished man'. Toland considered himself and his fellow pantheists to be the 'mysts and hierophants' of nature, an alternative priesthood to the contemporary clergy.[90]

Many commentators upon Toland's religious thought have dismissed his schemes as ludicrous extravagance. But these ideas were not the products of an inflamed imagination: they were the logical outcome of Toland's adherence to the tenets of classical religion. Many commentators, both contemporary and modern, have been unhappy with his continued and repeated assertion of his belief in Christianity, and the Church of England: he could only be a canting hypocrite. A man who attacked the mysteries of religion, the divinity of the priesthood and the doctrines of Christianity could surely not be credibly thought an orthodox member of the established Church. If, however, we consider Toland, as he did himself, as a Ciceronian philosopher, we can comprehend this apparent contradiction. Toland accepted the sacrament of communion as a token of the membership of the national Church; he considered it not as a canal of grace, but as a 'public sign whereby we commemorate the death of Jesus Christ, the founder of our religion, engage ourselves to obey his laws, and declare our hopes to enjoy the benefits of the same'.[91] As a Ciceronian Toland was bound to maintain the

---

86 Toland, *Pantheisticon*, 57.
87 This was for two reasons. First, the philosopher might be subject to the persecution of the populace if they were considered to be undermining their beliefs. Secondly, the philosopher ought not to devalue the persuasive potency of the public religion since this could become a source of civil instability.
88 Toland, *Pantheisticon*, 65, 67–71.   89 *Ibid.*, iii, 65, 67, 72, 84, 86, 96–7.
90 *Ibid.*, 95, 102–6.
91 Toland, *Collections*, II, 375. Worden, *Edmund Ludlow*, 40, argues that the Republicans of the 1690s were split into two camps, the Roman Whigs (centred on the Grecian Club and epitomized by Walter Moyle), and the Calves-head group. Toland is portrayed as straddling the two groups. It is apparent that Toland as a Ciceronian should be firmly placed in the Roman tendency, or perhaps that the distinction between Roman and Calves-head should be re-evaluated.

established religion; similarly he had a duty to attack the encroachments of superstition. As he wrote to Leibnitz in 1714, it was important to distinguish carefully 'religion from superstition; lest the one be unwarily involv'd in the censure of the other'.[92] Working within the same framework, Toland was able to applaud the practice of occasional conformity, indicted by the High Church as indicative of the hypocrisy of dissent, as the 'most Charitable, generous and Christian practice that can be'.[93]

The overriding theme of this tradition was of the necessity 'to accommodate religion to politick affairs'.[94] The premise of this injunction was that the tenets of public religion were to be calculated in terms of the needs of human society, and the vagaries of human nature. The transcendent principles of divinity were replaced by the injunctions of temporal comfort. The clerical estate should evangelize the state ideology; the dogmas and doctrines of religion, constructed of myth and fable, were calculated for easy popular digestion. While true religion had the capacity to direct and shape the structure and mores of society towards social harmony, priestcraft introduced discontent. Since the power of religion was so effective, one had to ensure that it was employed to 'good' ends. The objection to contemporary religion was that the clergy made use of 'religion' not for social benefit, but for their own private aggrandizement.

[92] Toland, *Collections*, II, 391.   [93] Toland, *State-Anatomy*, 71.
[94] G. Naudé, *Political Considerations* (1711), 156.

⟪ 7 ⟫

From theology to ethics

Henry Neville (1620–94), devout Ciceronian, author of the Harringtonian *Plato Redivivus* (1681), with his translation of Machiavelli's works in 1675, cemented a firm link between the Republicans and the tradition of 'politick religion'. Machiavelli epitomized the idea of civil religion by his favourable commendation of Numa Pompilius in his *Discourses* on Livy. Like Moyle, Machiavelli insisted on the value of religion as a tool of political manipulation. Neville, the probable author of *A True Copy of a Letter written by N. Machiavelli in Defence of Himself and His Religion* (1675), vindicated the Italian as a true Harringtonian Christian applauding his prescription of the civil uses of religion. This close identification was strengthened by John Dennis, who openly cited Machiavelli against High Church antagonists. Dennis, friend and associate of Walter Moyle, combated Sacheverell's sacerdotal proposition that 'the peace, happiness, and prosperity of the secular and civil power depends upon that of the spiritual and ecclesiastical'.[1] Following Machiavelli's indictment of the papacy in Italy, Dennis insisted that Christianity frequently operated as a fomentor of schism, rather than supporter of the state. In his *Vice and Luxury* (1724) the debt to the Florentine notion that religion was the 'sacred cement' of civil society was re-emphasized by citations from both the *Prince* and the *Discourses*. For Dennis, as for Machiavelli, a public religion was a necessary means to lead the populace to virtue.[2]

To appeal to the Machiavellian history of Roman religion and the idea of a politic legislator was anathema in Anglican eyes. As Raab has shown in *The*

---

[1] H. Sacheverell, *Political Union: A Discourse Showing the Dependence of Government on Religion*, (1700), 9; J. Dennis, *The Danger of Priestcraft* (1702), 5–8, 16.

[2] Dennis, *Vice and Luxury*, 22, 48, 81, 83, 85–7, 92–3. It is important to note that Harrington applauded Machiavelli repeatedly: according to Harrington, Machiavelli had designed a commonwealth that was a 'minister of God on earth, to the end that the world may be governed with righteousness'. Machiavelli had defended the 'Holy asylum' but was repaid by being 'pelted for it by sermons' (see Pocock, *Works*, 323, 392–3, 531).

196

English Face of Machiavelli (1964), orthodox Christians received such civil theologies with charges of irreligion and heresy. The forcefulness of Anglican counter-polemic has obscured the full meaning of Republican civil theology, dismissing it as mere politic device. This Anglican historiographical bias has been reinforced by the hysterical Christian reaction to the powerful anticlericalism of clandestine manuscripts like the *Traité des trois imposteurs* which dismissed all religion as 'human fictions' and as an 'empire of fable'. Republican civil religion has too easily been indicted with the legacy of Renaissance infidelity. The arguments of heretics like Cardano, Vanini and Pomponazzi were identical, at least in Trinitarian eyes, to those of Blount, Harrington and Toland. In pejorative Anglican terms a civil religion was no religion at all, but for the Republican (like Harrington, Moyle or Toland), appealing to transcendent principles different from those accepted by the Judaeo-Christian idiom of the clergy, the injunctions of nature, reason and virtue became true theology.[3]

In order to explore the transcendent principles that underlay Republican political thought in the 1690s and 1700s the editorial publications of John Toland are most significant. In particular his important edition of Harrington's works of 1700, and his pirated 1699 version of Shaftesbury's *An Inquiry Concerning Virtue* proposed a naturalistic, or neo-Stoic rereading of Republicanism: Harrington (in Toland's version) was more intent on pursuing virtue than the millennium. While Pocock's analysis, of both Harrington and the country ideologies of the 1690s, has presented the complex blendings of Machiavelli, the ancient constitution, polemics against patronage, corruption and credit, the religious dimension has remained unexplored.[4] In tracing

---

[3] On the *Traité des trois imposteurs*, see G. Brunet, *Le Traité des trois imposteurs* (Paris, 1867), i–lvi and BL Stowe 47 'The Famous Book Intitled De Tribus Impostoribus', folios 26r, 30v, 68r–v, 136–8.

[4] See J. G. A. Pocock, *The Ancient Constitution* (Cambridge, 1957), Pocock, 'James Harrington and the Good Old Cause', *Journal of British Studies* 10 (1970), Pocock, *Politics, Language, and Time* (1972), chapters 3–4; Pocock, *The Machiavellian Moment* (Princeton, 1975), Part III and *The Political Works of James Harrington* (Cambridge, 1977) are the best accounts of Harrington's thought, although Pocock insists Harrington should be read in a millennarian context, a view from which I differ. See also C. Blitzer, *An Immortal Commonwealth* (Yale, 1970); J. C. Davies, *Utopia and the Ideal Society* (Cambridge, 1981), chapter 8; H. F. Russell-Smith, *Harrington and His 'Oceana'* (Cambridge, 1914); M. Downs, *James Harrington* (Boston, 1977); J. W. Gough, 'Harrington and Contemporary Thought', *Political Science Quarterly* 45 (1930). The work of S. B. Liljegren is a much underestimated source for Harrington studies, in particular his indispensable, footnoted edition of *Oceana*, published in *Skrifter Vetenskaps-Societen* 4 (Heidelberg, 1924); see also Liljegren *Harrington and the Jews* (Lund, 1932), and 'A French Draft Constitution of 1792 Modelled on James Harrington's *Oceana*' K. *Humanistiska Vetenskapssam* 17 (1932). One of the more recent important discussions of the religious elements in Harrington's thought is M. A. Goldie, 'The Civil Religion of James Harrington' which, although admirable in the logic of its arguments, operates within a Pocockian idiom. See below for my objections to Pocock's theses on Harrington's millenarianism. For a later development, see J. D. Coates, 'Coleridge's Debt to Harrington: A Discussion of Zapolya', *JHI* 38 (1977).

the neo-Stoic idioms of Harrington's original statements, the significant re-emphasis of this Stoicism in Toland's edition of his *Works* in 1700, and the refinements of Shaftesbury's *Characteristicks* (1711), and the popularization of the same in Trenchard's and Gordon's periodical publications, *The Independent Whig* and *Cato's Letters*, the intention is to argue that Republican political theory was a holistic enterprise far different from the individualism of Lockean 'rights' theories. Neo-Harringtonianism, as read through Toland's edition, was concerned not only with political and economic realities, but with a discipline of the soul. The emphasis that Toland placed upon the metaphysical identification of the body natural and the body politic in Harrington's writings, was no innovation, but a commonplace of political metaphor. This notion of man's body as a microcosm of the world or the universe, was a trope rooted in pagan philosophy: Plato had considered the government of society to be an analogue of the government of man.[5] As William Temple insisted, the Republicans followed the method of the ancient philosophers, who concentrated not upon forms of government, but upon means to 'improve men's reason, to temper their affections, to allay their passions'. Toland's rereading of Harrington's Republicanism adopted the Socratic method and argued for the close link between theories of politics, psychology and ethics.[6]

TOLAND'S HARRINGTON: THE SOUL, VIRTUE AND THE STATE

The frontispiece of Toland's edition of Harrington's *Works* (1700) indicates the ancient tradition within which Toland intended Harrington's works to be appreciated: land, industry and commerce combine to produce a balanced and free state. The ancient legislators Numa, Solon, Lycurgus and Confucius are supplemented by the biblical Moses and the modern example of William III. Pocock has insisted that Harrington's thought, at least in the 1650s, should be treated within a millenarian idiom: the Toland edition of Harrington's *Works* proposed a pantheistic and Stoic version. As Worden has so capably demonstrated in *Edmund Ludlow: A Voyce from the Watchtower*

---

[5] For a general consideration of the role of the editor in the period, see R. Iliffe, 'Author-Mongering: "The Editor" between Producer and Consumer' (privately communicated paper: delivered at UCLA in January 1991). For a general discussion of the role of natural analogy in both political and scientific thought, see B. Barnes and S. Shapin (eds.), *Natural Order* (1979); B. S. Turner, *The Body and Society* (1984); E. M. W. Tillyard, *The Elizabethan World Picture* (1960); M. Macklem, *The Anatomy of the World Relations between Natural and Moral Law from Donne to Pope* (Minnesota, 1958); G. P. Conger, *Theories of Macrocosm and Microcosm in the History of Philosophy* (New York, 1922); for more specific discussions, see B. Williams, 'The Analogy of the City and the Soul in Plato's *Republic*', *Phroenesis* Supplement 1; P. Archambault, 'The Analogy of the "Body" in Renaissance Political Literature', *Bibliothèque d'Humanisme et Renaissance* 29 (1967); J. Daly, 'Cosmic Harmony and Political Thinking in Early Stuart England', *TAPS* 69 (1979).

[6] Temple, *Complete Works*, I, 'Of Popular Discontents', 257.

(1978) Toland employed his editorial capacities to adapt earlier works to the exigencies of the 1690s: this is evident, too, in his Harrington edition. Although, following Pocock's opinion, there is no suggestion that Toland significantly altered the text of Harrington's works, as he did Ludlow's, his inclusion of the possibly suppositious Harringtonian work *The Life of the Mechanics of Nature* significantly alters the meaning of Harrington's language in the 1700s. Pocock says little about the work, deciding neither one way nor the other about its authenticity, although in this state of ambivalence he choses to exclude the piece from his own edition. The question of the authenticity of the work is at once crucial and irrelevant. We have few means to prove the answer convincingly one way or the other as no surviving manuscript has (yet) been found. If we accept Toland's rather dubious insistence that the work was Harrington's, the explicit pantheistic hylozoism of *The Life of the Mechanics of Nature* seems sharply at odds with the picture of Harringtonian millenarianism. If, on the other hand, the work is the result of Toland's pen (perhaps an aphoristic precis of the last two pieces in *Letters to Serena*) we have to ask the question why Toland wished to foist the piece on Harrington, and what effect he intended it to create on the reception of Harrington's thought.

The *Mechanics of Nature* is concerned with the idea of nature and the relationship between matter and spirit, and body and soul. Nature is a fundamental and divine principle, not the inert and corrupt principle of Christian metaphysics. Both the world and humankind are a combination of nature and divinity. In order to understand the world, both nature and spirit must be examined. It is this hermeneutic that Toland intended to emphasize in Harrington's thought. In *Oceana* Harrington set out to examine the natural principle of government (that empire follows dominion) and the spiritual premises of this natural order (the idea of the soul as the form of both government and body). In his prefatory 'Life' of Harrington, Toland portrayed Harrington as an anatomist of civic constitutions. Harrington was addicted to the study of civil government, 'being ... convinced that no government is of so accidental or arbitrary an institution as people are wont to imagine, there being in societies natural causes producing their necessary effects, as well as in the earth or the air'.[7] Importantly, Toland eulogized Harrington's 'noble discovery' that empire follows the balance of property, as comparable to the discovery of printing, the compass, or Harvey's work upon the circulation of the blood. Harrington had investigated the histories of political 'constitutions', and in his work they were 'dissected and laid open

---

7 Toland, *Works of Harrington*, 'The Life of James Harrington', xvii; the *Mechanics of Nature* is at xlii–xliv. See also Trenchard and Gordon, *Cato's Letters*, III, 154: 'Now it seems to me, that the great secret in politicks is, nicely to watch and observe this fluctuation and change of natural power, and then adjust the political to it by prudent precautions and timely remedies.'

to all capacities'. Harrington had insisted that his project dealt not with 'notions, wandering, and ill abstracted from things' but that he had 'descended to practical observation'. Set before the histories of commonwealths, as the anatomist did so before the body, Harrington intended not to draw pictures of ideals but to examine the parts and functions of the body politic. Harrington explicitly appealed to the model of Harvey's anatomy; as the latter's principles had been gleaned from nature via the examination of particular bodies, his own ideas were achieved from the study of nature exemplified in the histories of states. The relationship between Harrington's idea of anatomy, and orthodox religious or medical perceptions of the value and purpose of anatomy, is a complex issue that needs fuller treatment elsewhere. Briefly, anatomy was considered by its religious and medical practitioners as a form of natural revelation: through the physical examination, dissection, and ocular exploration of the body the investigator could come to knowledge about the power of God. Isbrand de Diemerbroeck (translated by William Salmon) wrote in his *Anatomy of Human Bodies* (1689), that the anatomist's skill displayed nature that he 'might see and admire the skill and workmanship of the Divine hand in building a Tabernacle for the Soul'. Anatomy cut away superficial appearance and revealed the 'truth'. As one physician commented, anatomy could give a 'history of natural structure'. Just as the doctor insisted anatomy was 'an art which teaches the artifical dissection of the parts of the body of man, that what things in them can be known by senses, may truly appear', so Harrington was assured that 'political anatomy' displayed the true structure of the political organism.[8] Throughout Harrington's work political society was conceived of as a natural organism, a machine with principles of natural

[8] I. de Diemerbroeck, *Anatomy of Human Bodies* (1689), iii. See Pocock, *Works of Harrington*, 162, 403, 725. On Harvey, see R. G. Frank, 'The Image of Harvey in Commonwealth and Restoration England' in J. J. Bylebyl (ed.), *William Harvey and his Age* (Baltimore, 1979); C. Hill, 'William Harvey and the idea of Monarchy' *PP* 29 (1964). It is interesting to note that one of Harrington's associates in the Rota Club was William Petty, an expert anatomist who became the Tomlins Reader in Anatomy at Oxford. In his *Advice to Mr Hartlib* (1648), Petty had argued for the necessity of a central school of anatomical investigation, while in his later *The Political Anatomy of Ireland* (1691) he specifically employed anatomical analogy to discuss Irish politics and economics. The suppositious Sarpi work, *The Rights of Sovereigns and Subjects*, as late as 1725 proposed to examine 'the matter to the bottom, to anatomise it, to strip it of artificial disguise, and expose it naked to the whole world' (page 2). The role of 'anatomy' displays a further link between Harrington and Henry Neville's *Plato Redivivus*; the body-politic analogy was a common theme throughout Neville's work. Walter Moyle (*Works* 1727, 'Some Account of Mr Moyle', 27) argued that the English Gentleman in Neville's dialogue was supposed to represent William Harvey. The power of the anatomy analogy would repay further examination set in the context of anatomical practices. See, for example, C. Webster, *The Great Instauration* (1975), 247–55, 420–3, for a discussion of the connections between natural analogy and political anatomy. Note that between 1600 and 1650 some fifty works were published concerning anatomy, while between 1650 and 1700 230 pieces were written; see K. F. Russell, *British Anatomy 1525–1800* (Melbourne, 1963) 6.

regulation. A 'political anatomy' was undertaken to expose the 'natural nerves and ligaments of government'.

Toland, then, in his 'Life' and the inclusion of the *Mechanics of Nature*, intended to present Harrington's thought as an anatomical/metaphysical investigation of the analogical relationship between the 'human' and 'political' notions of the 'soul' and the 'body'. This conception of the relationship between the 'soul' and the 'body' owed more to ancient materialism than the Old Testament. This interpretation of Harrington's thought as operating within a naturalistic or pantheistic idiom, contradicts the recent analyses of J. G. A. Pocock and J. C. Davis. Pocock has claimed that Harrington should be interpreted in a millennial framework, a view which itself has been challenged by J. C. Davis' alternative suggestion that Harrington's thought is essentially secular. Harrington, as interpreted and projected by Toland in the 1700s (if not also of the 1650s), employed a naturalistic (i.e. neither millennial nor secular) method to understand politics. For example, Pocock uses Harrington's idea of an 'immortal commonwealth' to identify him as a millenarian. However, further evidence of Toland's rewriting of Harrington's thought (that supplements the *Mechanics of Nature*) directly answers Pocock's meditations on the idea of immortality in *Oceana*. This can be found in 'Appendix 1' to Toland's *Nazarenus* (1718). Here Toland dealt directly with Harrington's description of the immortal commonwealth: importantly, rather than using Judaeo-Christian ideas of the apocalypse or eschatology, Toland employed a passage from Cicero's *De Republica* (from Augustine's *City of God*, Book XXII, chapter 6). Immortality for Cicero and Harrington, according to Toland's reading, was premised upon the idea of the world's eternity. Politically, if reason and humanity could be perfected, the state should continue for ever. For Toland, Harrington's metaphysic had more to do with a pantheistic natural philosophy, than with Christianity. Toland explained that Cicero had denied the analogy between the death of an individual and the demise of government. Death to the individual was natural, and 'so very often desirable': but governments ought to be so regulated 'to be of *ETERNAL DURATION*'. Toland continued in explicit pantheistic vein:

For as the corruption of ever generating individuals neither lessens the matter, nor disorders the form of the world, but on the contrary perpetuates it: so the species of mankind, which is the matter of government, ever continuing; if such a temperament (as Cicero somewhere calls it) or such a libration (as Harrington) be fixt in the form, as to make it proof against all internal division and external force, that government will consequently be immortal.

In very much the same way as Harrington had commented in *Oceana*, Toland pointed out, 'such was the language of Plato and Aristotle before'. For Toland, and Harrington, the idea of an 'immortal government' was neither a millenarian hope nor a utopic 'whim', but something that could be naturally established according to the 'intrinsic nature and constitution of the Form itself'. It was Toland's point that the Jewish government and nation under the direction of the supreme legislator Moses had come closest to establishing the conditions for 'a Government Immortal', without the aid of divine providence.[9]

Harrington, particularly in *Oceana*, was concerned to explore the principles of 'nature' as a divine exercise. This was a seventeenth-century enterprise, and should not dupe the modern writer into attributing materialistic or secularistic motives to Harrington's work. Modern scholarship, preoccupied with Marxist theories of historical materialism, has tended to treat Harrington's principle of empire following property as the first modern economic analysis of politics. But this is to look at only one side of Harrington's arguments. His analysis of the natural grounds of political society is premised on a pantheistic metaphysic that implies the need to examine the idea of the 'soul' as well as that of 'nature'. Harrington's continual analogy between the principle of politics and the relationship between the body and soul is not merely an anachronistic literary trope, but a constitutive metaphysical argument.[10] As the authors of *Cato's Letters*

[9] Toland, *Nazarenus*, 'Appendix 1', 2, 6–7; Cicero, *De Republica*, (Loeb edition 211–13); see Pocock, *Works of Harrington*, 72, 86 on 'the millennial note' and 142–3: 'If Harrington's *Mechanics of Nature* is indeed a work of hermetic character, we can better understand Toland's insistence on its sanity.' On the relationship between Harrington's natural philosophy and his political beliefs, written within the Pocockian idiom, see C. Diamond, 'Natural Philosophy in Harrington's Political Thought', *JHP* 16 (1978). For an attack upon this analysis, see J. C. Davis, 'Pocock's Harrington: Grace, Nature, and Art in the Classical Republicanism of James Harrington', *HJ* 24 (1981), and *Utopia and the Ideal Society*, 211–12. It is here that the close connection with Winstanley can most fruitfully be made. A recurrent theme of Winstanley's theology was that divinity and reason were very similar quantities: man's relation to God is premised on freedom through reason rather than omnipotent divine power. See C. Hill, 'The Religion of Gerrard Winstanley', *PP* Supplement 5 (1978), and (ed.), *Winstanley: The Law of Freedom and Other Writings* (1973), passim. Harrington, too, insists that God can be treated as either 'infinite love' or 'almighty power'. True religion must be based on free submission rather than command, thus God has 'prepared before his empire, his authority or proposition'. For Harrington, Christ was to be understood as proposition rather than Godhead (see Pocock, *Works*, 373, 421, 539).

[10] Toland, *Works of Harrington*, 429–34. See Greenleaf, *Order, Empiricism, and Politics* for a misreading of the role of analogy in Harrington's thought. C. Blitzer, *An Immortal Commonwealth*, 89–108, discusses the idea of political anatomy at some length, although his arguments are faulted by the Whiggish premise that the political scientist and the political anatomist are the same man. Underestimating the rhetorical power of the body-politic analogy Blitzer writes: 'These are not meant to constitute proof of Harrington's arguments. Rather they are intended as inducement.' Again my argument is that the idea of natural analogy between city and soul is not a quaint anachronism on Harrington's part, but foundational for his thought. See P. Archambault, 'The Analogy of the "Body" in Renaissance Political Literature' which stresses (see pages 21–2): 'One of our fundamental contentions, in this study, is that the analogy of the body was never used loosely. The political writers of the late medieval and Renaissance periods did not consider it as an inert, neutral literary topos, but as capable of betraying certain political implications.' That this analogy

reiterated: 'Government is political, as a human body is a natural, mechanism; both have proper springs, wheels, and a peculiar organisation to qualify them for suitable motions.' Unless regulated by the physic of virtue the machine would decay.[11] This Harringtonian description of the organic nature of the body politic provided the intrinsic conceptual backcloth for the analysis of society proposed by such men as Henry Neville, Robert Molesworth, Walter Moyle and Toland.[12]

Harrington openly premised his notions of government upon the tenets of ancient prudence. *Oceana* (1656), Harrington's most important work, was conceived of as a handbook of these ancient traditions. According to the ancients the principles of government were twofold, 'the internal or the goods of the mind; and external, or the goods of fortune'. The description of 'power' was a material one resulting in the assertion that empire followed the balance of dominion, or property. Just as the idea of a human being was premised upon the existence of 'natural body', so the civil state was founded upon property and the goods of fortune.[13] The state was composed of both 'power' and 'authority', as the body natural was a composition of body and soul: the goods of mind and fortune 'meet and twine in the wreath or crown of empire'. When these two principles were confluent, the government came 'nearest to the work of God, whose government consists of heaven and earth'. Harrington's notion of 'authority' rested not upon any earthly prudence, but derived from 'heaven', or the image of God embodied in the soul of man. Government upon earth was capable of two types of rule, that of public interest (embodied in the pattern of ancient virtue), or of private interest epitomized in the priestcraft of modern prudence. This in itself was an analogy of the 'soul' of man, which was 'the mistress of two potent rivals, the one reason, the other passion, that are in continual suit; and according as she gives up her will to these or either of them, is the felicity or misery which man partakes in this mortal life'. Passion of the will, actualized into action brings forth 'vice and the bondage of sin', while reason enforced results in 'virtue and the freedom of the soul'.[14]

This analysis was extended into the sphere of the civil state: 'Now government is no other than the soul of a nation or a city: wherefore that which was reason in the debate of a commonwealth being brought forth by the result, must be virtue; and foreasmuch as the soul of a city or nation is the

was still vigorous in the early eighteenth century is confirmed by Toland's *State-Anatomy* (1717), a tremendously popular work: the title is a rather bad Harringtonian pun.
11 See Trenchard and Gordon, *Cato's Letters*, III, 150; see also III, 4.
12 See H. Neville, *Plato Redivivus* (1681), 71, 75, 81, 82, 95, 158–9, 160–7, 174, and Thomas Goddard's hostile reply *Plato's Demon, Or the State Physician Unmaskt* (1684), 61, 144, 146, 147–51, 156; Toland, *State-Anatomy*, 12–13, citing Cicero: 'As our bodies cannot be manag'd without a mind, so a government cannot without a law rule its several parts, analogous to nerves, blood and other members.'
13 Toland, *Works of Harrington*, 39, 448.   14 *Ibid.*, 44–5.

sovereign power, her virtue must be law'. Government which was bound by virtue embodied in law, saw empire and authority conflated. Moving gracefully from the relationship of the soul to the body, to that of the government and the state, Harrington explained: 'If the liberty of a man consists in the empire of his reason the absence whereof would betray him to the bondage of his passions; then the liberty of a commonwealth consists in the empire of her laws, the absence where of would betray her to the lust of tyrants.' As the man who rejected the divine dictates of reason rejected God, so did the state which attempted to rule above the law. In this way Harrington undercut the hieratic argument that since the soul was above the body, so the priesthood should govern the state.[15] When power and authority were united in either the human form or the body politic, it became like 'a holy altar, and breathing perpetual incense to heaven in justice and in piety, may be something, as it were, between heaven and earth'. The form of government Harrington attempted to prescribe rested upon his 'philosophy of the soul', which consisted in the necessity of deposing the rule of passion and, 'advancing reason to the throne of empire.'[16] The 'common right' or 'law of nature' argued that the interest of the whole commonwealth was superior to the 'right or interest of the parts only'. As it was the role of reason to establish the right interest of the individual, so 'the reason of mankind must be right reason'. This implied that the dictates of right reason would so cultivate correct 'orders' that would enable each individual to perceive the interest of the whole. This achieved, the commonwealth became 'as a magistrate of God unto mankind for the vindication of common right and the law of nature'. It is important to note that in arguing this point Harrington saw no impropriety in citing Hooker, Grotius, Cicero and Machiavelli, alongside the injunctions of Scripture, because all these texts shared the principles of nature and divinity. He wrote: 'The Heathen politicians, have written, not out of nature, but as it were out of Scripture: as in the commonwealth of Israel God is said to have been king; so the commonwealth where the law is king, is said by Aristotle to be the kingdom of God.'[17]

[15] *Ibid.*, 45.   [16] *Ibid.*, 242, 252.

[17] *Ibid.*, 46–7, 52, 195. See Aubrey, *Brief Lives*, I, 293: 'He was wont to say that right reason in contemplation, is vertue in action, et vice versa, vivere secundum naturam is to live vertuously, the Divines will not have it so ...' See Winstanley, *The Law of Freedom*: 'the great lawgiver in commonwealth government is the spirit of universal righteousness dwelling in mankind, now rising up to teach everyone to do to another as he would have another to do him', cited in Hill, 'The Religion of Winstanley', 44. On this point I would take issue with Hill's argument (at 55) that 'eighteenth century deism was so abstractly secular that it lacked the emotional appeal of Winstanley's ideas. Never again were serious revolutionary ideals to be expressed in religious forms in England.' See Trenchard and Gordon, *Cato's Letters*, III, 193–4: 'Nothing is so much the interest of private men, as to see the publick flourish ... every man's private advantage is so much wrapt up in the publick felicity, that by every step which he takes to depreciate his country's happiness, he undermines and destroys his own.' The

In his *System of Politics* Harrington succinctly conveyed his notions of government in the form of Hippocratic aphorisms. Here the concept of government as 'soul' was made even more explicit. He wrote 'as the form of man is the image of God, so the form of a government is the image of man'. The formation of government was the creation of a 'political creature after the image of a philosophical creature'. The 'soul' was that which gave life to the matter of the body and the state. Since the 'soul' of man was essentially a religious principle because of its contemplation of divine reason, so the 'soul' of the state became a theological principle. As language was the means of communication between the 'souls' of mankind, so religion was the means of communication between the 'soul' of man and God. The body politic had a 'soul' in the form of its government, so this, too, became a mediation with the divine.[18] In radical Erastian terms the mediating role of the clergy in the state was replaced with the idea of the 'soul' of government both at the individual and the national level. The 'soul' of each individual had to bind itself freely to reason, thus 'liberty' became the premise both of religion and politics.

This system would not arise of its own accord but had to be constructed. Government was an art (Harrington citing Hobbes), 'for in the art of man (being the imitation of nature) there is nothing so like the first call of beautiful order out of chaos and confusion, as the architecture of a well ordered Commonwealth'. Good government had to be composed from the natural materials available to man; such a building would remain erect as long as the materials remained incorruptible.[19] Following the classical

conflation of public and private interest was the central theme in Shaftesbury's *An Inquiry Concerning Virtue* (1699); see below, pp. 210–18. For an interesting discussion of public and private interest in Harrington, see J. A. W. Gunn, *Politics and the Public Interest in the Seventeenth Century* (1969), 109–52. Gunn points out that many of Harrington's arguments were commonplace and conventional. Gunn's general thesis that 'Liberal or republican thought in this era was largely based upon the premise that the public good was most obviously and immediately related to the preservation of private right' (*Politics and the Public Interest*, 300) is certainly misapplied to Harrington (144, 151). Gunn creates problems for himself by conflating the injunctions of reason and virtue: both should be read within a neo-Stoic context, rather than rather nebulous liberal conceptions of 'individualism' and 'rational self-interest'.

18 Toland, *Works of Harrington*, 499, 500. The same analogy is employed by J. Dennis in *An Essay Upon Publick Spirit* (1711) in *Selected Works* (2 volumes, 1727), I, 406–43, at 406: 'What the spirit of a man is to the body natural, that publick spirit is to the body politick.' Note that J. A. W. Gunn, *Beyond Liberty and Property* (Montreal, 1983), chapter 7, 'Public Spirit to Public Opinion', uses Dennis' work without acknowledging either the Harringtonian meaning or the analogical purpose of the argument.

19 Toland, *Works of Harrington*, 192, 211. See Cicero, *De Natura Deorum*, 76: 'Nature therefore cannot be void of reason, if art can bring nothing to perfection without it, and if the works of nature exceed those of art.' See Shaftesbury to Stanhope, 7 November 1709: 'So is architecture and its beauty the same, and founded in nature, let men's fancy be ever so Gothic; for there is a Gothic architecture which is false, and ever will be so, though we should all turn Goths, and lose our relish', B. Rand, (ed.), *The Life, Unpublished, Letters, and Philosophical Regimen of Anthony, Earl of Shaftesbury* (1900), 416–17. See below for a discussion of Shaftesbury's point, argued against both Hobbes and Locke, that aesthetic

tradition of Numa, Solon and Lycurgus, Harrington insisted that such a structure would be created by a politic legislator. Through the creation of 'orders' and laws, the mass of the people could be led to prefer the path of virtue, over that of appetite. Education was the 'plastic art of government' and was therefore a concern of the state. Harrington explained, 'now the health of a government, and the education of its youth being of the same pulse, no wonder it has been the constant practice of well-ordered commonwealths to commit the care and feeding of it to public magistrates'.[20] Harrington appealed to naturalistic metaphor to illustrate his point: man considered without 'orders' was a skeletal structure, once laws were created, flesh was put upon the body.[21] Harrington upheld the infallible political maxim, 'give us good orders, and they will make us good men'.[22]

Harrington suggested that the way to create a healthy body politic was for it to be directed by a rational soul, and to consist of members educated in the principles of virtue. The problem was how to effect this education.[23] In a society dominated by the clergy, morality and religious truth were disseminated from the pulpit: so too in Harrington's scheme was virtue to be evangelized in the Church. To this end Harrington insisted upon the necessity of a national Church, but one firmly under control of the civil power. The clergy were to have no independent wealth, or employment in the civil state; they were to be chosen and ordained by the people, who were also to contribute voluntarily to their income. Harrington's clergy were to exercise no coercive authority over matters of religion: they were merely teachers and scholars. Just as the conviction of the private conscience produced a private religion, so the belief of the body politic produced a national religion.[24]

beauty and moral truth are natural rather than conventional. For an excellent discussion of classical and Renaissance ideas of art and nature, see A. J. Close, 'Commonplace Theories of Art and Nature in Classical Antiquity and in the Renaissance', *JHI* 30 (1969), and 'Philosophical Theories of Art and Nature in Classical Antiquity', *JHI* 32 (1971).

20 Toland, *Works of Harrington*, 172.
21 Harrington explained at length: 'Diogenes seeing a young fellow drunk, told him that his father was drunk when he begat him. For thus in natural generation I must confess I see no reason; but in the political it is right. The vices of the people are from their governors; those of the governors from their laws or orders; and those of their laws or orders from their legislators. What ever was in the womb imperfect, as to their proper work, comes very rarely, or never at all to perfection afterwards; and the formation of the citizen in the womb of the commonwealth is his education' (Toland, *Works of Harrington*, 177; this notion is reminiscent of Marx's description of the natural determinism of society).
22 Toland, *Works of Harrington*, 75–6.
23 Harrington here addresses one of the central issues between the claims of liberty and duty: see also Hegel, *The Philosophy of History*, trans. J. Sibree (New York, 1956), 449: 'Plato in his Republic makes everything depend on the government, and makes disposition the principle of the state; on which account he lays the chief stress on education. The modern theory is diametrically opposed to this referring everything to the individual will. But here we have no guarantee that the will in question has the right disposition which is essential to the stability of the state.'
24 Toland, *Works of Harrington*, 58.

Since the Scriptures were a complex selection of works, the state had to provide means of disseminating the sacred tenets. Harrington explained, 'she must institute some method of this knowledge, and some use of such as have acquired it, which accounts to a national religion'. The duty of all men as rational creatures was to apply this 'reason' to understanding the injunctions of Scripture. Harrington enshrined this liberty of conscience in the *Art of Lawgiving* as a 'kind of state, where a man is his own prince'. The national Church was therefore non-coercive, compatible with the free exercise of reason in religion, but still provided a guide for those incapable of this liberty. The role of the national establishment was to teach the people to use their own reason in religious contemplation. In his Oceanic scheme Harrington provided for a council of religion, which would protect both the interests of the national Church, and the liberty of the private conscience.[25]

Harrington expressed his thought in terms of the analogy between the divinity of the body politic and that of the body natural. The relationship of the soul with the body was to be the explanatory instrument for elucidating his conception of 'political' authority. The business of the state was to establish the divine authority of reason as a means of rendering the 'soul' both of government and the individual closer to the pattern of God. The intention was to create a 'healthy' body which conformed to the dictates of reason, and transcended the private interest of passion and appetite. The implication of this system of government was that the function of authority was reduced to the issues of human psychology; the rational government was the one which encouraged the rational man. The rational and the religious were collapsed into a singular notion: the role of the state was to evangelize the claims of reason. It was this religious dimension to Harringtonianism that informed the thought of such men as Walter Moyle, John Toland and Thomas Gordon. There is some problem, at least for the Harrington of the 1690s, in describing these arguments as Christian and millenarian. Admittedly Harrington employs the Christian language of the 'soul', but in terms of a neo-Stoic framework of 'reason' and 'virtue' rather than traditional Trinitarian Christianity. Harrington's treatment is, in effect, a rereading of Christian theology into a civic theology.

The Harringtonian vision of government was similar in structure to the hierocratic: both systems aimed at providing a discipline for the 'soul' of mankind. The content of this discipline was distinct in each case. In the theocratic state, obligation to priestly authority was a religious duty, and the

---

25 Toland, *Works of Harrington*, 89, 127, 448–51, 505–508. Harrington's hermeneutic is an important but understudied facet of *Oceana*. Certainly he considered scriptural interpretation as a crucial weapon in the destruction of priestcraft. As he commented (Pocock, *Works*, 307): 'But in the searching of the Scriptures by the proper use of our Universities, we have been heretofore blessed with greater victories and trophies against the purple hosts and golden standards of the Romish hierarchy, than any nation.'

telos of salvation was placed in the afterlife. For Harrington, religious obligation was by the individual to the dictates of reason: the telos of conformity was civil salvation. Thus Harrington in turn indicted the contemporary clergy as the perpetrators of priestcraft, who claimed 'religious' authority not in order to dispense the lessons of virtue, but to usurp 'power' for their own interest.[26]

This analysis of the proscription of priestcraft and pursuit of virtue became a commonplace in the thought of Moyle, Toland, Trenchard and Gordon. The authors of *Cato's Letters* succinctly presented the idea that government rested upon the control of man's mind: 'The only way of dealing with mankind, is to deal with the passions; and the founders of all states, and of all religions, have ever done so: the first elements, or knowledge of politics, is the knowledge of the passions; and the art of governing, is chiefly the art of applying to the passions.'[27] Passions were linked to ideas, or opinions, about the world. It was through this connection that the clergy, by the creation of false (ideological) perceptions of the world and the duties of religion, had erected their corrupt dominion over society. The fundamental passion was self-love: 'Every man loves himself better than his own species.'[28] Each and every action of all individuals was governed by some form of self-interest; the necessity was to direct this motivating passion towards the interest of the whole. Man simply could not operate independently of passion; 'the passions of men, which are the only motions raised within us by the motions of things without us, are soothed or animated by external causes; it is hard to determine whether there be a man in the world, who might not be corrupted by some means and applications; the nicety is, to choose those that are proper.' When the motion of passion led men to do good to others, 'it is called virtue and public spirit, and when they do hurt to others, it is called selfishness, dishonesty, hurt, and other names of infamy'.[29]

Man as a machine governed by the passions of self-interest, could not be expected to follow the tenets of 'philosophical virtue', but through the skilful construction of obliging laws men could be directed to follow 'virtue as their interest'. The obliging character of law extended from self-interest, 'therefore in the making of laws, the pleasures and fears of particular men, being the

---

[26] Toland, *Works of Harrington*, 37–8, 59; see J. G. A. Pocock, *Virtue, Commerce, and History* (Cambridge, 1986), 66: 'What we used to think of as the age of reason may just as well be called the age of virtue.' in general on the psychological tenor of political theory of the period, see A. Hirschmann, *The Passions and the Interests* (Princeton, 1977); the author makes no reference to any classical tradition. An important text on the passions is Descartes' *Passions of the Soul* (1646) usefully discussed in R. B. Carter, *Descartes' Medical Philosophy* (Baltimore, 1983). See also N. O. Keohane, *Philosophy and the State in France* (Princeton, 1980); A. Levi, *French Moralists and the Theory of the Passions 1585–1689* (Oxford, 1964).
[27] Gordon and Trenchard, *Cato's Letters*, II, 47.
[28] *Ibid.*, II, 50–51, 53–4.
[29] *Ibid.*, II, 53.

great engines by which they are governed, must be consulted. Vice must be rendered detestable and dangerous, virtue amiable and advantageous'.[30] The role of government was not to 'subdue' the passions, for to do so would be to depart from nature: the intent was to 'control' the passions via the use of reason. The passions, like the body and politics, must be well balanced, 'with an impartial hand, and giving them all fair play, it is an equal administration of the appetites by which they are restrained from outrunning one another'. This conception of man's psychology was both mechanistic and organic: passion, appetite and opinion were the motors which governed all the motions of the mind. This was 'purely mechanical ... and whoever would govern him, and lead him, must apply to those passions; that is pull the proper ropes, and turn the wheels which will put the machine in motion'. The politician, like Plato's guardians, could employ human weakness to render the individual happy.[31] John Toland insisted that the efficient politician must learn to 'govern all men by the springs of their own passions, and to manage the whole machine by the chains and weights of prevailing opinions'. The idea of the psychological foundations of political order and the value of religion in creating this order was the same intention behind Harrington's 'orders'.[32] The ideal government was one that placed the individual in a structure designed to turn all movements towards the public benefit.

This was similar to the prescription advanced by such men as Trenchard, Toland and the third Earl of Shaftesbury: man had to be induced to the paths of virtue using the instrument of the mind's mechanism. The most effective method for establishing discipline in man's soul was through the sovereign masters of pain and pleasure. The appetites and passions of men were too strong for the restraints of reason and the injunctions of the law of nature, thus religion was

institued to regulate and quell them. For this end, it proposes as sanctions and restraints, the favour of God to the virtuous, and threatens his displeasure to the wicked, in this life, and, in the next, still more adequate rewards and punishments, even those of heaven and hell. This is the great design of religion; and it effectually answers the same, where its own honest and simple dictates are observed and followed.[33]

---

[30] *Ibid.*, II, 56, 67.   [31] *Ibid.*, II, 43–6, III, 332–3, 335.

[32] Toland, *Collections*, II, 377. The idea of mechanistic control is neatly presented in Harrington's description of a carnival pageant he had seen in Italy. He wrote: 'At Rome I saw one which represented a kitchin, with all the proper utensils in use and action. The cooks were all cats and kitlings, set in such frames, so tied and so ordered, that the poor creatures could make no motion to get loose, but the same caused one to turn the spit, another to baste the meat, a third to skim the pot and a fourth to make the green sauce. If the frame of your commonwealth be not such as causeth everyone to perform his certain functions as necessarily as this did the cat to make the green sauce, it is not right' (Pocock, *Works of Harrington*, 744).

[33] Gordon and Trenchard, *Independent Whig*, 313.

The radicals argued that men ought to be directed towards rational behaviour by the inclinations of their own passions. Individuals needed to be led along the paths of virtue. Hierocratic superstition had expelled virtue and morality from their terrestrial havens. The framework for these notions was not only Judaeo-Christian, but appealed to the classical neo-Stoic tradition.

NEO-STOICISM, SHAFTESBURY AND THE PURSUIT OF SOCIAL VIRTUE

Stoic ideas were readily available during the Augustan era. Justus Lipsius' seminal work *De Constantia* was translated in 1594, 1653, 1654 and 1670. Guilliame du Vair's French work also achieved two editions in the Restoration. The neo-Stoic influence extended throughout all forms of literature.[34] Original Stoic texts are fragmentary, so the bulk of their notions were transmitted in the commentaries of such men as Cicero and Diogenes Laertius, whose works were consistently available during the period. A useful epitome of Augustan perceptions of Stoicism can be found in Thomas Stanley's (1625–78) *History of Philosophy* (1655–62).[35] This work followed the example of Diogenes Laertius and intended to give an historical account of the origins and development of philosophy. Part VIII of the work dealt exclusively with the 'Stoick Philosophers'.[36] In this piece Stanley wove together a multiplicity of ancient sources including Diogenes Laertius' *History*, and Cicero's important works *De Officiis*, *De Finibus* and *Tusculan Disputations*.

For the neo-Stoic, reason was the most important facet of humanity. Reason was shared by man with the universe and God. It was a faculty endowed in man to direct him to a correct and natural pattern of virtue, and transcend the tyranny of opinion and the passions. To live according to reason was to follow God and nature. As Stanley explained:

[34] See G. Oestreich, *Neostoicism and the Early Modern State* (Cambridge, 1982); G. Monsarrat, *Light from the Porch Stoicism and Early Renaissance Literature* (Paris, 1984), especially chapter 2, 'Classical Stoicism, Texts, Translations, and Translators', 21–49; F. H. Sandbach, *The Stoics* (1975); G. B. Kerferd, 'Cicero and Stoic Ethics' in J. R. C. Martyn (ed.), *Cicero and Virgil Studies in Honour of Harold Hunt*, 60–74; J. M. Rist, *Stoic Philosophy* (Cambridge, 1969). An important discussion of the links between anticlericalism and the impact of neo-Stoicism is P. L. Rose, *Bodin and the Great God of Nature: The Moral and Religious Universe of a Judaiser* (Geneva, 1980). This focuses upon Bodin's manuscript, 'Colloquium Heptaplomeres de Rerum Sublimium Arcanis Abditis'. There is no study of the relevance of this work to the English context of the late seventeenth century. It is known that Milton possessed a copy, see C. Hill, *Milton and the English Revolution* (1977), 109–10. Bishop John Moore also owned a copy, which was deposited in Cambridge University Library in the early eighteenth century.

[35] The second edition was 1687, and a third in 1700. Jean Leclerc was to translate portions of the work into Latin.

[36] T. Stanley, *The History of Philosophy* (1687), 421–91.

To live according to this knowledge is all one, as to live according to virtue, not doing anything forbidden by our common law. Right reason, which is current amongst all, being the very same that is God, the governor of all. The virtue therefore, and the beautitude of a happy man, is, when all things are ordered to the correspondence of a man's genius, with the will of him who governs the universe.[37]

If we now turn to Cicero's work, in particular *Tusculan Disputations*, *De Legibus* and *De Republica*, the idea of the government of the state and the individual, by right reason, is given a fuller treatment. The central tenor of Cicero's work was to proclaim the 'all sufficiency of virtue'.[38] Reason is presented as the joint property of man and God: its injunctions follow the dictates of nature.[39] In the *Five Days Debate at Cicero's House in Tusculum* (1683), an English translation of the *Tusculan Disputations*, the idea of the rational government of man's passions and the pursuit of natural order is central. The homology between illness in the body and the corruption of the soul by passion and false opinion is firmly established. The passions were the result of false opinion contrary to right reason and nature. Reason was considered as a type 'of Socratick medicine'. Constancy and virtue were the fruit of knowledge: philosophy was the guide to life and the physic of the soul. Cicero explained:

O Philosophy thou guide of life, instructress of vertue, and correctress of vices, what could not only we be, by the very life of men without thee? thou hast founded cities; thou hast invited scatter'd men to live in communities; thou hast link'd them to one another, first in habitations, then in marriages, then in communication by letters and words; thou was the inventress of law; thou the mistresse of manners and discipline; we fly to thee.[40]

In the *De Republica* and *De Legibus* Cicero reinforced the role of reason and law in directing the civil community, as well as the individual, to virtue.

Charles Blount was one of the most committed promoters of this Stoic version of religion as a means for controlling man's passions. He boldly explained, 'for as philosophy applies itself to reason, so doth religion to passion'. It was in this context (rather than in the name of secularization) that such men as Blount, Toland and Shaftesbury were to evangelize the claims of reason. Reason was the natural psychological director of human-kind's actions. Nature had constructed humanity as a combination of

---

[37] Stanley, *History of Philosophy*, 462–5. For a useful account of neo-Stoicism and natural law, see M. C. Horowitz, 'The Stoic Synthesis of the Idea of Natural Law in Man: Four Themes', *JHI* 35 (1974).

[38] Cicero, *De Divinatione*, II, i.200.

[39] Cicero, *De Legibus*, I, vii, xv, xxi.408–17, 423. Also *De Republica*, III, xxii, 360, 408, 412–13, 418, 423, 360.

[40] *The Five Days Debate at Cicero's House at Tusculum* (1683), especially Book IV, 'The Government of the Passions' 217–18, 223, 226–48, 268 and Book V, 'The Chief End of Man', 268–9, 280. Note that Toland (*Pantheisticon* 72) cited this passage as crucial to the pantheist liturgy.

passion and mind, 'the passions therefore were given to be used', and reason 'set over them for their moderation and direction'. To infringe this exercise of reason either by proscription or manipulation was to 'invade the common charter of nature'. In this manner reason was lauded not as a secularizing principle, but as part of the 'spiritual' nature of humanity. It was this psychological theory that underpinned the radical polemic against priestcraft and their propagation of civil theology.[41]

Perhaps the most articulate priest of this neo-Stoic pursuit of virtue was Anthony Ashley Cooper, third Earl of Shaftesbury (1671–1713). Shaftesbury, educated by the philosopher John Locke, was steeped in the injunctions and eloquence of the classics. This was reflected in his private regimen, correspondence and published works. Shaftesbury was a central figure in the radicalism of the late 1690s and early 1700s: an associate of men as varied as Robert Molesworth, John Toland and the Republican rector William Stephens, as well as Continental luminaries like Pierre Bayle, Jean Leclerc and Pierre Coste. His *Characteristicks of Men, Manners, Opinions, and Times* (1711), a collection of his previous printed and unpublished works, is a convenient epitome of the radical Harringtonian redefinition of the *theologia christiana* into a deistical civil religion. For Shaftesbury religion should be reduced from 'the higher regions of divinity' to 'plain honest morals'. General Stanhope, writing to Sir John Cropley in April 1712, echoed this opinion in commenting: 'I cease not to study Characteristics, and find my value and admiration for the author increase daily, nor do I believe anything hath been writ these many ages so likely to be of use to mankind, by improving man's morals as well as their understandings.'[42] The premise of Shaftesbury's conception of the value and necessity of a civil theology rested

---

[41] Blount, *Great is Diana*, Preface, Sig. F3v; Blount, *Anima Mundi*, 124–5; Blount, *Miscellaneous Works*, 'Account of the Life and Death', Sig. A10r; Blount *Oracles of Reason*, Preface, Sig. B3r–v.

[42] Shaftesbury, *Characteristicks* (3 volumes, 2nd edition, 1714), I, 41. See B. Rand (ed.), *The Life, Unpublished Letters, and Philosophical Regimen* (1900), 500, note at 494, (Shaftesbury to Coste 5 June 1712) that Prince Eugene conveyed his enthusiasm for the recently published *Characteristicks*; see, passim, for correspondence with Bayle, Leclerc and Coste. On Shaftesbury, see R. Voitle, *The Third Earl of Shaftesbury 1671–1713* (Lousiana, 1984); A. O. Aldridge, 'Shaftesbury and the Deist Manifesto', *Transactions of the American Philosophical Society* 12 (1951); S. Grean, *Shaftesbury's Philosophy of Religion* (Ohio, 1967). Note that Grean makes no reference to Shaftesbury's Harringtonianism, but is content to make anachronistic statements about Shaftesbury as a 'defender of liberal religion', and being on the 'liberal left wing of Protestantism', at 99–107, also 119, 260; see also J. A. Bernstein, *Shaftesbury, Rousseau, and Kant* (Toronto, 1980). For more detailed work, see E. Tiffany, 'Shaftesbury as Stoic', *PLMA* 37 (1923), 642–85; A. O. Aldridge, 'Two Versions of Shaftesbury's Inquiry', *Huntingdon Library Quarterly* 13 (1950). On the emblems contained in the *Characteristicks*, see F. Paknadel, 'Shaftesbury's Illustrations of the Characteristicks', *Journal of Warburg and Courtauld Institute* 37 (1974); W. J. Ong, 'From Allegory to Diagram in the Renaissance Mind', *Journal of Aesthetics and Art Criticism* 17 (1958).

au fond in his neo-Stoic idea of human psychology. Following Harrington, he insisted that to understand the 'scheme of the passions' was the business of religion and government. Conducting his 'moral researches' into the 'social passions' he presented a succinct neo-Stoic conception of human nature.[43] In *Soliloquy: or Advice to an Author* Shaftesbury argued that man acted under impulse of the will which was the product of the conflicting injunctions of appetite and reason. The human mind was a muddled system of passions, fancies and appetites: the soothing balm of reason was intended to regulate and order this machine. 'The mint and foundery of the imagination' if left to its own devices would produce dangerous 'specters' which deformed the human agent. The role of reason was to defend the 'moral fortress' of the mind against the corrupting interest of fancy.[44] The end of reason was to direct the imagination to a true appreciation of good objects and to the development of 'right opinion': it was 'the regulation and government of those passions, on which the conduct of a life depends'. Although Shaftesbury cited Descartes' *Treatise of Passions* (1650) approvingly he insisted that the government of the passions was not simply a question of mechanistic direction, but more concerned with internal perceptions of the 'good'.[45]

The injunction to establish true and good perceptions and opinions was most evident in the issue of religion. Shaftesbury had argued in *A Letter concerning Enthusiasm* that religious impulses were powerful motivating forces: if left undirected they could result in absurdity and socially corrosive behaviour. The letter, originally written in 1709, focused upon a contemporary manifestation of religious excess. The French Prophets were a group of French refugees given to millenarian prophecy and self-resurrection. To the orthodox clergy such enthusiasm smacked of irreligion, impiety and Antichrist, but for Shaftesbury such actions were the result of ill-humour and diseased reason. The French Prophets were simply 'unnatural' examples of a natural religious inclination. To treat such disease with the full rigour of a coercive law was counter-productive: it would merely reinforce their 'melancholy' ways. The correct method would be to substitute benign enthusiasm for malignant. In Harringtonian terms 'ancient policy' indicated that wherever superstition and enthusiasm were treated mildly 'they never raged to that degree as to occasion bloodshed, wars, persecution and devastations in the world'. It was thus necessary that the 'people should have a public

---

[43] Shaftesbury, *Characteristicks*, I, 116, III, 143. The connection between Toland, Harrington and Shaftesbury is virtually unexplored: note that Shaftesbury sent at least two copies of Toland's edition of Harrington's works to Holland: see Russell-Smith, *Harrington and His Oceana*, 143. The whole of *Characteristicks*, at least in political and religious terms, seems to have been informed by Harringtonian ideas. The classic case is the *An Inquiry Concerning Virtue*. Rand, *Life, Letters, Private Regimen*, xxiii, suggests that Shaftesbury gave Toland an annual stipend in the late 1690s.
[44] Shaftesbury, *Characteristicks*, I, 187, 311, 320, 327; see also III, 101–4, 186, 196–200.
[45] *Ibid.*, I, 294–5.

leading in religion'.[46] One of the recurrent themes in this letter was that a 'good' conception of the deity was a fundamental premise for all religious belief: deviant enthusiasms modelled their opinions of the deity upon the inconstant and corrupt pattern of the human passions.[47]

This theme was given an extended treatment in Shaftesbury's *An Inquiry Concerning Virtue*, a text of contentious origins. The first published edition was anonymously propagated in 1699 by John Toland, who had (without permission) removed the manuscript from Shaftesbury's papers. The author was unimpressed with his protégé's illicit endeavour. Shaftesbury attempted to purchase and destroy every copy of the edition. Although he was publicly angered at the premature publication of the work, in private he made moves to engage Pierre Desmaizeux to make a French translation for Pierre Bayle. The work was finally published with authorial acknowledgement and meticulous correction in the *Characteristicks* (1711). The differences between the 1699 and 1711 editions are merely ones of style and orthography: Toland's pirated edition is testimony to the centrality of the text to the radical pursuit of virtue.[48]

The *Inquiry* attempted an assessment of the contribution of contemporary religion to the quest for virtue, and should be recognized as a 'realist' reply to the conventionalist arguments on ethics and morality proposed in both Hobbes' *Leviathan* (1651), and more importantly Locke's *An Essay Concerning Human Understanding* (1690). Writing to a clerical protégé, Michael Ainsworth (3 June 1709), Shaftesbury suggested that 'all those they call free writers now-a-days have espoused those principles which Mr Hobbes set a foot in this last age': Locke was included in this inheritance along with such men as Matthew Tindal. Arguing against Locke's position that ideas of God, order and virtue 'has no other measure, law, or rule, than fashion and custom', and that 'experience and our catechism teach us all'. Shaftesbury set out to describe: 'What honesty or virtue is, considered by itself; and in what manner it is influenced by religion, how far religion implies virtue; and whether it be a true saying, that it is impossible for an atheist to be virtuous, or to show any real degree of honesty, or merit.' Nature, rather than human opinion, provided injunctions for both political and ethical behaviour.[49] Shaftesbury made the startling suggestion that

---

[46] *Ibid.*, I, 15, 32, 17–18; see also Toland, *State-Anatomy*, 28. Note that Shaftesbury and Toland both cite Harrington directly here: Toland, *Works of Harrington*, 448. On the French Prophets, see H. Schwartz, *The French Prophets*, (1980).

[47] Shaftesbury, *Characteristicks* I, 39–40.

[48] See D. Walford, (ed.), *An Inquiry Concerning Virtue*, (Manchester, 1977), Introduction, 1–14; Rand, *Life*, xxii–xxiii, 385.

[49] Rand, *Life*, (Shaftesbury to Ainsworth) 403–5, and (Shaftesbury to Stanhope, 7 November 1709), 413–17; Shaftesbury, *Characteristicks*, II, 7. See Cicero, *De Legibus*, I, xvii.418: 'Goodness is not a mode of opinion, but of nature.' See Aubrey, *Brief Lives*, I, 294,

atheism did not necessarily imply immorality: religious belief and moral action were strictly bifurcated. The case of the 'moral' atheist suggested that contemporary religion was insufficiently coincident with the injunction to virtue. Shaftesbury's polemical point was that many 'religious' conceptions led men to actions and beliefs which were incompatible with virtue and merit. While insistent that naturally man had some conception of the eternal standard of right and wrong, he was also convinced that by 'superstition and ill custom' this perception could be warped. 'False imaginations', ideas of vengeful and inconstant deities, vague notions of tribes of unjust and uncaring divinities could easily dislocate enthusiasm from its naturally virtuous course and substitute a deviant and socially malignant zeal. As Shaftesbury commented,

> that as the ill character of a God does injury to the affections of man, and disturbs and impairs the natural sense of right and wrong; so on the other hand, nothing can more highly contribute to the fixing of right apprehensions, and a sound judgement or sense of right and wrong, than to believe a God who is ever, and upon all accounts, represented such as to be actually a true model and example of the most exact justice, and highest goodness and worth.[50]

To hold a deity in awe and terror, to be bound to good acts by fear of

'Harrington', citing Harrington's verse: 'The state of nature never was so raw / But Oakes bore acornes and ther[e] was a law / By which the Spider and the Silkworme span; / each creature had her birthright, and must man / be illegitimate! have no child's parte! / if Reason had no wit, how came in Arte?' Note also the correspondence between Shaftesbury and Gilbert Burnet (Rand, *Life*, 419–21), where the former attempted to gain a chaplaincy for Ainsworth in 1710. It is also interesting to note that Shaftesbury lamented that Ainsworth was in clerical orders; he wrote in 1711: 'You have been brought into the world, and come into orders, in the worst time for insolence, riot, pride, and presumption of clergymen that I ever knew or have read of, though I have searched far into the characters of high churchmen from the first centuries that they grew to be dignified with crowns and purple, to the late time of the reformation and to our present age' (Rand, *Life*, 434).

50 Shaftesbury, *Characteristicks*, II, 12–14, 34–5, 40, 44, 45, 50–1, 118–19. Shaftesbury here follows the argument proposed by Plutarch in *On Superstition*, a text much favoured by John Toland who intended to publish a translation and commentary entitled *Superstition Unmaskt*. It is important to note that in his commendation of Pierre Bayle, Shaftesbury made clear the distinction between private speculation and morality. Writing to his printer Mr Darby in February 1702, he commented on Bayle: 'Whatever his opinions might be, either in politics or philosophy (for no two ever disagreed more in these than he and I), yet we lived and corresponded as entire friends. And I must do him the justice to say that whatever he might be in speculation, he was in practice one of the best Christians, and almost the only man I ever knew who, professing philosophy, loved truly as a philosopher; with that innocence, virtue and temperance, humility, and contempt of the world and interest which might be called exemplary' (Rand, *Life*, 385). Shaftesbury commented on himself: 'But as in philosophy so in politics, I am but few removes from mere scepticism, and though I may hold some principles perhaps tenaciously, they are however, so very few, plain, and simple that they serve to little purpose towards the great speculations in fashion with the world' (Rand, *Life*, 367).

retribution was neither virtuous nor religious behaviour. Good acts must be appreciated as good in themselves.[51]

In his *Miscellaneous Reflections* Shaftesbury supplemented this abstract argument with an historical account of the corruption of religion and priestcraft. Temple had risen against temple, and priestcraft had become a 'science'. The heathen priests had forced a trade which had unbalanced the city. Rather than employing force, the priesthood had used their 'wits' to 'practice on the passions' of the vulgar. Employing a Harringtonian analysis, and the principles of 'political arithmetick', Shaftesbury insisted that 'the quantity of superstition (if I may so speak) will, in proportion, nearly answer the number of priests, diviners, soothsayers, prophets or such like who gain their livelihood, or receive advantages by officiating in religious affairs'. In place of this corruption Shaftesbury proposed an enthusiastic search for virtue. The natural esteem for virtue, and detestation of evil ought to be encouraged and awakened by the state.[52]

Virtue in Shaftesbury's civil theology was a concept that would both unite man to man, and man to God. Thus virtue was recommended 'for its own sake' as a state of natural harmony. Drawing upon Platonic ideas of the beauty and truth of natural order and harmony Shaftesbury presented the analogy between the beauty of the natural order of the universe and an equivalent natural state of social harmony for humankind. As the world was in an ordered and balanced ecology, so human society was potentially a theatre of beauty and symmetry rather than conflict and contentions.[53] Like Aristotle, Shaftesbury argued that political society was natural: the ideas of a state of nature and the contractual origins of society and government were chimerical. Unlike Aristotle's vision, Shaftesbury's naturalism was not based

---

[51] Shaftesbury, *Characteristicks*, II, 55: 'There is no more rectitude, piety, or sanctity in a creature thus reformed than there is meekness or gentleness in a tyger strongly chained, or innocence and sobriety in a monkey under the discipline of the Whip.' See Toland, 'A Project for a Journal' in *Collections*, II, 201–14 at 202, on the 'beauty, harmony, and reasonableness of virtue in-itself'; Toland *Clito* (1700), 19: 'Virtues its own reward'; and Trenchard and Gordon, *Cato's Letters*, II, 236: 'Virtue is its own reward.'

[52] Shaftesbury, *Characteristicks*, III, 42–59, 60; II, 64. This passage is a reference to Harrington, *The Prerogative of Popular Government* (Pocock, *Works*, 437–8), where in citing Diodorus Siculus on the Egyptian priesthood's land ownership, Harrington commented: 'Egypt by this means is the first example of a monarchy upon a nobility, at least distributed into three estates by means of a landed clergy, which by consequence came to be the greatest councellors of state and, putting religion unto their uses, to bring the people to be the most superstitious in the whole world.'

[53] Shaftesbury, *Characteristicks*, I, 120, 142, 353–4; II, 17, 66, 77–81; III, 180–1: See J. Dennis, *The Grounds of Criticism in Poetry* (1704), 6: 'The microcosm owes the beauty and health both of its body and soul to order, and the deformity and distemper of both, to nothing but the want of order. Man was created like the rest of the creatures, regular, and as long as he remained so he continued happy; but as soon as he fell from his primitive state by transgressing order, weakness and misery were the immediate consequences of that universal disorder that immediately followed in his conceptions, in his passions and actions.'

upon hierarchy and inequality but liberty and the pursuit of the good of the whole. Contrary to those who argued that man's self-interest would always override the needs of the common good, Shaftesbury argued that social affection was both natural to humankind and in its best interests. True self-interest should be followed by the pursuit of this 'common affection' rather than turning every passion 'towards private advantage, and narrow self-end'.[54] The 'health, wholeness or integrity of the particular cræture' was to be found in the 'social or natural affections' that contributed to the 'welfare and prosperity of that whole species, to which he is by nature form'd'.[55]

To establish this ordered and harmonious society it was necessary to create ordered and balanced individuals. Just as bodily health entailed a good proportion and natural order in the components of the body, so the mind needed a similar balance. The study of 'inward Anatomy' could create this harmony.[56] An understanding of the 'inward constitution' and the 'oeconomy of the passions' was crucial to the achievement of human happiness. Men were like different instruments which needed different tunings and timbres. By a 'moral kind of architecture' individual passions could be adjusted to their proper natures. When both internal and external balance could be established then both society and the individual would flourish in health and virtue.[57]

The most important passion to direct and regulate was religion. As a benign enthusiasm it ought to be nurtured. He explained, 'so far is he from degrading enthusiasm, or disclaiming it in himself; that he looks upon this passion, simply consider'd, as the most natural, and its object as the justest in the world'. Virtue itself was a noble enthusiasm 'justly directed, and regulated by that high standard which he supposes in the nature of things'. If this passion was left untended it could disjoint the natural frame of society.[58] A civil direction of religious passion would create a naturally divine society. Man would realize, 'he is not only born to virtue, friendship, honesty and faith, but to religion, piety, adoration, and a generous surrender of his mind to whatever happens from that supreme cause, or order of things, which he acknowledges intirely just, and perfect'. If religion could be established upon these civil affections mutual love and friendship would follow. Following

---

[54] Shaftesbury, *Characteristicks*, I, 106, 109–11, 120; II, 78–81; III, 144–6.
[55] *Ibid.*, III. 222. This argument is explicitly Harringtonian: see Toland, *Works of Harrington*, 46–7. Shaftesbury was certainly one route by which Harrington's ideas were carried to later thinkers, for example Rousseau: see M. Viroli, 'The Concept of Ordre and the Language of Classical Republicanism in Jean-Jaques Rousseau' in A. Pagden (ed.), *Languages of Political Theory in Early Modern Europe* (Cambridge, 1987), 160. See also M. Viroli, *Jean-Jacques Rousseau and 'the Well-Ordered Society'* (Cambridge, 1988), 13–16, 24–5.
[56] Shaftesbury, *Characteristicks*, II, 83; III, 180–1.
[57] *Ibid.*, II, 83–4, 94–6, 130–4, 135; III, 180.
[58] *Ibid.*, III, 33, 36–40.

Harrington, Shaftesbury argued that the duty of the civil state was to create a system of inducements to virtue and discouragements to vice, 'to remove all prejudices against it, create a fair reception for it, and lead men into that path which afterwards they cannot easily quit'.[59] In the *Moralists*, the discussion was extended to argue for the necessary connection between civil liberty and the 'native liberty' of morality. As temperance and virtue could free the mind from 'inborn tyrannies' so the moral dame and her 'political sister' could combine to free humanity from the social tyrannies of passion.[60]

REPUBLICAN 'PRACTICAL CHRISTIANITY' AND THE GOLDEN
RULE

For the Republican the only good and true religion was a social religion. As the authors of *The Independent Whig* commented, religion was designed by heaven for the benefit of man: 'It teaches us to moderate our desires, calm our passions and be useful and beneficial to one another.'[61] In this vision there was a transcendence of Lockean 'rights' theories to a more holistic conception of society. The radical argument was concerned more with creating good agents and social order than defining and protecting the individual. The business of government was not security and protection but a more creative conception of human flourishing in the pursuit of virtue.

The central characteristic of the Republican attitude towards religion was that it had to induce 'morality' or 'social virtue' into political and social life. Following Shaftesbury's injunctions, the role of religion was to integrate the individual with the collective, as a well-ordered and 'natural' organism. Morality was the science of the control of the passions and private interest.[62] Thomas Gordon clearly supported this vision in his translation of Barbeyrac's preface to Pufendorf's *Treatise of the Law of Nature*, published in 1722, subtitled 'the History of Morality'.[63] The text insisted that 'morality is

---

[59] *Ibid.*, I, 18–19; II, 63–4, 72–3; III, 143, 224. [60] *Ibid.*, II, 250–4.
[61] Gordon and Trenchard, *Independent Whig*, 8. See also page xlviii: 'Morality is a social virtue, or rather the mother of social virtues: it wishes and promotes unlimited and universal happiness to the whole world; it regards not a Christian more than a Jew or an Indian, any further than he is a better citizen; and not so much if he is not.' This argument clearly has continuities with Leveller polemics in favour of 'practical Christianity'; see, for example, J. C. Davis, 'The Levellers and Christianity' in B. Manning (ed.), *Politics, Religion and the English Civil War* (1973), and 'The Levellers and Religion' in J. F. McGregor and B. Reay, *Radical Religion*.
[62] Moyle, *Works* (1726), I, 'Mr Moyle's Charge to the Grand Jury at Liscard April 1706', 156–7.
[63] T. Gordon, *The Spirit of Ecclesiasticks*, 2. See R. Tuck, *Natural Right Theories* (Cambridge, 1979), especially 156, 158–9, 174–6 on Barbeyrac and the history of morality. Tuck makes no reference to this early Republican translation of Barbeyrac's work. Note that Gordon's translation received a hostile reply in the form of Z. Grey's *The Spirit of Infidelity Detected* (1723 and enlarged in 1735). S. B. Liljegren in 'A French Draft Constitution of 1792', 37–8, discusses the favourable reception of Gordon's works in France.

the daughter of religion, that she keeps even pace with her, and that the perfection of morality is the measure of religion'. The author noted that it was necessary to have divine injunctions behind the precepts of morality, to ensure that the passions directed men to obligation via the mechanism of interest.[64] Barbeyrac excoriated the influence of the 'ecclesiasticks' who had misdirected religion away from the promotion of 'solid virtue' towards self-interest. Many churchmen among the Early Fathers had created speculative principles that were irrelevant to the cause of morality.[65] Barbeyrac's work was used extensively by the authors of *The Independent Whig* who insisted that 'morality is the only religion which human society, considered as such, has any occasion to see practiced'. Morality was a social virtue, that needed to be supported by revelation, because man's capacity for virtue had been clipped by the fall of Adam.[66]

The same argument was the premise of John Toland's *Nazarenus* (1718). His theme was the 'Original plan of Christianity': he explained, that the

Gospel consists not in words but in virtue; 'tis inward and spiritual, abstracted from all formal and outward performances: for the most exact observation of externals, may be without one grain of religion. All this is done mechanically by the help of a little bookcraft, whereas true religion is inward life and spirit.

The historical purpose of Christianity was to improve knowledge 'of the law of nature, as well as to facilitate and inforce the observation of the same'.[67] Toland completed this analysis by citing both Cicero and Benjamin Whichcote applauding the practice of right reason and insisting 'that natural religion was eleven parts in twelve of all religion'. This equation of pristine Christianity with social morality was reiterated in his *Primitive Constitution of the Christian Church*. As we have seen, the reduction of religion to morality was also effected by the radicals' applause for pagan, Islamic and Judaic theology.

One of the most interesting and enigmatic expositions of virtue in the period was the anonymous text *Averroeana*, published in 1695. The text contains a selection of letters from Averroes, 'an Arabian Philosopher', to a Greek student discoursing upon various medical and scientific principles. Supplementing this are fabricated letters from Pythagoras to an Indian king

---

[64] Gordon, *Spirit of Ecclesiasticks*, 3: 'To give these ideas all the force they are capable of, to make them able to keep their grounds against the passions, and private interests; it is necessary there should be a superior being, a being more powerful than we are, which may compel us to conform ourselves to them invariably in our conduct, that may bind us so, that it may not be in our power to disengage ourselves at pleasure; in a word, that it may lay us under an obligation, properly so called, to follow the light of our Reason. This fear of a divinity, that punishes vice, and rewards virtue, has so great an efficacy.'

[65] *Ibid.*, 3–4, 5–8, 13–15.

[66] Gordon and Trenchard, *Independent Whig*, xlix, xlv, xlviii, 312–13.

[67] Toland, *Nazarenus*, v, 67; see also Blount, *Oracles of Reason*, 199.

discussing the nature of religion. Pythagoras stated, that 'religion, I mean, true religion, is the same in all places and at all times'. Religious ceremonies were not the *esse* of religion which was defined as 'a vertuous course of life'. True virtue was only to be achieved by 'living in a constant imitation of our creator, in being innocent, just and holy'. This was to be achieved through the exercise of reason and an arrival at true knowledge of divinity. Pythagoras asserted 'that a wise man can only properly be said to be a priest, a lover of God, and fit to pray; for he only can worship who confounds not the qualities of what he is to adore; but first making himself the sacrifice, erects a statue of God in his own breast, and builds in his soul a temple for the reception of the divine light'. Toland, following this thought, cited the Church Father Justin Martyr who maintained that those who lived according to reason, such as Socrates or Heraclitus, were not impious but true Christians. As Justin insisted, the Christian scheme was accessible to reason, it was 'reason itself transformed or become a man, and call'd Jesus Christ'.[68]

The Freethinkers insisted that the Christian religion was a moral creed. John Trenchard argued that, 'our saviour plainly intended to reduce men to natural religion, which was corrupted and defaced by the numerous superstitions of the Jews, and by the absurd idolatries of the gentiles'. His description of Christian doctrine was minimalistic, being reduced to the belief in one God 'and in doing good to men; and therefore he instituted a religion without priests, sacrifices and ceremonies: a religion, which was to reside in the heart, to consist in spirit and truth; and to show itself outwardly in virtuous actions'. Charles Blount in his 'Summary Account of the Deists Religion' in *Oracles of Reason* upheld similar beliefs; the deist intended to worship no image, to make no sacrifices, nor rely upon any mediating body but practised his religion 'by an imitation of God in all his imitable perfections, especially his goodness, and believing magnificently of it'. Blount proclaimed the moral content above the mystery of religion; living well was to be a better standard of orthodoxy than a set of sterile beliefs. The only theological 'heresy' was vice.[69]

The description of religion as morality can be illustrated in the repeated use of the Christian prescription of Matthew 7.12 that, 'whatever ye would that men should do to you, do ye even so to them'. John Toland considered this injunction as the central premise of toleration. Men were to be treated as they behaved towards one another, thus a man's beliefs should not be subject to the supervision of authority unless they led him to antisocial actions. The 'golden rule' was an 'eternal standard, whereby to distinguish persecution for speculative opinions and harmless rites, from lawful restraints upon

[68] Anon., *Averroeana*, 128, 129, 130, 133; Toland, *Primitive Constitution of the Christian Church* in *Collections*, II, 138–9, 140.
[69] Gordon and Trenchard, *Cato's Letters*, IV, 265–6; Blount, *Oracles of Reason*, 88–9, 91–3.

unlawful practices'.[70] The integration of private interest with concern for public welfare was similarly an application of the golden rule. The 'rules and maxims' of law were created for mutual convenience, 'so that no man can oppress or injure another, without suffering by it himself'.[71] Religion had been designed by God to create social happiness for man. It was not made for priestly persecution, but to teach the precepts of 'virtue and social duties', to inspire men 'with social virtue ... for social happiness'. Ultimately the concern was to create a 'public spirit', a Republican equivalent of Matthew 7.12, which embodied the principle, 'it is one man's care for many, and the concern of everyman for all'.[72] Thus the Bible was to be read not as a text containing 'a metaphysical science, made up of useless subtilties, and insignificant distinctions', but as a work teaching men 'how to live'. True religion was determined by social comfort and consisted of a 'comprehensive charity, this spirit of public benevolence'.[73]

Historiographically, the Republican polemic has been treated as a symptom of the advent of the *saeculum rationalisticum*. Thus, as Dunn has noted, after Locke there was a profound caesura in political thought: Hume and Smith, for example, heralded the 'abandonment of theocentrism'.[74] Traditionally the radical has been seen to promote modern ideas like 'science', 'progress', 'popular rights' and 'democracy'. Writers like Toland and Moyle were, however, far more comfortable with the relationship between religion and politics than modern historians have been prepared to accept. The Republicans composed historical polemics against priestcraft based on a defence of biblical injunctions like Matthew 7.12 ('Do unto others') and John 18.36 ('My Kingdom is not of this world'). Both Anglican and Freethinker shared a common theme: the business of politics and religion were fused, and 'true religion' was the telos of political society. The precise description of 'true religion' was the bone of contention. For the Anglican the pulpit was a font of sacrament and piety, for the Republican it was an instrument for annunciating virtue and morality. For both, the Church was to shame vice and dishonesty from the community, but for the radical the clerical body was a creature of the state, no independent 'fairy dominion'. The Republican Church was to enforce the injunctions of 'practical holiness', and 'every social and civil duty'. Persuasion and good example were the only tools available to this clerical body. To attempt to gain any other power was to

---

70 Toland, *The Second Part of State-Anatomy*, 76–8.
71 Gordon and Trenchard, *Cato's Letters*, IV, 24–5.
72 *Ibid.*, II, 113, 291–4.
73 Gordon and Trenchard, *Independent Whig*, 58–62, 344–5, 429–439, 440.
74 J. Dunn, 'From Applied Theology to Social Analysis: The Break Between John Locke and the Scottish Enlightenment' in *Rethinking Modern Political Theory* (Cambridge, 1985), 66–7.

introduce the 'ghostly craft' of popery, rather than to animate a 'public spirit' in the nation.[75]

The Republican aphorism, 'liberty is salvation in politics', with its mixture of political and spiritual language, should alert us to the point that the radicals examined in this book did not employ the idea of 'liberty' simply in a juristic sense.[76] As Toland and Shaftesbury made clear (following Cicero) *libertas* did not imply licentiousness (an equation Anglican opponents repeatedly tried to make) but free obligation to rational law. For 'natural rights theories' the Republicans substituted a language of natural virtue. As Pocock has recently pointed out, 'alongside the history of liberalism, which is a matter of law and right, there existed throughout the early modern period a history of republican humanism, in which personality was considered in terms of virtue'.[77] Following from this, it is the argument of this book that, Republican ideas of *religio* must be explored side by side with those of *virtus* in order to grasp the full meaning of the radical polemic. Until this story of the displacement of the priestly caste from the temple and the substitution of the 'rational' body politic as a mediator between the individual and 'divinity' has been accepted as a central achievement of Republican thought, the tale of the mutation of this metaphysical ideal of the body politic into the secular idea of the 'modern' state will remain obscure.

[75] Gordon, *Works of Tacitus*, III, 222, 224–6, 226–7, 228–30, 245–55. The argument between Anglican and radical over who were the correct and legitimate promoters of virtue extended into the dispute between the High Church Jeremy Collier and John Dennis over the immorality (or not) of the stage. See J. Collier, *A Short View of the Immorality of the Stage* (1698) which vilifies the corruption of the theatre, and Dennis' reply, *The Usefulness of the Stage* (1698), which defends the stage as a competent propagator of virtue. Dennis extended this thesis in his *The Grounds of Criticism in Poetry* (1704) which called for a rebirth of poetic virtue. See also Dennis, *An Essay on the Operas* (1706) in *Selected Works*, I, 444–71 and C. Gildon in *An Apology for Poetry* written for Walter Moyle: 'The Ancients termed poesie a more excellent king of philosophy, which should from our childhood inform our lives, and teach us with pleasure, what our manners, our passions, and our actions ought to be' (*Miscellaneous Letters and Essays* (1694), 20–1).

[76] Trenchard and Gordon, *Cato's Letters*, III, 65. It seems then that the English radicals of the late seventeenth and early eighteenth century pre-empted the ideas of the 'high' Enlightenment: see D. Beales, 'Christians and "Philosophes": The Case of the Austrian Enlightenment' in D. Beales, and G. Best (eds.), *History, Society and the Churches* (Cambridge, 1985), 171–2, citing Diderot: 'Reason is in respect to the philosophe what grace is in respect to the Christian ... Civil society is, so to speak, a divinity on earth for [the philosophes]; he worships it ...'

[77] J. G. A. Pocock, 'Virtue, Rights and Manners' in *Virtue, Commerce and History*, 45; see on the juristic tradition, Tuck, *Natural Rights Theories*, passim.

---------------- ⫷ *8* ⫸ ----------------

Conclusion

We know, and what is better, we feel inwardly, that religion is the basis of civil society and the source of all good and all comfort. In England we are so convinced of this that there is no rust of superstition with which the accumulated absurdity of the human mind might have crusted it over in the course of all ages, that ninety nine in a hundred of the people in England would not prefer to impiety.[1]

Writing in 1790 against the revolutionaries in France and England Burke insisted that the 'coat of prejudice' should be protected against the 'smugglers of adulterated metaphysics' and 'naked reason'. It was a commonplace for Burke that tradition or 'prejudice' was essential to the stability of political and social order, 'it previously engages the mind in a steady course of wisdom and virtue ... Through just prejudice ... duty becomes part of ... nature'. For Burke religion and the established Church were the 'first of our prejudices': the consecration of the state was a necessity. Part of Burke's polemic against English and French radicals was that they had attempted to destroy the social mystery of the Church by naked speculation and 'metaphysics'. This defence of Anglicanism as a fundamental political theology and the assault on the incursions of philosophic cabals, atheists and infidels can be taken as an apt framework for the ideological battles of the late seventeenth century studied in this book. Burke's picture of late eighteenth-century society resting on the unity of the established Church, the monarchy and the aristocracy, unchallenged by Enlightenment metaphysics, is premised on the perceived opposition between the clergy and the coffeehouse philosopher. While not accepting Burke's interpretation of late eighteenth-century English society as dominated by the Anglican alliance of priest and monarch, his notion of religion as a prejudice which provided the moral and political matrices of that culture is pertinent for my work. I have focused on the crucial period between the Restoration and the early eighteenth century as an intellectual moment when (in Burkean terms) 'tradition' and 'metaphysics' engaged each other head on. So far there is little

[1] E. Burke, *Reflections on the French Revolution*, (ed) J. G. A. Pocock (Indianapolis, 1987), 72.

223

new in such a claim: as long ago as 1935 Hazard wrote of a 'crisis of conscience' in the European mind at the turn of the eighteenth century. Reason triumphed over superstition, the scientist mechanized the world picture, and Locke shattered the medieval twilight ideas of divine monarchy. To borrow Kuhn's language, there was a paradigmatic shift from religion to reason. This triumph of the modern intellect is sharply at odds with Burke's description of the 1790s: in the same way this book is not intended to embroider the traditional interpretation which allies Freethinking reason with the triumph of liberal modernity. Rather than deal with what Burke called the 'naked reason' of radical polemic against the Church my intention has been to focus on how the radical Republicans of the late seventeenth century employed history to attack established Christianity.[2]

As stated in the introduction, this work is conducted with the intention of emphasizing the religious context of the period. That is to say, whilst it does not intend to discuss the complexity of religious disputes *in toto* between 1660 and 1730, it takes the claims of theology, of religious conviction and of ecclesiastical politics as primary concerns of intellectual debate. The intention has been to examine how those who challenged the traditional role of the Church or of the priest set about demystifying and exposing the historical prejudices that shored up the clerical status quo. The thrust of my argument is that the radical counter-polemic was not sustained by the transparent power of rational argument alone, but by the careful construction of counter-histories. Part of my argument here is implicitly directed at what modern historians of political thought have taken as the proper focus of their scholarship; put bluntly, rather than examining the 'naked reason' of political ideas, my intention has been to explore how certain ideas came to be articulated in the form of historical argument. Christianity as an ideology is not simply a set of articles of faith but includes a necessary historical dimension. Individuals not only believed in Christian doctrine (the Trinity, transubstantiation, original sin) but also in Christian history (Christ's miracles, the Resurrection, the Primitive Church). Writing in an English context about Christian belief becomes an even more historical enterprise given that Anglicanism, as a schism from the Roman Catholic faith, rests its validity on the legitimacy (or not) of the historical events of the Reformation. Seventeenth-century Anglicans had to be aware not only of the 'Articles of Faith', but also of the unique historical probity of the transactions of the 1530s, 1540s, 1550s and 1560s.

If we accept that the seventeenth-century mind was deeply rooted in a complex set of religious beliefs and that the historical dimensions to these beliefs were crucial in inducing, confirming, or overturning conviction, then it is apparent that the idea of history in a modern sense becomes a problem.

2 *Ibid.*, 76–7, 80–1.

Consider an example: a devout Anglican, who believes in the Trinity, *de jure divino* episcopacy and monarchy, and treats Heylyn's *A Help to English History* as a cynosure of historical truth, encounters Burnet's abridged history of the Reformation. As a devout and conscientious Christian the individual can either reject Burnet's history out of hand or can attempt to arbitrate between the claims of the different works. In terms of the necessities of faith (the need to secure true beliefs in order to be saved) the conscientious Christian ought to choose that history which is the truest or most reliable. It is this picture of history as a seedbed for moral conviction that is the second major premise of this book (the first being the overarching importance of things sacred).

In chapter 2 I hope to have pointed out the duality of the historiography of the period: the fundamental tension between history as *res gestae* (the facts about the past) and history as *disciplina* (organizing these facts about the past). Contrary to the arguments of modern scholarship, which has attempted to divorce seventeenth-century history writing from its moral context and place it in the genealogy of modern academic practice, the force of my work in this chapter is to suggest that the historiography of the period is to be firmly anchored, not in the positivistic tradition of the birth of modern scholarship, but in the didactic ideals of humanist rhetoric. History was written to explain, justify and, most of all, to persuade. The past was not resurrected 'for its own sake', but in order to display the moral rectitude of a particular set of facts. The importance of 'true history' for 'true principles' cannot be underscored too heavily: for example, Catholic historians like Bossuet were trying to catch Burnet out, not just as a poor historian, but as a corrupt theologian. During the Restoration, theologians and natural philosophers became acutely aware of the persuasive potential of 'matters of fact'. As Shapin and Schaffer have stated succinctly, 'the matter of fact was a social as well as an intellectual category'.[3] Just as Boyle and his fellow members of the Royal Society sought to convey experimental accounts as transparent value-free matters of fact, so historians like Burnet created a set of methodological rules concerned to define the correct way a 'matter of fact' might be applied to induce true belief. Documents, testimonies and probabilities conspired to show the truth. The voice of historical impartiality set out to insinuate principles of partisan interest. As Locke asserted in the *Essay*, God had only afforded man a 'twilight' knowledge, and existential necessity forced humanity to rely on the probability of 'matter of fact' created by confidence in 'many and undoubted witnesses'. If 'historians of credit', contradicted by no writer, identified a matter of fact then 'a man cannot avoid believing it'.[4] On the same grounds, if Burnet addressed the impartial

---

[3] S. Shapin and S. Schaffer, *Leviathan and the Air-Pump*, 69.
[4] Locke, *Essay*, IV, xvi.8–11.

Christian conscience with the matter of fact that the Reformation displayed the subordination of the Church to state (and Locke's conditions held sway) then a 'man cannot avoid believing it'. The point was that while adversaries shared a common conviction in the value of 'matter of fact' they incessantly disagreed about the 'correct' truthful interpretation of such facts.

History was then a resource which intellectuals could employ to enshrine their particular ideals. As already stated above, the central theme of the book is the importance of the religious dimension to disputes in the period: without wishing to state the obvious, religion was not, however, a unitary notion. The Restoration saw many rival claims to be the true religion. As a necessary preamble to discussing how the radicals attempted to deconstruct the historical prejudices that upheld the established Church, chapters 2 and 3 have set out to sketch the parameters of rival clerical interpretations of the history of the Church. These chapters have sampled the varieties of Anglicanism, ranging from the High Church Heylyn, the latitudinarian Burnet, and the arch-Erastian William Denton. These chapters are intended to be illustrative of the types of historical arguments clerical apologists presented in order to justify their visions of the legitimate Church. While the treatment involves a selective rather than all-encompassing account of the complex history of Restoration apologetics, the intention is to describe the general shape of ecclesiological argument which radicals like Toland, Tindal and Gordon reacted against.

The Reformation idea of two regiments (Church and state) left many conceptual tensions: the purpose of chapters 2 and 3 is to provide a brief account of the potential readings of the ecclesiological legacy of the Reformation. The case of Peter Heylyn presents us with the defence of sacerdotalism: his belief in *de jure divino* episcopacy and of the spiritual superiority of the clergy over the laity, provides an excellent example of what writers like Hobbes and Toland would call priestcraft. Heylyn's historical defence of the clericalist principle 'non est sacerdotium nisi in ecclesia, non est ecclesia sine sacerdotio' is a necessary conceptual backcloth for providing some sense of what the radicals attacked. The studies of Twysden and Denton are included to indicate the diverse ways theorists justified the position of the Church within the state: some concentrated on the historical case for the imperial royal supremacy while Denton and Twysden proposed a more radical Erastianism that described the role of the civil sovereign less as an architectonic device to protect the true Church, than as an instrument of anticlericalism directed against all forms of clerical independence. While Heylyn and the other subjects of chapter 3 all claimed to be just and truthful historians they achieved no long lasting historical monuments. In chapter 3 I also moved on to discuss the works of Stillingfleet and Burnet: the purpose of this study being twofold. First, both works (Stillingfleet's *Origines Britannicae* and Burnet's *History of the Reformation*) are qualitatively different from the other histories discussed in the chapter. While Heylyn's historical writing was learned, it was never erudite: although Heylyn always pleaded the truthfulness of his historical narrative, he wrote consistently as a controversialist with a point to make. Stillingfleet and Burnet don the mantle of scholarship. Both works were conceived as authoritative, exhaustive and complete histories of the Church of England from the days of St Paul to the Reformation. They were public, collaborative and scholarly enterprises. Burnet in particular, with his almost irritating pleas for corrections and addenda, intended his history as definitive and unchallengeable. Secondly, in spite of (or perhaps more accurately because of) the public insistence on impartial scholarship, both Stillingfleet and Burnet designed their histories with the intentions of justifying their particular interpretations of correct ecclesiology. As Burnet was ever ready to point out, there was no conflict between scholarship and true religion; thus, if an opponent set out to undermine his academic abilities, his religion was implicated, too.

Thus, the first chapters of this book set out to illustrate the context of the radical attacks on the established Church. Following from the premise that religion, or the relationship between religion and politics, was the central driving force of intellectual debate, and that historical perspectives on this relationship were crucial to the authority of any given enterprise, the initial chapters have been intended to give illustrative examples of clerical historiography. Politically, the Church held authority in the pulpit; intellectually, history had been colonized by a priestly past. The staple diet of ecclesiastical history legitimated the role of the priesthood. Readers consumed documentary histories of the Church of England, be they Heylyn's heroic vision of episcopacy, Prynne's eulogy of the royal supremacy as biblical reformer, or Burnet's vision of a pastoral clergy. Although Heylyn and Burnet are at different ends of the theological and ecclesiological spectrum they shared certain common beliefs as Christians: the truth of Christ's mission and the idea of the Church being two fundamental principles. While they disputed the precise content of such notions, they both insisted on the 'truth' of the Christian religion. The different histories composed by writers like Burnet, Stillingfleet and Heylyn are treated as a common clerical heritage: a fundamental prejudice or intellectual resource which justified the Anglican status quo in the late seventeenth century. The second half of this work has examined how the radical Freethinkers and Republicans set about unpicking the elaborately embroidered tapestry of historical prejudices in order to substitute their own.

As the case of Tindal's *Right of the Christian Church* (1706) was intended to illustrate, the attack on the *auctoritas* of the Christian Church was initially conducted as a radical exercise in orthodox ecclesiological discourse. Tindal wrote as a radical Reformation Erastian: he used commonplace discussion of Church and state, the language of *regnum* and *ecclesia*, to justify the civil state as an instrument for deconsecrating the Christian priesthood. Just as clerical histories had lovingly documented the *res gestae* of holy bishops and godly princes, so Freethinkers began to frame counter-histories. As the cases of Tindal and the Unitarian polemicists discussed in chapter 4 indicates, one of the primary historical exercises was to reinvestigate the past described by the clerical historians in order to invest the Judaeo-Christian *saeculum* with different meaning. Thus, surprisingly, given the allegedly secularistic intentions of the radical enterprise, writers like Stephen Nye, Henry Stubbe and John Toland engaged themselves in serious, erudite and devoted studies of the Christian past. Far from writing histories to justify the clerical order the radicals rewrote the history of the Church as 'corruption' and in so doing redefined their conception of Christianity and the priesthood. The apogee of this strategy was John Toland's *Nazarenus* (1718) which recast the triumphalist interpretation of the Christian past (i.e. that Christianity was the sole true religious economy) into a synthesis of Judaism, Christianity, and Islam that undercut the orthodox idea of a singular true religion. Writers like Stubbe, Toland and Blount participated in a crucial change in historical mentality: rather than treating the past as morally significant only in a narrow Christian sense they broadened their historical canvas to evaluate the meaning of non- and even anti-Christian pasts. This intellectual disestablishment of clerical history, as described in chapters 5 and 6, was not merely a redefinition of the Christian past, but was the premise for an alternative model of religion. Clerical histories were premised upon a narrow and confined reading of the past: Christianity was the true religion and true religion could only be Christian. As the Christian religion was unique and true, so all other theologies were by definition false, profane and spiritually meaningless. Christians like Ficino, Erasmus, and later still Cudworth, had attempted to address the problem of 'other religions' but had resolved the issue by assimilating pagan and heathen religion (in their purest forms) into Christianity. Writers like Toland, Spencer and Trenchard preferred to adopt a wider definition of religion which attempted to assess the value of past religions not as a unitary Christian concept but as universal cultural phenomena located in precise political, social and historical circumstances. Thus Spencer undertook a detailed comparative analysis of Egyptian and Jewish religion; Toland felt that it was within his interpretative licence to assess Druidical theologies, the Koran, classical metaphysics and the canon of Christian Scripture all in the same breath. While clerical historians had examined documents like the 'Dinoth Ms' or the Cranmer Manuscript to draft the history of the Church, Toland *et al.* examined religion itself as a cultural artefact or document. Proceeding from this scrutiny of religion as a political or social phenomenon the radicals examined how human psychology contributed to religious behaviour. All this was not conducted with the purpose of furthering the cause of disinterested scholarship. Although such writings could be seen as the first moves towards later Enlightenment exercises in the history of civilization and manners, or the nineteenth-century disciplines of comparative religion of biblical interpretation, the Freethinkers conceived their writings as directed against the false priestcraft of seventeenth-century Anglicanism.

In the final chapters I have shown that treating religion as an object of intellectual investigation did not imply that men like Toland, Shaftesbury and Trenchard devalued or rejected religion. The radicals had concentrated on undermining the clerical notion of independent sacerdotal authority: *sacerdos* was a false ideology that corrupted religion and humanity. While the Freethinkers criticized the Christian priest as legitimate physician of the human soul they did not abandon the idea of an established Church, but appealed instead to the classical Ciceronian idea of *religio* or civil religion. As Robert Molesworth stated, 'the character of priest will give place to that of true Patriot'.[5] Writers like Moyle, Toland and Shaftesbury rejected Christian theology unreservedly, and substituted a metaphysics of virtue and reason. For the cleric, the salvation of the soul was the *telos* of Church and state; for the radical, salvation was a terrestrial possibility identified with the establishment of an harmonious, virtuous and rational society. As the clerical version insisted on the central role of the Church and clergy as dispensers of sacraments and keepers of the faith, so the Republican idea of civil theology (exemplified most clearly in Harrington's *Oceana*) suggested the need for an order of teachers to inculcate true principles of reason and virtue in the soul of each individual. As Toland had shown in his essay on 'prejudices' reason was easily capable of deformity and falsehood, therefore a civil priesthood was important to secure the claims of true reason.

Indeed, we should not confuse the radicals' plea for rationality with the cause of secularization or liberal modernity. Certainly for Toland or Shaftesbury 'reason' was a primary tool in dismantling the false metaphysics of priestcraft. If to be 'secular' one must call for the abolition of sacerdotalism then these men were secularists: in these terms the Reformation itself might be seen as a secular rather than a religious revival. The modern individualist trinity of freedom, equality and toleration has traditionally been seen as the achievement of 'reason' triumphing over religion. Although thinkers like Toland insisted on the 'reasonableness' of religious belief and

---

[5] Molesworth, *Account of Denmark*, Sig. B3r.

practice, their immediate aim was not the Lockean ambition of a separation of Church from state. Arguing tactically, against the false Anglican monopoly of true religion, the radicals could and did defend (on epistemological grounds) the right to a political toleration of different beliefs (what Toland called an 'indifference of temper'). They did not, however, abandon all to intellectual and religious pluralism. As the case of Toland clearly indicates, the hierarchical epistemology (embodied in the distinction between an exoteric and esoteric philosophy), central to the idea of a civil theology, distinguishes between 'reason' as a human faculty, and the state of rationality which could not be achieved by the majority of the people unaided. Civil society needed a didactic institution that could educate individual reason into a perception of true rationality. Reason was enshrined, for the radicals, not simply because it endowed each individual with a potential political and ethical autonomy, but because to be rational was to have achieved the highest state of human existence. True religion and reason became one and the same thing. The ambiguous position of these thinkers, straddled as they were between Christian theology and the modern world, can be illustrated by one final example.

John Dennis, as discussed above, anathematized priestcraft but insisted that a public religion was necessary to lead the populace to virtue. In a 'Short Discourse' appended to his *Vice and Luxury Public Mischiefs* (1724) Dennis discussed in detail the relationship between uncorrupted Christian theology and the public religion. As Dennis noted, some malicious people might argue that the logic of his arguments tended to 'put all religion upon an equal foot', but he wished to make it clear 'that I prefer the Christian religion to all the rest together'. Dennis' definition of Christianity was far from orthodox. The design of all religion was 'the happiness of those who embrace it': only the true religion could effect this happiness. Man's existential misery was the result of 'a discord continually reigning among the faculties of the soul; a cruel war between the passions, the senses, and reason'. Prior to the Fall man was 'holy, innocent, perfect': his intellectual and animal powers were in harmony. Human presumption and the 'design of growing independent, of shaking off the government of Him who made him, and finding his felicity apart from God', shattered the original harmony. Interestingly, Dennis conceived of the Fall not as an historical decline from God's grace, but as an internal state of human psychological disharmony. Salvation is described not as an extra-historical regeneration of human innocence, but as the restoration of 'the harmony of the human faculties'. The clerical equation of sin, sacraments and salvation is abandoned. For the bulk of humankind reason and philosophy are insufficient to establish harmony: thus Christian revelation, epitomized as the virtues of love and charity, 'performs in a moment' what philosophy has 'for Ages in vain attempted'. Put simply, for Dennis, the

Christian religion was the best social theology, 'so agreeable to the nature of man, whether considered as an individual, or a member of a vast society'. Charity makes 'the happiness of particulars tend to the felicity of the whole community; and whereas justice is satisfyed with the restraining of men from the doing harm, charity, the most active and best natured of all the virtues, engages him to the doing good'.[6] Christianity becomes a social ideology: for Dennis there is no soteriological theorizing about sin, grace and the Last Judgement. Religion was to be a belief system created to render men good and happy: salvation was identified with human well-being, creating social felicity for both individual and community.

It is worth now, as a final conclusion, having established the way in which the radical Republicans of the late seventeenth and early eighteenth century were concerned to rebut the priestcraft of the established Church, attempting some assessment of the significance of this moment. In order to do so it is worth briefly attempting a general consideration of the current state of the historiography. As described in the introduction there is one broad interpretation of the period which acknowledges the deist controversy in England as marking a discontinuity with the clericalism of the old order of the early modern period. As the first drafts of essays in the use of reason the English contribution to that wider intellectual and historical moment termed the Enlightenment, because of its unique conservative priestly nature, was overshadowed by the far more weighty, learned and devastating critiques of the *ancien régime* executed by the *philosophes* proper.[7] Perhaps the most articulate and extensive example of this position, dealing in particular with the case of John Toland, has been the work of R. Sullivan. Basing his arguments upon the triumph of a rationalistic and moralistic interpretation of Anglican latitudinarianism after 1689, Sullivan, discussing the elusiveness of deism, proposes that Toland's arguments and intentions were merely an extension of the theological liberalism of the dominant religious idiom. The Freethinking programme provoked liberal Anglicanism to face up to the implications of their rational moralism: in confronting this logic the Church of England assimilated reason into providing a foundation stone for the stable consensus of Georgian ecclesiology. Deism then, for Sullivan, is interpreted as part of a long tradition of Anglican compromise between the claims of reason and revelation.[8] Sullivan's case is well argued, and in parts attractive, although one suspects that High Church men like Atterbury, Leslie and Lowth might have objected to his characterization of early eighteenth-century Anglicanism as triumphantly rational. Indeed recent scholarship has argued convincingly that there is good reason to suspect that

---

6 Dennis, *Vice and Luxury*, 'A Short Discourse', 106, 108, 112–15, 117, 121–2.
7 See above, pp. 1–18.
8 Sullivan, *Toland*, 35, 55, 67, 213, 218, 227; see also 251, 272–3.

even liberal Anglicanism was still committed to notions of grace and priesthood as the *esse* of Christianity.[9] Ranged against this religious interpretation of Freethought is the irreligious or atheistic treatment. Although its proponents lay different emphasis upon how far the English radicals travelled the road to secularity they share a common insistence that the Freethinkers ought to be examined as significant within the history of unbelief. This secularist account of Freethought itself has two broad strands: the first, articulated *in extremis* by D. Berman, and most convincingly by D. Wootton, suggests that the late seventeenth century saw the uncovering of a widespread unbelief. By the 1700s effective and powerful arguments against god and revelation were prevalent.[10] For this interpretation atheism or Freethought is a question of intellectual or propositional arguments: to this end it is an idealist treatment, in the sense of suggesting that atheism or unbelief is a catagory of thought, rather than a political disposition. The victory (and the language of triumph and warfare is significant) of Freethought was achieved by developing a coherent intellectual case against Christianity. Such arguments were successful or unsuccessful only if they were perceived as right or wrong. For this position there is a logic of unbelief that leads from Renaissance to the Enlightenment: this transition saw the evolution of a correct philosophical (as opposed to irrational) account of God and matter.

In contra-distinction to this idealist interpretation which suggests that English Freethought should be understood as a route to a true transcendent model of philosophical atheism, the work of M. C. Jacob proclaims the centrality of politics and ideology. As she writes: 'The crisis of the late seventeenth century brought the legacy of the first great modern revolution into the mainstream of continental thought where it merged with indigenous traditions of anticlericalism, philosophical heresy, and anti-absolutism.' Stating boldly that the 'English Enlightenment begins in 1689' Jacob argues that prior to the 1750s the English experience of Freethought was significant in developing the threefold inheritance of the English revolution of the 1640s: materialism, Republicanism and social levelling. The radical coterie, with Toland at its centre, rejected the 'most basic assumptions of Christian metaphysics' and (continues Jacob) 'formulated an entirely new religion of nature and gave it a ritualistic expression within Freemasonry'.[11] One of the themes that unites the atheistic argument with Jacob's interpretation is the

---

[9] See Emerson, 'Latitudinarianism and the English Deists', esp. 33–43.

[10] See essays by Wootton and Berman in Hunter and Wootton (eds.), *Atheism*; and Berman, *History of Atheism*, passim; Berman, 'Deism, Immortality and the Art of Theological Lying'; for Wootton, see 'Lucien Febvre and the Problem of Early Modern Unbelief', *Journal of Modern History* (1988), and 'Unbelief in Early Modern Europe', *History Workshop* (1985).

[11] M. C. Jacob, 'Hazard Revisited', 251, 252, 254–5; Jacob, *Radical Enlightenment*, 22–3, 25, 84.

emphasis laid upon the covert, clandestine or shadowy nature of the movement. Much has been made of the private, as opposed to the public, nature of radical Freethought. Berman writes of a 'deep, covert atheism', while Jacob lays much of her claim for the influence of the radical Enlightenment on an entire, and clandestine, network of Continental Freemasonry. To accept this characterization of the impact and significance of English Freethought as a private moment concerned to alter the philosophical dispositions of shadowy individuals, is to underestimate the intentions and meaning of the authors examined in this book.[12]

Confronted with the rival interpretations of deism as a movement (as Emerson has neatly put it) on the margins of Anglican thought, or as a moment in the development of the cause of unbelief, this book has attempted to suggest a compromise. In setting the significance of late seventeenth- and early eighteenth-century Freethought in continuity with the series of crises of religion that dominated the political culture of the period, the intention is to insist upon the relevance of both the religious and infidel readings. Understanding the attacks upon the role of the Church and the priest between 1660 and 1730 as the culmination of a conflict that initially came to a head in the precise Protestant objections to the popery of Archbishop Laud in the 1630s suggests that Freethought participated in a public debate about true religion rather than the conventicles of private infidelity. In this manner perhaps we can place the radicals of the period in the religious camp, on the margins of theology. In doing so, however, it is important to be precise about the meaning of the category 'religious'. Suggesting that writers like Toland, Blount and Shaftesbury operated within a religious or theological idiom is not to agree with Sullivan's argument that they are merely 'latitudinarian exegetes'. One common theme of both the religious and unbelief arguments plays down the anticlerical content of Freethinking: an element this book deems central to their polemic. Sullivan, in particular, has stressed that Freethought is to be identified with the rationalization of revelation. The reading of John Toland as an apostle of theological liberalism epitomizes this tradition. Berman, on the other hand, has identified Toland (and in particular his *Clidopherous*) as the cynosure of private atheistical philosophy.[13]

It seems worthwhile, briefly, to focus on the case of Toland, as indicative of the debate. Both the religious and the unbelief interpretations treat the arguments of men like Toland as simple propositions: so for Sullivan, Toland is derivative, pedantic and amateur in his biblical criticism. For Berman, his

---

12 See *ibid.*, passim; Berman, 'The Art of Theological Lying', 77. It is the overarching argument of Berman's work that atheism was covert: this has led to some rather exceptional interpretations of certain texts. Much emphasis is laid upon Toland's *Clidopherous* as pronouncing the hidden method. I hope to show elsewhere that this is a misreading of an epistemological argument, for a pragmatic one.
13 Sullivan, *Toland*, 41, 47, 120, 251.

achievement lies in articulating a profound and importantly esoteric materialism. The balance lies between the two. First, it is clear that Toland devoted much of his life's work to publishing his investigations and innovative researches into Scripture. His early work on the canon, his constant rereading of the Old Testament, and finally the fully blown synthesis of *Nazarenus* suggest indeed that Toland could be considered as a full-time theologian.[14] If Toland is to be considered as a theologian, however, it should be an appreciation that insists that he had contrived an innovative vision of Christianity. Toland's reading of Scripture led him to a conception of Christianity that was distinct from the liberal Christianity of the post-1689 Church in its profound anticlericalism. Toland's criticism was calculated to historicize Christian belief and institutions: in doing so he struck at the very roots of the sacerdotal authority of the priesthood. It was this concern to attack the political role of the Church that places English Freethought out of kilter with both the religious and unbelief interpretations.[15] The case of Toland is again significant. Using the Protestant vernacular of anticlericalism, he undercut the traditional vision of the Church: importantly this campaign was conducted in the public arena rather than in a clandestine manner. Toland self-consciously projected his scriptural researches as public monuments: it was central to his intention of reforming the halo of sanctity of the Church of England into a true civil theology that his alternative readings of biblical traditions were voiced in the public forum. The importance of Toland's polemic was not, then, the development of the arcane esoterism of *Pantheisticon*, but the unorthodox ecclesiology of *Nazarenus*.

Having argued that the Republican and deist articulation of a civil theology could be considered as a renovation of the traditional conception of the Church: that is, that the reform was conceived and created from within a religious idiom, it is important also to be aware of the innovative implications of this polemic. Put simply, the driving force of the radical attack was premised upon an analysis of power rather than theology. In attacking the human agency of priestcraft as a corruption of natural religion, writers like Toland and Blount came to a different understanding of religion from the traditional conception. This new step was not so much towards a philosophi-

---

[14] See D. Patrick, 'Two English Forerunners of the Tübingen School: Thomas Morgan and John Toland', *Theological Review* (1877) where the author remarks upon the 'really startling' coincidences between the arguments of *Nazarenus* and Bauer's 'The Christ Party in the Corinthian Church' in *Tübingen Zeitschrift* 1831. As Patrick points out, Toland was the first to argue that the idea of a canon was merely a list of books rather than a rule of faith. For these reasons he claimed that it was 'by no means irrelevant' to argue for the primacy of English theological interpretation over German (see 593–9).

[15] See M. A. Goldie, 'Ideology' in T. Ball, J. Farr and R. L. Hanson (eds.), *Political Innovation and Conceptual Change* (Cambridge, 1989), 272–3.

cal atheism, as towards the development of an anthropological conception of religion.[16] In investigating the rhetorical question, 'whether the historical part of the Christian religion ... be a true History, or a legend or fiction', the radicals came to consider the 'matters of fact' of a variety of other religions. As Charles Blount commented: 'I was bound, to study with an impartial mind, not only all the severall religions; but likewise the controversies amongst them in Diverse Ages, languages and countries.'[17] This process led the Freethinkers to articulate a notion of natural religion as the historical premise for their civil theology. This conception of natural religion was, however, a revision of the natural religion proposed, for example, in the Erasmian syncretism of the Cambridge Platonists. The radical conception went beyond the suggestion that all societies have a common or shared religion, to argue that religion was man-made.

The distinction is subtle but important. For the eirenic position of Cudworth or even Stillingfleet, natural religion was a deontological truth, universally accessible to all humanity irrespective of language or geography. This natural religion was God-given. It had a divine ontology distinct from human convention. The fundamentals of such a natural theology are at the same time, then, both normative and universal. Although, certainly in the case of Blount's reliance upon Herbert of Cherbury's researches into the five common notions of religion, the Freethinkers, particularly in their notion of the historical corruption of a *prisca theologia*, relied in some sense upon this normative conception of natural religion, they also went beyond it. The anthropological refinement suggested, not that a natural religion that all could perceive without the aid of priest or revelation existed, but that all societies as human communities generated religion for their own purposes. The argument was that while historical research showed that there were structural elements coincident in the religious practice of different places, these cross-cultural similarities were not components of a divinely ordained template. For the radicals, religion was, in this sense, real and part of humanity's existential condition.

As each culture produced its religion in an autochthonous manner, so the standards by which to interpret and assess the value of worship were of human or social origins rather than divine. The radical argument, however, was aware that for the bulk of the population, given the very nature of the

[16] See M. T. Hogden, *Early Anthropology* (Pennsylvania, 1964); P. Harrison, *'Religion' and the Religions*, passim. The latter work, which only came to my attention in the final stages of this book, argues for a similar moment of anthropological awareness. Harrison's enterprise is distinct from mine in his emphasis upon tracing the rise of a natural history of religion as a 'secular study of the religious'. Harrison sees this as driven by a 'new and much vaunted scientific method': my argument would suggest that the new perspective evolved from the polemical dimensions of the radical attack upon priestcraft.

[17] S. Nye, *A Discourse Concerning Natural and Revealed Religion* (1696), 128; C. Blount, *Religio Laici* (1683), 3.

religious impulse, all organized religions assumed the garb of divinity. To dismiss these aspirations, or the 'priestly nature' of common humanity, would, as Toland repeatedly acknowledged, have been foolhardy. The radicals therefore tried to reform Christianity rather than overthrow it. It could be argued that in trying to reform Christianity without the central element of priestly *sacerdos* the Freethinkers abandoned any claims to the titles 'Christian' or 'religious'. This was precisely the argument of their religious contemporaries.[18]

As I have shown, however, the radicals did consistently, and sincerely, support the existence of a national Church: there was a clear role in their thought for some form of established clerical organization. The point was as Toland complained in 1714, that the Church of England 'is not what we would wish it'. It was thus important to 'endeavour to alter and amend by degrees, as far as is practicable'.[19] Whether this interpretation passes muster, on a transcendent definition of what it is to be Christian or religious, is in terms of the intentions of the radicals a marginal issue. The composition of the history of religion, which substituted a sociological explanation of the function of religion for the soteriological meaning of the clerical idea of the history of Christianity, was a significant moment in the history of early modern ideas. Religion was conventional not deontological: as such, it had a human history. Such theologies and Churches were created by civil society: they could be reformed by the same agency. Traditionally this moment of challenging the hegemony of Christianity has been located in the theorizing of the French High Enlightenment: the *philosophes* (Voltaire, d'Holbach and Diderot) dethroned God and theology. The intention of this book has been to suggest a contrary picture: the primary essays of desacralization were composed by the Freethinking Republicans, in their indictments of the priestcraft of the Church of England between 1660 and 1730.

---

[18] The phrase 'priestly nature' is Marx's: describing man's emancipation from the rule of religion he wrote: 'But if Protestantism is not the true solution it was at least the setting out of the problem. It was no longer a case of the layman's struggle against the priest outside himself, but of his struggle against his own priest inside himself, his priestly nature'; see *A Contribution to the Critique of Hegel's Philosophy of Law* in Marx and Engels, *On Religion*, 46.

[19] Toland, *Collections*, II 222, 246–7.

BIBLIOGRAPHY

MANUSCRIPT WORKS

THE BRITISH LIBRARY

Add. 4295, Birch 4465: Papers, Letters and Miscellanies of John Toland
Add. 20780: Thomas Gordon's History of Britain
Add. 23215: 'Muslim Reports' Sir John Finch to Lord Conway, February 4/14, 1675
Sloane 388, 1024: R. Smith, 'Observations on the Report of a Blasphemous Treatise by some affirmed to have been of late years published in print of Three Grand Imposters'
Sloane 2039: 'Manuscript De Tribus Impostoribus 1709'
Stowe 47: 'The Famous Book Intitled De Tribus Impostoribus'

CAMBRIDGE UNIVERSITY LIBRARY

Dd.10.58: J. Bodin, 'Colloquium Heptaplomeres'
Add. 41 f. 255: P. Heylyn, 'Ecclesia Restaurata 1674; Notes on, 1700'
Add. 7113: S. Ockley, 'Letters to Him'
Add. 2610: J. Spencer, 'De Legibus Hebraeorum; material for second edition of'
Add. 4. no. 27: H. Wharon, 'Anglia Sacra; extracts'
Add. 7647: Letters between John Woodward and John Edwards
Add. 8286: 'John Woodward's Letters'

LAMBETH PALACE

Ms. 673: 'Systema Theologicae Socinianae'

PUBLIC RECORDS OFFICE

PRO/30/24/47/4: Walter Moyle, 'Reflections Upon Ye Roman = Commonwealth'

ST JOHN'S COLLEGE, CAMBRIDGE

K 27: 'Letters from Mr Moyle and Mr Reynolds', 1705/6 30 January to 10 May 1720

237

PRIMARY WORKS

Addison, L., *The First State of Mahumedism* (1679)
　West Barbary: Or a Short Narrative of . . . Fez and Morrocco (Oxford, 1671)
Agrippa, C., *The Vanity of Arts and Sciences* (1684)
Anon., *An Account of the Life . . . of Spinoza* (n.d.)
　Acts of Great Athanasius (1690)
　An Answer to Mr Fontenelle's History of Oracles (1709)
　Averroeana (1695)
　*The Conduct of the Reverend Dr White Kennet . . . being a very proper supplement
　　to his Three Letters to the Bishop of Merks* (2nd ed. 1717).
　The Faith of One God (1691)
　King Edward VI His Own Arguments against the Pope's Supremacy (1682)
　The Life of Lucilio Vanini (1730)
　The Life of Mr John Toland (1722)
　The Life of the Most Learned Father Paul (1676)
　Mahomet No Impostor, Written in Arabick by Abdulla Mahumed Omar (1720)
Aristotle, *Rhetoric: Or the True Grounds and Principles of Oratory* (1686)
Ashwell, G., *The History of Hai Ebn Yockdan an Indian Prince: Or the Self-Taught
　　Philosopher* (1686)
Atterbury, F., *The Christian Religion Increas'd by Miracle* (1694)
　The Scorner Incapable of True Wisdom (1694)
　Rights, Powers, and Priviledges of an English Convocation (1700)
　Sermons and Discoveries on Several Subjects and Occasions IV (9th ed. 1774)
　The Epistolary Correspondence, 4 vols. (1789)
Aubrey, J., *Brief Lives*, 2 vols., ed. A. Clark (Oxford, 1898)
　'Remaines of Gentilisme and Judaisme', in J. Buchanan-Brown (ed.), *Three Prose
　　Works* (Sussex, 1972)
Augustine, *The City of God*, ed. D. Knowles (1972)
Bacon, F., *Of the Advancement of Learning* (1693)
Barclay, R., *An Apology for the True Christian Divinity* (1678)
Barnard, J., *Theologicus-Historicus, or the True Life of Peter Heylyn* (1683) in
　　P. Heylyn, *Ecclesia Restaurata*, 2 vols. (Cambridge, 1849)
Barrow, I., *The Theological Works*, 9 vols. (Cambridge 1859)
Basire, I., *The Ancient Liberty of the Brittanick Church* (1661)
Baxter, R., *Treatise of Episcopacy* (1681)
　The Second Part of the Non-conformists' Plea for Peace (1680)
Bayle, P., *General and Historical Dictionary*, 10 vols. (1734–41)
Bedwell, W., *Mohammedis Imposturae* (1615)
Bekker, B., *The World Bewitch'd* (1695)
Bibliothèque Universelle et Historique (Amsterdam, 1699)
Bisbie, N., *An Answer to a Treatise out of Ecclesiastical History* (1691)
　Unity of Priesthood necessary to the Unity of Communion in a Church (1692)
Blount, C., *The First Two Books of Philostratus, concerning the Life of Apollonius*
　　(1680)
　Janua Scientiarum (1684)
　The Last Sayings and Dying Legacy of Mr Thomas Hobbs (1680)
　Great is Diana of the Ephesians (1680)
　Miscellaneous Works (1695)
　Miracles No Violations of the Laws of Nature (1683)

The Oracles of Reason (1693)
Religio Laici written in a letter to John Dryden (1683)
Blount, T. P., *Essays on Several Subjects* (1691)
A Natural History (1693)
Bodin, J., *Method for the Easy Comprehension of History*, trans. B. Reynolds (New York, 1945)
Bolton, E., *Hypercritica: Or a Rule of Judgement* (Oxford, 1622)
Hypercritica: Or a Rule of Judgement in J. Haslewood (ed.), *Ancient Critical Essays*, II (1815)
Bossuet, J., *History of the Variations of the Protestant Churches*, 2 vols. (Antwerp, 1742)
Boulainvilliers, H., *Life of Mahomet* (1731)
Boyer, A., *The Political State of Great Britain* XXIII (1722)
Bradley, J., *An Impartial View of the Truth of Christianity* (1699)
Braithwaite, R., *The Scholar's Medley* (1614)
A Survey of History or a Nursery for Gentry (1638)
Brett, T., *An Account of Church Government and Governours* (1701)
Tradition Necessary to Explain and Interpret the Holy Scriptures (1718)
Broughton, R., *A True Memorial of the Ancient ... State of Great Britain* (1650)
Browne, P., *A Letter in Answer to a Book Entitled Christianity Not Mysterious* (1697)
Browne, T., *Miracles Works Above and Contrary to Nature* (1683)
Bruno, G., *The Expulsion of the Triumphant Beast*, ed. A. D. Imerti (Rutgers, 1964)
Burke, E., *Reflections on the Revolution in France*, ed. J. G. A. Pocock (Indianapolis, 1987)
Burnet, G., *A History of My Own Times*, 2 vols. (1723, 1734)
A Letter from Gilbert Burnet to Mr Simon Lowth ... occasioned by his late book of the subject of church power (1685)
The Abridgement of the History of the Reformation (1682)
History of the Divorce of Henry VIII and Katharine of Arragon (1688)
History of the Reformation, 3 vols. (1679–1714)
A Continuation of Reflections on Mr Varillas' History of Heresies (Amsterdam, 1687)
A Defence of the Reflections on the Ninth Book ... of Varillas' History of Heresies (Amsterdam, 1687)
A Letter Occasioned by the Second Letter to Dr Burnet (1685)
A Letter to the Bishop of Coventry and Litchfield (1693)
A Letter to Mr Thêvenot (1689)
Reflections on ... the Rights, Powers, and Privileges of an English Convocation (1700)
Reflections on Mr Varillas' History of the Revolutions (1689)
Reflections on the Relation of the English Reformation (1689)
Reflections upon a Pamphlet entitled Some Discourses (1696)
Utopia Translated into English (1684)
The History of the Reformation, 7 vols., ed. N. Pocock (Oxford, 1865)
Burnet, T., *Archaeologiae Philosophicae* (1692)
The Sacred Theory of the Earth (1690)
Burton, R., *The Anatomy of Melancholy* (Oxford, 1621)
Bury, A., *The Naked Gospel* (1690)
Care, H., *The Weekly Pacquet of Advice: Or the History of Popery* (1678–1683)

Casaubon, I., *De Libertate Ecclesiastica* in G. Hickes, *Two Treatises on the Christian Priesthood* (1711)
Cicero, *The Five Days Debate at . . . Tusculum* (1683)
    Five Books of Tusculan Disputations (1715)
    The Treatises of Marcus Tullius Cicero, ed. C. D. Yonge (1853)
Claget, W., *Of the Authority of Councils and the Rule of Faith* (1687)
    The Queries Offered by T.W. to the Protestants . . . Answered (1688)
Coghan, T., *The Haven of Health* (4th ed., 1636)
Collier, J., *An Answer to Some Exceptions in Bishop Burnet's . . . History* (1715)
    An Ecclesiastical History (1708, 1710)
    A Short View of the Immorality of the English Stage (1698)
    Some Considerations on Dr Kennet's Second and Third Letter (1717)
Collins, A., *A Discourse of Freethinking* (1713)
Cowper, W., *The Anatomy of Humane Bodies with Figures Drawn from Life* (1698)
Craig, J., *Rules of Historical Evidence* (1690) ed. G. A. Nadel, *HT* supplement 4
Cressy, S., *The Church History of Brittanny . . . to the Norman Conquest* (1668)
Cunaeus, P., *Of the Commonwealth of the Hebrews* (1653)
Darnell, W. N., (ed.), *The Correspondence of Isaac Basire* (1831)
Davis, J., *Instructions for History* (1680)
De Beer, E. S. (ed.), *The Correspondence of John Locke* V (Oxford, 1979)
Dennis, J., *The Danger of Priestcraft to Religion and Government* (1702)
    The Grounds of Criticism in Poetry (1704)
    Priestcraft Distinguished from Christianity (1715)
    Selected Works 2 vols. (1727)
    The Usefulness of the Stage (1698)
    Vice and Luxury Publick Mischiefs (1724)
Denton, W., *Jus Caesaris et Ecclesia Vera Dictae* (1681)
    Some Remarks Recommended unto Ecclesiasticks (1690)
Dodwell, H., *The Doctrine of the Church of England* (1694)
    A Vindication of the Deprived Bishops (1692)
Earbery, M., *A Serious Admonition to Dr Kennet* (1717)
Edwards, J., *A Complete History or Survey of all the Dispensations and Methods of Religion*, 2 vols. (1699)
    The Socinian Creed (1697)
    Socinianism Unmasked (1696)
Elwall, E., *Idolatry Discovered and Detected* (1744)
    A Declaration Against All the Kings and Temporal Powers (1741)
    Memoir of Edward Elwall (Liverpool, 1817)
Elys, E., *A Letter to . . . Sir Robert Howard* (1696)
Evelyn, J., *The Diary*, 2 vols. (1952)
Fiddes, T., *Remarks on the State-Anatomy in a Letter to a Member of Parliament* (1717)
de Fontenelle, B., *The History of Oracles and the Cheats of the Pagan Priests* (1688)
Foxe, J., *Acts and Monuments*, 3 vols. (1684)
Freke, W., *A Vindication of the Unitarians* (1690)
du Fresnoy, L., *A New Method for Studying History* (1730)
Fuller, T., *Appeal of Injured Innocence* (1659)
    The Church History of Britain (1655)
Fullwood, F., *A Parallel: Wherein it Appears that the Socinian Agrees with the Papist* (1693)
    The Socinian Controversy Touching the Son of God (1693)

Goddard, T., *Plato's Dream: Or the State-Physician Unmasked* (1684)
Goodwin, F., *A Catalogue of the Bishops of England* (2nd ed., 1615)
  The Bishop of Carlisle's Speech in Parliament (1679)
Gordon, T., *The Spirit of Ecclesiasticks of all Sects and Ages* (1722)
  The Works of Tacitus, 4 vols. (2nd ed., 1737)
Grimeston, E., *The Histories of Polybius* (1634)
Harrington, J., *The Works*, ed. J. Toland (1700)
  The Works, ed. J. G. A. Pocock (Cambridge, 1977)
Harris, J., *The Divine Physician* (1676)
Hearne, T., *Remarks and Collections* (Oxford, 1875)
Herbert, E., *A Dialogue Between a Tutor and His Pupil* (1768)
  De Religione Laici, ed. H. T. Hutcheson (Yale, 1944)
  The Antient Religion of the Gentiles (1705)
Heylyn, P., *A Help to English History* (1671)
  Aerius Redivivus: Or the History of the Presbyterians (1670)
  Cyprianus Anglicanus (1668)
  Ecclesia Restaurata: The History of the Reformation of the Church of England
    (3rd ed., 1674)
  Examen Historicum (1659)
  The Historical and Miscellaneous Tracts of Peter Heylyn (1681)
Heywood, T., *The Two ... Histories both written by C. C. Sallust* (1608)
Hickes, G., *Some Discourses upon Dr Burnet and Dr Tillotson* (1695)
  Two Treatises on the Christian Priesthood, 3 vols. (Oxford, 1847)
Hickman, H., *Historia Quinqu-Articularis Exarticulata* (1659 and 1673)
  Plus Ultra, or England's Reformation Needing to be Reformed (1661)
Hilliar, A., *A Brief and Merry History of Great Britain* (n.d.)
Hoadly, B., *The Nature of the Kingdom of Christ, or the Church of Christ* (1717)
Hobbes, T., *Art of Rhetoric* (London, 1681)
  Eight Books of the Peloponnesian Warre Written by Thucydides (1634)
  A True Ecclesiastical History from Moses to the Time of Martin Luther (1722)
  An Historical Narration Concerning Heresy (1680)
  Leviathan (1651)
Hody, H., *A Letter from Mr Humphrey Hody to a Friend* (Oxford, 1692)
  Case of Sees Vacant (1693)
  Reflections on a Pamphlet Entitled on the Occasional Paper Numb. VIII (1698)
  The Unreasonableness of a Separation from the New Bishops (1691)
Howard, R., *A History of Religion* (1696)
  *A Twofold Vindication of the Late Archbishop of Canterbury and the Author of
    the History of Religion* (1696)
Hughes, J., *Miscellanies in Verse and Prose* (1737)
Hume, D., *The Natural History of Religion*, ed. A. W. Colver (Oxford, 1976)
Inett, J., *Origines Anglicanae*, 2 vols. (Oxford, 1704 and 1710)
Jones, T., *Of the Heart and its Right Sovereign* (1678)
Keill, J., *The Anatomy of the Human Body Abridg'd* (1701)
Keith, G., *An Account of the Oriental Philosophy* (1674)
Kennett, W., *A Letter to the Lord Bishop of Carlisle* (1713)
  Ecclesiastical Synods and Parliamentary Convocations (1701)
King, J., *Mr Blount's Oracles of Reason Examined* (Exeter, 1698)
King, W., *A Vindication of the Answer to the Considerations* (Dublin, 1688)
  An Answer to the Considerations which Obliged Peter Manby (Dublin, 1687)

Klopp, O., (ed.), *Correspondence de Leibnitz avec l'électrice Sophie*, 3 vols. (1874)

Le Grand, J., *Histoire du divorce* (Paris, 1688)

Leclerc, J., *Mr Leclerc's Extract and Judgement on the Rights of the Christian Church* (1708)

Parrhasiana, or Thoughts of Several Subjects (1700)

Leland, J., *A View of the Principal Deistical Writers*, 2 vols. (1764)

Leslie, C., *The Theological Works*, 7 vols. (Oxford, 1882)

Lloyd, W., *An Historical Account of Church Government* (1684)

Considerations Touching the True Way to Supress Popery (1677)

Papists No Catholics and Popery No Christianity (1679)

Locke, J., *An Essay Concerning Human Understanding* (1690)

A Letter Concerning Toleration (1690)

The Reasonableness of Christianity (1695)

A Vindication of the Reasonableness of Christianity (1695)

A Collection of Several Pieces of Mr John Locke, ed. P. Desmaizeux (1720)

Lowth, S., *Ekalogai: Or Exerpts from the Ecclesiastical History* (1704)

Historical Collections Concerning Church Affairs (1696)

Of the Subject of Church Power (1685)

Manby, P., *A Reformed Catechism* (1687)

The Considerations Which Obliged Peter Manby (1687)

Mandeville, B., *Freethoughts on Religion, the Church, and National Happiness* (1720)

Mangey, T., *Remarks upon Nazarenus* (1718)

Martin, M., *A Description of the Western Islands of Scotland* (1716)

Marvell, A., *A Short Historical Essay Touching General Councils* (1680)

Middleton, C., *The History of the Life of Marcus Tullius Cicero* 2 vols. (1741)

Milbourne, L., *A False Faith Not Justified By Care for the Poor* (1698)

Mysteries in Religion Vindicated (1692)

Molesworth, R., *An Account of Denmark* (1694)

Francis Hotman's Francogallia Translated (1711)

Montesquieu, C., *Reflections on the Causes of the Grandeur and Declension of the Romans* (1734)

Œuvres Complètes, 3 vols. (Paris, 1950)

Morgan, J., *A Complete History of Algiers*, 2 vols. (1728)

Mahometanism Fully Explained, Written in Spanish and Arabick in the Years MDCIII for the Instruction of Moriscoes in Spain 2 vols. (1723–5)

Morgan, T., *The Moral Philosopher*, 3 vols. (1737)

Moyle, W., *The Whole Works of Walter Moyle* (1727)

The Works of Walter Moyle, 2 vols. (1726)

Munroe, A., *A Letter to Robert Howard* (1696)

Naish, T., *The Diary of Thomas Naish*, ed. D. Slatter (Wiltshire Archaeological and Natural History Society, 1964)

Naudé, G., *Political Considerations upon Refin'd Politicks* (1711)

Neville, H., *Plato Redivivus* (1681)

A New and Further Discovery of the Isle of the Pines (1668)

The Works of Machiavelli (1675)

Nicholls, W., *A Conference with a Theist* (1696)

An Answer to the ... Naked Gospel (1691)

Nichols, J., (ed.) *Letters ... to and from William Nicolson*, 2 vols. (1809)

Nicolson, W., *The English Historical Library*, 3 vols. (1696–9)

A Letter to the Reverend Dr White Kennet (1702)
A True State of the Controversy (1704)
The London Diaries of William Nicolson, 1702–1728, ed. G. Holmes and C. Jones (Oxford, 1985)
Nouvelles de la Republique des Lettres (Amsterdam, 1686)
Nova Bibliotheca Lubecensis VII (Lubaecae, 1756)
Nye, S., *Brief History of the Unitarians, Called also Socinians* (1687)
   A Defence of the Brief History of the Unitarians (1691)
   A Discourse Concerning Natural and Revealed Religion (1696)
   An Historical Account: A Defence of the Canon of the New Testament (1700)
   Letter of Resolution Concerning the Doctrines of the Trinity (1695)
   Life of Firmin (1698 and reprinted 1791)
Ockley, S., *An Account of the Arabick Manuscripts in the Bodlean Library* (1712)
   An Account of South West Barbary (1713)
   The Conquest of Syria, Persia, and Aegypt by the Saracens (1708)
   The History of the Saracens (1718)
   The Improvement of Human Reason (1708)
Orme, W., *Bibliotheca Biblica* (1824)
Osborne, F., *Advice to a Son* (Oxford, 1658)
   A Discourse Upon Nicholas Machiavelli (1662)
   Political Reflections Upon the Government of the Turks (Oxford, 1662)
Petty, W., *The Political Anatomy of Ireland* (1691)
Philoclerus, *Speculum Salisburianum* (1714)
Pitts, J., *A Faithful Account of the Religion and Manners of the Mahometans* (1737)
Plutarch, *Plutarch's Morals*, 5 vols. (1694)
Pocock, E., *Philosophus Autodidactus sive Epistola* (Oxford, 1671)
Pomponazzi, P., *Tractatus de Immortalitate de Animae* (Haveford, 1938)
Prideaux, H., *A Discourse for the Vindication of Christianity* (1697)
   The True Nature of Imposture Fully Displayed in the Life of Mahomet (1697)
Prideaux, M., *An Easy and Compendious Introduction for Reading all Sorts of Histories* (5th ed., Oxford, 1672)
Priestly, J., *The Triumph of Truth* (1775)
Prynne, W., *An Exact and Chronological Vindication* (1666)
Radicati, A., *A Parallel between Mahumed and Sosem* (1732)
Rapin-Thoyras, R., *Instructions for History* (1680)
   The Modest Critick: Or Remarks on the Most Eminent Historians (1691)
Reland, A., *Four Treatises Concerning the ... Mahometans* (1712)
Richardson, J., *The Canon of the New Testament Vindicated* (1699)
Robbins, C. (ed), *Two English Republican Tracts* (Cambridge, 1969)
Rochester, J., *The Letters of Rochester*, ed. J. Treglown (Oxford, 1980)
Ross, A., *Pansebeia: Or a View of all the Religions in the World* (6th ed., 1696)
Rycaut, P., *The Present State of the Ottoman Empire* (1668)
Sacheverell, H., *The Political Union: A Discourse Showing the Dependence of Government on Religion* (1700)
Saint-Evremond, C., *The Letters of Saint-Evremond*, ed. J. Hayward (1930)
Sale, G., *The Koran, Commonly Called the Alkoran of Mohammed* (1734)
Sarpi, P., *A Treatise of Matters Beneficiary* (1680)
   Advice Given to the Republick of Venice (1693)
   The History of the Inquisition (1639)
   The Rights of Sovereigns and Subjects (1725)

Selden, J., *De Synedriis et Praefecturis Juridicis Veterum Ebraeorum* (Frankfurt, 1696)

Sewell, G., *An Introduction to the Life and Writings of ... S–m* (1714)

Shaftesbury, A., *Characteristicks of Men, Manners, Opinions, and Times*, 3 vols. (1714)

Sheeres, H., *The Histories of Polybius*, 2 vols. (1693)

Sherlock, W., *An Apology for Writing against Socinians* (1693)

Spelman, H., *Concilia* (1639)

Spencer, J., *De Legibus Hebraeorum Ritualibus et Earum Rationibus* (1685)

Spaher, M., *A Survey of the Microcosm* (1695)

Spinoza, B., *A Treatise Partly Theological and Partly Political* (1689)

Stanley, T., *The History of Philosophy* (2nd ed., 1687)

Stephens, W., *A Sermon Preached before the House of Commons* (1700)
　An Account of the Growth of Deism in England (1696)

Stillingfleet, E., *A Discourse Concerning the Doctrine of Christ's Satisfaction* (1696)
　Irenicum: A Weapon-Salve for the Church's Wounds (1661)
　The Mysteries of the Christian Faith Asserted (1696)
　Origines Britannicae, or the Antiquities of the British Churches (1685)

Strype, J., *Annals of the Reformation* (1709)
　Ecclesiastical Memorials 3 vols. (1721)
　The Memorials of Thomas Cranmer (1694)

Stubbe, H., *An Account of the Rise and Progress of Mahometanism*, ed. H. M. Khan Shairani (Lahore, 1954)
　An Essay in Defence of the Good Old Cause (1659)

Sutcliffe, M., *The Subversion of Robert Parsons* (1606)

Swift, J., *A Discourse of the Contests and Dissentions ... in Athens and Rome*, ed. J. F. Ellis, (Oxford, 1967)
　A Full and True Account of the Battle Fought Last Friday ... the Antient and Modern Books in St James Library (1704)
　A Preface to the B...p of S.r.m.'s Introduction (1713)

Temple, W., *Complete Works* 2 vols. (1720)

Tillotson, J., *Sermons* 4 vols. (1704)

Tindal, M., *A Defence of the Rights of the Christian Church* (1709)
　A Letter Concerning the Trinity and Athanasian Creed (1694)
　Christianity as Old as the Creation (1730)
　The Rights of the Christian Church Asserted (1706)

Toland, J., *Adeisdaemon Sive Titius Livius A Superstitione Vindicatus* (The Hague, 1709)
　(ed.), *The Agreement of the Customs of the East Indians with those of the Jews* (1705)
　Amyntor, or a Defence of Milton's Life (1699)
　Anglia Libera (1701)
　An Apology for Mr Toland (1697)
　Art of Governing by Parties (1701)
　Christianity Not Mysterious (1696)
　Clito: A Poem on the Force of Eloquence (1700)
　Collection of Several Pieces of Mr John Toland, 2 vols. (1726)
　A Critical History of the Celtic Religion and Learning (1820)
　Cicero Illustratus (1712)
　The Danger of Mercenary Parliaments (1722)

Hodegeus, or the Pillar of Cloud and Fire (1720)
Letter from an Arabian Physician (Paris, 1706)
Letters from the Late Earl of Shaftesbury to Robert Molesworth (1721)
Letters to Serena (1704)
The Life of John Milton (1699)
Mangoneuteus: Being a Defence of Nazarenus (1720)
Miscellaneous Works of Mr John Toland, 2 vols. (1747)
Nazarenus Or, Jewish, Gentile, and Mahometan Christianity (1718)
(ed.), *Oceana of James Harrington and His other Works* (1700)
Origines Judicae (The Hague, 1709)
Pantheisticon (1751)
The Second Part of the State-Anatomy (1717)
Socinianism Truly Stated (1705)
The State-Anatomy of Great Britain (1717)
Tetradymus (1720)
Two Essays Sent in a Letter of Oxford to a Nobleman in London (1695)
Vindicius Liberius or Mr Toland's Defence of Himself (1702)
Touchet, G., *Historical Collections out of Several Grave Protestant Historians* (1673)
Townley, J., *The Reasons of the Laws of Moses* (1827)
Trenchard, J., *A Natural History of Superstition* (1709)
Trenchard, J., and T. Gordon, *Cato's Letters; Or Essays on Liberty, Civil and Religious*, 4 vols. (1737)
The Independent Whig (1721)
Twysden, R., *An Historical Vindication of the Church of England* (1657 and 1675)
Ussher, J., *Britannicarum Ecclesiarum Antiquitates* (2nd ed., 1687)
A Discourse of the Religion Anciently Professed by the British and Irish (1687)
The Power Communicated by God to the Prince (1688)
The Reduction of Episcopacy (1656)
Warburton, W., *The Divine Legation of Moses*, 5 vols. (1765)
Wharton, H., *A Specimen of Some Errors and Defects in the History of the Reformation* (1693)
Wheare, D., *The Method and Order of Reading both Civil and Ecclesiastical Histories* (1694)
Whiston, W., *An Account of the Convocations Proceedings* (1711)
An Account of Mr Whiston's Prosecution (1718)
Historical Memoirs of the Life of Dr Samuel Clarke (1730)
Mr Whiston's Memoirs (1749)
A New Theory of the Earth (1696)
Primitive Christianity Reviv'd, 5 vols. (1711–12)
Scripture Politicks (1717)
Williams, D., *A Vindication of the Sermons of His Grace John Archbishop of Canterbury, concerning the Divinity and Incarnation of our B. Saviour* (1695)
Winstanley, G., *The Law of Freedom and other Writings* ed. C. Hill (1973)
Woodward, J., 'Of The Wisdom of the Ancient Egyptians' *Archaeologia* 4 (1777)
Wotton, W., *Reflections upon Ancient and Modern Learning* (1694)

SECONDARY WORKS

Aldridge, A. O., 'Two Versions of Shaftesbury's Inquiry', *Huntington Library Quarterly* 13 (1950)
'Shaftesbury and the Deist Manifesto', *TAPS* 12 (1951)
Alic, M., *Hypatia's Heritage* (1986)
Allen, D. C., *Doubt's Boundless Sea: Scepticism and Faith in the Renaissance* (Baltimore, 1964)
Althusser, L., *Politics and History: Montesquieu, Rousseau, Marx* (1982)
Aquilecchia, G., 'Nota su John Toland Traduttore di Giordano Bruno', *English Miscellany* 9 (1958)
'Schedu Bruniana: La Traduzione "Tolandiana" dello Spaccio', *Giornale Storico della Letteratura Italiano* 152 (1975)
Arberry, A., *The Cambridge School of Arabic* (Cambridge, 1948)
The Koran Interpreted, 2 vols. (1955)
Archambault, P., 'The Analogy of the "Body" in Renaissance Political Literature', *Bibliothèque d'humanisme et renaissance* 29 (1967)
Armstrong, D., *Political Anatomy of the Body* (Cambridge, 1983)
Ashcraft, R., *Locke's Two Treatises of Government* (1987)
Ashcraft, R. and M. M. Goldsmith, 'Locke, Revolution Principles and the Formation of Whig Ideology', *HJ* 26 (1983)
Aspelin, G., 'Ralph Cudworth's Interpretation of Greek Philosophy', *Götesborgs Hogskolas Årsskrift* 49 (1943)
Atkinson, G., *Les Relations de voyages du XVII siècle et l'évolution des idées* (Paris, 1926)
Avis, P., *Foundations of Modern Historical Thought from Machiavelli to Vico* (1986)
Axon, W. E. A., 'On the Mohammedan Gospel of Barnabas', *Journal of Theological Studies* 3 (1901–2)
Aylmer, G. E., (ed.), *The Interregnum* (1972)
Baker, H., *The Race of Time: Three Lectures on Renaissance Historiography* (Toronto, 1967)
The Wars of Truth (Massachusetts, 1969)
Barnes, B. and S. Shapin (eds.), *Natural Order: Historical Studies of Scientific Cultures* (1979)
Barzily, I., 'Toland's Borrowings from Simone Luzzato', *Jewish Social Studies* 31 (1969)
Beales, D. and G. Best (eds.), *History, Society and the Churches* (Cambridge, 1985)
Bedford, R. D., *The Defence of Truth. Herbert of Cherbury and the Seventeenth Century* (Manchester, 1979)
Behrens, B., 'The Whig Theory of the Constitution in the Reign of Charles II', *CHJ* 8 (1941)
Bennett, G. V., 'King William and the Episcopate', in Bennet, G. V. and J. D. Walsh, (eds.), *Essays in Modern Church History* (1966)
'The Convocation of 1710: An Anglican Attempt at Counter-revolution', *Studies in Church History* 7 (1971)
The Tory Crisis in Church and State. The Career of Francis Atterbury 1688–1730 (Oxford, 1975)
Bennett, H. S., *English Books and their Readers 1603–1640* (Cambridge, 1970)
Berger, P., *The Social Reality of Religion* (1968)

Berman, D., 'Deism, Immortality and the Art of Theological Lying', in J. A. Leo Lemay, *Deism, Masonry and the Enlightenment* (Newark, 1987)

A History of Atheism in England (1988)

'Disclaimers as Offence Mechanisms in Charles Blount and John Toland', in M. Hunter and D. Wootton (eds.), *Atheism from the Reformation to the Enlightenment* (Oxford, forthcoming)

Bernal, M., *Black Athena: The Afro-Asiatic Roots of Classical Civilisation* (1987)

Bernstein, J. A., *Shaftesbury, Rousseau, and Kant: An Introduction to the Conflict between Aesthetic and Moral Values in Modern Thought* (1980)

Berti, S., '"La Vie et l'esprit de Spinoza" (1719) e la prima traduzione Francese dell' "Ethica"', *Rivista storica italiana* 98 (1986)

'The first edition of the *Traité des trois imposteurs*, and its debt to Spinoza's *Ethics*' in M. Hunter and D. Wootton (eds.), *Atheism from Reformation to Enlightenment* (Oxford, forthcoming)

Betts, C. J., *Early Deism in France* (The Hague, 1984)

Biddle, J. C., 'Locke's Critique of Innate Principles and Toland's Deism', *JHI* 37 (1976)

Blitzer, C., *An Immortal Commonwealth. The Political Thought of James Harrington* (New Haven, 1960)

Bolgar, R. R., *The Classical Heritage and Its Beneficiaries* (Cambridge, 1954)

(ed.), *Classical Influences on European Culture 1500–1700* (Cambridge, 1976)

Bonante U., *Charles Blount: Libertismo e Deismo nel Seicento Inglese* (Florence, 1972)

Bonner, S. F., *Roman Declamation* (1949)

Boon, J. A., *Other Tribes, Other Scribes. Symbolic Anthropology in the Comparative Study of Cultures, Histories, Religions and Texts* (Cambridge, 1982)

Bosher, R. S., *The Making of the Restoration Settlement* (1951)

Boss, R. I., 'The Development of Social Religion: A Contradiction in French Freethought', *JHI* 34 (1973)

Bossy, J., *Christianity in the West 1400–1700* (Oxford, 1985)

Bowersock, G. W. *et al.* (eds.), *Edward Gibbon and the Decline and Fall of the Roman Empire* (Harvard, 1977)

Braddick, M., 'State Formation and Social Change in Early Modern England: A Problem Stated and New Approaches Suggested', *Social History* (1991)

Brooks, C., and K. Sharpe, 'Debate: History, English Law, and the Renaissance', *PP* 72 (1976)

Brown, K. (ed.), *Hobbes Studies* (Oxford, 1985)

Browning, R., *The Political and Constitutional Ideas of the Court Whigs* (Louisiana, 1982)

Brunet, G., *Le traité des trois imposteurs* (Paris, 1867)

Bryant, J. A., 'Milton and the Art of History', *Philological Quarterly* 24 (1950)

Buckley, M., *At the Origins of Modern Atheism* (New Haven, 1987)

Buick-Knox, R., *James Ussher, Archbishop of Armagh* (Cardiff, 1967)

Bullock, J. M., *Thomas Gordon the Independent Whig* (Aberdeen, 1918)

Buranelli, V., 'The Historical and Political Thought of Boulainvilliers', *JHI* 18 (1957)

Burke, P., 'A Survey of the Popularity of Ancient Historians', *HT* 5 (1966)

The Renaissance Sense of the Past (New York, 1966)

Burrow, J., *A Liberal Descent. Victorian Historians and the English Past* (Cambridge, 1983)

Campbell, L. B., *Tudor Conceptions of History and Tragedy in a Mirror for Magistrates* (Berkeley, 1936)

Capp, B., *The Fifth Monarchy Men* (1967)

Astrology and the Popular Press: English Almanacs 1500–1800 (1979)

Carabelli, G., 'John Toland e G. W. Leibnitz: Otto Lettere', *Rivista Critica di Storia della Filosophia* 29 (1974)

Tolandiana (Florence, 1975)

Cargill-Thompson, W. D. J., 'Strype as a Source for the Study of Sixteenth Century English Church History', *Studies in Church History* 11 (Oxford, 1975)

Carrithers, D. W., *The Spirit of Laws by Montesquieu: A Compendium* (Berkeley, 1977)

Carroll, R. S., *The Commonsense Philosophy of Bishop Edward Stillingfleet* (The Hague, 1975)

Carter, R. B., *Descartes' Medical Philosophy: An Organic Solution to the Mind–Body Problem* (Baltimore, 1983)

Cassirer, E., *The Philosophy of the Enlightenment* (Princeton, 1951)

The Platonic Renaissance in England (1953)

Castillejo, D., *The Expanding Force in Newton's Cosmos* (Madrid, 1981)

Chadwick, H., *The Early Church* (1968)

Chadwick, O., *The Secularisation of the European Mind in the Nineteenth Century* (Cambridge, 1990)

Chew, S., *The Crescent and the Rose* (1958)

Cirrillo, L. and M. Fremaux, *L'Evangile de Barnabé: recherches sur le composition et l'origine* (Paris, 1977)

Clark, J. C. D., *English Society 1688–1832* (Cambridge, 1985)

Revolution and Rebellion (Cambridge, 1986)

'On Hitting the Buffers: The Historiography of England's Ancien regime', *PP* 117 (1987)

Close, A. J., 'Commonplace Theories of Art and Nature in Classical Antiquity and the Renaissance', *JHI* 30 (1969)

'Philosophical Theories of Art and Nature in Classical Antiquity', *JHI* 32 (1971)

Coates, J. D., 'Coleridge's Debt to Harrington: A Discussion of Zapolya', *JHI* 38 (1977)

Cohen, M., *Sensible Words* (Baltimore, 1977)

Colie, R. S., *Light and Enlightenment* (Cambridge, 1957)

'Spinoza and the Early English Deists', *JHI* 20 (1959)

'Spinoza in England', *TAPS* 107 (1963)

Condren, C., 'From Premise to Conclusion: Some Comments on Professional History and the Incubus of Rhetorical Historiography', *Parergon: Bulletin of the Australian and New Zealand Association for Medieval and Renaissance Studies* 6, *Festschrift for Sir Geoffrey Elton* (1988)

Conger, G. P., *Theories of Macrocosm and Microcosm in the History of Philosophy* (New York, 1922)

Conzelmann, H., *History of the Primitive Church* (1973)

Cornforth, M. (ed.), *Rebels and Their Causes* (1978)

Costello, W. T., *The Scholastic Curriculum at Early Seventeenth-Century Cambridge* (Cambridge, 1958)

Cotton, J., 'James Harrington and Thomas Hobbes', *JHI* 42 (1981)

Cragg, G. R., *The Church and the Age of Reason* (1965)

Cranston, M., *Philosophers and Pamphleteers: Political Theorists of the Enlightenment* (Oxford, 1986)

Cressy, D., *Literacy and the Social Order* (Cambridge, 1980)

Daly, J., 'Cosmic Harmony and Political Thinking in Early Stuart England', *TAPS* 69 (1979)

Damrosch, L., 'Hobbes as a Reformation Theologian', *JHI* 40 (1979)

Daniel, N., *Islam and the West* (Edinburgh, 1980)

Daniel, S., *John Toland: His Methods, Manners, and Mind* (McGill, 1984)

Davidson, W. L., *The Stoic Creed* (New York, 1979)

Davies, L. J., 'A Social History of Fact and Fiction; Authorial Disavowal in the Early English Novel' in E. Said (ed.), *Literature and Society* (1980)

Davis, H., *Worship and Theology in England from Andrewes to Baxter and Fox 1603–1690* (Princeton, 1975)

Davis, J. C., 'The Levellers and Christianity' in B. Manning, *Politics, Religion and the English Civil War* (1973)

'Pocock's Harrington: Grace, Nature, and Art in the Classical Republicanism of James Harrington', *HJ* 24 (1981)

Utopia and the Ideal Society (Cambridge, 1981)

'Radicalism in a Traditional Society: The Evaluation of Radical Thought in the English Commonwealth 1649–1660', *HPT* 3 (1982)

Fear, Myth and History (Cambridge, 1986)

Dean, L. F., 'Sir Francis Bacon's Theory of Civil History Writing', *ELH* 8 (1941)

'Bodin's Methodus in England before 1625', *Studies in Philology* 38 (1942)

Deporte, M. V., *Nightmares and Hobbyhorses, Swift, Sterne and Augustan Ideas of Madness* (San Marino, 1974)

Dewhurst, K. E. 'Locke and Sydenham on the Teaching of Anatomy', *MH* 11 (1958)

Diamond, C., 'Natural Philosophy in Harrington's Political Thought', *JHP* 16 (1978)

Dickens, A. G. and J. Tonkin, *The Reformation in Historical Thought* (Oxford, 1985)

Dickinson, H. T., *Liberty and Property* (1977)

Dieckmann, L., *Hieroglyphs: The History of a Literary Symbol* (Washington and St Louis, 1970)

Downs, M., *James Harrington* (Boston, 1977)

D'Oyly, G. D., *The Life of William Sancroft*, 2 vols. (1824)

Dory, T. A. (ed.), *Tacitus* (1969)

Douglas, D. C., *English Scholars 1660–1730* (1951)

Drabble, J., 'Gilbert Burnet and the History of the English Reformation: The Historian and his milieu', *Journal of Religious History* 12 (1983)

Duffy, E., 'Whiston's Affair: The Trial of a Primitive Christian 1709–1714', *JEH* (1976)

Dunn, J., *The Political Thought of John Locke* (Cambridge, 1968)

'The Politics of Locke in England and America in the Eighteenth century', in Yolton, J. W. (ed.), *John Locke: Problems and Perspectives* (Cambridge, 1969)

Rethinking Modern Political Theory (Cambridge, 1985)

Eagleton, T., 'Text, Ideology, Realism', in E. Said (ed.), *Literature and Society* (1980)

Eisenach, E. J., *Two Worlds of Liberalism: Religion and Politics in Hobbes, Locke, and Mill* (1981)

'Hobbes on Church, State, and Religion', *HPT* 3 (1982)

Eliade, M., *The Sacred and the Profane: The Nature of Religion* (1959)

Elshtain, J. B., *Public Man, Private Woman* (1981)

Emerson, R.L. , 'Heresy, the Social Order and English Deism', *Church History* 37 (1968)

'Latitudinarianism and the English Deists', in J. A. Leo Lemay (ed.), *Deism, Masonry and the Enlightenment. Essays Honoring – Alfred Owen Aldridge* (Newark, 1987)

Every, G., *The High Church Party, 1688–1718* (1956)

Ferguson, A. B., *Clio Unbound* (North Carolina, 1974)

Ferguson, J. P., *An Eighteenth Century Heretic: Dr Samuel Clarke* (1976)

Fermia, J. V., *Gramsci's Political Thought* (Oxford, 1981)

Figgis, J. N., *The Divine Right of Kings* (New York, 1965)

Fink, Z., *The Classical Republicans* (Evanston, 1945)

Finlayson, M., *Historians, Puritans and the English Revolution: The Religious Factor in English Politics before and after the Interregnum* (Toronto, 1983)

Fisch, M. H., 'Review of M. Rossi's *La Vita, Le Opera: Tempi di Edoard Herbert di Cherbury*', *Journal of Philosophy* 48 (1949)

Fleischmann, W. B., *Lucretius and English Literature 1580–1740* (Paris, 1964)

Fletcher, J., 'The Spanish Gospel of Barnabas', *Novum Testamentum* 18 (1976)

Florida, R. E., 'Voltaire and the Socinians', *SVEC* 122 (1974)

'British Law and Socinianism in the Seventeenth and Eighteenth Centuries', in L., Szczucki (ed.), *Socinianism* (Warsaw, 1983)

Force, J. E., *William Whiston: Honest Newtonian* (Cambridge, 1985)

'The Origins of Modern Atheism', *JHI* 50 (1989)

Fox, A., *John Mill and Richard Bentley* (Oxford, 1954)

Fox, L., (ed.), *English Historical Scholarship in the Sixteenth and Seventeenth Centuries* (Oxford, 1956)

Fox-Bourne, H. R., *The Life of John Locke*, 2 vols. (1876)

Foxcroft, H., *A Life of Gilbert Burnet* (Cambridge, 1907)

Frank, R. G., and B. Shapiro, *English Virtuósi in the Sixteenth and Seventeenth Centuries* (Los Angeles, 1972)

'The Image of Harvey in Commonwealth and Restoration England', in J. J. Bylybyl (ed.), *William Harvey and His Age* (Baltimore, 1979)

Franklin, J. H., *Jean Bodin and the Sixteenth Century Revolution in the Methodology of Law and History* (New York, 1963)

John Locke and the Theory of Sovereignty (Cambridge, 1978)

Franz, R. W., *The English Traveller and The Movement of Ideas 1660–1732* (New York, 1968)

Fremaux, M., *L'Evangile de Barnabé recherches sur la composition et l'origine* (Paris, 1977)

Freud, S., *The Origins of Religion* (1985)

Fulton, A. S., (ed.), *The History of Hayy Ibn Yockdan* (1929)

Furley, O. W., 'The Whig Exclusionists', *CHJ* 13 (1957)

Fustel de Coulanges, N. D., *The Ancient City* (Baltimore, 1980)

Gascoigne, J. A., *Cambridge in the Age of the Enlightenment* (Cambridge, 1989)

Gaskin, J. C. A., *Hume's Philosophy of Religion* (1978)

Gauthier, D. P., *The Logic of Leviathan* (Oxford, 1969)

Gawlick, G., 'Cicero and the Enlightenment', *SVEC* 25 (1963)

Gay, P., *The Enlightenment: an Interpretation: The Rise of Modern Paganism* (1967)

Gentile, G., 'Eighteenth-Century Historical Methodology: De Sovia's *Institutions*', *HT*, 4 (1964–5)

Gibbs, G. C., 'Review of M. Jacob's *Radical Enlightenment*', *British Journal for the History of Science* 17 (1984)

Gilley, S., 'Christianity and the Enlightenment', *History of European Ideas* (1981)

Gilmore, M., *Humanists and Jurists* (Harvard, 1966)

Ginsburg, C., 'High and Low Knowledge in the Sixteenth and Seventeenth Centuries', *PP* 73 (1976)

Giuntini, C., 'Toland e Bruno: ermetismo rivoluzionario', *Rivista di Filosophia* 66 (1975)

Goar, R. J., *Cicero and the State Religion* (Amsterdam, 1972)

Godelier, M., *Perspectives in Marxist Anthropology* (Cambridge, 1977)

Godwin, J., *Athanasius Kircher: A Renaissance Man and the Quest for Lost Knowledge* (1979)

Goldie, M. A., 'The Roots of True Whiggism 1688–1694', *HPT* 1 (1980)

'The Nonjurors, Episcopacy and the Origins of the Convocation Controversy', in Cruickshanks, E., (ed.), *Ideology and Conspiracy* (Edinburgh, 1982)

'John Locke and Anglican Royalism' *Political Studies* 31 (1983)

'Obligations, Utopias and their Historical Context', *HJ* 26 (1983)

'The Civil Religion of James Harrington', in Pagden, A. (ed.), *Languages of Political Theory In Early Modern Europe* (Cambridge, 1987)

'Ideology' in T. Ball, J. Farr and R. L. Hanson (eds.), *Political Innovation and Conceptual Change* (Cambridge, 1989)

Goldmann, L., *The Philosophy of the Enlightenment* (1968)

Goldsmith, M. M., *Hobbes' Science of Politics* (1966)

Gooch, G. P. and H. Laski, *English Democratic Ideas in the Seventeenth Century* (Cambridge, 1954)

Gordon, A., 'The Primary Document of English Unitarianism', *Christian Life* 18 (1892)

Heads of Unitarian History (1856)

Gough, J. W., 'Harrington and Contemporary Thought', *Political Science Quarterly* 45 (1930)

Gramsci, A., *Selection from the Prison Notebooks* eds. Q. Hoare and G. Nowell (1971)

Grean, S., *Shaftesbury's Philosophy of Religion* (Ohio, 1967)

Green, I. M., *The Re-Establishment of the Church of England* (Oxford, 1978)

Greenleaf, W. H., *Order Empiricism, and Politics: Two Traditions of Political Thought 1500–1700* (Oxford, 1964)

Grene, M., (ed.), *Spinoza and the Sciences, Boston Studies in the Philosophy of Sciences* 91 (1986)

Grodynski, D., 'Superstitio', *REA* 76 (1974)

Gunn, J. A. W., *Politics and the Public Interest in the Seventeenth Century* (1969)

Beyond Liberty and Property (Montreal, 1983)

Gunther, R. T., *Early Science in Oxford* 14 (Oxford, 1945)

Gwynn, R., *Huguenot Heritage* (1986)

Hacking, I., *The Emergence of Probability* (Cambridge, 1984)

Hall, J., *Lucian's Satire* (New York, 1981)

Haller, W., *Foxe's Book of Martyrs and the Elect Nation* (1963)

Hamilton, A., *William Bedwell and the Arabists 1563–1632* (Leiden, 1985)

Hampshire, S., *Spinoza* (1978)

Hampson, N., *Will and Circumstance* (1983)

Hargreaves, M. and H. Macdonald, *Thomas Hobbes: A Bibliography* (1952)

Harris, T., *London Crowds in the Reign of Charles II* (Cambridge, 1987)
Harris, T., *et al.* (eds.), *The Politics of Religion in Restoration England* (Oxford, 1990)
Harrison, P., *'Religion' and the Religions in the English Enlightenment* (Cambridge, 1990)
Harvey, R., 'The Problem of Social and Political Obligation for the Church of England in the Seventeenth Century', *Church History* 40 (1971)
Hazard, P., *The European Mind 1680–1715* (1973)
Heinemann, F. H., *John Toland and The Age of Enlightenment* (Oxford, 1949)
Hennecke, E., *New Testament Apocrypha* (1963)
Hill, C., 'Republicanism after the Restoration', *NLR* 3 (1960)
  'William Harvey and the Idea of Monarchy', *PP* 27 (1964)
  Intellectual Origins of the English Revolution (Oxford, 1965)
  Puritanism and Revolution (1972)
  (ed.), *Winstanley: The Law of Freedom and Other Writings* (1973)
  The World Turned Upside Down (1975)
  Milton and the English Revolution (1977)
  'The Religion of Gerrard Winstanley', *PP* Supplement 5 (1978)
  Some Intellectual Consequences of the English Revolution (1980)
  The Experience of Defeat (1984)
Hirschmann, A., *The Passions and The Interests* (Princeton, 1977)
Hodgen, M. T., *Early Anthropology in the Sixteenth and Seventeenth Centuries* (Pennsylvania, 1964)
Holmes, G. A., *British Politics in the Age of Queen Anne* (1967)
Holt, P. M., *Historians of the Middle East* (Oxford, 1962)
  Studies in the History of the Near East (1973)
Hood, F. C., *The Divine Politics of Thomas Hobbes* (Oxford, 1964)
Horowitz, M. C., 'The Stoic Synthesis of the Idea of Natural Law in Man: *Four Themes*', *JHI* 35 (1974)
Howell, W. S., *Logic and Rhetoric in England 1500–1700* (New York, 1961)
Hunter, M., 'The Royal Society and the Origins of British Archeology', *Antiquity* 45 (1971)
  John Aubrey and the Realm of Learning (1975)
  'The Problem of "Atheism" in Early Modern England', *TRHS* (1985)
Hunter, M. and D. Wootton, (eds.), *Atheism from the Reformation to the Enlightenment* (Oxford, forthcoming)
Huppert, G., *The Idea of Perfect History* (Urbana, 1970)
Hutcheson, H. R., (ed.), *Lord Herbert of Cherbury's De Religione Laici* (Yale, 1944)
Innes, J., 'Jonathon Clark, Social History and England's *Ancien Régime*', *PP* 115 (1987)
Iverson, E., *The Myth of Egypt and its Hieroglyphs in European Tradition* (Copenhagen, 1961)
Jacob, J. R., *Henry Stubbe, Radical Protestantism and the Early Enlightenment* (Cambridge, 1983)
Jacob, M. C., 'John Toland and Newtonian Ideology', *JWCI* 32 (1969)
  The Newtonians and the English Revolution 1689–1720 (1976)
  'Newtonianism and the Origins of the Enlightenment: A Reassessment', *Eighteenth Century Studies* 11 (1977)
  The Radical Enlightenment (1981)
  (ed.), *The Origins of Anglo-American Radicalism* (1984)

'Hazard Revisited' in M. C. Jacob and P. Mack (eds.), *Politics and Culture in Early Modern Europe* (Cambridge, 1987)
James, F. G., *North Country Bishop: A Biography of William Nicolson* (Yale, 1956)
Jameson, F., 'Religion and Ideology' in F. Barker *et al.* (eds.), *1642: Literature and Power in the Seventeenth Century* (Essex, 1981)
Janik, L., 'Lorenzo Valla: The Primacy of Rhetoric and the Demoralisation of History', *HT* 12 (1973)
Jardine, L., *Francis Bacon and the Art of Discourse* (Cambridge, 1974)
Johnson, J. W., *The Formation of English Neo-Classical Thought* (Princeton, 1967)
'The Classics and John Bull 1660–1714', in H. T. Swedenborg (ed.), *England in the Restoration and Early Eighteenth Century* (California, 1972)
Johnston, D., *The Rhetoric of Leviathan: Thomas Hobbes and the Politics of Cultural Transformation* (Princeton, 1986)
Jones, J. R., 'The Green Ribbon Club', *Durham University Journal* (1956)
The First Whigs: The Politics of the Exclusion Crisis, 1678–1683 (Durham 1961)
Jones, J. R., (ed) *The Restored Monarchy* (1979)
Kamen, H., *Inquisition and Society in Spain in the Sixteenth and Seventeenth Centuries* (Indiana, 1985)
Katz, D. S., *Philosemitism and the Re-admission of the Jews to England* (Oxford, 1982)
Kaufman, P. I., 'John Colet's *Opus de Sacramentis* and Clerical Anticlericalism: The Limitation of the "Ordinary Wayes"', *Journal of British Studies* (1982)
Kearney, H., *Scholars and Gentlemen* (1970)
Kelley, D. R., 'History, English Law, and the Renaissance', *PP* 65 (1974)
The Foundations of Modern Historical Scholarship (New York, 1970)
The Beginning of Ideology (Cambridge, 1983)
Kennedy, G., *Classical Rhetoric and its Christian and Secular Tradition from Ancient to Modern Times* (North Carolina, 1980)
Kenworthy, F., 'The Toleration Act of 1689', *Transactions of the Unitarian Historical Society* 7 (1939–42)
Kenyon, J. P., *The Popish Plot* (1972)
Revolution Principles; The Politics of Party 1689–1720 (Cambridge, 1977)
The History Men (1983)
Keohane, N. O., *Philosophy and the State in France* (Princeton, 1980)
King, A. D., (ed.), *Buildings and Society* (1980)
Knowles, D., *The Evolution of the Medieval Mind* (1962)
Koch, G. A., *Republican Religion: The American Revolution and the Cult of Reason* (New York, 1933)
Kontler, L., 'The Idea of Toleration and the Image of Islam in the Early Enlightenment English Thought', in E. H. Balzacs, (ed.), *Sous le signe des lumières* (Budapest, 1987)
Kors, A., 'The Preamble of Atheism in Early-Modern France', in A. Kors and P. J. Korshin (eds.), *Anticipations of the Enlightenment in England, France and Germany* (Philadelphia, 1987)
A History of French Atheism (Yale, 1989)
Kossok, M., (ed.), *Studien über die Revolution* (Berlin, 1975)
Kra, P., 'Religion in Montesquieu's Lettres Persanes', *SVEC* 52 (1970)
Krabbe, O. C. *The Apostolic Constitutions* (New York, 1848)
Kramnick, I., 'Augustan Politics and English Historiography 1720–35', *HT* 6 (1967)
(ed.), *Lord Bolingbroke: Historical Writings* (Chicago, 1972)

'Religion and Radicalism: English Political Theory in the Age of Revolution', *Political Theory* 5 (1977)
'Republican Revisionism Revisited', *AHR* 87 (1982)
Kristeller, P. O., *Eight Philosophers of the Italian Renaissance* (California, 1964)
'The Myth of Renaissance Atheism and French Freethought'. *JHP* 6 (1968)
Kritzeck, J., 'Moslem–Christian Understanding in Medieval Times', *Comparative Studies in Society and History* 4 (1961–2)
Kuhn, A. J., 'English Deism and the Development of Romantic Mythological Syncretism', *PMLA* 71 (1956)
Kummel, W. G., *The New Testament: The History of the Investigation of Its Problems* (Nashville, 1972)
Lacey, D., *Dissent and Parliamentary Politics in England 1661–1689* (New Jersey, 1969)
Lamont, W., *Marginal Prynne* (1963)
   Godly Rule: Politics and Religion 1603–1660 (1969)
   Richard Baxter and the Millenium (1979)
Lange, F. A., *The History of Materialism*, 2 vols. (1925)
Larrain, J., *The Concept of Ideology* (1979)
Laski, H., *Political Thought in England from Locke to Bentham* (1920)
Laslett, P., *The World We Have Lost* (1979)
Laslett, P. and J. Harrison, *The Library of John Locke* (Oxford, 1971)
Lathbury, T., *A History of the Convocation of the Church of England* (1853)
Leach, E. and A. Alcock, *Structuralist Interpretations of Biblical Myth* (Cambridge, 1983)
Leff, G., *Medieval Thought* (1958)
Levi, A., *French Moralists and the Theory of the Passions* (Oxford, 1964)
Levine, J., 'Ancients, Moderns and History: The Continuity of Historical Writing', in Korshin, P. J. (ed.), *Studies in Change and Revolution* (Menston, 1972)
Levy, F. J., *Tudor Historical Thought* (California, 1967)
Levy, L. W., *Treason Against God* (New York, 1981)
Lievsay, J. L., *Venetian Phoenix: Paolo Sarpi and Some of His English Friends, 1606–1700* (Kansas, 1973)
Liljegren, S. B., 'James Harrington's *Oceana*', in *Skrifter Vetenskaps-Societeten* 4 (1924)
   'A French Draft Constitution of 1792', in *K. Humanisticka Vetenskapssam* 17 (1932)
   'Harrington and the Jews' *K. Humanisticka Vetenskapssam* 4 (1931–2)
Lillywhite, B., *London Coffee Houses* (1963)
Lovejoy, A. O., 'The Parallel of Classicism and Deism', *Modern Philology* 29 (1931)
Lupton, J. H., *Life of Dean Colet* (1909)
Macklem, M., *The Anatomy of the World: Relations between Natural and Moral Law from Donne to Pope* (Minnesota, 1958)
Maclear, J., 'Popular Anticlericalism in the Puritan Revolution', *JHI* 17 (1956)
Macpherson, C. B., *The Political Theory of Possessive Individualism: Hobbes to Locke* (Oxford, 1962)
Mainusch, H., *John Toland: Gründe für Einbügerung der Juden in Grossbritannien und Irland* (Stuttgart, 1965)
Malament, B., (ed.), *After the Reformation* (Pennsylvania, 1980)
Malcolm, N., *De Dominis: Venetian, Anglican, Ecumenist and Relapsed Heretic* (1984)

Manuel, F., *The Eighteenth Century Confronts the Gods* (Harvard, 1959)
　The Changing of the Gods (Hanover, 1983)
Marshall, J. W., 'The Ecclesiology of the Latitude-Men 1660–1689: Stillingfleet, Tillotson and "Hobbism"', *Journal of Ecclesiastical History* 36 (1985)
Marx, K., *Collected Works* I (1975)
　On Religion (Moscow, 1976)
Marx, K. and F. Engels, *Selected Works* (Moscow, 1968)
Massa, D., 'Giordano Bruno's Ideas in Seventeenth Century England', *JHI* 38 (1977)
Mayor, J. E. B., *Cambridge Under Queen Anne* (Cambridge, 1911)
McGregor, J. F., (ed.), *Radical Religion in the English Revolution* (Oxford, 1984)
McLachlan, H., 'Seventeenth-Century Unitarian Tracts', *Transactions of the Unitarian Historical Society* 2 (1919–22)
　The Religious Opinions of Milton, Locke, and Newton (Manchester, 1941)
McLachlan, H. J., 'Links between Transylvania and British Unitarians from the Seventeenth Century onwards', *Transactions of the Unitarian Historical Society* 17 (1979–82)
　Socinianism in Seventeenth-Century England (Oxford, 1951)
McNeilly, F., *The Anatomy of Leviathan* (1968)
Mendelsshon, M., *Jerusalem and Other Writings*, (New York, 1969)
Mengel, E. F., (ed.), *Poems on Affairs of State 1678–81* (Yale, 1965)
Miel, J., 'Ideas or epistemes: Hazard versus Foucault', *Yale French Studies* 49 (1973)
Miller, J., *Popery and Politics in England 1660–1688* (Cambridge, 1973)
Momigliano, A. M., *Studies in Historiography* (1969)
　Essays in Ancient and Modern Historiography (Oxford, 1977)
Monk, J. H., *The Life of Richard Bentley* (1830)
Monsarrat, G., *Light from the Porch Stoicism and Early Renaissance Literature* (Paris, 1984)
Monter, W., *Ritual, Myth and Magic in Early Modern Europe* (Sussex, 1983)
Montgomery, R. M., 'A Note on the Acts of Parliament Dealing with the Denial of the Trinity', *Transactions of the Unitarian Historical Society* 6 (1935–8)
Morrill, J. S., 'The Religious Context of the English Civil War', *TRHS* (1984)
　'The Attack upon the Church of England in the Long Parliament', in D. Beales and G. Best (eds.), *History, Society, and the Churches* (Cambridge, 1985)
Morton, A. L., *The World of The Ranters* (1975)
Mosse, G. L., 'Puritan Radicalism and the Enlightenment', *Church History* 29 (1960)
Nadel, G. H., 'The Philosophy of History before Historicism', *HT* 3 (1963–4)
　'History as Psychology in Francis Bacon's Theory of History', *HT* 5 (1966)
Neilson, K., *An Introduction to the Philosophy of Religion* (1982)
Neilson, M. E., 'Cicero's *De Officiis* in Christian Thought 300–1300', *Essays and Studies in English and Comparative Literature* (Michigan, 1933)
Nicolson, M. J., (ed.), *The Conway Letters* (Yale, 1930)
Norman, E., *Christianity and the World Order* (Oxford, 1979)
Novak, M. E., *Realism, Myth, and History in Defoe's Fiction* (Nebraska, 1983)
Oake, R., 'Montesquieu's Religious Ideas', *JHI* 14 (1953)
Oakley, F., *Omnipotence, Government and Order* (1984)
O'Brown, N., 'The Prophetic Tradition', *Studies in Romanticism* 21 (1982)
Oestreich, O., *Neostoicism and the Early Modern State* (Cambridge, 1982)
O'Higgins, J., *Anthony Collins the Man and his Works* (The Hague, 1970)
　Yves de Vallone: The Making of an Esprit Fort (The Hague, 1982)
Okin, S. M., *Women in Western Political Thought* (1980)

Olgilvie, R. S., *Latin and Greek: A History of the Influence of the Classics on English Life from 1600–1918* (1967)

Oliver, H. T., *Sir Robert Howard 1626–1698* (North Carolina, 1963)

Ong, W. J., 'Hobbes and Talon's Ramist Rhetoric in England', *Transactions of the Cambridge Bibliographical Society* 1 (1951)

'From Allegory to Diagram in the Renaissance Mind', *Journal of Aesthetics and Art Criticism* 17 (1958)

Owen, A. L., *The Famous Druids: A Survey of Three Centuries of English Literature on Druids* (Oxford, 1962)

Owens, J., *Sceptics of the Italian Renaissance* (New York, 1893)

Paknadel, F., 'Shaftesbury's Illustrations of the Characteristicks', *JWCI* 37 (1974)

Parrinder, G., *Jesus in the Qu'ran* (1965)

Pascoe, L. B., *Jean Gerson: Principles of Church Reform* (Leiden, 1973)

Passmore, J., *The Perfectibility of Man* (1974)

Patrick, D., 'Two English Forerunners of the Tübingen School: Thomas Morgan and John Toland', *Theological Review* 14 (1877)

Patrides, C. A., *The Cambridge Platonists* (Cambridge, 1969)

Patterson, A. M., *Marvell and the Civic Crown* (Princeton, 1978)

Paul, H. G., *John Dennis, his Life and Criticism* (New York, 1911)

Paulin, D. A., 'Herbert of Cherbury and the Deists' *The Expository Times* 94 (April, 1983)

Attitudes to Other Religions (Manchester, 1984)

Pelli, M., 'The Impact of Deism on the Hebrew Literature of the Enlightenment in Germany', *Eighteenth Century Studies* 6 (1972–3)

Perkins, M. L., 'Civil Theology in the Writings of the Abbé de Saint Pierre', *JHI* 18 (1957)

Piggott, S., *William Stukeley: An Eighteenth-Century Antiquary* (Oxford, 1950)

The Druids (1974)

Pines, S. (ed.), *Maimonides Guide to the Perplexed* (Chicago, 1963)

'The Jewish Christians of Early Christianity according to a New Document', *Proceedings of the Israel Academy of Sciences and Humanities* 2 (1968)

Plumb, J. H., *The Growth of Political Stability in England 1675–1725* (1967)

Pocock, J. G. A., *The Ancient Constitution and the Feudal law* (Cambridge, 1957 and reissue 1987)

'James Harrington and the Good Old Cause', *Journal of British Studies* 10 (1970)

Politics Language and Time (1972)

The Machiavellian Moment (Princeton, 1975)

(ed.), *The Political Works of James Harrington,* Introduction (Cambridge, 1977)

'Contexts for the Study of James Harrington', *Il Pensiero Politico* (1978)

'Post-Puritan England and the Problem of the Enlightenment' in P. Zagorin (ed.), *Culture and Politics: From Puritanism to the Enlightenment* (1980)

Three British Revolutions: 1641, 1688, 1776 (Princeton, 1981)

'English Historical Thought in the Age of Harrington and Locke', *Topoi* 2 (1983)

'Clergy and Commerce: The Conservative Enlightenment in England', in *Eta dei Lumi. Studia Storici sul Settecento Europeo in onore di Franco Venturi* (Naples, 1985)

Virtue, Commerce and History (Cambridge, 1986)

Pocock, N. (ed.), *G. Burnet's History of the Reformation,* 7 vols. Introduction (Oxford, 1865)

Popkin, R. H., (ed.), *Pierre Bayle's Historical and Critical Dictionary* (New York, 1965)
The History of Scepticism (1979)
'Spinoza and the Conversion of the Jews', in C. de Deugd, (ed.), *Spinoza's Political and Theological Thought* (Amsterdam 1984)
'Spinoza and Samuel Fisher', *Philosophia* 15 (1985)
'Serendipity at the Clark: Spinoza and the Prince of Condé', *The Clark Newsletter* 10 (1986)
Isaac La Peyrère 1596–1676 (Brill, 1987)
'The Dispersion of Bodin's Dialogues in England, Holland, and Germany', *JHI* 49 (1988)
Popkin, R. H. and J. E. Force, *Essays on the Context, Nature, and Influence of Isaac Newton's Theology* (The Netherlands, 1990)
Porter, R., (ed.), *The Ferment of Knowledge* (Cambridge, 1980)
'The Rage of Party: A Glorious Revolution in English Psychiatry', *Medical History* 27 (1983)
Porter, R. and M. Teich, (eds.), *The Enlightenment in National Context* (Cambridge, 1981)
Potts, L. J., (ed.), *Aristotle on the Art of Fiction* (Cambridge, 1959)
Preston, J. H., 'English Ecclesiastical Historians and the Problem of Bias 1559–1742', *JHI* 32 (1971)
'Was there an Historical Revolution?', *JHI* 38 (1977)
Preus, J. S., 'Machiavelli's Functional Analysis of Religion', *JHI* 40 (1979)
Explaining Religion: Criticism and Theory from Bodin to Freud (Yale, 1987)
Pruett, J. H., *The Parish Clergy under the Later Stuarts* (Illinois, 1978)
Purpus, E. R., 'Some Notes on a Deistical Essay Attributed to Dryden', *Philological Quarterly* 29 (1950)
Raab, F., *The English Face of Machiavelli* (1964)
Rademaker, C. S. M., *The Life and Works of Gerardus Vossius* (Assen, 1981)
Ragg, L. L., 'The Mohammedan Gospel of Barnabas', *Journal of Theological Studies* 4 (1904–5)
The Gospel of Barnabas (Oxford, 1907)
Rand, B., *The Life, Unpublished Letters, and Philosophical Regimen of Anthony, Earl of Shaftesbury* (1900)
Ranum, O., *Artisans of Glory* (North Carolina, 1980)
'D'alembert, Tacitus, and the Political Sociology of Despotism', *Transactions of the Fifth International Congress of the Enlightenment* 2 (Oxford, 1981)
Reay, B., (ed.), *Popular Culture in Seventeenth-Century England* (1985)
Reay, B. and J. F. McGregor, *Radical Religion in the English Revolution* (Oxford, 1984)
Rebelliau, A., *Bossuet: historien du protestantisme* (Paris, 1861)
Redwood, J. A., 'Charles Blount, Deism, and English Freethought', *JHI* 37 (1976)
Reason, Ridicule and Religion: The Age of Enlightenment in England 1660–1752 (1978)
Reedy, G., 'Mystical Politics: The Imagery of Charles II's Coronation', in P. J. Korshin (ed.), *Studies in Change and Revolution* (Menston, 1972)
The Bible and Reason: Anglicans and Scripture in late Seventeenth-Century England (Philadelphia, 1985)
Rees, T., *The Racovian Catechism* (1818)
Reesink, H. J., *L'Angleterre et la littérature anglaise* (Paris, 1931)

Reeves, W., *The Culdees of the British Isles* (Dublin, 1864)
Renan, E., *Averroes et l'averroisme* (Paris, 1852)
Rendell, J., 'Scottish Orientalism from Robertson to James Mill', *HJ* 25 (1982)
Reventlow Graf, H., 'Judaism, and Jewish Christianity in the Works of Toland', *Proceeding of the Sixth World Congress of Jewish Studies* 3 (1977)
The Authority of the Bible and the Rise of the Modern World (1984)
Reynolds, B., 'Shifting Currents in Historical Criticism', *JHI* 14 (1953)
'Latin Historiography: 1400–1600', *Studies in the Renaissance* 2 (1955)
Rice, W. G., 'Early English Travellers to Greece and the Levant', *Essays and Studies* (Michigan, 1939)
Richardson, A., *History Sacred and Profane* (1964)
Robbins, C., *The Eighteenth-Century Commonwealthsmen* (Harvard, 1959)
Two English Republican Tracts (Cambridge, 1969)
Robertson, J. M., *A History of Freethought: Ancient and Modern to the Period of the French Revolution*, (1936)
Robinson, C., *Lucian and his Influence in Europe* (1979)
Robinson, J. A., *The Glastonbury Legends* (Cambridge, 1922)
Ronalds, F. S., *The Attempted Whig Revolution 1678–81* (Illinois, 1937)
Roosbroecke, G. L. van, *Persian Letters before Montesquieu* (1932)
Rose, P. L., *Bodin and the Great God of Nature: The Moral and Religious Universe of a Judaiser* (Geneva, 1980)
Rossi, P., *Philosophy, Technology and the Arts* (New York, 1970)
The Dark Abyss of Time (Chicago, 1985)
Royle, E., *Radicals, Secularists and Republicans. Popular Freethought in Britain 1866–1915* (Manchester, 1980)
Rule, J. C., 'Bibliography of Works in the Philosophy of History 1945–1957', *HT* Supplement 1 (1961)
Russell, K. F., *British Anatomy 1525–1800* (Melbourne, 1963)
Russell-Smith, H. F., *Harrington and His Oceana* (Cambridge, 1914)
Said, E., *Orientalism* (1978)
(ed.), *Literature and Society* (1980)
Sailor, D. B., 'Moses and Atomism', *JHI* 25 (1964)
Salvatorelli, L., 'From Locke to Reitzenstein: The Historical Investigation of the Origins of Christianity', *The Harvard Theological Review* 22 (1929)
Sandbach, F. H., *The Stoics* (1975)
Sandys, E., *A History of Classical Scholarship* 3 vols. (Oxford, 1930)
Saunders, J. J., 'Mohammed in Europe: A Note on Western Interpretations of the Life of the Prophet', *History* 39 (1954)
Schaffer, S., 'The Political Theology of Seventeenth-Century Natural Science', *Ideas and Production* (1983)
Schaffer, S. and S. Shapin, *Leviathan and the Air Pump* (Princeton, 1986)
Schellhase, K. C., *Tacitus in Renaissance Political Thought* (Chicago, 1976)
Schmitt, C. B., 'Renaissance Averroism Studied through the Venetian Editions of Aristotle-Averroes', *Atti Dei Convegni Lincei* 40 (1979)
Schwartz, H., *The French Prophets* (1980)
Schwartz, J., 'Hobbes and the Kingdoms of God', *Polity* 18 (1985)
'Liberalism and the Jewish Connection: A Study of Spinoza and the young Marx', *Political Theory* 13 (1985)
Scott, J., *Algernon Sidney and the English Republic 1623–1677* (Cambridge, 1988)

'England's Troubles: Exhuming the Popish Plot', in T. Harris *et al.* (eds.), *The Politics of Religion* (Blackwell, 1990)

'Radicalism and Restoration: The Shape of the Stuart Experience', *HJ* 31 (1988)

Shackleton, R., *Montesquieu. A Critical Biography* (Oxford, 1960)

Shaffer, E. S., *Kubla Khan and the Fall of Jerusalem* (Cambridge, 1975)

Shapin, S., 'Pump and Circumstance: Robert Boyle's Literary Technology', *Social Studies of Science* (1984)

Shapiro, B., *Probability and Certainty in Seventeenth-Century England* (Princeton, 1983)

Sharpe, A., 'The Manuscript Version of Harrington's *Oceana*', *HJ* 16 (1973)

Sharpe, E. J., *Comparative Religion: A History* (1975)

Shaw, E. K., (ed.), *English and Continental Views of the Ottoman Empire 1500– 1800* (Los Angeles, 1972)

Sherlock, R., 'The Theology of Leviathan: Hobbes on Religion', *Interpretation* 10 (1982)

Sheroner, C. M., 'Rousseau's Civil Religion', *Interpretation* 8 (1979)

Shklar, J., 'Ideology Hunting: The Case of James Harrington', *American Political Science Review* 53 (1959)

'Jean D'Alembert and the Re-habilitation of History', *JHI* 42 (1981)

Montesquieu (Oxford, 1987)

Simms, J. G., 'John Toland (1670–1722): A Donegal Heretic', *Irish Historical Studies* 16 (1969)

Singer, D., *Bruno, His Life* (New York, 1950)

Skinner, Q., 'History and Ideology in the English Revolution', *HJ* 8 (1965)

The Foundations of Modern Political Thought, 2 vols. (Cambridge, 1978)

Slomp, J., 'The Gospel in Dispute', *Islamochristiana* 4 (1978)

Slymovics, P., 'Spinoza: Liberal Democratic Religion', *JHP* 23 (1985)

Smith, B. P., *Islam in English Literature* (Lebanon, 1939)

Smith, H. P., *Essays in Biblical Interpretation* (1921)

Smith Fussner, F., *The Historical Revolution* (1962)

Sommerville, C. J., *Popular Religion in Restoration England* (Gainesville, 1977)

'The Destruction of Religious Culture in Pre-industrial England', *Journal of Religious History* (1988)

Sommerville, J. P., *Politics and Ideology in England 1603–1640* (Essex, 1986)

Southern, R. W., *Western Views of Islam in the Middle Ages* (Harvard, 1962)

Sox, D., *The Gospel of Barnabas* (1984)

Speck, W. A., *Stability and Strife 1714–1760* (1977)

Tory and Whig: The Struggle in the Constituencies, 1701–1715 (1978)

Spink, J. S., *French Freethought from Gassendi to Voltaire* (1961)

'The Reputation of Julian the Apostate in the Enlightenment', *SVEC* 57 (1967)

Springborg, P., 'Leviathan, the Christian Commonwealth Incorporated', *Political Studies* 24 (1976)

Spufford, M., *Small Books and Pleasant Histories* (Cambridge, 1981)

Spurr, J., 'Latitudinarianism and the Restoration Church', *HJ* 31 (1988)

'"Rational Religion" in Restoration England', *JHI* 49 (1988)

'The Church of England, Comprehension and Toleration in 1689', *English Historical Review* 104 (1989)

'Schism and the Restoration Church' *Journal of Ecclesiastical History* 41 (1990)

The Restoration Church of England 1646–1689 (Yale, forthcoming)

Stephens, L., *English Thought in the Eighteenth Century*, 2 vols. (1949)
Stoughton, J., *Religion in England*, 8 vols. (1881)
Strafford, W., *Socialism, Radicalism, and Nostalgia* (Cambridge, 1987)
Strauss, L., *The Political Philosophy of Hobbes* (Oxford, 1936)
  Spinoza's Critique of Religion (New York, 1965)
Struever, N., *The Language of History in the Renaissance* (Princeton, 1970)
Sullivan, R., *John Toland and the Deist Controversy* (Harvard, 1982)
Sykes, N., *From Sheldon to Secker* (Cambridge, 1959)
Szczucki, L., (ed.), *Socinianism* (Warsaw, 1983)
Szemler, G., 'Religio, Priesthood, and Magistrates in the Roman Republic', *Numen* 18 (1971)
Thomas, K. V., *Religion and the Decline of Magic* (1978)
  The Perception of the Past in Early Modern England (The Creighton Trust lecture, 1982)
Thompson, E. P., *The Poverty of Theory and Other Essays* (1978)
Thompson, E. T., *Letters of Humphrey Prideaux to John Ellis 1674–1722* (Camden Society, 1875)
Thompson, M. P., 'The Reception of Locke's *Two Treatises of Government* 1690–1705', *Political Studies* 24 (1976)
Thrower, J., *The Alternative Tradition: Religion and the Rejection of Religion in the Ancient World* (The Hague, 1980)
  Marxist-Leninist 'Scientific Atheism' and the Study of Religion and Atheism in the USSR (Berlin, 1983)
Tierney, B., *The Foundation of Conciliar Theory* (Cambridge, 1955)
  Religion, Law and the Growth of Constitutional Thought, 1150–1650 (Cambridge, 1982)
Tiffany, E., 'Shaftesbury as Stoic', *PLMA* 37 (1923)
Tillyard, E. M. W., *Milton's Private Correspondence* (Cambridge, 1932)
  The Elizabethan World Picture (1960)
Tindal, W. Y., 'James Joyce and the Hermetic Tradition', *JHI* 15 (1954)
Tompkins, J. M. S., 'In Yonder Grave a Druid Lies', *Review of English Studies* 22 (1946)
Torrey, N. L., *Voltaire and the English Deists* (Yale, 1967)
Townley, J., *The Reasons of the Laws of Moses* (1827)
Trevor-Roper, H., *William Laud* (1965)
  Religion, the Reformation and Social Change (1967)
Tuck, R., *Natural Right Theories* (Cambridge, 1979)
Tully, J., *A Discourse on Property: John Locke and His Adversaries* (Cambridge, 1980)
Turner, B. S., *The Body and Society* (1984)
Tuveson, E., *Millennium and Utopia* (California, 1972)
Tyacke, N., *Anti-Calvinists: The Rise of English Arminianism c. 1590–1640* (Oxford, 1987)
Van Leeuwen, H., *The Pursuit of Certainty in English Thought, 1630–1690* (The Hague, 1963)
Venturi, F., *Utopia and Reform in the Enlightenment* (Cambridge, 1971)
  Italy and the Enlightenment (1972)
Villey, P., 'L'Influence de Montaigne sur Charles Blount et sur les deistes anglaises', *Revue du seizième siècle* 1 (1913)
Viroli, M., 'The Concept of Ordre and the Language of Classical Republicanism in

Jean-Jacques Rousseau', in A. Pagden, (ed.), *The Languages of Political Theory in Early Modern Europe* (Cambridge, 1987)

Jean-Jacques Rousseau and the "Well Ordered Society" (Cambridge, 1988)

Voitle, R., *The Third Earl of Shaftesbury 1671–1713* (Louisiana, 1984)

Wade, I. O., *The Clandestine Organisation and Diffusion of Philosophic Ideas in France* (Princeton, 1938)

The Intellectual Origins of the French Enlightenment (Princeton, 1971)

Wagar, W. W. (ed.), *The Secular Mind* (New York, 1982)

Walbank, F. W., *Polybius* (1972)

Walker, D. P., *The Decline of Hell* (1964)

The Ancient Theology (1972)

Wallace, D. D., 'Socinianism, Justification by Faith, and the Sources of John Locke's *The Reasonableness of Christianity'*, *JHI* 45 (1984)

Wallace, R., *Antitrinitarian Biography* 3 vols. (1850)

Walzer, M., *The Revolution of the Saints* (Harvard, 1982)

Wand, J. W. C., *A History of the Early Church* (1937)

Wardman, A., *Religion and Statecraft among the Romans* (1982)

Warrender, H., *The Political Philosophy of Hobbes* (Oxford, 1957)

Webb, C. J., *Studies in the History of Natural Theology* (Oxford, 1915)

Webster, C., *The Great Instauration* (1975)

Western, J. R., *Monarchy and Revolution* (1972)

White, H., *Tropics of Discourse Essays in Cultural Criticism* (Baltimore, 1978)

White, R. J., *Dr Bentley* (1965)

Whittaker, W., 'The Open Trust Myth', *Transactions of the Unitarian Historical Society* 1 (1917–18)

Wiener, M., 'John Toland and Judaism', *Hebrew Union College Annual* 16 (Cincinnati, 1941)

Wilbur, E. M., *A History of Unitarianism in Transylvania, England and America* (Harvard, 1952)

Willey, B., *The Seventeenth-Century Background* (1979)

Williams, B., 'The Analogy of the City and the Soul in Plato's *Republic'*, *Phronesis*, Supplement 1 (1973)

Williams, G., 'Some Protestent Views of Early British Church History', *History* 37 (1953)

'The Concept of 'egemonia' in the Thought of Antonio Gramsci', *JHI* 21 (1960)

Williams, J., *The Idea of the Novel in Europe 1600–1800* (1979)

Williams, R., 'Base and Superstructure in Marxist Cultural Theory', *NLR* 82 (1973)

Wiseman, T. P., *Clio's Cosmetics* (Leicester, 1979)

Witcombe, D., *Charles II and the Cavalier House of Commons* (Manchester, 1966)

Wolin, S., *Politics and Vision* (Boston, 1960)

Wolper, R. S., 'Circumcision as Polemic in the Jew Bill of 1753', *Eighteenth-Century Life* 7 (1982)

Wootton, D., *Paolo Sarpi between Renaissance and Enlightenment* (Cambridge, 1983)

'Unbelief in Early Modern Europe', *History Workshop Journal* (1985)

'Lucien Febvre and the Problem of Early Modern Unbelief', *Journal of Modern History* (1988)

'New Histories of Atheism', in M. Hunter and D. Wootton (eds.), *Atheism from the Reformation to the Enlightenment* (Oxford, forthcoming)

Worden, A. B. (ed.), _Edmund Ludlow: A Voyce from the Watchtower_, 'Introduction' (Camden Society, 1978)

'Classical Republicanism and the Puritan Revolution in A. Lloyd-Jones, V. Pearl and A. B. Worden, (eds.), _History and Imagination_ (1981)

'Toleration and the Cromwellian Protectorate in W. J. Sheils (ed.), _Persecution and Toleration: Studies in Church History_ 21 (Oxford, 1984)

Wormald, B., 'The Historiography of the English Reformation', _Historical Studies_ (1958)

Wrightson, K., _English Society 1580–1680_ (1982)

Wrightson, K. and D. Levine, _Poverty and Piety in an English Village: Terling 1525–1700_ (New York, 1979)

Wylie-Sypher, G., 'Similarities between the Scientific and Historical Revolutions at the End of the Renaissance', _JHI_ 26 (1965)

Yolton, J. W., _Thinking Matter; Materialism in Eighteenth-Century Britain_ (Oxford, 1983)

Yonge, C. D., (ed.), _The Treatise of Marcus Tullius Cicero_ (1853)

Zagorin, P., _A History of Political Thought in the English Revolution_ (1965)

(ed.), _Culture and Politics from Puritanism to the Enlightenment_ (1980)

Zaller, R., 'The Continuity of British Radicalism in the Seventeenth and Eighteenth Centuries', _Eighteenth-Century Life_ 6 (1980–1)

UNPUBLISHED THESES

Burnett, G. A. 'The Reputation of Cicero among the English Deists 1696–1776', California Ph.D., 1947

Cargill Thompson, W., 'The Two Regiments', Cambridge Ph.D., 1960

Gascoigne, J., 'The Holy Alliance: The Rise and Diffusion of Newtonian Natural Philosophy and Latitudinarian Theology within Cambridge from the Restoration to the Accession of George II', Cambridge Ph.D., 1981

Goldie, M. A. 'Tory Political Thought 1689–1714', Cambridge Ph.D., 1978

Harris, T., 'The Politics of the London Crowd in the Reign of Charles II', Cambridge Ph.D., 1985

Holt, P. M., 'Arabic Studies in Seventeenth-Century England', Oxford B.Litt., 1950

Kararah, A., 'Simon Ockley. His Contribution to Arabic Studies and Influence on Western Thought', Cambridge Ph.D., 1955

Malcom. N., 'Thomas Hobbes and Voluntarist Theology', Cambridge Ph.D., 1983

Pritz, R. A., 'The Jewish Christian Sect of the Nazarenes', Hebrew University Ph.D., 1981

Schaffer, S., 'Newtonian Cosmology and the Steady State', Cambridge Ph.D., 1980

Scott, J., 'The Early Life and Writings of Algernon Sidney', Cambridge Ph.D., 1986

Sommerville, J. P., 'Jacobean Political Thought and the Controversy over the Oath of Allegiance', Cambridge Ph.D., 1981

Stephenson, H. W., 'Thomas Firmin 1632–1697', 3 vols. Oxford D.Phil., 1949

Wickenden, J. N., 'Early Modern Historiography as Illustrated by the Work of G. J. Vossius 1577–1649', 2 vols. Cambridge Ph.D., 1963

INDEX

Cambridge Studies in Early Modern British History

Titles marked with an asterisk are also available in paperback.